ROMAN · IMPERIAL · POLICY

from JULIAN *to* THEODOSIUS

STUDIES IN THE HISTORY OF GREECE AND ROME

Robin Osborne, P. J. Rhodes, &

Richard J. A. Talbert,

editors

•

R. Malcolm Errington

ROMAN

IMPERIAL

POLICY

from JULIAN

to THEODOSIUS

The University of North Carolina Press

Chapel Hill

© 2006
The University of North Carolina Press
All rights reserved

Designed by Eric M. Brooks
Set in Adobe Garamond and Trajan
by Tseng Information Systems, Inc.
Manufactured in the United States of America

This book was published with the assistance
of the William R. Kenan Jr. Fund of the
University of North Carolina Press.

Library of Congress
Cataloging-in-Publication Data
Errington, R. M. (Robert Malcolm)
Roman imperial policy from Julian to
Theodosius / by R. Malcolm Errington.
p. cm. — (Studies in the history of
Greece and Rome)
Includes bibliographical references and index.
ISBN-13: 978-0-8078-3038-3 (cloth: alk. paper)
ISBN-10: 0-8078-3038-0 (cloth: alk. paper)
1. Rome—History—Empire, 284–476.
2. Rome—Politics and government—284–476.
3. Byzantine Empire—History—To 527.
4. Byzantine Empire—Politics and
government—To 527. I. Title. II. Series.
DG319.E77   2006
937'.09—dc22   2006005195

10 09 08 07 06   5 4 3 2 1

FOR · CATHERINE

again

CONTENTS

Preface · ix

Chronology · xi

I Introduction · 1

PART I · ACTORS & EVENTS

II Emperors and Dynasties · 13

III Foreigners and Frontiers · 43

PART II · EAST & WEST

IV The Government · 79

V Rome · 111

VI Constantinople · 142

PART III · RELIGION & THE STATE

VII Julian's Successors · 171

VIII Theodosius · 212

Epilogue · 261

Notes · 267

Bibliography · 313

Index · 325

PREFACE

This small book has been long in the making. Since the Magnum Opus of A. H. M. Jones appeared in 1964, late antiquity in general has experienced a boom in historical activity, but relatively little further attention has been directed to the functioning of the state, perhaps on the assumption that Jones had said it all. For his generation, he had. More recent historical work on the law codes, however, suggests that a new approach to the extant legislation might offer a more realistic view of the apparently monolithic structure of the later Roman state in traditional historical accounts. Also, a more critical approach to the function of imperial panegyric has opened new ways of looking at the imperial governmental apparatus. In this book I have tried to draw attention to some central areas where a fresh handling of important sources seems to offer the prospect of fruitful results.

I am grateful to students in a series of Marburg seminars, where the ideas worked out in this book were first tried out; those ideas were then further developed in detail in articles published in *Chiron* and *Klio*. I have not attempted to give an exhaustive coverage of all aspects of the late Roman state—that would doubtless have taken me another twenty years—and, given the huge amount of international academic production, I imagine I have missed important contributions to the subjects I have covered. I apologize to their authors. There are also many other areas illuminated by the extant legislation where a critical approach might be equally fruitful: the forthcoming Marburg doctoral dissertation of Sebastian Schmidt-Hofner on aspects of the legislation of Valentinian I will treat some of these and show the kind of thing that remains to be done.

I wish to thank all who have tolerated my obsession with the later fourth century over the past twenty years, but in particular Hans-Ulrich Wiemer, whose own work grew along with my own and who in frequent discussions listened to raw ideas and at a later stage read a version of the manuscript, contributing substantially to its final shape. Noel Lenski, an anonymous reader for the University of North Carolina Press, and Richard Talbert as series editor made a series of constructive criticisms of an earlier draft, which have led to substantial improvements in structure and readability. My wife, Catherine, read the text as an "outsider," pointing out, as always, grammatical illogicalities, shortening sentences, and removing commas. To all I am most grateful for their help, particularly, however, to Catherine, whose constant tolerant support over the last forty years has made fruitful academic work in our home both possible and a pleasure.

CHRONOLOGY

363 · Death of Julian in Mesopotamia; appointment of Jovian as emperor and treaty with Persia.

364 · Death of Jovian; appointment of Valentinian I and Valens; division of empire.

365 · Usurpation of Procopius (East); Valentinian I begins campaigns against Alamanni (West).

366 · First consulate of Valentinian's son Gratian; birth of Valens's son Valentinianus Galates; election of Damasus as bishop of Rome.

367 · Eight-year-old Gratian becomes Augustus; Count Theodosius begins operations in Britain (West); Valens begins war against Goths (East).

368 · Gothic war continues in East.

369 · First consulate of Valens's son Valentinianus Galates (East); beginning of investigation of magical practices in Rome (West).

370 · End of Gothic war (spring); Valens takes up residence in Antioch (East).

371 · Birth of Valentinian II (West).

372 · Trials for magical practices in Antioch.

373 · Death of Athanasius in Alexandria; Count Theodosius begins operations in Africa against Firmus.

374 · Election of Ambrose as bishop of Milan.

375 · Death of Valentinian I; appointment of Valentinian II as Augustus; death of Count Theodosius; retirement of Theodosius to Spain (West).

376 · First crossing of Goths into Thrace (East).

377 · Increasing tension with Gothic refugees in Thrace (East); the younger Theodosius has a command on the Danube (West).

378 · Battle of Adrianople; death of Valens; Gratian at Sirmium.

379 · Appointment of Theodosius as Augustus (January) (East); Illyricum becomes temporarily Eastern.

380 · War against Goths in the Balkans directed from Thessalonica;
Theodosius enters Constantinople in November (East).

381 · Gratian's court moves permanently to Milan; Illyricum is
restored to West; church councils in Constantinople and
Aquileia; election of Nectarius as bishop of Constantinople.

382 · Peace treaty with Goths in the East.

383 · Theodosius's son Arcadius becomes Augustus in January (East);
usurpation of Magnus Maximus and death of Gratian;
installation of regime of Valentinian II in Milan (West).

384 · Symmachus *praefectus urbi* in Rome; birth of Theodosius's son
Honorius; death of Damasus and election of Siricius as bishop
of Rome.

385 · First consulate of the child Arcadius; Eastern praetorian prefect
Cynegius travels in the Levant and encourages destruction of
temples.

386 · Magnus Maximus's praetorian prefect Euodius consul together
with Theodosius's son Honorius.

387 · Magnus Maximus invades Italy; Valentinian II flees to
Thessalonica.

388 · Theodosius defeats and kills Magnus Maximus and takes up
residence in Italy.

389 · Valentinian II takes up residence in Trier; Theodosius visits
Rome.

390 · Massacre of Thessalonica and subsequent tensions between
Theodosius and Ambrose.

391 · Theodosius returns to Constantinople.

392 · Death of Valentinian II; usurpation of Eugenius (West);
destruction of Sarapeion in Alexandria (East).

393 · Theodosius's son Honorius becomes Augustus in January;
Eugenius in Italy.

394 · Civil war: Theodosius defeats Eugenius's troops at the battle of
the Frigidus and returns to Milan; deaths of Eugenius, Arbogast,
and Virius Nicomachus Flavianus.

395 · Death of Theodosius.

ROMAN · IMPERIAL · POLICY

from JULIAN *to* THEODOSIUS

CHAPTER I

INTRODUCTION

The thirty years following the death of the apostate emperor Julian in Mesopotamia in the summer of 363 constituted one of the most dynamic periods in the history of the later Roman Empire. The responses of the imperial government to the challenges posed both by external and by internal forces changed and conditioned the structure of the empire in such enduring ways that it would be difficult to overestimate their importance. With the death of Julian the Constantinian dynasty ended, and we see with Valentinian, Valens, and Gratian, followed by Valentinian II and Theodosius, the successful creation of a new dynastic structure at the center of the empire, which lasted until 454 and preserved a certain level of unity. But at the same time the empire split into two parts, which gradually developed separate histories. This split did not first happen in 395 on the death of Theodosius I, but was already in place in 364, after which no serious effort was ever made to stop the gradual development of separate administrations in East and West. They cooperated indeed quite closely on occasion, and they certainly maintained the existential constitutional myth that all emperors always ruled everywhere, thereby upholding the idea that the empire was a single governmental and jurisdictional unit. But the regional division of responsibilities that Valentinian and Valens agreed on in early summer 364 was a real turning point, and this was a deliberate decision, not merely the accident of a sudden death. After 364 no Western emperor ever again exercised practical jurisdiction in the East and—apart from Theodosius's engagement in civil wars, which brought him twice briefly to Pannonia and Italy—no Eastern emperor ever again governed directly in the West, or even thought of doing so, until Justinian in the sixth century tried to turn the clock back and reconquer for Constantinople Rome and a Western empire, which by then had long been transformed by invading Germanic peoples.

These central years of the fourth century are a period of tension, of experiments, of breaks with tradition, while at the same time the great past of Rome formed the backdrop against which all events and developments took place, challenging and questioning the new. The practical governmental challenge posed by the sheer size of the empire was met by Valentinian and Valens pragmatically—and not for the first time—by dividing the empire into two areas of equal responsibility. The problem was old, the solution chosen not new, but this time it was enduring. As long as the city of Rome had been not only the ideological and name-giving center of the empire but also the center of administration and imperial residence, the imperial structure had been conceived in the traditional terms of the ruling center and the ruled periphery.

Whereas even an intensely active (and therefore frequently absent) soldier-emperor such as Trajan, or a restless traveler like Hadrian in the second century, never called the centralizing function of the city of Rome into question—though through their very restlessness they demonstrated in practice that the governmental center was not Rome, but wherever the emperor happened to be, and that other governmental structures were at least conceivable, if not conceived—the military crises of the third century and the structural political turmoil that they created left the city of Rome as a political backwater. Military necessity had by then transferred the emperors' main activity to the frontier districts; many never even visited the city; and when at the turn of the century under Diocletian and the tetrarchy a certain level of stability was again reached, the internal political map of the empire had changed out of all recognition. Communication with the frontier districts had become and remained of paramount importance; and if the emperor (or emperors) resided anywhere at all for longer periods, then it was with this factor in the foreground: instead of Rome, Milan and Aquileia became the main political centers in Italy; but rivals in Gaul (Trier and Arles), in the Balkans (Sirmium and Thessalonica), and in the East (Nikomedeia and Antioch) claimed the imperial presence much more often than did Rome.

The formal geographical division of administrative responsibility introduced by Diocletian, with several emperors each chosen by him and each ruling regionally in the name of all, soon collapsed when Constantine reverted to a traditional dynastic policy, but the idea of centrality, which the dynasty was supposed to personify, was immediately watered down again when Constantine founded his eponymous city on the Bosphorus as "New Rome." Its gradual development in the fourth century, especially favored by Constantius II and Valens, to become under Theodosius a real capital city, a long-term imperial residence and administrative center—called by at least some Easterners, even in semiofficial contexts, "the ruling city"—produced over time a permanent shift of the power balance toward the eastern part of the empire. Constantine and in the end Constantius II (followed in this respect by Julian and Jovian in their brief reigns) had nevertheless upheld the original dynastic imperial principle of "one empire, one emperor", and by more or less effective delegation of regional responsibilities to loyal subordinates or members of the dynasty maintained the fiction that the imperial government was a pyramid with one man, the emperor, at its peak. This changed when the troops who elected Valentinian in 364 at the same time insisted that he choose a partner in rule; they thereby brought about a practical division of equal responsibility that permanently altered the ethos of the empire and led in due course, through the almost inevitable separate development of the two "*partes imperii*," to its gradual dissolution as a recognizable single unit.

It was a long process, and various practical factors contributed to it. At Sirmium in 364 the brothers Valentinian and Valens divided up the existing administrative staff and the army units between them. Henceforth the tendency was very strong for future recruitment both to the administration and the army also to be regionally separate, and only in periods of severe crisis did exchanges of personnel from one part of the empire to the other take place. Individual careers became increasingly—but by no means exclusively—limited to one area or the other. This tendency was encouraged by the nature of the regional administration whereby the provinces were grouped into dioceses under *vicarii*, who in turn were subordinate representatives of the praetorian prefects; under Constantius II there emerged a group of three praetorian prefects who divided the administration of the empire among themselves with three geographically defined areas of responsibility. After the division of the empire between Valentinian and Valens, more or less along the line of division between Greek and Latin speakers — the main anomaly was that the Balkan peninsula at first remained Western — the East had one praetorian prefect (*Orientis*), while in the West there were two, the Gauls (*Galliarum*), which included Britain and Spain, and the central prefecture of Italy, Africa, and Illyricum. It seems to lie in the nature of bureaucratic structures that the longer they exist, the more independent and self-sufficient they become, each developing its own internal structure and ethos, its own history and documentary archive. These structures are not unalterable, but the dead weight of tradition and vested interest makes fundamental change difficult. Only a major crisis produces the impetus to reform, and even then tradition can be reasserted. Our period is one of development, of controlled change within preexisting structures, but during this time innovative administrative traditions were established as well.

The security factor also played a role in allowing the *partes imperii* to grow apart. This was indeed a major consideration when Valentinian divided up the army units between himself and his brother Valens. The main aim was that each should be responsible for the security of his own sector, so that the military weakness caused in the West by Julian's stripping Gaul of its best troops to fight his civil war against Constantius and then to participate in the invasion of Sassanid Mesopotamia would not be repeated. The separation seems in general to have worked reasonably well. But frontier activity is not just decided by the defenders, who cannot always choose the place or intensity of their actions. It was the misfortune of the Eastern sector in our period to be confronted with a grave, indeed epochal, crisis when large numbers of Goths asked Valens for asylum in Roman territory in Thrace in 376. When their dissatisfaction at their treatment by the Roman authorities turned them into enemies once they had arrived on Roman soil, the crisis was there, and the resulting war cost Valens his life. Thereafter the Goths remained in our period largely an Eastern problem, even though the Western emperor Gratian was also affected by the war and sent specialists and troop reinforcements to help his uncle. But even after Valens's death in the battle at Adrianople in 378 Gratian had no thought of taking on full responsibility for the East himself. He and his advisers saw the only possible solution to the crisis in the continuation of the division of the empire: they sought a replacement for Valens who would solve the Eastern problem for them —while preventing it from becoming a serious Western one also—and then continue to rule the East separately, as the unfortunate Valens had done. The crisis was therefore put to rest when Theodosius finally settled the war-weary Goths on lands on the lower Danube and subsequently offered many of their young men employment in his Eastern army.

Internal security also played its part in consolidating the divisions. Usurpations—military challenges to a ruling emperor—could by their nature only begin regionally, since no challenger was so foolish or so well organized as to challenge both emperors, who were nearly always thousands of kilometers apart, at the same time. Three such attempts took place in our period. The first was an Eastern challenge to Valens in 365 by Procopius, who claimed Constantinian connections; its defeat had no further effect beyond stabilizing Valens's Eastern regime and proving the effectiveness of the recent partition of the empire. The other two challenges are more interesting. Magnus Maximus and his British troops felt that Gratian was inadequate as emperor and so removed him in 383. Their aim, however, was purely Western. Theodosius in the East was not challenged. Indeed, quite the opposite: Maximus's negotiations with Theodosius aimed at mutual recognition as partners in rule and nothing more. In the end it was Theodosius who found the arrangement unsatisfactory, but not because he wanted to revert to the unitary governmental model of Constantius and Julian, rather because he seems to have felt that a continuation of Maximus's rule in the West might endanger the succession of his sons; and the same basic consideration applied to his reaction to the usurpation of Eugenius in 393. The empire could and should remain partitioned, as long as both parts stayed in the family. Theodosius's interventions in Western affairs were, therefore, intended to uphold the division of responsibilities introduced by Valentinian and Valens, but on his own conditions. The usurpations, however, showed that not all found the dynastic argument convincing.

A third major area of interest in which the thirty years saw a significant development was that of the relationship of the representatives of

the state to those of organized Christian religion. Constantius II, following in the steps of his father, Constantine, had aimed to create a single
official imperial church in order to give the empire the moral and institutional support he thought it needed. Since his ecclesiastical advisers
felt this could only be achieved if everybody belonging to the official
church accepted exactly the same formula of belief, down to the precise form of words in which it was expressed, this requirement caused
severe and ongoing problems, in particular in the tricky philosophical
question of how to express the precise relationship of the members of
the Holy Trinity to each other. Emperors from Constantine onward had
felt obliged to make efforts to get their bishops to agree on such a formula and take measures to have it generally accepted. Shortly before
Constantius II died in 361 he had pressured recalcitrant bishops in East
and West to accept a new formula, changing that agreed on at Nikaia,
which, however, met severe resistance in the West and was only forced
through in the East because the emperor, who was present, used his secular authority to do so. When the apostate Julian took over as emperor,
he announced a policy of universal tolerance, hoping for the chaos of
disunity; and when he died a few months later, his successors were confronted with a natural split in the church between the almost universal
Western acceptance of the Nicene formula and the almost universal acceptance in the East, by those bishops supported in office by Constantius who were still there, of the new so-called homoian formula. Valentinian and Valens were pragmatic enough to leave things largely as they
found them, and no new empire-wide initiative was started. This meant,
of course, that incumbents of bishoprics in East and West tended to
regard each other as heretics, and the later victorious catholics had no
hesitation in calling the emperor Valens himself one, though he did no
more than accept the status quo. In this way the religious factor, instead
of aiding the unity of the empire as Constantine and Constantius had
intended, had just the opposite effect and tended in this period to cement the separation of the *partes imperii*, which for other, more practical
reasons of imperial administration the two emperors had agreed on.

Had Valens survived the Gothic war of 378, the Eastern church might
well have remained "homoian" in perpetuity and thus have formally

separated from the Western church much earlier than in fact happened. Theodosius was, however, in this respect less conciliatory than his predecessor Valens. A Western catholic advised by Western catholics who wished those ecclesiastics living in his area of residence and supporting him also to be catholics, he immediately began replacing "homoian" bishops with catholics—who were in the meanwhile in rather short supply in the East—as soon as he came to Constantinople. His idea, however, seems to have been restricted to doing what he thought right doctrinally, and had little to do with global visions of a united church helping to unite the empire, as was envisaged by Constantine and Constantius. For Theodosius the doctrinal question seems to have been separate from the division of the empire, which he simply accepted as given. Once the Gothic war seemed manageable and he moved to Constantinople in 380, he strictly rejected attempts by Western ecclesiastics to interfere in Eastern church affairs.

These developments, on different planes of consciousness, make the period from Julian to Theodosius one of central importance for the development of the empire. It is, however, not the intention of this book to explore every last detail of the period. The aim here is above all to focus on the changing role of the state and its structures and mechanisms, its reaction to crisis and to the tensions between tradition and renewal. Much recent work on the fourth century has neglected the state, concentrating largely on social or intellectual developments. The time has perhaps come to begin to take a new look at the functions of the emperor and the way the Roman state was run in the fourth century. Concerning the early and middle Empire, there has been a great deal of discussion in the last decades stimulated by Fergus Millar's epochal book *The Emperor in the Roman World* (1977), about the nature of imperial government. The basic question raised by Millar was whether the central government of the empire broadly speaking developed its own active policies, or rather simply reacted to problems and proposals presented to it. In general Millar's views that government was in most ways for most of the time reactive remain most convincing. But the model of the reactive emperor has not yet been systematically tested in application to the post-Constantinian period, for which it offers an equally convincing interpretative instrument—despite the different nature of the source material at our disposal. A secondary purpose of this book is therefore to attempt a contribution to an extended debate, to explore some material that has usually been interpreted differently, and to produce some arguments for the validity of the reactive model in the fourth century, and perhaps beyond.

There are, of course, structural differences in the post-tetrarchic fourth century that affected the detailed mechanisms of "petition and response." In particular in the latter part of the century, with which I am primarily concerned, the division of the empire into the two "*partes*" and the consolidation of the regional governmental structure within each of them according to the praetorian prefectures were major changes in the form of government from that of the pre-tetrarchic phase. Also, the gradual division of the provinces into much smaller geographical units from the time of the tetrarchy onward altered the lower levels of the administrative structure. On the one hand, this made it easier for local authorities and interested parties to contact the responsible provincial governor; on the other hand, the multiplication of governors also increased the possibility of local dissatisfaction. Because more people were directly involved in governing, there were simply more chances of something going wrong, and this development in itself may well have stimulated an increasing number of direct approaches to the central authorities, or at least have raised the number of official requests for advice from the larger number of overcautious local officials. One further area was, since Constantine, quite new: the official tolerance followed by the active favoring of the Christian church. It would, of course, be false to deny that here the imperial center developed initiatives that made themselves felt throughout the empire (and then under Julian produced an equally centralized hostile reaction), in each case beginning with the will of the emperor personally. Once, however, the major decision to favor the church had been taken, the church authorities adapted astonishingly quickly to the new climate, and in the last resort they found no better way of representing their interests or solving local disciplinary, or even dogmatic, problems than by approaching the emperor and eliciting an imperial response to their petition. This was no different in principle from the centuries-old behavior of generations of city administrations, who since the Republic had always communicated in just the same way with the central authorities of the empire. The broad policy in this area, as in many others, was indeed that of the emperor, but the knotty problems associated with its realization in detail, which required much more governmental attention, could, it seems, still only be resolved by a steady stream of imperial responses to locally generated problems and petitions.

The problems of the population of the empire continued to be brought to the notice of the emperor and his court, whether by representative embassies or by individuals, by official notification or requests for advice or instructions on how to act by the lower bureaucracy in the provinces (*consultationes*). Global policies could indeed be conceived centrally, but their local application depended to a great extent on two-way communication between center and periphery, which can be subsumed under Millar's shorthand phrase "petition and response." In some cases it is possible to discern central policies that seem to have developed out of a series of similar ad hoc decisions ("responses"). Each replied to a perceived local or regional problem that provoked a local solution; but taken together such replies suggest a tendency, an inclination, to decide similar things in similar ways, thus finally creating the impression of a considered policy, which, once appreciated, might be articulated in a general law summarizing but also perhaps systematically going beyond individual decisions. This practice was certainly not new in the fourth century; it merely continued existing procedures. Continuity in basic governmental practice therefore seems a more likely model than a fundamentally different approach.

The chapters that follow are each devoted to one specific theme relating to the development of the structure and mechanisms of the empire. We begin at the top in part 1 with the emperors, their aims, and the chief events affecting them, especially the embryonic building of new dynastic structures in the post-Constantinian world. The next chapter illustrates the government in action in foreign and frontier policy. With the scene thus set, part 2 lays out in three longer chapters some internal organizational problems of the period. We look first at the broad administrative structure of the empire, emphasizing the regional and often reactive nature of imperial administration and legislation, and examining how this affected governmental practice and what the regional, reactive model means for the historical interpretation of our legal sources. The role and development of the two great cities of the empire, Rome and Constantinople, belong to our survey of the forms of regional government. Finally, part 3 addresses the role of the state in religious affairs at this dynamic phase of the development of the Christian empire. The conclusions to be drawn offer much support for extending Millar's thesis of the fundamentally reactive emperor to the later empire.

PART · I

ACTORS & EVENTS

CHAPTER II

EMPERORS · & · DYNASTIES

The purpose of this chapter is to explore and relate the changes at the topmost level of the empire, that of the emperors themselves, which the crisis caused by the sudden death of Julian brought about. We shall examine the way in which, despite further military and political crises, the dynastic principle continued to be the most widely favored—it seems almost the inevitable—form of imperial government at the highest level of the empire. Because after Julian the Constantinian dynasty offered no further acceptable candidate for the imperial purple, decisions taken by the leading military men, who hoped to be able to channel the loyalties of their troops to reinforce their choice, conditioned the processes through which new emperors were created. The men chosen were, foreseeably, themselves military men, who then tried to fulfill the expectations of their electors by regularly taking the field at the head of an army and thus in a traditional Roman way gaining and strengthening charismatic legitimacy through repeated military victory.

At the same time, however, the charisma that the post-Julian emperors won tended to be exploited in order to promote members of their own family—even small children—in the public view, in the hope that they would themselves in due course acquire sufficient public acceptance in the decisive circles of the empire to seem inevitable successors and thus be able to renew the dynastic imperial system created centuries ago under great difficulties by Augustus and most recently restored by Constantine. By the time of Theodosius's death in 395 the dynastic principle was once more sufficiently well established for his two quite unmilitary sons Arcadius and Honorius, basking in the light of their father's charisma, to take over the rule in East and West unchallenged. A new—but by no means wholly happy—phase in the history of the Roman empire had begun. This chapter will outline and explain how it became possible.

The End of the Constantinians

The death of the emperor Julian in June 363 on campaign beyond the eastern frontier in Mesopotamia brought to a head the structural political crisis of the empire, which Constantine's dynasty, through a mixture of luck, good management, and great expense of energy, had disguised for a generation. Constantine, not least through the sheer length of his rule, had created a complex network of loyalties to himself and his sons within the army and the administrative elite, so that on his death no alternative to the succession of one or more of the sons was seriously considered; these loyalties were also strong enough to survive the brutal series of murders and internal disagreements that again and again produced dangerous tensions. In the 350s they allowed Constantius II to overcome the usurpation attempt of a Gallic pretender, Magnentius, caused by a regional army's feeling itself disadvantaged by its current regional emperor, Constantius's younger brother Constans.[1]

The division of spheres of responsibility on a geographical basis made possible the relatively unproblematic succession of the three sons of Constantine in 337. The innate centrifugal tendencies of such a gigantic geographically defined political structure as the Roman Empire were counteracted by the postulated internal dynastic loyalty of each of the Augusti to each other and by the employment in each area of the system of dynastic patronage developed by Constantine. This implied the retention of almost identical administrative and personnel structures. Additionally the ideological theory that all acted as one—for instance, all legislation, even if only of local or regional application, was formally issued in the names of all ruling emperors listed in order of seniority— served to maintain the surface public impression of a unified political structure. A series of accidents and external events strained the system to the breaking point: in particular the unexpected death, in 340, of Constantine II, who as the eldest surviving son had begun a dispute with Constans over responsibility for the central area of the empire— Italy, Africa, and the great military recruitment area Illyricum—created a massive imbalance. Constans reacted to the event by simply taking over Gaul in addition to the disputed central area without even consulting his elder brother Constantius in the East. That was followed ten years later by the murder of Constans by the minions of the military usurper Magnentius, which in effect left Constantius, once he had defeated Magnentius, as sole legitimate ruler and thus shattered the Constantinian dynasty as well as shaking the imperial governmental system based on it to its foundations.

Here we see the fundamental dilemma facing every emperor. Over the centuries of its existence the empire had simply become too big and too complex for one person at the top, however energetic, to administer effectively; yet the complex system of personal loyalties and interdependencies within the upper classes and military commanders in the different regions, which was an essential stabilizing factor for the empire, nevertheless still seemed to require an active military man who was prepared to travel, show himself, and if necessary lead his army in the fight, not just a sedentary figurehead sitting in some palace complex issuing instructions. To establish his legitimacy and to rule effectively a Roman emperor needed wide consensual acceptance—particularly among the military and high administrative classes—which did not come about and continue automatically by some magical process but required constant personal attention. The use of violence by a competitor or a usurper against a ruling (that is, already accepted) emperor who fulfilled the expectations of these influential classes of people virtually excluded that essential empire-wide acceptance which in the last resort constituted legitimacy and provided the only effective basis for long-term success.[2] In practice the only person who could appoint a joint ruler without causing serious institutional problems for himself and his candidate was a ruling and accepted emperor himself. Thus an attack on one member of an established imperial college tended to be regarded as an attack on the others also—and on the "loyalty system" as a whole. Constantius does not seem to have hesitated long before deciding to go to war against his brother's murderer, Magnentius, although he was far away in Antioch in Syria when he heard the news. This decision was taken despite the facts that Magnentius in Gaul was anxious to negotiate, that his support in the West—even in Rome—was by no means negligible, and that many highly placed Easterners would have been happy to retain Constantius and his court in the East in order to avoid a civil war fought largely at their expense and, it must have seemed to many, for merely dynastic reasons.[3] But Constantius and his closest advisers automatically took the view that Magnentius could never be accepted as a legitimate colleague in rule because he had shown such massive disloyalty to the imperial governmental system by challenging, and then murdering, Constans. Despite initial tensions between the brothers, in the last resort Constantius had accepted Constans fully as his colleague and as joint guarantor for the dynastic system of regionally divided responsibilities. By the time of Magnentius's putsch, a challenge to one brother was seen as a challenge to both.

There was, however, a serious practical problem caused by this mindset. If Constantius went to the West to fight against Magnentius, the question immediately arose as to who was to rule the East in his absence, who was to constitute the controlling peak of the imperial patronage system there? It was clearly desirable to have somebody represent the empire in person — not just a high administrative official or general — particularly in view of the ongoing tensions with the Sassanian Persians on the Mesopotamian frontier. But there were no family members left who had sufficient experience and ability to rule the East as Constantius's equal; there was nobody who could immediately succeed to Constans's place in the imperial college and share as a colleague the burdens and rights of an emperor, bearing that highest title available for a Roman ruler, "Augustus." Despite this problem Constantius showed no intention of going outside the family "firm" for his choice of helper because embarrassing questions could then be raised about the point of fighting a civil war for dynastic reasons, if the only result was to be the appointment of someone else outside the family. He therefore reanimated the institution of the "Caesar" — a kind of junior emperor, a status that he and his brothers had all enjoyed under their father until Constantine's death — and appointed in great haste his half cousin (son of his father's half brother) Constantius Gallus, who promptly took up residence in Antioch in 351.

Gallus's brutal and unpopular activities in Antioch rapidly showed his inadequacy for the imperial role he was intended to play; and after the final defeat, in 353, of Magnentius, who conveniently committed suicide,

Gallus was recalled and discreetly eliminated in a provincial prison, far away from major military or urban centers that might object: a failed Caesar had no future, either at court or in private life. But the governmental problem was not solved by this act of summary justice. One man alone, even with loyal and efficient subordinates, could not adequately rule the whole empire. Constantius had no choice if he wanted to retain the dynastic structure. He himself had no male children, and there was only one surviving Constantinian adult male left, Gallus's younger half brother, Julian. Despite serious doubts about his suitability for an imperial function, Julian, not yet twenty-five years old, was summoned to the court at Milan and in 355 made Caesar with special responsibility for Gaul.[4] This enabled Constantius in due course to return to the East and the Mesopotamian frontier, but once again the dynastic choice caused as many problems as it solved. Not that Julian was unsuccessful in his job—indeed, quite the opposite. The Gallic army under his nominal command went from victory to victory, so that by 360 both Julian and his army were dissatisfied with his junior status as Caesar, and in a ceremony staged at Paris he asserted his formal equality with Constantius: Julian became Augustus.

Constantius, who had not been consulted, reacted formalistically and stiffly refused to negotiate, beginning immediate preparations for military action against his half cousin. He now regarded Julian as a usurper—inevitably so, given his inflexible view that all legitimacy as a ruler flowed from his own sovereign decision—and a betrayer of the dynastic collegiate principle, within which he as Augustus was the senior and all-deciding figure. Once again the weaknesses of dynastic rule were glaringly apparent. Family ties and blood relationship alone certainly offered no absolute guarantee of efficiency (though that could in itself be compensated for by attentive staff work), but it had now become shockingly clear, and not for the first time, that there were circumstances in which they guaranteed not even a minimum level of obedience and personal loyalty. This time the empire was lucky in its misfortune. Forestalling another civil war, which, given the potential combatants, could only have had devastating effects on the fundamental dynastic loyalties on which the governmental system depended, Constantius suddenly became mortally ill. Before his death on 3 November 361 he demonstrated statesmanship and dynastic solidarity by accepting the inevitable and publicly recognizing Julian as Augustus. Julian himself, hurrying from Gaul with his military challenge, had already reached Naissus (Niš in Serbia) by the time the news reached him. It enabled him to drop his military threats and to march on to Constantinople as recognized single legitimate emperor of the whole empire.

Less than two years later, on 26 June 363, Julian was also dead, the most prominent victim of the invasion of Sassanid Mesopotamia, which he had undertaken with great enthusiasm that same spring. He had taken no precautions for the event of his premature death or for any other eventuality concerning the rule of the empire, though a rumor that he had secretly encouraged Procopius, a relative on his mother's side, to grasp the purple should he die in the war, was later circulated. However, this rumor was probably propagated by Procopius himself, when he indeed launched a usurping claim to the purple late in 365.[5] The soldiers of the expeditionary army that Julian had led against the Persians were now stranded in Mesopotamia without commander or emperor, since Julian had occupied both functions, and were surrounded by aggressive Persian troops. Their immediate problems were existential, much more urgent than any longer-term emotional considerations of dynastic loyalty. Had Procopius been with them on the spot, he might possibly have been able to play the dynastic card, even in the emergency; but he was hundreds of miles away, safe in Roman territory, and the imperial army, surrounded by the enemy in the middle of enemy territory, felt not only that it needed an emperor and commander immediately but also that it was entitled to attend to its own pressing problems and choose one. The historian Ammianus Marcellinus was present with the expeditionary force, though he did not belong to the inner circle that participated in the deliberations leading to the appointment as Augustus of the senior guards officer (*primicerius domesticorum*) Jovian, whose origins were in Illyricum (he had been born at Singidunum [Belgrade]). Ammianus was therefore unable to discover precisely why Jovian had been chosen by the caucus of leading military and court officials. He records only that he was a compromise candidate, acceptable both to the Western group of officers who had supported Julian's usurpation in Paris and accompanied him from Gaul and to the residual Eastern staff members, whom Julian had taken over with most of Constantius's entourage when he arrived at Constantinople. Ammianus, who did not approve of Jovian as emperor, sardonically comments that perhaps the virtues of his father, Varronianus, a retired commander of the guards (*comes domesticorum*), had recommended him, thereby hinting, one might suppose, that an Illyrican faction among the senior officers had been largely responsible for the selection.[6]

However, nobody present doubted the validity of this precipitate election. Jovian himself only saw problems regarding a challenge from the West. As soon as he had extracted the army from Mesopotamia by making a highly unfavorable and much criticized peace treaty with the Persian king Shapur,[7] he sent off a group of officers posthaste to inform his father-in-law, Lucillianus, a temporarily retired general currently living at Sirmium, that he should make senior military appointments in the West in his name and generally work to establish Jovian's authority in the West. According to Ammianus, the new emperor feared that forces in Gaul or Illyricum might challenge him once they heard how he had been chosen.[8] He traveled westward as fast as he could in order to show himself personally. This was sensible enough. His purpose was to try to create the type of personal loyalty and interdependency between himself as emperor and his most influential subjects — here particularly the soldiers and the traditional administrative elites in the West — which in general had served Constantine's dynasty, despite all internal disputes, satisfactorily. This operation would inevitably cost the empire much money for donations to the troops and posts for the most influential members of the upper classes, but it was generally expected and was politically the right thing to do. Jovian even began immediate public relations work on proving that he also had the wherewithal to build an imperial dynasty: his father-in-law, Lucillianus, was foreseen as supreme commander (*magister equitum et peditum*) in the West;[9] his retired but well-respected father, Varronianus, was intended to share the inaugural consulship of 364 with him;[10] and a baby boy, also called Varronianus, was born to him at about the time of his election as emperor, thus providing immediate and visible hopes for a dynastic future.[11]

Jovian clearly set out with the best intentions to make good the disaster of Julian's Mesopotamian expedition, but was plagued by accident and misfortune. Lucillianus, a key figure in his plans, was soon killed in a military mutiny at Reims,[12] and his father, Varronianus, died before he could enter on his consulship on 1 January. He was replaced on short notice by his homonymous six-month-old grandchild, who was, of course, incapable of carrying out even the most straightforward parts of the formal inauguration ceremonial—he would not keep still and cried all the time—so giving gratuitous offense to traditionalists, who felt, not unreasonably, that the ancient office, still the most prestigious distinction the state had to offer, had been trivialized.[13] But worse was still to come: during the westward march from Ankara, where the consular inauguration ceremonies had taken place on 1 January[14] and where the court spent the deepest part of the winter, halt was made on 17 February at the provincial frontier station Dadastana. Those responsible for waking the emperor found him the next day dead in his bed, overcome, it seems, by poisonous fumes emitted from a charcoal-burning stove in the room.[15] Eight months had passed since the death of Julian. Tragic events seemed indeed to be repeating themselves as farce.

The Valentinians

The court moved on to the nearest large city, the Bithynian provincial capital, Nikaia, where the highest military and civilian officials of the empire who happened to be in the area met in conclave to choose yet another emperor. Ammianus again seems well informed, knowing of discussions about two candidates, neither of whom for one reason or another met general approval, until at last Valentinian's name convinced the caucus. Valentinian, another Illyrican army man—he was born at Cibalae in Pannonia—as were both rejected candidates, had retired from the army under Julian but then joined Lucillianus in his efforts to win acceptance for Jovian in the western provinces. He had escaped from Reims during the mutiny in which Lucillianus was killed and had brought the bad news to Jovian in Anatolia. Valentinian stayed behind at Ankara for some reason when the court left the city, and he was still there when he was summoned to Nikaia by the news of his election as emperor; he was invested with the purple on 26 February.[16] The empire had survived the ten-day vacancy. The army was not, however, satisfied that this decision of the officers' caucus was in itself an adequate guarantee of stability at the top, and demanded that Valentinian immediately choose and name a joint emperor to share the responsibility of rule. In view of recent events the aim was legitimate enough: to exclude a repetition of the governmental crisis that had now repeated itself three times in as many years, each instance caused by the constitutional vacuum following the sudden death of an emperor who had chosen to rule without a colleague.[17] Valentinian, however, was irritated at the army's interference and postponed his compliance with their wishes, asserting that he needed time to find a capable man whom he trusted, but he also admitted that there was no escaping the pressure in the long term. By the time the troops reached Constantinople he had decided. On 28 March, at the suburban barracks known as Hebdomon ("Seven-Mile"), Valentinian's brother Valens was presented to the troops and formally acclaimed by them as Augustus.[18] The period of one-man rule was over, and as long as the united empire in East and West existed, it did not recur. Dynastic considerations had, however, once again defeated any thought of choosing "the best man."

Toward the end of April the new emperors left Constantinople together on the great military road through the Balkans, moving via Serdica (Sofia) and Naissus (Niš) to Sirmium (Srmska Mitrovica). Valentinian was eager to waste no time in imposing his presence on the West, which had not seen a legitimate Augustus in person since Constantius left Illyricum to return to Constantinople in 359, and where in Britain, on the Rhine, and on the Danube, as well as in Africa, the frontier zones were under pressure.[19] His recent experience as Jovian's envoy with Lucillianus will have convinced him of the urgency. As the two emperors journeyed, they made plans and worked out global policy patterns: at Naissus they decided how to divide up the highest military officers and the existing army units between them, and by the time they arrived in

Sirmium in July they had also agreed on a division of the empire along geographical lines. Valentinian, as senior Augustus, had first choice and chose the West; he then hurried on to Milan. Valens accepted his lot and returned to Constantinople to govern the East.[20] On 1 January 365, with each in his own temporary residence, Valentinian in Milan, Valens in Constantinople, the brothers celebrated the New Year and the inauguration of their first joint consulship. However, after separating at Sirmium they never saw each other again.

The Eastern imperial propagandist Themistius, who delivered a speech in the Senate at Constantinople sometime before Valens's first consular inauguration on 1 January 365, emphasized the closeness of the relationship between the two brothers but also addressed the division of responsibility and the particular interest of Valens in Constantinople. These brothers, said Themistius, were different from those of recent experience—he meant the Constantinian dynasty—because they offered security and order; the geographical division of the empire that they had agreed on was depicted as part of an improved imperial security system, ensuring that "the emperor" was—by a flight of rhetorical fantasy—at the same time in Italy and on the Bosphorus, in Britain and in Syria. The empire was thus paradoxically united and strengthened by being geographically divided; these brothers in their mutual trust and divinely protected interdependence were the ideal solution to the governmental problems of the empire.[21] So the propaganda for highly placed Eastern doubters. Valens's spokesman Themistius continued over the next period of years to emphasize the mutual trust and cooperation of the two brothers, but in fact their regions presented totally different problems to their governments, incorporating as they did quite different political and cultural traditions. It was therefore virtually inevitable, given the lack of real regular contact between them, that they began increasingly to develop in different ways. Because of the great distances involved, consultation was never possible when precipitate action was required, and this fact—a fundamental reason for the division of responsibility in the first place—also inevitably encouraged independent action and provoked separate long-term developments.

The first internal challenge to the new emperors and their system of government occurred in the East, where Valens, an unsophisticated Balkan soldier who knew little or no Greek, had serious difficulties in making himself acceptable to Constantinopolitan society, despite his assiduous employment of Themistius's rhetorical talents as propagandist. In late September, while Valens was on the road headed for Antioch and the eastern frontier, Procopius, claiming to be the last remaining adult male of the Constantinian dynasty—he was in fact a maternal relative of Julian's—declared himself emperor in Constantinople. He was supported by some troops who happened to be passing through the city and to whom he promised a rich donative, as well as by various highly placed friends, ex-officials, and disappointed beneficiaries of the Constantinian dynasty. He even drafted into his movement Constantius II's widow, Faustina, and their little daughter, Constantia, who were living in Constantinople, to support his Constantinian image building. A great deal, as always when such challenges occurred, would now depend on the attitude of the main body of troops on the spot, and in the last resort Procopius's generals and their men were not prepared to battle it out against Valens, whose formal legitimacy, created by his brother's choice and the acclamation of the massed troops assembled at the Hebdomon in March 364, no military man who had participated in the ceremony could reasonably deny.[22] It still took several months, however, before Valens had mobilized his own troops for the decisive confrontation that ended the usurpation attempt in spring 366.[23]

Valentinian did nothing to help his brother. After it was all safely over, the prominent Roman senator Symmachus, visiting Trier on an official mission and making a public speech at court, could flatter Valentinian's public spirit—while looking back from a safe distance—by citing a reason for his staying in Gaul: while the Alamanni were enemies of the whole empire, Procopius was only a "private enemy," a view echoed in Ammianus Marcellinus's account of the events.[24] A contemporary Greek writer, Eunapius of Sardis, himself no friend of Valens, had a different interpretation: Valentinian refused to send help to somebody who took insufficient care of what had been entrusted to him.[25] It seems, therefore, that military help might have been welcome (though we have no evidence that Valens made a formal request), but in the event there certainly was none. Valens, however, did not hesitate to inform Valentinian of his success in the traditional way by sending Procopius's severed head to Trier, and two highly placed Gauls who had served Procopius as urban prefect (*praefectus urbi*) at Constantinople and as master of the offices (*magister officiorum*), Phronimius and Euphrasius, were also sent to Valentinian for trial.[26] Valens thus survived his first crisis as emperor, a fairly serious challenge to his rule backed by at least some members of the Eastern political establishment, thanks to the troops' recognition of his undeniable legitimacy. The power placed at his disposal by his brother had in the last resort been adequate for the purpose. Valentinian's lack of interest in the East was doubtless a sign of his own priorities, as Symmachus suggested, but the system, the regional division of responsibilities on which the brothers had agreed, had been proved viable and had withstood its first major test.

It is therefore scarcely surprising that the next years show no sign of closer practical cooperation between the Augusti and that the official speech that Themistius delivered in Constantinople effectively announcing the end of the persecution of Procopius's sympathizers did not so much as mention Valentinian.[27] Valens's initiative in beginning a war against the Goths on the lower Danube, some of whom had supported Procopius, and for which he needed three annual campaigns (367–69), was, however, taken only after consultation with Valentinian, whose responsibility for the security of neighboring Pannonia might well have been affected by Valens's activities.[28] Efforts to induce the public to accept that a dynasty was in the making also began as early as 366, when Valentinian's six-year-old son, Gratian, was made consul along with the general Dagalaifus. A year and a half later, on 24 August 368, after Valentinian suffered a serious illness, Gratian was declared to be Augustus, like his father and uncle. Gratian's elevation was also widely celebrated in the East, as shown by an official inscription from Antioch by Pisidia that honors Gratian in phrases strictly speaking belonging to his uncle in the immediate aftermath of Procopius's rebellion, as "champion of the Roman constitution and of liberty."[29] Any potential Western criticism of the appointment of the child as Augustus was stifled in a public speech by Symmachus, still (or again) at court in Trier, who summoned history to his aid in the search for precedents—though none of his examples truly paralleled the case of the eight-year-old emperor. In the end nobody present can have minded much, since Symmachus finally confirmed, for those attuned to interpreting imperial panegyric, that Gratian would have no practical ruling function, not even as a regional puppet. He did so by formulating the absurd conceit that in contrast to Valentinian and Valens, who each had only part of the empire, Gratian possessed it all.[30] Gratian's teacher, Ausonius, managed to trump this by developing a rhetorical flight of fancy that compared the imperial governmental structure of the three Augusti with the structure of the Holy Trinity.[31] The message was well taken.

Valens forced the pace even more in respect to dynasty building. His own son, Valentinianus Galates, had been born on 18 January 366, during the revolt of Procopius, but reached the consulship already on 1 January 369 with Valens's general Victor as colleague. The inauguration ceremony took place at the imperial winter quarters at Marcianopolis in Thrace. Once again Themistius was there to suggest to the assembled dignitaries in the elegant obscurity of panegyrical rhetoric what they should think and expect: as with Gratian's precedent, the consulship was, asserts Themistius, for a child born in the purple merely the first public step in his own advancement to it. Currently the empire possessed three Augusti; soon the East would draw level and restore the parallelism with the West.[32] Hopes for this scenario were, however, dashed almost as quickly as they were raised. By 373 at the latest the boy Galates was dead, and Themistius, speaking at the ceremony celebrating Valens's tenth year of rule (*decennalia*) in that year, was publicly expressing official hopes for a replacement.[33] They were disappointed, and worse was still to come. In November 375, during a campaign on the middle Danube, Valentinian, aged only fifty-four, suddenly died at Brigetio. Gratian, who had been left at Trier, was still just sixteen, but with suitable advisers might conceivably have been able to grow into the office. Valentinian's military staff officers on the spot, however, in particular the infantry general (*magister peditum*) Flavius Merobaudes, who had moved on from Brigetio to Aquincum (Budapest), were dissatisfied at this prospect, doubtless suspecting that with the young Gratian as sole Western Augustus, already equipped with his own favored circle of advisers, they themselves might not be able to exert as much influence as they had been accustomed to and thought desirable. They therefore acted quickly, taking advantage of the nearby presence of Valentinian's ambitious second wife, Justina, and her four-year-old son, also named Valentinian, to "elect" the child as successor to his father as Augustus and have him acclaimed by their troops, who were happy enough to act as emperor makers since they could anticipate a sizable donative to help assuage their consciences, if indeed conscience was a factor.

Given that neither of the existing Augusti, neither Valens nor Gratian, had even been consulted about this decision, and that there was no way in which the four-year-old could himself "rule", the action reeked of usurpation by a clique, despite the fact that the little boy (now for us Valentinian II) was already being groomed for a life in the purple by his father. Before his sudden death he had designated the boy for the consulship of 376 together with his uncle Valens.[34] The pattern for the public promotion of children of the dynasty was by now familiar. However, Valentinian II's promoters seem to have expected trouble with Gratian and his advisers at Trier, which in the event did not materialize. The timescale is uncertain. Soon after Valentinian I's death Valens sent Themistius to Rome and on to Trier, where he delivered a speech praising Gratian, which he later published in the East. According to this speech only two Augusti were in control of the empire—clearly Valens and Gratian—and they were planning to meet at Rome. To arrange this meeting may indeed have been the main purpose of Themistius's long journey from Antioch. Since his speech cannot be dated much earlier than spring 376, it follows that neither Gratian nor Valens had by then recognized Valentinian II as Augustus.[35]

Events, however, favored the child and his backers, for the meeting of the two Augusti at Rome never took place. Just that spring Valens was confronted by a massive movement of Goths from their settlement areas in modern Romania, where they were threatened by wandering Huns, toward the lower Danube frontier. The leader of the Gothic tribe of the Tervingi now requested asylum for his people south of the river in the Roman province. Only six years before, Valens had fought three difficult

EMPERORS & DYNASTIES
27

campaigns to prevent periodic Gothic incursions over the river; now permanent settlement was supposed to happen by agreement. Valens and his army were still resident in northern Syria, based at Antioch, and busy on the eastern frontier, while at the same time he was forced to negotiate with the Goths. This combination of circumstances was doubtless the main reason why he could not travel to Rome to meet Gratian and his advisers, as he and Themistius had planned, to discuss the particularly delicate dynastic problem caused by the coup-like elevation of Valentinian II. If Gothic immigration could not be prevented, a well-controlled agreement might at least try to keep it in check. The integrity of the Danubian provinces seemed threatened by the Goths' movements, and this was seen to be more urgent than the notional stability of the dynastic order. As the immigrants proved less amenable to accommodation than Valens had hoped, he asked Gratian for military help; Frigeridus was sent immediately with Pannonian troops and was operating in Thrace as early as 377.[36] The potential Gothic emergency on the Danube impinged on both parts of the empire too strongly to risk an internal dispute with Valentinian's military officers about the legitimacy of their action in acclaiming Valentinian II as Augustus. The looming crisis made his recognition inevitable, and there would be time to find him some kind of function after it was over. Gratian therefore showed no open displeasure at the action of the caucus of Valentinian's officers at Aquincum and accepted his half brother into the imperial residence at Trier, where he would grow up under the supervision of Gratian's own advisers. The formal balanced structure of the empire that Valentinian and Valens had created was put out of equilibrium, but this solution was certainly less dangerous than to allow a son of Valentinian I—particularly in view of the looming ambitions of his mother, Justina—to live somewhere independently of the main court of the West with his own imperial establishment, where he might easily serve as a focus for undesirable or dangerous elements.[37]

The Gothic crisis, however, had more shocks in store. In spring 378 Valens felt compelled to take personal responsibility for military activities in Thrace. After appealing to Gratian for more emergency help he left Antioch for the scene of the action. This time Gratian decided to come personally, but before he and his army could arrive from Germany Valens committed his troops to battle against the Goths near Adrianople on 9 August 378 and was never seen again.[38] Gratian was still some 200 miles away with his army when the news of the lost battle reached him, and he returned at once to the main city of central Illyricum, Sirmium, where he awaited events. The extent of the disaster and his uncle's disappearance were announced to him in due course.[39] The single, if bitter, consolation was that so many senior officers of the Eastern army had also been killed in the battle that there was little danger of any of the survivors achieving such a high level of acceptance—even supposing the shattered Eastern army retained sufficient corporate spirit to act at all—to seriously challenge Gratian's authority as Augustus by electing a successor to Valens from their own ranks. All prominent Eastern military men had participated in the defeat, and the young senior Augustus with an intact Western army was relatively close and doubtless able and ready to deal with any precocious ambition.

The Theodosians

The fact that it took five months to appoint another Augustus for the East suggests that Gratian and his advisers had no quick recipe on hand to meet the dynastic governmental crisis in the East. Strictly speaking, it was not constitutionally necessary to appoint a new man. Valentinian I's imperial system of maintaining imperial unity through geographical division of responsibilities within the dynasty required two Augusti, and two were available. Theoretically Valentinian II could have represented the empire in the East, if militarily and administratively competent and trustworthy advisers were available. Fifteen years later this proved an acceptable model both in East and West. But the military disaster seemed to call for a man at the top who could make strategic decisions in his own right, unfettered by considerations of court protocol; and no prominent Easterner with adequate military experience was now available, all being dead or tainted by defeat. Nor, it seems, was there much enthusiasm among Gratian's own senior generals for taking on the troubles of the East—Merobaudes, for instance, *magister peditum* and ex-consul of

377, the emperor maker of Aquincum, could doubtless have done the job well enough but, it seems, was not even considered for it.[40]

By 19 January 379, when the inauguration took place at Sirmium, the choice had fallen on the recently promoted cavalry general (*magister equitum*) Theodosius, who under Valentinian I had already had several years of campaign experience on the Danube. He was the son of one of Valentinian's most prominent generals, the *comes* Theodosius, who, however, had fallen foul of influential civilian officials and had been killed at Carthage early in 376. The younger Theodosius had withdrawn to the family estates near Cauca in Spanish Galicia around this time, but after Valentinian's death his and his father's political enemies lost their hold on power and the family made a political comeback. Theodosius's paternal uncle, Flavius Eucherius, had become Gratian's finance minister (*comes sacrarum largitionum*) by 29 March 377 at the latest, probably some months earlier, and another relative by marriage, Flavius Claudius Antonius, was already in office as praetorian prefect of the Gauls on 23 May 376.[41] Theodosius soon emerged from his retirement and is recorded in active service in Moesia or Pannonia early in 378 as part of Gratian's flanking measures protecting his section of the Danube frontier. Successful fighting against a Sarmatian attack won him immediate promotion to *magister equitum* from Gratian, and thus he was on the spot and sufficiently senior to be entitled to access to the council of state when Gratian withdrew to Sirmium after Adrianople. By January 379 Theodosius had become the official choice for solving the emergency in the East. He was only thirty-three years old.[42]

Theodosius and his direct descendants ruled the empire for more than seventy years, eventually linking East and West in a dynastic union, like that practiced by Valentinian and Valens, which lasted more than half a century. But the structure first needed to be set in place, and in 379 few would have given Theodosius much chance of surviving more than a short time. A mixture of pragmatism involving the undogmatic cultivation of those influential circles in East and West that the empire relied on and a readiness to take realistic chances, coupled with more than a mere touch of good fortune, were all factors in his success. When Theodosius suddenly died in 395, the imperial structure he had by then set in place suffered no caesura, no shattering crisis, no sudden usurpation of power. The planned and well-prepared succession of his young sons, Arcadius in Constantinople and Honorius in Milan, took place without a hitch, each young emperor enjoying—or at least tolerating—the advice and guidance, amounting in effect to control, of trusted and tried associates of their father. The type of crisis at the center of the empire that had occurred on each sudden imperial decease since Julian's did not happen, and this was perhaps Theodosius's most important lasting contribution to the stability of the empire. The fact that his sons and their advisers rapidly began to disagree over the precise way the imperial responsibility was to be divided between East and West hardly makes a difference in this regard because his solution was not in itself challenged.

But first there was the Gothic war, which Theodosius ended with a pragmatic but far-reaching stalemate treaty in 382.[43] In the meanwhile appointments to the two annual consulships demonstrated to the world the unity of the governing class in East and West. In 379 the consuls were Gratian's teacher, Ausonius, promoted in 378 to be praetorian prefect for the whole of the West, and the polyonymous Quintus Claudius Hermogenianus Olybrius, who was Theodosius's own first praetorian prefect of the East. Olybrius had accompanied Gratian to Sirmium as praetorian prefect for Illyricum, and as the most senior and influential civilian official on the spot he must have played a prominent part in solving the crisis and "managing" Theodosius's appointment as emperor. He was also a member both by birth and by marriage of two of the most influential Roman clans of the time, the Anicii and the Petronii. Then in 380—the first year in which Theodosius was already emperor on 1 January—Gratian and Theodosius themselves demonstrated with joint consulates imperial unity, but after them came another series of well-deserving officials and influential friends: in 381 the Gaul Syagrius, now praetorian prefect of Italy, who had been Gratian's master of the offices and therefore also presumably present with the court at Sirmium in 378 at the time of Theodosius's appointment, was consul together with Theodosius's paternal uncle Eucherius; in 382 another Syagrius, together with Theodosius's relative by marriage Flavius Claudius Antonius, occupied this highest decorative office in the state; in 383 Gratian's general and éminence grise Flavius Merobaudes was consul for the second time together with Theodosius's chief general and negotiator of the peace with the Goths, Flavius Saturninus. The governing class in East and West, led by the example of the two Augusti, was demonstratively showing unity in and after the crisis. Valentinian II played no part in all this.[44]

Not all were convinced that these men offered the best possible government for the empire. In the East Theodosius seems to have been safe enough at Constantinople, despite some criticism of his too generous peace with the Goths. It was rather Gratian who came under fire, particularly in Gaul, where he had spent much less time since the outbreak of the Gothic war; in the spring of 381 he seems to have left Trier and transferred his residence permanently to Milan, taking his half brother Valentinian II with him. The move to northern Italy may have had strategic reasons, but it did not please the Gauls, who lost their direct access to the court, and it brought Gratian into a politically much more sensitive region, in which he showed no great tact or ability. He quickly fell under the influence of Ambrose, the aggressively assertive bishop of Milan, and then severely offended highly influential traditionalists in the Roman Senate by bowing to Christian pressure and canceling imperial subsidies for traditional Roman state cults; the altar of Victoria, which the first emperor Augustus had set up in the Senate House to commemorate his all-decisive victory at Actium, the birthplace of the imperial governmental system, was also removed from its traditional place because of its pagan associations.[45]

More important for Gratian in the short term was his growing personal unpopularity among the main military units in the provinces. With them he won the dubious reputation of neglecting the most important units while favoring a small troop of Alan archers above all others —he was himself passionately fond of archery, which was not a traditionally respectable Roman military accomplishment, unsuitable even as a hobby for the imperial commander in chief.[46] Early in 383 a revolt broke out in Britain, where the troops of the garrison, scarcely spontaneously, acclaimed their local commander Magnus Maximus as Augustus. Maximus was an experienced commander who as a young man had served with Theodosius under the latter's father in Britain. Moreover, like Theodosius he was a Spaniard, and he was, it seems, a relative by marriage of Theodosius. Also like Theodosius he was a baptized catholic. By early summer Maximus had crossed the Channel to the continent, and Gratian, who was already operating with his army north of the Alps, where he had been dealing with some troublesome Alamanni in southern Germany, hastened north to confront him. In July the armies met up near Paris, but no battle took place. Instead Gratian's troops began gradually to desert him, and even the mighty Merobaudes, consul of the year for the second time, abandoned his unloved imperial archery enthusiast and joined Maximus. Gratian fled south, escorted by his favorite troop of Alan archers, and reached Lyon before he was overtaken at one of the bridges by Maximus's right-hand man, Andragathius, was invited to a meal—to which he naively went without the protection of his bodyguard!—and was assassinated.[47]

As soon as the news of Maximus's revolt arrived in Constantinople, Theodosius prepared to intervene; but when envoys from Maximus arrived offering negotiations, all military preparations were promptly stopped.[48] By then Theodosius must also have known that Gratian was dead and that he therefore had little immediate alternative to negotiation. Since the Western army had abandoned Gratian, it was highly improbable that it would show much enthusiasm for the cause of the child Augustus Valentinian II—not, at any rate, to the extent of fighting a civil war for him. Since his initial consulate in 376, arranged for him by his father before his death as his introduction to public life, Valentinian II seems to have been deliberately kept out of public view by his brother, and he therefore now enjoyed no special relationship with the army, which might have engendered a wider military loyalty in the crisis. Moreover, Theodosius's Eastern army had still not recovered from the heavy losses suffered at Adrianople and had not been strong enough, even with some Western help, to defeat the Goths as comprehensively as Theodosius would have wished. What chance of success would it then have against Maximus's well-tried, intact Western legions? In any case, even a success in battle would not solve the governmental and dynastic problem because Theodosius's own son Arcadius, whom he had just

promoted to Augustus in January, thus triumphantly opening the celebration of his own quinquennial year, was still merely six years old and
so even younger than Valentinian II. He needed at least ten more years,
and preferably even more than that, before he could reasonably be seen
as capable of ruling in his own right, above all in the eyes of the soldiers
and their officers, whose acceptance was critical.

Maximus's overwhelming advantage lay in his acceptance by the Gallic legions and, it seems, also by large sections of the Gallic aristocracy,
who were offended by Gratian's recent neglect, including representatives
of the catholic church, into which he had already been baptized before
his revolt. A better man for the job was hardly available, and Theodosius was pragmatic enough to acknowledge the fact.[49] Perhaps he was
not too displeased, for Valentinian II's mere existence in Milan offered
him arguments based on dynastic legitimacy, should he wish for an opportunity to gain more influence in the West, in which case he could
always claim the role of honest broker between the two Western Augusti.
The negotiations with Maximus must have dragged on over the winter,
since Theodosius did not recognize Maximus's self-proclaimed consulship, which began on 1 January 384.[50] His own candidates—inevitably
under the circumstances both Easterners—were his general Richomeres
and Clearchus, a senior administrator and recent urban prefect at Constantinople. Nevertheless, by the time of his imperial anniversary on
19 January everybody knew that no military action had taken place, or
would take place, and the official orator Themistius could assert that
"Western aggression" had been curbed by the mere threat of action.[51]

What this meant became evident somewhat later in the year when the
praetorian prefect of the East, Cynegius, on a visit to Egypt, publicly
showed official portraits of Maximus in Alexandria, in this way demonstrating that Theodosius had officially accepted him into the college of
the Augusti.[52] Negotiations also took place in the West, where Maximus
made repeated attempts to gain control of the person of Valentinian II,
whose entourage sent the Milanese bishop Ambrose to Trier to represent
his interests.[53] The result of this diplomacy seems at first to have been a
geographical division of administrative responsibilities along the lines of
the great praetorian prefectures: Maximus in Trier accepted that of "the

Gauls" (*Galliarum*), which also included Britain, the Rhine provinces, and Iberia, while Valentinian II in Milan retained the strategically critical bridging central prefecture of Italy, Africa, and Illyricum.[54] Some kind of formal agreement to this effect seems to have existed, and Theodosius apparently also gave his agreement to it. It might at least informally have included the provision that Maximus keep a relatively low public profile outside his praetorian prefecture of the Gauls, for he did not take another consulate until 388, by which time the agreement had broken down and war with Theodosius already threatened. But until then unity of purpose was the public message, and this was expressed by the choice of consuls: in 385 Arcadius served together with Valentinian II's chief general, the Frank Bauto; in 386 Maximus's competent and severe praetorian prefect, Euodius, was recognized as consul both in East and West, and his colleague was none other than Theodosius's sixteen-month-old son Honorius, who in this by now traditional way received his earliest official introduction to the interested public; in 387 East-West unity was again displayed by the joint consulate of Valentinian II and the Eastern administrator and intellectual Eutropius.[55]

By mid-387, however, the honeymoon was over. Ambrose, among others, had traveled to Trier again late in 385, only to hear the accusation that he had misled Maximus on his first embassy and that the regular contacts that Valentinian's court upheld with Theodosius were a cause for mistrust.[56] Maximus's irritation may well have been justified, for a series of men with known Eastern contacts held posts in Valentinian's administration during these years.[57] But we do not really know why Maximus chose to invade Italy in 387. The only source providing a motive says that Maximus was dissatisfied with holding merely Gratian's part of the empire and wanted more—in particular, the removal of Valentinian.[58] But this motivation cannot be correct, since it is based on the false assumption that Gratian in his lifetime had granted Valentinian II an independent area of rule. Because getting his hands on Valentinian's person, as Gratian had done, and so preventing his vestigial prestige being manipulated against him, had been one of Maximus's chief political aims since 383—at that time it was thwarted by Ambrose's first embassy—it would be comprehensible enough if it remained so.

As time went by it might well have seemed ever more urgent, given the continually increasing chance that Valentinian's advisers could establish a long-term independent role for him. Why this question suddenly became acute in 387 remains, however, obscure.

Two current factors may have tipped the balance. The state of security in Illyricum after Valentinian took control of the central prefecture in 383 following Gratian's death left much to be desired and was a cause of serious concern. In 387 Maximus offered troop reinforcements to protect Pannonia, and already in 385 he had complained to Ambrose that Bauto "let loose barbarians on him," that is, he was failing to control the frontiers adequately.[59] There was also a religious factor. Valentinian, under his mother's influence, favored the modified Arian ("homoian") version of the Christian faith, whereas Maximus, like Theodosius, was a strictly orthodox Nicene "catholic." The collection of papal and imperial correspondence known as the *Collectio Avellana* contains two letters written by Maximus on religious matters: one to Valentinian complaining of the damage his lack of orthodoxy was doing, and one to the Roman bishop Siricius, in reply to a lost letter of Siricius's, protesting Maximus's own orthodoxy.[60] That Maximus's religion could lead him to take action is shown clearly enough by his condemnation and execution, in 385, of Priscillian of Avila, whose views seemed to many, including Maximus, perversely extreme and were regarded as dangerous to the state because they involved what appeared to be magical practices.[61] Theodosius was much more pragmatic and reserved on such questions, and there is no indication, even in sources hostile to Theodosius, that he might have encouraged Maximus to invade Italy. But Maximus may well have trusted to Theodosius's well-known laid-back pragmatism. He had already experienced it in the negotiations after Gratian's death, and perhaps he thought he had a good chance in the interests of administrative and military efficiency of persuading Theodosius to accept a fait accompli again, once he had taken Valentinian and his entourage into custody and gained administrative control of the strategically vital central prefecture—especially when such a move was accompanied by the bonus of religious orthodoxy.

Had Maximus managed to capture Valentinian and Justina, this might indeed have happened, but in the early summer, perhaps in connection with some military action planned for Pannonia, they left Milan and moved to Aquileia. Since Maximus came across the Cottian Alps from Gaul, making a direct approach to Milan from the west through modern France, they had the opportunity of escaping eastward and eventually reached the easternmost major city of Valentinian's great central prefecture, Thessalonica.[62] Resistance in Italy itself, it seems, was not an issue, but Maximus had again come up short of achieving his central objective, that of gaining control of the person of Valentinian. His initial diplomacy had failed to secure Valentinian's cooperation; now not even a military coup d'état had succeeded in capturing the young emperor and his entourage. Few in Italy can have regretted Valentinian's departure. The spokesman for the Roman Senate (*princeps senatus*) Symmachus lost little time in attending on Maximus with one of his famous panegyrical speeches—perhaps on the occasion of Maximus's Western consulate on 1 January 388.[63] How Ambrose and other great men in Milan and northern Italy reacted to the arrival of an orthodox usurper we do not know; Ambrose's attitude toward Maximus was recorded only after the latter's defeat and Valentinian's return to Italy, and by then the safely dead Maximus was for everybody, including Ambrose, simply "the tyrant." But a pragmatic temporary accommodation, as notoriously practiced by Symmachus, cannot be excluded.

When Maximus invaded Italy, Theodosius's attitude was critical. Valentinian and Justina had appealed to him from Thessalonica, but they were not invited to Constantinople. Moreover, it seems to have taken several months before Theodosius and his senior advisers made up their minds to travel to Thessalonica to talk to them in person. There was thus no immediate enthusiasm for civil war with Maximus, and Theodosius clearly wanted to see what advantages negotiations might bring.[64] Valentinian and Justina were more than ever an embarrassment. Belated loyalty to the ghost of Gratian can scarcely have stimulated Theodosius to take action, though this was the only motive the official version of events seems to have allowed.[65] The contemporary ecclesiastical historian Rufinus added that Valentinian converted to orthodoxy under pressure from Theodosius,[66] while the hostile tradition emanating from Eunapius of

Sardis contributed an intimate personal nuance: the recently widowed Theodosius was introduced by Justina to Valentinian's pretty sister Galla and was so impressed that he married her, on her mother's condition that he fight Maximus to avenge Gratian and restore Valentinian.[67] The marriage was fact; the associated motivation for the war mere romantic fancy. From all this it emerges that the cause of the war was a puzzle also to contemporaries, who fled to explanations of sudden extravagant dynastic loyalty or sexual enticement to explain it to themselves. Maximus also was taken by surprise when in late spring 388 he heard that Theodosius was actually marching against him.[68] His rapidly fielded army was beaten twice in Pannonia, once near Siscia and once near Poetovio, before Maximus could be captured and promptly beheaded at Aquileia on 28 August.[69] His son Victor, whom he had appointed Augustus sometime after his own elevation and had left in Gaul as his deputy, was also speedily eliminated.[70] Neither would be able to tell their version of their political contacts with Theodosius. Valentinian and his mother returned to Italy by ship (thus elegantly preventing any suspicion that the young man might have participated in the victory), but Justina died soon afterward, and the personal loss deprived him of such driving force as he had ever had.

What had all this to do with the governmental problems of the empire? Theodosius was further than ever from setting up an adequate government, having just destroyed the one man whose wide acceptance by the army, aristocracy, and church in the West might have provided a guarantee of acceptance, efficiency, and stability. Theodosius himself seems to have been at a loss as to the immediate future. He had left his elder son, Arcadius, now twelve years old and an Augustus since 383, officially in charge of the East—though controlled by experienced senior advisers—in his absence, which lasted for three full years, until the summer of 391. This was much longer than Theodosius's recorded activities could possibly justify. The only satisfactory explanation for the delay in returning to Constantinople is that he was seriously exploring the possibility of filling the gap at the head of the empire by taking over the West in person, with the dynastically awkward Augustus Valentinian II granted a minimal formal responsibility—even then only under reliable guidance—for a specific prefecture, to bind together such loyalties as he represented and otherwise to keep up the appearance of legitimacy.

In the spring of 389, a few months after his return to Italy, Valentinian duly departed for Gaul, accompanied by the efficient and experienced Frank Arbogast as his master of the soldiers (*magister militum*). Arbogast was, of course, appointed by Theodosius, whose goodwill he had earned by his speedy elimination of Maximus's son Victor in Trier the previous summer.[71] This could have provided a satisfactory governmental model for the immediate future, at least until Honorius, who accompanied his father when he visited Rome in triumph in 389,[72] was old enough to take over part of the empire himself. The empire could in fact have been satisfactorily run from Milan, Aquileia, Siscia, or Sirmium—indeed, from virtually anywhere within the European parts of the central "hinge" prefecture of Italy, Africa, and Illyricum—as long as reliable subordinates, whatever their formal status, looked after their own areas efficiently, and communications functioned adequately. The Augusti, even if they did not rule, would serve to maintain the dynastic loyalty system.

It is by no means clear that when Theodosius returned to the East in 391, he must have abandoned long-term plans to settle in the West. A few more years spent in Constantinople keeping Arcadius on the right lines and waiting for Honorius to grow up could only improve the general age-structure of the Theodosian family. Moreover, the public religious tensions that the power-hungry bishop of Milan, Ambrose, had provoked with the court during its period of residence in his city can only have made Constantinople, where the flexible Nectarius had been made bishop in 381 in an election much influenced by Theodosius, at least temporarily a more attractive place to live. Ambrose was twelve years older than Theodosius, and one might even have hoped for a natural solution to the tensions between bishop and emperor before Honorius was old enough to take an active part in imperial government.[73]

Theodosius's schemes—if these they were—were, however, thwarted from an unexpected quarter. Valentinian II, tired of playing the puppet and of being treated as a semiprisoner by Arbogast, who made no pretense about where his loyalties lay or of the fact that Theodosius, not Valentinian, had appointed him, committed suicide on 15 May 392.[74]

Arbogast seems to have thought at first that he could operate just as well without an Augustus, as long as Theodosius supported him; but negotiations with this aim went badly wrong, presumably because they crossed Theodosius's long-term plans for his sons. Arbogast acting alone would be emperor in all but name, effective perhaps but virtually uncontrollable, and certainly impossible to replace without war or assassination. A non-Roman, a Frank, openly ruling a major part of the empire, however loyal to it he might be, was still unthinkable, and in the end Arbogast and his advisers seem to have realized this. Moreover, Theodosius must now have regarded Arbogast, whose insensitive treatment of Valentinian had driven the labile young man to suicide, as an unsuitable person to be entrusted with Honorius (who was still only nine years old), although putting the boy under the Frank's tutelage would technically have solved the problem of maintaining dynastic representation in the West. Honorius was far too important for the future of the dynasty to take any such risks, and in any case other plans had already been made for him.

Before he became emperor, Theodosius had adopted his niece Serena, and she had come with him to Constantinople as part of his family. In 384 she was married to the brilliant young guards officer Stilicho, son of a Romanized Vandal cavalry officer and a Roman mother—therefore a Roman citizen—who had distinguished himself on an embassy to Persia in 383 and was commander of the guards regiment (*comes domesticorum*) in later campaigns. Their child Maria, born in 384/85 and almost of an age with Honorius, was thus Theodosius's grandchild by adoption; another child, Eucherius, born to Serena and Stilicho at Rome during the court's visit there in the summer of 389 and named after Theodosius's uncle Fl. Eucherius—the man who had been influential in drawing Theodosius to Gratian's attention in 378—guaranteed the male line. Stilicho was being groomed for a great career.[75]

It is unclear whether Arbogast and his advisers realized that Valentinian's suicide had robbed them not of a pawn but in the truest sense of their king; by August frustration with Theodosius's apparent indecisiveness reached the point where Arbogast set up his own emperor, Eugenius, a Roman senator and man of letters, who had earlier taught grammar and rhetoric and then become an important figure in Valentinian II's civil administration. The man was worthy enough, not undistinguished in his social contacts with the Italian aristocracy, but he was politically Arbogast's puppet. By appointing Eugenius without consultation with the senior Augustus and thus offending against both Theodosius's unspoken dynastic plans and imperial protocol, Arbogast had, in effect, challenged Theodosius's perceived rights as senior Augustus in an existential question. No amount of negotiation subsequently offered by Eugenius could change this, though as long as the usurpers stayed in Gaul and merely negotiated with leaders of Italian opinion, such as Ambrose and Symmachus, action could be postponed until all desirable preparations had been made in the East. Theodosius's first answer to Eugenius was his refusal to accept him as consular colleague on 1 January 393, the year of his own *quindecennalia*, appointing instead one of his senior generals, Abundantius. A few days later, on 23 January, Honorius was declared Augustus, under the circumstances a clear challenge to Eugenius. During the spring of 393 Eugenius and Arbogast came down to Italy and took up residence in Milan, and so by their uninvited and unwelcome presence in the heart of the old Western Empire made the depth of their provocation clear for all to see.[76]

The matter was too important to be decided without adequate preparation, both military and civil: it is perhaps no surprise that 393 saw the largest number of laws issued at Constantinople in any year of Theodosius's rule.[77] The ground was being cleared for a longer period of absence. The future of the dynasty in the West was at stake, and with it the formal unity of the empire. The new Augustus Honorius was to be installed in his realm. This time the delay brought Theodosius no accusation of lethargy from hostile commentators, as had happened at the time of Maximus's threat, when it had been suggested that he merely preferred to enjoy the luxury of his Eastern capital city to doing the right thing. He had, indeed, nothing to gain from excessive haste. Arbogast was at least as experienced a military commander as Maximus had been, and he led a war-tested army. He had spent the winter on the Rhine operating against invading Franks, whereas Theodosius would have to rely in large measure on Gothic auxiliaries.[78] He could not afford to have anything go wrong. By the time all preparations were complete, it was early in the summer of 394. The day before the army left, Theodosius's young wife, Galla, sister of Valentinian II, died in childbirth, thus further isolating Theodosius emotionally and emphasizing the importance of the sons he already had.[79] Galla it was, says Zosimus following Eunapius, who had particularly pressed Theodosius to "avenge" her brother Valentinian, whose obscure death was now officially interpreted in the East as murder.[80]

As in the campaign against Maximus, Arcadius was left behind at Constantinople and was formally in charge of the East. Stilicho, now promoted officially to master of the soldiers (*magister militum*), was intended to play a major role in the campaign and thereby gain in political and military profile for his share in the victory. Zosimus depicts Honorius as traveling to Italy with his father and the army, which, though wrong, shows that his source Eunapius recognized the dynastic importance of the occasion.[81] In fact Honorius was far too valuable to risk in the uncertainties of the campaign, and he was summoned to Italy only after the decisive battle at the river Frigidus, on the Italian side of the last pass on the main road leading through the Julian Alps from Emona (Ljubljana) to Aquileia, where victory was won following a severe two-day struggle on 6 September.[82] Eugenius died on the field, and two days later Arbogast, who had retreated to Aquileia, committed suicide. The way was finally open for Theodosius to fulfill his dynastic plans.

After working so long and with such stubbornness at his dynastic structure Theodosius did not enjoy his success for long. If his favored model had been for himself to reside in Italy with direct responsibility for the central prefecture while his sons, as Augusti with nominally equal but in essential respects subordinate court establishments in Gaul and in Constantinople, ruled their own prefectures in the name of the dynasty, this was never realized in practice. A few months after the victory, during the New Year celebrations in Milan in early January 395, Theodosius suddenly became acutely ill, and on 17 January, two days before he would have celebrated the completion of sixteen years as Augustus, unexpectedly died. The machinery he had created for the dynastic succession was, however, in place, if only just, and swung smoothly into action. Stilicho claimed, perhaps even rightly, that on his deathbed Theodosius had entrusted him with guardianship of both brothers, thus claiming for himself the role that Theodosius personally would have liked to fulfill.[83] In practice, however, the division of responsibility between East and West on the lines already drawn up by Valentinian I for himself and Valens in 364 was merely confirmed by the succession of Theodosius's sons.[84] Stilicho had neither the charisma nor the authority of his deceased father-in-law, so that in practice he was unable to exert influence in the East from Milan. Paradoxically his aim and claim to be continuing what Theodosius had planned led, as a result of the negative reaction by the Eastern government, to a further gradual loosening of the bonds linking East and West. The emperors were indeed the brothers Honorius and Arcadius; the real rulers in the East, however, would not allow Stilicho to interfere outside his own immediate area of responsibility and simply refused to recognize his claimed superiority of authority. This could not conceivably have happened to Theodosius, and it shows what the empire had lost with his premature death.

The three decades following the extinction of the Constantinian dynasty on Julian's death illustrate the fundamental importance of the dynastic idea for the government of the Roman Empire. Even given much bad experience in the past with inadequate emperors having blood ties, the notion that a family structure was in the last resort the best way of ensuring stability at the peak of the imperial government seems by this time to have been so firmly entrenched in the minds of the ruling classes of the empire that all attempts to revise it were faced with major problems of acceptance. Despite the external and internal tensions of the period Theodosius, building on the familial loyalties set in place by Valentinian and Valens, managed to create a new dynastic structure that was strong enough to keep itself in place for the next sixty years. It would provide the traditional type of focus for loyalty enabling the empire to face with some success the ever-increasing challenges to its integrity. It was only when the Theodosian dynasty collapsed, and with it the mental attachment of the governing classes to the ruling family, that the innate centrifugal tensions of the empire finally became irresistible.

CHAPTER III

FOREIGNERS · & · FRONTIERS

Emperors as military leaders, real or nominal, held a primary responsibility for the security of the empire. The post-Julianic ruling emperors, with whom we are concerned in this book, were, with the exception of Gratian and Valentinian II, experienced military men who enjoyed the support of the troops and the officer corps, and who devoted themselves intensively to activities associated with securing safe living conditions for their main tax base, the farmers and traders living within the confines of the empire. This chapter, without going into full detail about the military operations themselves, offers a survey of the regions and areas in which the emperors marshaled their forces, thus illustrating imperial priorities. That survey will then serve as a foil to the examination of the internal structural aspects of the imperial administration to be treated in the following chapters.

The external security of the empire was inextricably related to the regulation of frontiers and "foreign policy," they being by the mid-fourth century almost indistinguishable. It was for this reason, above all, that the Romans retained a large standing military capability; and it was in the frontier zones that emperors, ever since the challenges of the later second century, had proved themselves and had been continually engaged. In view of the highly personal nature of the foreign relations of the empire—in the last resort, for any decision of importance the emperor personally was both chief negotiator and guarantor for treaties made for the empire—still in the fourth century the emperors were expected to be personally engaged in frontier activities. The regular show of personal interest in potentially or actually endangered areas was intended to encourage the local Roman population—the taxpayers—and to frighten and impress potential enemies. Challenge and response had been the Roman tradition now for centuries, whereby the challenge almost always came from outside—Julian's invasion of Mesopotamia was a precedent that did not recommend emulation.[1] Active defense was thus the main strategy, but to be effective it required the personal attention of the emperors in the areas regarded as central: on the Rhine, on the Danube, and on the Euphrates.

Official Roman foreign policy had for centuries been restricted to regulating contacts with peoples and powers immediately bordering the empire; relations with peoples and states further afield were left to the private initiatives of traders or other travelers, who themselves only became seriously relevant for the imperial administration when they were assessed to pay customs duties on the goods they brought back with them. This basic attitude had been a fundamental principle since the earliest stages of Roman expansion, and it led to a not always clearly defined zone of contact with neighboring peoples who, if friendly, were integrated by one means or another, formally or informally, into the Roman governmental system. Although questions of security and loyalty formally dominated these relationships, informally economic and cultural transfers increasingly influenced and shaped them.

The empire had grown piecemeal, and an official standing army was only created by the first Augustus, who at the end of his long period in power undertook the first tentative attempts to outline the limits of Roman rule. The limits lay in identifying the provinces where Roman administration and Roman taxation could be applied, since up to then these territories were legally still merely the areas of responsibility of Roman officers, defined more by the nature of the job to be done than by geography. Such an operation was in itself, however, not too difficult; it was much more demanding to spell out the long-term status vis-à-vis Rome of friendly peoples who for one reason or another were not included within the areas directly administered by Rome and made subject to a Roman provincial governor, but whose stability and welfare directly affected conditions in the Roman frontier provinces. In most cases the zones within which the Romans drew up their provincial (taxation!) boundaries might indeed offer a natural, easily recognized geographical dividing line—that is, a major river, like the Danube, the Rhine, or the Euphrates. In terms of culture or economics, however, the major river valleys often presented on the ground not so much a barrier as a means of communication: hence the Roman use of the word *limes* for "frontier," which originally meant "path" or "way." (This problem of definition did not occur, of course, with unfriendly neighboring peoples: they were merely "the enemy" (*hostes*) and served as a never-ending source of material for the perpetuation of Roman victory myths.) A Roman *limes*—even the most spectacular, Hadrian's Wall—was never intended to block traffic altogether. At the most the point was to control passage, probably also to tax it, and the level of control aimed at varied enormously from area to area and from time to time.

This situation makes it virtually impossible to generalize on the nature of frontier activity and its effect on the empire as a whole. Nevertheless, by the fourth century certain differences had begun to emerge between the problems caused by the European frontier peoples (in Britain, on the Rhine, and on the Danube), and those having to do with the Africans and the Asians (especially in Syria and Armenia), which led to forms of action and reaction characteristic for each area. Since the security problems facing the Asian areas proved more amenable to diplomatic solutions, and thus in the last resort demanded less manpower and other resources, the government in Constantinople found it relatively easy in the long term to stabilize its tax base and maintain its administrative structure, whereas the problems in Britain and on the Rhine and the Danube called for military methods, which in the long term sapped the strength and destroyed the tax base of the West.[2]

It would, however, be wrong to depict frontier problems as existing in a political vacuum, as distant, isolated occurrences unrelated to other areas of imperial concern. The second half of the fourth century was a time when the interaction of internal and external factors affecting the general security of the empire became particularly intense. This began already under Constantius, who by employing Alamannic troops against Magnentius certainly defeated the usurper, but who thereby also demonstrated to the participating Alamannic tribes how feeble the locally available units of the central forces of the empire really were; thus began more than a decade of serious instability in the area, with repeated raids and counteractions on the Upper Rhine and Danube. Julian was not much better in this respect. After initial successes against the Alamanni and other tribes bordering the Rhine, he used them not to consolidate his gains locally but to challenge Constantius for the imperial throne; as a result he abandoned the West and its irritatingly sporadic problems for a much more spectacular Eastern enemy, the Persians. The use of external forces for internal purposes, however, could be imitated. In 365 Procopius intended to employ Goths for his usurpation against Valens, and a few years later it was above all recently settled Gothic auxiliaries who made up a significant part of the armies with which Theodosius defeated his civil war enemies, Magnus Maximus and Eugenius.

Julian's neglect of the West led to an immediate reaction under his short-lived Western-born successor, Jovian, who set an immediate priority in the West,[3] and given these circumstances it was little wonder that Valentinian in 364 lost no time in setting the same priority for himself and his brother: the priority of the West can be read from the urgency with which he as senior Augustus took immediate personal responsibility for Western affairs. The treaties that Julian had made with several of the Alamannic tribal leaders needed the constant presence of an emperor and an army to maintain their efficacy, particularly since at least some of the agreements seem to have required regular "presents" from the Romans. Valentinian reached Milan by October 364, and he remained there for almost a year. During the winter delegates representing some of the Alamanni expressed dissatisfaction with their treatment at the court: they were received with less respect than they had expected, and the presents given to them were less valuable than past ones had been.[4] Although it is not clear whether these circumstances were intended as Roman policy or resulted from mere diplomatic inadequacy, Alamannic raiders crossed the middle Rhine in the autumn of 365, by which time Valentinian had transferred the court to Paris. Here he received news of Procopius's usurpation against his brother on the same day, it was said, as that of the Alamannic invasion. According to Ammianus Marcellinus, Valentinian's immediate inclination was to race off to protect Illyricum, where he had been born, in case Procopius should march westward, but his local advisers were able to convince him of the greater urgency for his personal presence in Gaul, since, as he then asserted, Procopius was an enemy merely of his family, whereas the Alamanni were enemies of the whole Roman world.[5] His local hearers can only have welcomed his personal commitment to their welfare.

Gaul and the Rhine

True to the principle that kept him from chasing Procopius, Valentinian remained resident in Gaul, from the autumn of 367 onward usually in Trier, until he left on his last journey in 375. It was an important period for the security of the West, which Valentinian labored to uphold. The main problems were frequent Alamannic raids on the middle and upper Rhine, though one could not ignore the lowlands of the lower Rhine, where the external enemies were Franks and Saxons. Traditional Roman policy on the Rhine over centuries had been a mixture of carrot and stick. Indubitable military superiority needed to be established in order to cow and impress the Germans, and the power and permanence of the Roman presence was demonstrated in bricks and mortar by extending or repairing military installations, whether they were bridges, roads, towns, forts, or canals.

Much of this activity was in a sense a routine search for imperial military success, appropriately stylized in dispatches, the terms of which exaggerated in the conventional way both the traditional threats to the stability of the empire and the long-term positive prospects resulting from imperial action. But if the empire was not threatened in its existence by the activities of the transrhenane Germans, the local annoyance of regular (or even of sporadic) raids was real enough and justified the emperor's show of force. Both sides needed a periodic show of force to maintain the status quo.[6] There followed respectfully worded treaties that, while maintaining the peace for Rome, also guaranteed recruits for service in auxiliary units, or even in the legions. Since local nobles found officer posts in the Roman army attractive, Rome provided honorable employment and regular activity to large numbers of young men who might otherwise have been inclined to undertake booty-hunting expeditions on their own initiative and at Roman expense. As "friends of Rome" Germanic tribal leaders received the support of the Roman name for internal or intertribal political struggles, cash payments as "presents" (*munera*) to demonstrate the efficacy and power of their Roman friends, and the respect due to those deemed worthy of a treaty relationship with the great power, perhaps even negotiated dramatically before an admiring public with the all-powerful emperor personally.

In 365 Valentinian was at the beginning of the first stage of this program, and the neglect of recent years made itself felt. His response was longer-lasting and more systematic than had been seen since the tetrarchy; it did not aim at extension or fundamental change, but rather at renewal and consolidation. The bands of raiders, one of which had reached as far as Chalons sur Marne before it could be stopped, had to be defeated and killed, or a least driven back across the Rhine; punitive attacks into enemy territory, *pour décourager les autres*, were the only logical consequence. Valentinian showed the importance he attached to protecting the civilian taxpayers by participating personally in expeditions into the lower Neckar and Main valleys, where newly founded forts on the right bank of the Rhine demonstrated the intended permanence of the Roman presence on the left bank.[7] In 369 Valentinian's success on the Neckar against the Alamanni of King Macrianus was so impressive that he was able to employ the defeated Alamanni to help with the building of a Neckar fort (though Macrianus himself escaped); at court propagandists even played with the notion of creating a new province called Alamannia.[8]

Diplomacy without the backing of military force was less successful. An arrangement to cooperate with the Burgundians against the Alamanni on the Neckar and exploit for Roman purposes an ongoing dispute between the two neighboring peoples concerning some sources of salt—perhaps near Schwäbisch Hall—collapsed when Valentinian's troops failed to turn up.[9] We are not told why. A couple of years later a Roman expeditionary force operating through Aquae Mattiacae (Wiesbaden) into the valley of the Main penetrated fifty miles inland and caused substantial destruction, but it too failed to capture Macrianus, who had good reason to mistrust the Romans, since Julian had failed to respect the treaty made with him and in 359 had even invaded his territory. Valentinian tried a new tack, "appointing" a new king Fraomar for these Alamanni (Ammianus calls them "Bucinobantes," an otherwise unknown name), but since the area had so recently been thoroughly devastated by the Romans, Fraomar and two other nobles had no effective means of ruling and were therefore taken into the Roman army as officers of an Alamannic unit and then transferred to Britain.[10]

It was two more years before Valentinian was prepared to accept a peace with Macrianus, and even then only under pressure of circumstances, for his presence was needed by now on the middle Danube. Ammianus describes the dramatic scene on the banks of the Rhine opposite Mainz as follows:

> The king received a polite invitation to come to the vicinity of Mainz, since it was thought that he also was inclined to accept a treaty. On the day appointed for the meeting he came to the bank of the Rhine with an appalling show of arrogance, as if it were his attitude toward the peace that would be decisive. He stood on the river bank with his head held high, surrounded by his native troops noisily beating on their shields. On the opposite bank of the river the emperor and his large entourage of military officers boarded river boats and safely approached the other bank, a brilliant sight with their gleaming military standards. When the arrogant posturing and the incomprehensible chatter of the barbarians had calmed down, speeches were made on both sides and a modest friendship was agreed to and sealed with oaths. When this was accomplished the king, who had caused so much trouble in the past, departed meekly and remained our ally from that time onward. Until the very end of his life the record of his fine actions underlined the conviction with which he stood to his agreement.[11]

It was a classic piece of diplomatic stage management on both sides, stylized to cater for the political needs of both rulers, who were both personally center stage, while reaching a mutually desirable agreement on the suspension of hostilities. The peace achieved in this sector, supported by the visible investment in new forts and strong points, outlived both peacemakers.

With this success the Alamannic problem on the middle Rhine was largely solved for a generation. The lower Rhine was less easy to deal with, since the open coasts attracted seaborne attacks from Saxon raiders moving down from Holstein that were difficult to prevent on a permanent basis. The native population on the right bank of the Rhine north of Köln (Cologne) consisted of various groups of Franks, some with a closer, some with a more distant attachment to the empire. Like the Alamanni, the Franks had also for a long time been welcome recruits into the Roman army, and some of their nobles reached its very highest ranks. This ambivalent relationship suited both sides well enough, though it was important to Rome for ideological reasons to uphold the impression of military superiority. Julian had also been active in this area, in Toxandria (North Brabant) and on the lower Rhine, where he had restored forts near Nijmegen, Kleve, and Xanten, and tried to impress the Salian Franks with the seriousness of Roman intentions.[12]

Among the immediate threats to the empire that Ammianus Marcellinus lists at the time of Valentinian's accession, he names explicitly Saxon raids on Britain (along with those of Scoti [i.e., Irish], Picts, and "Attacotti");[13] under Julian Saxon raiding activity had already severely hampered the transport of grain from Britain to the lower Rhine. Given that no emperor had been seen in Gaul for six years when Valentinian arrived in Paris in the autumn of 365, it is hardly surprising that these problems not only continued but became even more pressing. In detail their extent and importance are not easy to assess, since our sources are particularly concerned to draw general attention to the successes of the father of the later emperor Theodosius, "Count" Theodosius, and give little reliable detail. Nevertheless, we hear of activity on the lower Rhine and the Waal (in modern Holland), which presumably was connected with impressing the local Franks, as well as sea battles (or a sea battle) against Saxons, doubtless in the same area. This seems to have been around 366/67.[14] It brought no long-term success, since in 370 Saxons attacked Salian Franks in Toxandria (North Brabant) and could only be destroyed by an act of miserable ill faith by the Roman commander on the spot, Severus.[15] The Saxon threat simply could not be eradicated with the means then available; the Roman aim could be no more than to reduce the raids and their associated violence to an acceptable level and as far as possible to limit their geographical extent.

A Saxon attack on southeastern Britain in the summer of 367 seems to have been more serious, since the raiders managed to kill both of the responsible Roman military commanders, Nectaridus, "count of the Saxon shore" (*comes litoris Saxonici*), and Fullofaudes, "duke of the British provinces" (*dux Britanniarum*). Valentinian was returning to Trier from Amiens, where he had been seriously ill—so seriously that in the emergency, on 24 August, he had appointed Gratian Augustus—when he heard the news. He sent off his guard commander (*comes domesticorum*) Severus at once, soon replacing him with his cavalry general (*magister equitum*) Iovinus who, however, quickly decided that no glory would be won without major troop reinforcements, and promptly returned to the continent. It was Count Theodosius's big chance, and he took it in 368–699, driving out the invaders in the South and in the North, restoring military discipline to the troops stationed in the island and reestablishing both civil and military administration under Civilis as deputy of the praetorian prefect (*vicarius*) and Dulcitius as *dux*.[16]

Pacatus, whose panegyric on the general's son, the later emperor Theodosius, recalled Theodosius senior's "driving the Scoti back into their bogs," and Ammianus Marcellinus, who also wrote under the emperor Theodosius, are full of enthusiasm for Theodosius senior's successes and achievements in Britain. Ammianus's statements remain, however, very general and are not easily confirmable, being conditioned no doubt by contemporary notions of political correctness. London "had been drowning in the extreme depths of the emergency, but was suddenly saved, quicker than could have been hoped for; Theodosius entered joyously, as if celebrating a triumph." This was after he had "attacked wandering bands of the enemy, who were heavily laden with their plunder; when they were driven off, he took their booty off them, including men in chains and animals, which had belonged to the miserable taxpayers, and restored it to the owners, except for a small portion for his tired troops."[17] The account of activity in the North is just as conventionally successful and just as imprecise in detail, but it extends to the restoration of towns and military camps, comparable to what the emperor was doing on the Rhine. None of this activity recorded by Ammianus—neither the destruction (or mere dilapidation) nor the restoration—has left any clearly recognizable archaeological record, which suggests that neither the damage done nor the restoration procedures were as earth-shattering as Ammianus depicts them. The threat seems to have been to the administrative superstructure rather than to the economic infrastructure, though those who lost animals and friends or family members to the Saxons doubtless saw that differently.[18]

Valentinian's operations seem to have been so successful that even though "total peace" was not achieved—given the general conditions prevailing in the area, it can scarcely have been his aim—the amount of violence on the Rhine and in Britain (as far as we know) fell to a tolerable level, despite the series of military and political emergencies that shook the administrative structure of the empire in the years after his sudden death in 375. These activities can again best be summarized as "challenge and response," and they continued after his death, being part and parcel of the Roman military system on the Rhine, and carrying no fundamental threat to the Roman governmental system, though occasionally the accidental effects were serious enough. One such occasion occurred in 378, when the Lentienses, an Alamannic people living on the upper Rhine in northern Switzerland, chose the very moment when Gratian was preparing to hasten to the Balkans with reinforcements for his uncle Valens to attack Roman territory. The challenge called for an immediate response, with the result that when Valens joined battle at Adrianople with the Goths on 9 August 378, Gratian and the fastest part of his army were still 200 miles away. Roman territory on the Rhine had, however, been protected, and a signal given to the local civilian population that even in a major emergency the emperor cared about them.[19] A different example shows the system functioning well enough without suffering such unfortunate side effects. The Frankish *rex* Mallobaudes, who had served in the Roman army since Constantius's time and risen to be guard commander (*comes domesticorum*) under Gratian, was responsible for the death of Valentinian's old treaty partner Macrianus in 380. For whatever reason, Macrianus's Alamanni had attacked their neighbors, Mallobaudes's Franks, and Mallobaudes in his dual capacity as Frankish *rex* and Roman commander coped adequately with the problem, doubtless satisfying both his loyalties.[20]

The troubles in the East had stretched the West, but Valentinian's priorities sustained control on the Rhine. The period of Western usurpations beginning with Gratian's death in 383 could theoretically have threatened the system, but in practice, since in both cases—Magnus Maximus and Eugenius-Arbogast—extremely competent military men took real responsibility for general security, the frontier system reasserted by Valentinian suffered no perceptible deterioration (though since Ammianus Marcellinus's history ends in 378, the inferior source situation for the subsequent period may have contributed to this impression). Only in connection with political crisis situations, when Germanic raiders could expect the Romans to be less decisive in their response, do we hear of major incursions. In 387 or 388, while Magnus Maximus was in Italy preparing his response to Theodosius's unexpected attack from the East, some Franks crossed the Rhine near Köln and penetrated at least as far as the Ardennes, where they were beaten up by the *magistri militum*, Nannienus and Quintinus, and driven back. Quintinus attempted a counterattack over the Rhine near Düsseldorf, but was badly mauled on difficult ground. The status quo was restored.[21]

After Maximus's defeat and death, his efficient *magistri militum* were, of course, replaced because of their loyalty to the defeated usurper, and the court entourage of Valentinian II arrived at Trier in the summer of 389. Valentinian's protector, Arbogast, like many other military men a Frank who had sought and found a career in the Roman army, resolved in his new role to reassert Rome's military authority among the Franks.[22] Immediate security was established by negotiating the giving of hostages with the chiefs of the transrhenane Franks, but while Valentinian was still alive Arbogast conducted an aggressively destructive winter campaign from Köln across the Rhine. Then after Eugenius's proclamation a scene resembling the encounter of Valentinian I and Macrianus was staged, this time, it seems, near Köln: "After this the usurper Eugenius prepared a military force and went to the frontier on the Rhine in order to undertake the traditional renewal of the old treaties with the Alamannic and Frankish kings, and to put on a show for those wild folk of—for that period—enormous military strength."[23] From about the same time a famous, but badly broken, inscription evidences the repair of some major piece of Köln's infrastructure at public expense, thus suggesting that Valentinian I's frontier system was in principle still intact.[24] Since Eugenius had been recognized as emperor in the West, he had no difficulty in recruiting Alamannic and Frankish units for his and Arbogast's army, which faced Theodosius at the battle of the Frigidus in September 394;[25] but their total defeat there and Arbogast's subsequent suicide provided a suitably dramatic end to a series of extremely prominent Franks in Roman service, which by then had lasted for several generations. On the Rhine frontier itself the usurpation and its defeat left less of a trace. In 395 Stilicho, as *magister militum* for Honorius, toured the frontier after Theodosius's sudden death, asserting the Roman presence and reaffirming treaties with the Germanic neighbors.[26] Valentinian's restored system had survived the internal crises of the empire and in 395 promised good service for the future. The traditional symbiotic strategy, with its objective of keeping the Germans under control in their homelands while having them available for military recruitment, thus integrating their most adaptable leaders into the social structure of the empire, was still in place and on Theodosius's death, it seemed, in principle still achievable.

Illyricum and the Danube

The river Danube constituted the same kind of riverine frontier as the Rhine, providing both a means of transport and a readily recognizable geographical feature separating Roman direct administration from the neighbors. Because of its great length it presented, even more than the Rhine, a complexity of peoples, traditions, relationships, and challenges. The upper reaches were peopled by Alamannic groups, who were traditionally treated by the Romans in the same way as those on the Rhine. In the third century Rome had yielded to Alamannic pressure and given up the so-called *agri decumates* (roughly the Black Forest region) and with it the shorter land *limes* across southern Germany from the middle Rhine to the upper Danube. This made the river the administrative frontier of the provinces Raetia and Noricum.

Further down the river the neighboring peoples did not remain constant over the centuries. In Czechia and Slovakia (Bohemia and Moravia) the trans-Danubian neighbors were the Marcomanni and the Quadi, who belonged to the group of Suebian Germans, and by the middle of the fourth century their territory stretched as far East as the Danube "knee," between Brigetio and Aquincum (Budapest) in modern Hungary. Here they came into contact with the Iranian Sarmatians, who had entered the Banat—the fertile plain between the Carpathians and the river Theiss, north of Belgrade—at some time during the previous centuries and provided an unsettled and unsettling neighbor for the provincials of Pannonia and Upper Moesia. East of the Iron Gates, on the territory of modern Romania, the Roman province of Dacia, created by Trajan in the second century, had been evacuated by Roman troops and administrators under Aurelian by 270. Since then the area had received different groups of Goths, who settled among the remaining ex-Roman population, and since 332 under Constantine some of them had had some kind of a treaty relationship with Rome. When Valentinian and Valens divided responsibility for the empire in 364, this area on the lower Danube, bordering the Roman provinces of Moesia Prima, Dacia, and Moesia Secunda, was attributed to Valens together with the regulation of relations with the Goths.

The division of responsibility between Valentinian and Valens, and later between Gratian and Theodosius, did not prevent a consistent attitude to the problems posed by this frontier, despite the Gothic emergency that developed on the lower Danube in the last years of Valens's reign. Relations among these peoples and between them and the empire were unstable. During the early and middle empire repeated wars were followed by the establishment of a modus vivendi through "client kings" and the recruitment of soldiers into Roman auxiliary units. Trade seems to have led to Roman-type settlements in parts of Bohemia; and though raids and attacks on the Roman border provinces in Pannonia and Moesia by groups of Quadi and Sarmatians did not cease and led to repeated Roman military action in this hinge area—most recently by Constantius II operating from Sirmium in 358 [27]—a kind of symbiosis in the frontier region, as on the Rhine, was established, whereby the regular raids across the river, however infuriating locally for the Romans, had

become in effect part of the system. The Roman army, though occasionally requiring the personal presence of an emperor to shock and awe the
enemy, as most recently under Constantius, was always able to restore
order. The vigorous young men of the barbarian peoples gained war experience and some booty, learned to respect the Roman army, and in
many cases were more than happy to join it.[28]

By 374 a new fighting generation had grown up among the Quadi
and Sarmatians since the losses of 358/59, and Valentinian seems to have
misread the signs. During the early years of his reign he treated the Pannonian frontier as he treated the Rhine. There is archaeological evidence
for the repair of bridgehead forts (some of which, however, being not
precisely datable, might possibly have been Constantius's work) and literary evidence for the building of one or more garrison camps—called
praesidiaria castra by Ammianus[29]—on the territory of the Quadi. Roman internal politics also raised its ugly head: the ambitious jealousy
of Valentinian's praetorian prefect of the Gauls, Maximinus (himself,
like the emperor, a Pannonian), for the career of his son Marcellianus
led to his criticizing the responsible general (*magister militum*), Equitius, for not completing the work with the desirable speed; it then led
to the appointment of Marcellianus as the responsible military sector
commander of the province Valeria (*dux Valeriae*).

Marcellianus immediately adopted an aggressive policy, in the course
of which he broke trust with the Quadi and had their king, Gabinius,
assassinated during a banquet to which he had invited him. In combination with existing suspicions about the purpose of the newly built
transfluvial fort(s), this irresponsibly brutal and faithless act provoked
a major incursion of groups of Quadi and Sarmatians on a broad front
into the provinces Valeria, Pannonia Secunda, and Moesia Prima—from
around Budapest to about Belgrade. On the eastern sector of their front
the young Theodosius, exercising his first independent regional command as *dux Moesiae*, successfully repelled the invading Sarmatians; further west the difficulties were greater. The praetorian prefect of Illyricum and Italy, Petronius Probus, who was personally present at Sirmium
on official business at the time, found himself shut up by the raiders
within the walls, which he immediately set about having repaired, con-

veniently using building materials that had been intended for a theater. The young Constantia, daughter of Constantius II, who was traveling westward from Constantinople to marry Gratian, only escaped capture by the skin of her teeth and also sought the protection of the newly strengthened walls of Sirmium. Still farther west in Valeria two Roman legions suffered severe losses.[30]

As a result of these events the military situation in Illyricum in the autumn of 374 seemed so serious that Valentinian, who had already sent troop reinforcements, felt compelled to plan for a personal response the next year, and in the spring he duly set off for Carnuntum, east of Vienna. After making organizational arrangements he crossed the river into the territory of the Quadi opposite Aquincum (Budapest) in late summer, employing the same terror techniques he had used against the Alamanni on the Rhine, and with the same success. Valentinian had withdrawn to Brigetio in search of suitable winter quarters when envoys from the Quadi arrived seeking peace. On the advice of Equitius, who was eager to repair the political damage caused by Marcellianus's murderous aggression, negotiations were begun, and as they continued the irascible emperor worked himself up into such a violent fit of anger that he suffered a seizure that killed him within a few hours.[31]

A treaty on conditions that Ammianus describes as favorable to Rome —the Quadi offered recruits and "other things of advantage to the Roman state"[32]—presumably was, however, agreed to before this event. For the rest of our period no further serious military activity seems to have occurred on the upper and middle Danube. In this sector the empire returned to an "acceptable level of violence," which meant that in 378 Theodosius had no serious difficulty in repelling a routine Sarmatian raid—though political correctness in our panegyrical sources inevitably overemphasized the exceptional skill and effort required[33]—as also Gratian in 383 when Raetia was attacked by raiding Juthungi from their homelands in western Bohemia.[34] The internal crises of the empire caused by the usurpations of Magnus Maximus and Eugenius seem also to have stimulated no major unrest in this area.

Lack of activity in the upper and middle Danube was more than compensated for by the Gothic crisis in Valens's sector lower down the river.

Relations with the Goths had presented Rome with a standing problem on the lower Danube since the first recorded Gothic raids in the third century. After Rome evacuated Dacia under Aurelian, the area was occupied by various Gothic groups or tribes, which the Roman writers only gradually learned to distinguish from one another. The first known treaty with Goths, probably with the clan known to later authors as Tervingi, was negotiated under Constantine after a successful war and dates from 332.[35] Its terms, however, are unclear. The only clause explicitly mentioned, though by a dubiously reliable source, provides that the Gothic treaty partners supply troops,[36] and the king's son, together with other nobles, certainly came to Constantinople as a hostage to guarantee the peace.[37] On the other hand a generation later Julian, mocking Constantine, alleges payment of "a sort of tribute" to barbarians, but the context is quite imprecise and gives no good reason for thinking Goths might be meant, since the giving of gifts as a goodwill gesture was a traditional method of Roman diplomacy.[38]

By the 360s a new generation had grown up among the Goths, and raids across the Danube into Roman territory already disturbed Julian.[39] In 365 Valens sent reinforcements toward the frontier, which, however, did not arrive there, since Procopius managed to win them over for his usurpation while they were passing through Constantinople.[40] Procopius then utilized his relationship with the Constantinian dynasty to invoke the old treaty obligations and was able to recruit 3,000 Gothic mercenaries for his civil war against Valens. They unfortunately arrived just in time to be too late, and they were arrested and interned by the victorious Valens.[41] This Gothic support for the usurper was used by Valens as a formal pretext for changing his strategic plans for operations in the East and launching a war against the Goths, although coordination of the operations with his brother, who in 365, as we know, issued orders to the local commander (*dux*) of the Danube frontier in Dacia Ripensis to strengthen fortifications,[42] suggests that agreed-upon longer-term strategic interests may have been the decisive factor.

This war, like so many other wars, turned out to be much more difficult and much more expensive than had been foreseen, so that already after one tiresomely indecisive campaign Valens and his advisers used the occasion of the celebration of his fifth anniversary of rule (*quinquen-nalia*) in March 368 to prepare public opinion for a possible peace without victory.[43] In 368 the Danube spring floods prevented all effective action; and although in 369 a campaign was again possible, no resounding victory was won, and once the army had returned to winter quarters in Marcianopolis, peace talks began. These culminated in a well-publicized midstream personal confrontation between the two leaders, Valens and Athanaric (whose title the Romans translated as *iudex*, "governor" or "judge"—for the Romans a *iudex* was both). The dramatic confrontation of the leaders, staged before the eyes of the assembled armies on both sides, had a ceremonial function similar to that of the meeting between Valentinian and Macrianus near Mainz a year later, and indeed may even have provided a model for it.[44]

Athanaric presumably was already aware of basic Roman attitudes toward frontier peoples, since he was probably a son of the aristocratic guarantee hostage brought to Constantinople by Constantine after 332; his personal prestige was in any case sufficient for him to be able to agree to a binding peace treaty. In it the Goths, who had been hard pressed but not militarily defeated in the war, agreed not to attack Roman territory but also had to accept restrictions on travel and trade: only two centers were to be allowed for commercial exchange, doubtless to prevent the continuation of unrestricted transfluvial commercial, and other private, access, which had proved difficult to control in the past.[45] It had been a recent Roman custom—whether or not it was a treaty clause going back to Constantine—to send regular presents to the Gothic kings. This diplomatic practice had, of course, stopped during the war and was not now resumed.[46] If Valens had not won a great victory, he had at least restored a measure of stability to the frontier zone. Realistically, nothing more could be achieved. The emperors celebrated by all three taking the title *Gothicus Maximus*, any success being better than none,[47] and Valens and his army departed immediately for Antioch.

The lower Danube frontier remained stable until 376. Within the area inhabited by the Goths, Athanaric used the peace to carry out a persecution of Gothic Christians, perhaps because of their inevitable association with the Christians of the empire. Particularly problematic for the Gothic leader seemed to be the contacts with a group of Christian Goths who had been allowed to settle near Nikopolis in Lower Moesia during an earlier persecution in the late 340s, and who could not resist the temptation of trying to missionize among the still pagan Goths beyond the Danube.[48] At about the same time all inhabitants of the trans-Danubian area—in particular the Gothic Tervingi and Greutungi, but also their northern neighbors the Alani—came under pressure from marauding groups of Huns who were migrating south and westward from Southern Russia in large numbers. The Gothic tribes were unable to develop any agreed-upon form of resistance to the Huns, since they were fragmented in their personal loyalties; this lack of unity was reflected in their differing reactions to the threat. At this time the "judge" Athanaric lost the support of several large groups who, it seems, saw no practicable possibility of resisting the Huns, and by 376 he and some of his closest followers had been forced to seek refuge in the southern Carpathians. The greater part of the Tervingi and some of the Greutungi, however, favored a different, less military solution and appealed to Valens, who was still in Antioch, for permission to migrate across the Danube into Roman territory and settle in Thrace, where they hoped to find land to till and security from the marauding Huns.[49]

When Valens granted their request, he was not creating a precedent. Thrace in particular, ever since the first Augustus, had been the place where trans-Danubian peoples, sometimes in very large numbers, had been settled on the land as farmer-producers and potential soldiers—the most recent example was that of the Christian Goths settled in Moesia under Constantius.[50] The exact conditions under which migrant populations were settled in Roman territory are surprisingly difficult to discover. It is doubtless correct to assume that in general defeated enemies were normally treated worse than voluntary immigrants, though even this premise owes more to common sense than to good historical evidence. The need of the empire for farmer-producers (that is, in the last resort, taxpayers of one category or another) and for young men as recruits for the army was always insatiable and had never been greater than in the fourth century.

The diocese of Thrace, judging by the relative frequency of new settlements on the land there over the centuries, was for reasons unknown to us almost always capable of absorbing new settlers. Neither the request of the Tervingi and Greutungi nor Valens's positive response to it were therefore in principle unusual. What was unusual was that the local Roman administration, in advising the emperor, seems to have had no real idea of the numbers of Goths who wanted to cross the river, and when it came to the point appallingly mishandled the settlement of the refugees. The original negotiated terms on which settlement was agreed are unknown. Ammianus reports that the Goths offered the Romans the prospect of long-term military service while the Romans wanted to guarantee the Goths logistical support for the migration and supplies for the transitional period of the settlement, and these terms must have been part of the deal. Whether the Romans interpreted the Gothic request as a legally binding unconditional surrender (*deditio*) also remains uncertain. The contemporary Ammianus Marcellinus does not say that they did, and he had no reason for concealing the the matter if he had understood it in this way.[51]

The crucial fact, however, is that whatever the original agreement may have been, it was not put into practice. The numbers of men, women, and children wishing to cross the river had been massively underestimated, and the transport for them was therefore inadequate and underorganized; no proper provision had been made for the large numbers arriving, so that when the Greutungi, who had had further to come, reached the river after the Tervingi had already crossed, the Roman commanders on the spot tried to physically prevent them from crossing and making the existing chaos even worse.[52] As it was, there simply were not sufficient troops present to keep control of the new immigrants, and the Roman officers—Ammianus mentions especially Lupicinus, the local commandant of the sector (*comes rei militaris*)—began to exploit the chaotic situation to their own private advantage, even deploying tricks to deprive the Goths of their recognized leaders, as when Alavivus was captured at Marcianopolis after accepting an invitation from Lupicinus and was never heard of again.[53]

It was a disastrous way to prepare the Goths for future military cooperation and long-term peaceful symbiosis with the Romans in Thrace.

Faced by the incompetence and bad faith of the responsible Roman officials, the Goths began to organize themselves, and by 377 a full-scale
crisis had broken out in Roman lands south of the Danube, as the Goths
despairingly took matters into their hands and spread out uncontrollably
in larger or smaller groups in all directions, but particularly to the south
and the west. By the end of the year reports reaching Valens in Antioch
made him see the need for his army and his personal presence in Thrace,
and he even requested support from Gratian, since Illyricum seemed to
be threatened by this mass movement, which would, of course, pay no
attention to Roman administrative boundaries. The immediate result
was a further devastating shock to the Roman governmental system. On
9 August 378, in the open country near Adrianople, the massive superiority of the united Gothic forces over the Eastern Roman army under
Valens (who had joined battle without waiting for Gratian and the Western reinforcements, still 200 miles away) was shattering. As a result the
whole lower Danube sector of the frontier zone fell unchallengeably into
Gothic hands, and bands of Gothic warriors overran the whole Balkan
area as far as Macedonia and even beyond, some reaching Pannonia.
They met effective resistance at first only from strongly walled cities,
which they had neither the patience nor the military technique to capture.[54]

A crisis of these dimensions at the hands of invaders had not been experienced by a Roman army for a century or more—historically minded
contemporaries even liked to compare it with the defeat at Cannae[55]—
and its solution reshaped the structure of Roman rule, at first merely in
the immediate area, but after several decades in the whole of the empire. For the Goths had come not as raiders but as settlers, with wives,
children, and civil impedimenta, and now had nowhere else to go. They
had neither the wish nor the intention of returning to the lands north
of the Danube, despite the vigorously optimistic early war propaganda
of the new emperor of the East, the Westerner Theodosius, that he intended to drive them back to where they had come from. At first he
operated from Thessalonica, where his land communications with the
West were less easily threatened, staying there for nearly two years after
his appointment by Gratian at Sirmium on 19 January 379. During this

time he succeeded in driving out most of the invaders from Macedonia and Dardania, where they threatened the land route to the West.

In November 380 Theodosius then moved his headquarters to Constantinople and promptly gave the impression of having landed a major diplomatic coup, for shortly after his own arrival and just before the anniversary celebrations of his coming to power (his *dies imperii*) on 19 January none other than the old Gothic "judge" Athanaric turned up at Constantinople, now seeking asylum in the city where his father had served as hostage. Received with extravagant honors, Athanaric seemed to offer the possibility of a negotiated solution to the Gothic problem. However, his very arrival at Constantinople at this time suggests that his prestige among his own people and his influence on the younger Gothic leaders who had crossed the Danube in 376 was by now at the most only moderate. He, unlike them, had not shared the common miserable experience of the botched reception of the immigrants and, while hiding from the Huns in his Carpathian refuge, had not participated in the varying fortunes of the war against the Romans. Hope on the Roman side was nevertheless sufficient to allow Theodosius's propagandist Themistius to hint at the new possibility of imminent peace with the Goths in a hasty insertion in the speech that he had prepared for the anniversary celebrations. It was too late, however, to change the general tenor of the well-prepared formal speech, and Themistius duly announced to the assembled worthies of Constantinople, doubtless in conformity with the emperor's wishes, that Theodosius would soon drive all the Goths back over the Danube.[56]

Old Athanaric could not personally have fulfilled the hopes the Romans placed in him, even if he had not died a mere ten days after his arrival in Constantinople. The quality of his residual influence on his people was thus never put to the test. Theodosius, however, tried to make the best of a half-chance and made efforts to impress Athanaric's Gothic entourage by putting on a splendid funeral ceremony for him. At the same time he demonstrated to whoever might take notice in Constantinople that in his view not all Goths, not even all old enemies, need be enemies of Rome for ever. The idea of negotiating was certainly now on the agenda, and it seems that alongside further military activity in

Thrace the two generals currently responsible for the day-to-day operations of the war, the *magistri militum* Fl. Saturninus and Fl. Richomeres, at some point indeed began to talk to the Gothic leaders. This all took some time, but by October 382 a modus vivendi had been found by negotiation and, it seems, formally agreed to in a treaty that was made after a formal capitulation (*deditio*) by the Gothic leaders. This diplomatic arrangement allowed Theodosius to talk of victory for home consumption, while in practice agreeing to the permanent settlement of Goths in Thrace.

The terms of the treaty are nowhere recorded, but they seem to have been particularly favorable to the Goths. The years of warfare and widespread plundering and ravaging of the land must have made a settlement easier to organize than it had been in 376. One gets the impression from Themistius, in a speech celebrating the consulship of the senior peacemaker Fl. Saturninus on 1 January 383 and held in Constantinople before the most influential men living in the city, that when the settlement took place the land assigned to the Goths was not only in a neglected state but also depopulated, that farmers were no longer available to work it. Without the Goths the government would have had to import farmers from Asia Minor, he suggests, looking on the bright side. He compares the Gothic settlement with that of the Celtic Galatians, who had occupied part of central Anatolia in the third century B.C., and had only gradually become integrated into the empire, but who now paid taxes, contributed soldiers, received Roman governors, and obeyed the same laws as the Romans did: "So within a short time we shall also experience the Skythians [i.e., the Goths]: at present their offenses are still fresh, but in the not too distant future we shall have them sharing our religious celebrations, joining our banquets, serving alongside us in the army, and paying taxes as we do."[57]

Since it would have suited Themistius much better to be able to assert that the Goths had a contractual obligation to do all those things immediately, we must assume that the treaty left them untaxed and without a formal military obligation. Moreover, since Themistius does not even express hope for "common laws," he admits by implication that the Goths would be allowed to live under their own rules without the inter-

vention of a Roman governor. This means that their settlement area—
probably in the frontier zone between the river and the Haimos moun-
tain range most affected by the recent troubles—must have been granted
to them freehold and en bloc, and presumably that their current leaders
(whose names, extraordinarily, are not known) organized the details of
the settlement themselves without Roman interference.

This was a far cry from the placative "pushing them back over the
Danube" of January 381. What had the Romans won by this treaty?
Above all two things: first and most important, peace and—at least on
the Danube—security. Once established as farmers in Roman territory
south of the river, the Goths were doubtless enthusiastic enough to defend themselves and their new settlements and possessions against aggression of whatever source from beyond it. Second, Theodosius gained
a source of recruits for the army, young men willing, perhaps even eager,
to adapt to Roman ways and earn good money to help support families
and friends. Two standing units of the central imperial field army of the
East were formed from Goths during Theodosius's reign, listed as "Visi"
and "Tervingi" in the official army list of the *Notitia Dignitatum* drawn
up shortly after his death.[58] Gothic auxiliaries serving under their own
commanders participated in Theodosius's civil war campaigns against
Magnus Maximus in 388 and Eugenius in 394, and there are hints that
some Gothic recruits were accepted into the existing units of the field
army, and so were fully integrated into the Roman military system.[59]

Themistius emphasizes moral rather than legal attachments, the importance of their social integration, and the abandonment of now anti-
quated friend-foe attitudes. Goths had been invited to the consular celebrations of the chief peacemaker; the once hated name was now pleasing
to the ear, and they participated in celebrating their own defeat. That
the Goths might have had a different view of the balance of advantage
in the treaty could not be Themistius's theme, nor that the settlement
of the Gothic war had created a situation that at least in its dimensions
and long-term implications was quite new. Themistius's talk of integration and consensual agreement would remain merely pious hope if he
was thinking of those rural Goths who had now been allowed to take
up residence in a Roman province without being required to adapt their

lives to Roman rules. The legal distinction between Roman and non-Roman territory and status was being obscured precisely at the point where it had always been clearest: at the frontier, where Roman province and administration bordered on *barbaricum*. Whereas Valentinian and Valens had tried to mark the limits by building bridgeheads across the river frontier, the Theodosian settlement in Thrace in effect allowed a bridgehead of *barbaricum* to be established within a Roman frontier province.[60] The precedent might well have seemed alarming.

The Eastern Frontier

Julian's expedition into Mesopotamia and his death in enemy territory led in practice to the stabilizing of the Eastern frontier for more than a century. A fairly neutral statement on the peace agreement is found in Orosius: "Since Jovian could find no way out, restrained as he was by the difficulties of the terrain and surrounded by enemies, he made a treaty with the Persian king Shapur, which, even though some think it unworthy, was urgent enough. It foresaw, in order to rescue his army from enemy attack and the dangers of the terrain, the transfer of the city of Nisibis and part of upper Mesopotamia to the Persians."[61] The contemporary Ammianus Marcellinus, who was present with the army in Mesopotamia, pours scorn on the peacemakers — "we would have done better to fight ten times over, rather than give up any of those territories"[62] — but also fills in details of the "lost territories." They were Rome's most distant possessions east of the Euphrates, the lands of Arzanene, Moxoene, Zabdicene, Rehimena and Corduene, including fifteen castles, the cities of Nisibis and Singara, and the fortress Castra Maurorum.[63]

The inhabitants of these areas, particularly those of Nisibis, who were evacuated into Roman territory and people like the Antiochene Ammianus, who felt that the transfer of Roman territory out of Roman hands was a scandal to be avoided at whatever the cost, regarded the terms of the treaty as disastrous and immoral. Yet Jovian's peace treaty with the old enemy, unsatisfactory compromise though it seemed to be at the time, held for some 140 years and doubtless contributed to the ability of the Eastern part of the empire to cope with the threats on the lower Danube, and thereafter to support a much more stable financial and administrative structure than the Western parts of the empire managed to achieve. No further major wars were fought on the Eastern frontier until the reign of Anastasius; no changes in the frontiers took place.

Such conflicts as there were concerned the control of (or, at least, dominant influence in) the mountainous client kingdoms of Armenia and Iberia (southern Georgia), which for centuries had served as buffer states between the two major powers, suffering the whole range of tensions and struggles for influence, both internal and external, that such states are prone to. Both Ammianus Marcellinus and the internal Armenian historical tradition relate that, as part of Jovian's treaty with Shapur, the Romans agreed not to intervene militarily to support the current Armenian king, Arsak, against Persia.[64] It was doubtless envisaged that Armenian aggression should not be supported, but the formulation was so general that Shapur felt entitled to attack, and when the Romans reacted in a moderate way, each side could feel justified in accusing the other of breaking this clause of the treaty.[65]

The fact was, however, that as long as tensions remained restricted to the client kingdoms of Armenia and Iberia, neither side was prepared to risk a major confrontation elsewhere. Low-level interference occurred sporadically from both sides under Valens and Theodosius. In Iberia, which along with Armenia suffered Persian interference immediately after 363, the Romanizing king Sauromakes was deposed, and some time later, in 370, the kingdom was divided up after a brief Roman military intervention, with Sauromakes regaining the western portion and a pro-Persian client taking the eastern section.[66] In Armenia, encouraged by the loose and strongly regional structure of Armenian society and politics,[67] interference was regular from both sides until around 387, when an internal agreement, brought about by Roman and Persian diplomacy, produced, as in Iberia, a division of the country that left the much smaller western sectors bordering on the Roman provinces in the hands of pro-Roman Armenians and their king Arsak, while the rest of the land became a Persian client with its own king, Chosro.[68]

When we compare the Eastern frontier with the Rhine and Danube frontiers in this period, the major difference is that here — and here alone

—the Roman Empire had a direct border with a major state that, at least locally, was quite capable of challenging Rome militarily and winning. In the East it was therefore potentially dangerous to challenge a once-established status quo; the Persians, unlike the Alamanni or the Sarmatians, were not likely to be impressed by mere short-term punishment raids, nor did the upper echelons of Persian society see service in the Roman army as a desirable alternative to living under their own king, so that social pressure for the integration into the empire of actively dangerous sections of the "foreign" society was largely missing. Only political exiles came into question, but they moved in both directions. Treaties were therefore made and largely respected on both sides; diplomacy was the chief means of communication.[69] Casual treaty breaking, so long experience told, could lead to massive retaliation, in which the outcome could not reasonably be forecast by either side.

The problem of the kingdom of Armenia, lying as it did in a physically inaccessible region and having a strong tradition of independence, could not be solved by either side's occupying the territory without provoking massive internal resistance to the occupying power and small- or medium-scale intervention by the other major player. To the combination of internal Armenian circumstances that led to the agreement of 387 should perhaps, however, be added the fact, scarcely accidental, that the agreement was reached at just about the time when Theodosius was finally preparing to attend to the problem of the usurpation of Magnus Maximus in the West. Presumably he was therefore particularly happy to accept the Armenian partition agreement at this time as a guarantee of stability in the East, which allowed him to concentrate on the war against the western usurper. Internal Roman considerations seem once more to have made their contribution to reaching a decision concerning an important frontier district—this time in favor of peace and stability.

Further south, in the provinces of Palaestina and Arabia, the frontier was the desert, inhabited by nomadic clans whom the Romans called "Saracens" and who made a practice of maintaining their independence by supporting whichever of the major powers, Rome and Persia, happened to suit their ever-changing internal requirements.[70] Raids on the settled territory of the Roman provinces were part of the normal way of life in the area, but only rarely did these become so serious as to threaten the basic security of the provinces. Under Diocletian a fortified road had been built leading south from Callinicum on the Euphrates, the strata Diocletiana, and joining up with the southern road through the Nabataean desert built by Trajan, the via Traiana nova. There is evidence that under Valens some forts on the desert frontier in Jordan were built or repaired, beginning, it seems, in 368,[71] and that some new standing military units were formed and became part of the regular garrison stationed in the area.[72]

Only one episode of more than routine dimensions seems to have disturbed this relatively stable structure during the period with which we are concerned. It is not altogether easy to assess its importance for the region, since our main secular literary sources, Ammianus Marcellinus and Zosimus, do not mention it at all (thus perhaps suggesting it was not of major significance). The orthodox ecclesiastical historians, following the contemporary Rufinus, who was in the area at the time and whose account they used as their source, are only concerned with it because it shows some Saracen interest in Christianity, a discomfiting defeat for one of their pet enemies, Lucius, the "homoian" bishop of Alexandria, and the unusual apparition of a woman taking over the leadership of Saracen invaders after the death of their sheikh, her husband.[73] These events were therefore not likely to have presented a great long-term threat to the security of the provinces, even though Rufinus writes in his contextualizing bridging passage of a violent war shaking the towns and cities of the provinces Palaestina and Arabia; Sozomenus, probably using a local tradition, since he was born in the area, expands on this and claims to know that the coastal province Phoenicia was also affected by Saracen raiders. But the whole point of their story is that the female warrior Mavia quickly came to terms after inflicting some defeats on the local Roman garrison troops, who were sufficiently frightened to summon help from the regional legionary forces under the command of the *magister militum*. She settled for peace when the Roman authorities agreed to allow a Saracen monk, appropriately called Moses, to be installed as their bishop.

Rufinus and his historiographical followers are really only interested in the story of Moses—how he was brought to Egypt to be consecrated and how he then refused ordination in Alexandria at the hands of Lucius and finally had to receive the ceremony from true catholic bishops exiled by Lucius, all of which was organized by the Roman authorities because it was the condition for the peace treaty they so much desired. The edifying literary context makes it virtually impossible to know how much of the background to this pious story is historical. For Rufinus and his followers it would have lost most of its point if the appointment of Moses, in itself nothing very unusual, had not at least signaled the end of a major confrontation, and this overriding purpose of the narrative can easily have led to rhetorical exaggeration to the greater glory of Moses. Local traditions stemming from those who suffered from the raids no doubt helped to obfuscate the matter.

The date of the event is also quite uncertain, since there is no reason to believe that Sokrates, who was merely following Rufinus's story but setting it into the different literary context of his own narrative, had any evidence for his dating the event after Valens had left Antioch for the Gothic war in 378; and Sozomenus, who is merely following Sokrates closely here, has no independent authority for the date.[74] The late chronographic source Theophanes dates the peace treaty to 376/77, but since he also dates the Gothic appeal to Valens to this year, which is approximately correct, he may have had some reason for rejecting the later date he found in Sozomenus.[75] Sozomenus's dating, in itself unlikely, was perhaps imposed by Sokrates merely to explain the slight embarrassment to the claim of authenticity for the story that the emperor Valens himself was not personally involved in this alleged major war (though he was in the general area), which was brought to an early end not by imperial operations but by the choice of a good catholic bishop and sealed by the marriage of Valens's Sarmatian general Victor with one of Mavia's daughters. Moreover, Saracen troops are known to have accompanied Valens when he left Antioch, and at the time they were regarded as reliable, since some of them were left as part of the garrison of Constantinople when Valens went on to Adrianople.[76] If this episode had really been a major war fought while Valens was resident in the area, it remains more than just surprising that he himself did nothing about it.

All in all, the evidence therefore points to a fairly routine series of incidents sometime after Lucius's arrival in Alexandria in 373—larger than normal-scale raids on the settled territories by the nomads, skirmishes with the local garrison troops, who were taken by surprise, whereby significant amounts of blood might well have been spilled, at least one confrontation with an imperial army, followed up by the usual palaver and negotiations to restore security and save face on both sides. Nothing of sufficient seriousness took place to shatter the belief that Saracen troops would remain reliable allies or to require the personal presence of the emperor at the scene of the action. The only later evidence for difficulties in the area is a brief mention in Pacatus's panegyric on Theodosius, held in Rome in summer 389, that rebellious Saracens who had broken a treaty had been punished.[77] This too cannot have been a major incident, and it may have been included in the speech merely for its exotic flavor.

Africa

Compared with the regular military activity in the northern and eastern frontier zones, Roman Africa—roughly speaking, the coastal strip of North Africa—was a relatively untroubled backwater, which, apart from Diocletian's visit to Egypt, had not seen an emperor for more than a century. When Valentinian and Valens divided the empire, Africa, with the exception of Greek-speaking Cyrene and Egypt, became Western. The whole of this Western area had been gradually integrated into the empire over the centuries since the fall of Carthage in 146 B.C., and a population consisting of native "Libyans," Phoenicians, and Roman settlers had benefited from the imperial peace and created an affluent city culture dominated by the rebuilt Carthage, but based on a largely undisturbed agricultural infrastructure. North Africa was firmly attached to Italy— the government of the "proconsulate" of Africa with its administrative seat in Carthage remained even in the fourth century a preserve of Roman senators. Italy was also the main market for agricultural surpluses, and tax in kind from Africa provided bread for the Roman plebs in the fourth century, just as tax in kind from Egypt supplied the bread for Constantinople. It was important to be able to defend these fertile agricultural areas against marauding desert tribes; but while the neighbors on the desert side who were not integrated into the urbanized provincial way of life caused recurring local annoyance with their occasional raids, they represented no fundamental threat to the way of life of the majority of the population.

In the fourth century security could in general be adequately maintained in the western sector by forts manned by small numbers of frontier troops (*limitanei*) under the overall command of the count of Africa (*comes Africae*);[78] a separate command under the *comes Tingitaniae* was responsible for the area of the Strait of Gibraltar.[79] The eastern section, especially Egypt, had larger military garrisons, including legions of the field army (*comitatenses*), which reflected both the more exposed position of the Nile valley and its critical importance as producer of wealth and above all of grain for Constantinople and the armies.[80] Egypt's economic significance is illustrated by the particular attention paid to its civil administration by Valens and Theodosius during their Gothic wars, which culminated in Theodosius's separation of Egypt from the diocese Oriens in 380 and his setting up a separate Egyptian diocese based at Alexandria and governed by the new "Augustal Prefect" (*praefectus Augustalis*).[81]

The security of the North African provinces was not noticeably affected by the internal and external troubles of the empire consequent on the death of Julian. Between Julian and Theodosius only two incidents are known to have caused problems, and they occurred in the western section under Valentinian. Both are related by our main source for the period, Ammianus Marcellinus, at unusual length because of the involvement of the supreme military commander in Africa (*comes Africae*) Romanus in a corruption scandal, which not only cast light on the morals of the highest members of Valentinian's administration but also unnecessarily exacerbated the security situation, for which Romanus was officially responsible. In 364 country districts of the easternmost province, Tripolitania, in the area around the major city Leptis Magna, were ravaged by raiding Austoriani. Incursions were a regularly recurring problem in the area, which the frontier troops were intended to be able to keep under control, and normally could, but this time the raids were more serious than usual.[82] Moreover, the newly appointed *comes* Romanus demonstrated both insouciance and incompetence, thus provoking further raids, including a weeklong abortive attempt on Leptis itself. Ammianus offers no further information on events on the ground at this point, following them up with a report on how Romanus's corrupt friends at court managed to prevent a proper investigation of the complaints of the provincials. Presumably the military situation resolved itself in due course.[83]

The other incident in which Romanus was initially involved not only caused his dismissal but had much more far-reaching consequences, and indeed shook the internal fabric of North African provincial life. Romanus had a talent for making himself unpopular, but his highly placed friends ensured that he did not suffer. He gained a reputation for being a persecutor of the schismatic Donatists, who had a large following, particularly in Numidia;[84] he had provided inadequate help to the Tripolitanians, as we have seen; and his disagreement with one of the leading Romanized Moorish families in the province of Mauretania Sitifensis led to a rebellion against him and his supporters of such dimensions that the *magister militum* Theodosius, the father of the later emperor, had to be sent from Gaul to Africa in 373 with units of the imperial field army, after the leader of the rebellion, Firmus, had taken the diadem and so in effect challenged the authority of the emperor himself.[85] This could not be tolerated, and in the end, after some two years of largely guerrilla fighting, Firmus's local troops proved no match for the imperial professionals, and he committed suicide.[86] But it was a warning that the stability of the African provinces depended on the proper functioning of the administration and due respect being paid to the leaders of provincial opinion, which included having a light hand in matters of religion: Firmus had sought and received support from those very schismatic Donatists whom Romanus had been persecuting.[87] It is therefore scarcely surprising that it was more than thirty years before any further serious attempt was undertaken by the imperial administration to address the Donatist schism in Africa,[88] or that Firmus's brother Gildo, who had joined Theodosius in opposing Firmus, himself rose to be supreme com-

mander of all forces in Africa (*magister militum*) by 386.[89] The administration had learned, it seems, from Romanus's heavy-handed mistakes.

.   .   .

This survey of Roman frontiers and foreign policy in the generation after
Julian's death has shown a strong continuity in principle from earlier
periods, but there were inevitably some significant major developments
in detail, which cast a shadow over the future. On the Rhine and upper
Danube Roman policy continued the centuries-old practice of trying to
contain the transfluvial peoples by regular demonstrations of power and
through the subsequent integration of influential young Germans into
the Roman military establishment. Periodic violence was part of normal
life in this region. In North Africa also the general strategic situation remained effectively unchanged, and had it not been for the self-seeking
aggressive incompetence of the *comes* Romanus, which provoked a serious rebellion requiring the presence of a major Roman army to quell it,
we would merely register routine here in these years.

In the East Julian's disaster in Mesopotamia and Jovian's peace treaty,
though condemned as unacceptable by several eloquent contemporaries,
produced a new and settled situation on the Euphrates frontier, which
aggressive Roman policy in the area over a span of generations had failed
to achieve. That in the mountainous borders between the Persians and
Romans in Armenia low-level tensions continued until under Theodosius a compromise was finally found should not blind us to the momen-
tous nature of the fact that by and large peace prevailed between the two
major powers for nearly 150 years, which was a direct result of Julian's
disaster and Jovian's inability to reject Persian conditions.

On the lower Danube the Goths dominated frontier activities in the
period. The Gothic wars, fought by Valens and Theodosius, changed the
face of the empire—in the long term not just in the immediate region—
and Theodosius's settlement in 382 created the ominous political precedent of allowing the Goths who settled on Roman land in Thrace after
the war to live according to their own rules of life and not be directly
subject to Roman administrative law. It was indeed a decision born of

perceived necessity, but once taken it was impossible to reverse and was capable of multifarious imitation.

In all these geographical areas we see the Roman authorities in essence always reacting to situations created, or even imposed by, their enemies or opponents: in Gaul the attacks of the Alamanni, Franks, and Saxons stimulated Roman reaction; in Africa and Palestine raids by desert nomads on the settled taxpaying territories provoked Roman responses; Jovian's peace with Persia was dictated in effect by Shapur; and Valens's Gothic enterprises were provoked in the first instance by Gothic initiatives. Despite the variations of challenge confronting the Roman authorities in these years, and the wide-ranging innovation that emerged as solutions to these challenges, the basic Roman attitude remained what it had been for centuries: Roman military actions, however systematic, professional, and well planned they may have been, remained responses to challenges imposed from outside; they were never themselves a result of considered Roman initiative.

PART · II

EAST & WEST

CHAPTER IV

THE · GOVERNMENT

The creation of a more effective regionally based government by Diocletian in the last years of the third century bore within it the seeds of regional separation. The grouping of provinces into regional administrative units, the dioceses, and the grouping of dioceses into very large regionally based praetorian prefectures, in which each prefect as the head of the administrative pyramid was directly answerable to the emperor as a kind of regional prime minister, was intended to curb centrifugal tendencies and did indeed allow the empire to weather the storms threatening it from many sides at the end of the third century. It created an internal cohesion that also provided the strength for the empire to survive the rapid collapse of the tetrarchic system that Diocletian had devised for the central government, composed of four chosen emperors, two senior (with the title Augustus) and two junior (the Caesares). His aim was to maintain the unity of the empire through establishing several equally legitimate, but not dynastically founded, centers of imperial power in the regions.

The system began to collapse as soon as successors for the first Augusti and Caesares had to be found, and once Constantine finally won the civil war against Licinius in 324, his long-term policy for the center of imperial government aimed at promoting his own family and setting up a dynasty. The regional praetorian prefects remained responsible for the regional administration, and as a group made their publicistic contribution to the objective of showing unity at the center by formally asserting in their official publications their joint responsibility for all administrative acts made by each of them in his own region. Under this system, as long as the empire knew only one emperor, who by constant travel tried to keep up personal contact with the elite of each major area, innate centrifugal tendencies could be curbed, since there was no single geographical center of government to secede from, the government being always there where the emperor was. Constantine's death, however, despite all pretensions of dynastic unity, ushered in a divisive period under his sons, each of whom, despite formal equality, went his own way in his own region until finally Constantius II restored the Constantinian single-emperor structure after the unanticipated deaths of his brothers.

Constantius's problems with his Caesars Gallus and Julian are well known, and they eventually led to Julian's ruling alone; Jovian also seems to have made no attempt, in his few months as emperor, to find another pair of competent shoulders to help bear the burden of imperial rule; and had the troops not insisted that Valentinian appoint another Augustus shortly after his own imperial acclamation, the double structure instituted by Valentinian and Valens in 364 might also never have emerged, or at least would not have been created so soon. For the government of the empire it was a decisive moment, since once again, as under the sons of Constantine, or even earlier under Diocletian's tetrarchy, more than one formally equal emperor, each bearing the supreme title Augustus, received his own area of regional administrative responsibility, and this time the potentially divisive structure was in principle there to stay. Even military cooperation occurred only at times when both parts of the empire were endangered, that is, when the common border in Illyricum was threatened. Valentinian did not even feel obliged to aid his brother during the usurpation of Procopius, serious though it was, setting his priorities firmly on the restoration of order in his own area in the upper Rhine frontier zone.

Regions and Prefectures

The first post-Constantinian regional division of the empire, that among Constantine's three remaining sons, set an administrative structural precedent and conditioned the shape of future divisions; in particular it seems to have formalized the structure of the praetorian prefectures as the highest administrative units in the empire. The division into three left Constantine II with Gaul, Spain, and Britain; Constans with Italy, Africa, and Illyricum (which then included the dioceses of Dacia and Macedonia); and Constantius with the Greek East, with the exception of Macedonia. Since each of the brothers needed a praetorian prefect as chief executive, these three areas in which they ruled quickly developed into standing units of administration, each under its own praetorian prefect; and the division into three, which had this purely dynastic origin, proved extraordinarily durable and long survived the changes of emperors consequent on dynastic turbulence, since existential questions of taxation, military recruitment and supply, or the administration of the law were all structured according to the praetorian prefectures: the praetorian prefecture *Galliarum*; the praetorian prefecture *Italiae, Africae, Illyrici*; and the praetorian prefecture *Orientis* thus became fixed entities within the imperial administration. Occasionally responsibility for the dioceses of Illyricum was separated from administrative responsibility over Italy and Africa for some particular reason; until the death of Theodosius, however, Illyricum usually remained attached to the other parts of the central "hinge" prefecture. When Constantius became sole ruler, he still retained the triple division of the regional administration, as did Julian after him. Had Constantine left two (or four) sons capable of ruling, the administrative structure of the empire after their decease would probably have been quite different, since the existing division into three was by no means a "natural" one; others would have been equally conceivable.

When Valentinian and Valens divided the empire into only two parts in 364, the question of the line of division arose immediately. What was to happen to the three existing prefectures? The gigantic central prefecture of Italy, Africa, and Illyricum, which Constantius had retained as a single administrative unit, particularly seemed to lend itself to division —and indeed was divided later. Illyricum alone consisted at the time of three large dioceses—Pannonia, Dacia, and Macedonia—and thereby stretched from the Danube west of Vienna as far as Crete, and included both Latin- and Greek-speaking areas. It was a historically grown structure, not a rationally designed one. The decision about its disposition was taken at the latest when the imperial brothers reached Sirmium, the administrative center of the Illyrican part of the central prefecture: the senior Augustus Valentinian, like his brother born at Cibalae in central Illyricum, proved in practice to be fundamentally conservative in this respect and seems never even to have considered the possibility of splitting up the three Illyrican dioceses. They therefore remained together and attached to the West.[1] There were doubtless good technical administrative reasons for this decision. In Europe Valens received therefore only the diocese of Thrace, which he administered from Constantinople through his praetorian prefect of *Oriens*.[2] During the greater part of the joint rule of the brothers and beyond, from 365 until perhaps as late as 377, Illyricum remained administratively attached to Italy and Africa and enjoyed the administrative attentions of the Roman aristocrat Sextus Petronius Probus from 368 until sometime after Valentinian's death in late 375.[3]

Only when in 376 the Gothic settlement in Thrace turned sour and serious war threatened the area was Illyricum temporarily separated administratively from Italy and Africa and given its own prefect. This change, temporary though it was, was important, since the praetorian prefect was responsible, among his other duties, for organizing military supplies, and the appointment of a special official for the Illyrican area implies increased attention by the Western government to such matters. The appointment was therefore part of the flexible response by the administration to the deteriorating security situation in the area. By the time the crisis peaked in 378, the experienced Italian senator Quintus Clodius Hermogenianus Olybrius had taken over,[4] but the effects of the military disaster of Adrianople dominated the affairs of Illyricum (and inevitably affected the imperial administration of the area) for the next several years; so the military crisis and its resolution drew a question mark over the current division of territorial responsibility within the central prefecture, which up to this time had remained remarkably stable since Constantine's death.

Gratian himself sat out the crisis after Adrianople at Sirmium, where the court settled in for the months immediately following the battle and where Theodosius was appointed emperor on 19 January 379. Part of the bargain that Theodosius struck with Gratian was that he should receive responsibility for the whole of Illyricum until the war against the Goths was over.[5] This gave Theodosius the immediate backing of the military and financial resources of the three populous and rich Illyrican dioceses for the war and is the first indication that the administrative structure created by Constantine's sons and reaffirmed by Valentinian and Valens did not have to be permanent. For Illyricum Theodosius appointed as successor to Olybrius the Aquitanian Eutropius, who had come out to the East under Constantius and then accompanied Julian on the Persian expedition; he had stayed on under Valens, whom he served as *magister memoriae* (head of one of the central administrative and legal departments [the *scrinia*]), and proconsul of Asia. He dabbled in history and had written a short Latin history of Rome (a *breviarium*) for Valens. Experienced both in East and West, in administration and in law, Eutropius was a high-grade appointment for the crisis, and a particularly suitable one for the multicultural Illyrican dioceses.[6] Olybrius, now relieved of Illyricum, joined Theodosius as his top administrator, his first praetorian prefect of the East, while Theodosius himself stayed in Illyricum, taking up residence in Thessalonica, the main city of the Macedonian diocese. From there he conducted the first stages of his Gothic war. By the beginning of the financial year ("indiction") 382 on 1 September the Illyrican administration was, however, again in Western hands. By then the war was effectively over, and Theodosius kept to his agreement with Gratian.[7]

Even in the West the Eastern crisis made its mark on the ruling elite within the imperial administration. Before April 378 Gratian's old teacher and confidant, Decimus Magnus Ausonius, had been appointed praetorian prefect of the Gauls, and after Adrianople he additionally took on responsibility for Italy and Africa. Here, however, he received some reliable assistance, since his son Hesperius was somehow associated with him in office. The precise arrangement is not known, but in practice Hesperius seems to have carried full responsibility, since all extant laws after this date are addressed to him alone.[8] Moreover, in 379, in the months between Olybrius's joining Theodosius as his praetorian prefect of the East and the transfer of Illyricum to Theodosius on 1 September 379, Hesperius also had responsibility for Illyricum.[9] However, by the end of the year 379 the double burden was shed. We know that his successor in Gaul, Siburius, was already in office before 3 December 379,[10] and in Italy Fl. Syagrius had taken over before 18 June 380.[11] Since the last known law addressed to Hesperius dates from 3 August 379,[12] it would be reasonable to assume that he (perhaps along with Ausonius) was relieved of his administrative burden at the time when the Illyrican dioceses were transferred to Eastern administration on 1 September 379.

By the end of Theodosius's reign Illyricum had been permanently split between East and West. The two easterly dioceses, Dacia and Macedonia, now belonged to Constantinople and received their own praetorian prefect of Illyricum, appointed by the Eastern emperor, while Pannonia remained attached to Italy and Africa.[13] How and when this division came about is unclear, but we have some indications. The Eastern section of the *Notitia Dignitatum*—the official listing of the administrative structure of the empire and one of our main sources for it—was written down in the form we have it around 401, and by then the division had already happened.[14] But when Magnus Maximus invaded Italy in 387, Valentinian II and his entourage fled to Thessalonica, which at the time was still the most easterly major city of his own western part of the empire and was not yet administered by Theodosius from Constantinople. It was at Thessalonica that plans and preparations for the war against the usurper were made, and it was from Thessalonica that the expedition started.[15]

Since Valentinian II returned to Italy by sea and played no effective part in the military campaign, Theodosius must have exercised, at least for the duration of the war, formal rights over the Illyrican administration, which, as in his arrangement with Gratian in the early 380s, must have included use of the tax income and military recruitment potential. It seems indeed quite feasible that the main costs of the war against Maximus could have been covered by Illyrican (that is, officially Western) funds. Theodosius's formal responsibility for Illyricum at this time is firmly evidenced by his issuing a law from Stoboi to the praetorian prefect Trifolius as early as 14 June 388.[16] Later in the year Trifolius was praetorian prefect in Italy, and his appointment in the spring and his receiving a law directed to him at that time by Theodosius show that one result of the negotiations with Valentinian II in Thessalonica 387/88 must indeed have been the transfer of formal responsibility for the central prefecture to Theodosius.[17] This formal legitimation also helps to explain why Theodosius seems to have met no resistance in Illyricum until he reached Pannonia, where Maximus was operating in the field, and confronted the usurper's army at Poetovio (Ptuj).

The war was speedily won, and Theodosius spent the next three years in Italy, during which time he certainly remained formally responsible for Thessalonica, and therefore for the Illyrican dioceses, as is shown by the affair of the massacre carried out by his garrison troops and his political battle about it with Ambrose in Milan.[18] After the defeat of Magnus Maximus, Valentinian II remained restricted to the prefecture of the Gauls for the rest of his short life. Theodosius's long-term plans may be uncertain, but the appointment of Virius Nicomachus Flavianus as praetorian prefect for Italy, Africa, and Illyricum on his departure for Constantinople in the summer of 391 was certainly made by him,[19] not by Valentinian, and it soon became clear that the whole of the huge central prefecture of Italy, Africa, and Illyricum, which Valentinian I had claimed for the West against his brother in 364, now belonged to Theodosius. This vital block of territory had therefore passed administratively to the East, at least for as long as Theodosius resided there. There is no evidence for a division of Illyricum at this time.

When Eugenius and Arbogast entered Italy in 393, they were joined by Theodosius's appointee Virius Nicomachus Flavianus, whom Eugenius confirmed in office. One reason for Flavianus's willingness to join the usurpers may have been that he had already been deprived of two-thirds of his area of responsibility by Theodosius. A law issued on 15 February 393 in Constantinople to the praetorian prefect Apodemius describes his area of responsibility (uniquely!) as Illyricum and Africa.[20] This was three months before the death of Valentinian II in May, therefore before the usurpation, and thus was not a reaction to it, but reflects a deliberate decision by Theodosius to reduce Flavianus's area of responsibility to Italy alone. Later in the year Apodemius received two further laws concerning Illyricum, but it was not until news arrived in Constantinople of the defection of Flavianus to the usurper that his title was extended in a law issued on 9 June 393 to the full prefecture, now including Italy.[21] These laws were all issued by Theodosius from Constantinople, but where Apodemius resided is not known.

After the law of 9 June the prefect disappears from our evidence. Whether Apodemius was another yet unrecognized victim of the usurpers or he had simply served his term for Theodosius, to be replaced after the battle at the Frigidus by someone who has left no record in the extant legislation, is not known. What is clear, however, is that the war against Eugenius offered no good reason for splitting up Illyricum between the two parts of the empire. That would have necessitated long-term cooperation and successful negotiation, based on a systematic analysis of what was practical and functional for a symbiotic system of government, as well as the willingness of the authorities both in the East and the West to compromise and settle their differences. Such a rational procedure was, however, unthinkable during the usurpation.

In the whole decade since the death of Gratian a first prospect for reorganizing Illyricum administratively emerged in September 394 after the battle of the Frigidus. In the few months before his death in January 395 Theodosius made dispositions for the future administrative structure of the empire, and among these arrangements must have been the division of Illyricum that we find recorded in the *Notitia Dignitatum*.[22] On the surface it was rational and practical, attributing as it did the administration of the mainly Greek-speaking dioceses of Illyricum to the East and the Latin-speaking to the West. The division became permanent when it was accepted and maintained by Theodosius's heirs, but the partition along the linguistic dividing line was in practice another nail in the coffin of imperial unity, which further encouraged the administrative separation of the Greek and Latin provinces of the empire. A dynastic system was to prevail instead as unifying factor, but it soon became clear that a unified Illyrican administration, once it was irretrievably gone, had indeed served as an important hinge on which the interests of both sections of the empire turned. The eventual division was now preprogrammed and is traceable to this day, reflected by the areas dominated by the orthodox and catholic churches respectively.

Summarizing the results of this section we can note that the formal division of government for the major regions of the empire, structured according to praetorian prefectures, was in effect created by the Constantinian brothers in the division of the empire after Constantine's death, and that after the end of the dynasty it remained firmly in place. Valentinian and Valens made no perceptible change to the system they had grown up with, and only the pressure of events during the Gothic war after their deaths made a more effective structure for the administration of the war zone in Illyricum seem imperative. The first stage was the emergency temporary transfer of Illyricum to Theodosius for the conduct of the war, but although Illyricum returned to Western administration after peace was made, the same administrative problem emerged at the time of the civil war against Magnus Maximus. Once again Theodosius in the East took over administrative responsibility for Illyricum and the war zone. This time he retained it until his death. Nevertheless, the experience gained in these years of crisis seems to have convinced him and his advisers that the best solution for this area of the empire would be a permanent division of the Illyrican dioceses along the lines of the linguistic frontier; and this appears to have been the division that he recommended to his sons and successors in 395. It doubtless removed an administrative anomaly and made communication within each of the separate divisions of the empire easier. At the same time, however, it made communication between the divisions structurally less necessary, since common or overlapping interests became fewer. The development of separate governmental structures then seemed more natural and was easier to justify.

The Theodosian Code

A new look at administrative developments in the fourth century would be impossible without the stimulus of much recent work on our sources, especially on the main single source for state activity in the fourth century, the Theodosian Code. It will be important for what follows to state my view on this major source here, since it differs in some respects from the results of recent research. The Theodosian Code was a compilation made with the support of Theodosius's grandson Theodosius II and completed in 438; it was aimed at collecting all "general" laws issued since Constantine's defeat of Maxentius (312)—laws, that is, that were applicable not just to individual cases, even if directed in the first instance to a particular local or regional problem. The compilers were to abbreviate the texts to their central legal substance, to arrange them chronologically within material rubrics—which sometimes led to separate paragraphs of the same law being arranged under different rubrics—and to record the name and office of the official to whom the law was originally directed and its place of issue.[23]

Large parts of this codification have survived, since it was much used in the medieval West, and it provides the basis of our knowledge of lawgiving and administration in the fourth century. It is therefore important to dwell on it briefly. One factor must be emphasized above all, and this is the nature of late Roman imperial legislation in the areas covered by the Code. In a society that did not know the institution of the public prosecutor, laws (*leges*) issued by the emperors as edicts, letters (*epistulae*), or replies to specific questions (*rescripta*) were each intended in the first instance as an instruction to the person or group of persons receiving the communication. If a private person requested an imperial decision on a particular point of civil law that was in dispute (as in the case of a disputed will), the *rescriptum* was initially valid for that instance alone. If, however, the recipient was a public official, the imperial instruction—in whatever form it was issued—was initially valid for him and for his area of responsibility, and in principle gave the recipient instructions on how he was to proceed in his function as judge (*iudex*) in cases brought before his tribunal that were covered by the relevant imperial pronouncement. (All of the higher public officials who received imperial communications directly functioned as judges.)

Such general imperial administrative instructions were normally made public by being posted at the official office in the city in which the recipient resided. How widely and how quickly new legislation became known was thus directly dependent on the administrative function of the recipient and his officials. An official letter directed to the governor of a single province will in most cases have originated in a request from him for information or for instructions on a particular issue (*consultatio*) and will have been published, apart from being known in the imperial chancery which issued the document, only in the province of the recipient.[24] Such a law therefore in the first, and perhaps in the last, instance was only to be applied there (unless, as was often the case, it was a mere reminder of a wider ruling already practiced elsewhere). Such laws are recognizable in the Code where the recipient and his subordinate office are explicitly named.[25] If the recipient was, however, a praetorian prefect, then—depending on the efficiency of the bureaucratic machinery—a copy of the law probably ought in due course to have reached each of his subordinates, that is, each provincial governor within the prefecture, and have been posted at each official residence there. Such laws are also recognizable in the Code.

Since the compilers, especially from the earlier part of their period, had only inadequate central archives to work from, as John Matthews has recently again made adequately clear, they were forced to rely on certain local, or even private, collections, based on what had been posted at some provincial administrative center. Some laws collected from such local sources were doubtless instructions issued to the local or regional representative of the central administration, recognizable as such when he is named explicitly as the recipient; it cannot, however, be excluded that some such locally applicable laws might have been culled from the archive of the issuing authority. Laws addressed to and passed down to his subordinates by the praetorian prefect and collected at the provincial point of publication, however, retained the name of their central addressee but were regularly marked with the date and place where they were posted, or with some formulation that allows this conclusion.[26] The covering letter of the praetorian prefect to his subordinate was, of course, not included in the Code, even though it had perhaps been originally posted, as some examples surviving outside the Code suggest happened.[27]

Unless a law was deliberately sent at the same time to other praetorian prefects—which, especially after the division of the empire in 364, only occurred in particularly important cases, in which common action was agreed upon by the emperors—the law would not necessarily ever become known outside the prefecture of the man who originally received it. When this did happen—the preserved evidence for which is extremely slight—textual changes seem to have been made to adapt to regional conditions, and the form of the official communication from the receiving consistory to the chosen recipient in its own area was in each case that of a new law. Even within the *partes* this seems to have been the case. Theodosius issued laws on Manichaeans to his praetorian prefect of Illyricum, Eutropius, and then with a delay of almost a year to his praetorian prefect of the East, Florus. Florus, however, received a text with significant changes, which justified its separate inclusion in the Code.[28]

A Western example (though later than the period with which we are concerned) is offered by a series of laws issued in the summer of 425 from Aquileia regulating the restoration of ecclesiastical privileges revoked by the recently defeated Western usurper Johannes. The law sent to Amatius, the praetorian prefect of the Gauls, is preserved in full (though not in the Code), and other laws on the same subject, some textually closer, some more distant from this, are preserved in the usual abbreviated form in the Code. They are addressed respectively to the *comes rerum privatarum*, the urban prefect of Rome, and the proconsul of Africa, all of whom were formally independent of the praetorian prefect of Italy, Africa, and Illyricum and normally received their official communications directly from the emperor.[29] It is remarkable that in this case no law issued to the praetorian prefect of Italy, Africa, and Illyricum was used by the compilers of the Code, and that the law issued to the praetorian prefect of the Gauls also escaped their notice. The historical problem, however, is to ascertain whether there ever was such a law issued to a praetorian prefect of Italy.[30] A final answer is not possible, since it is not even clear that there was yet a praetorian prefect in post in Italy after the reconquest of the West. The solution to the problem may perhaps lie therein. The first known praetorian prefect of the central prefecture after the reconquest (already in post by 6 March 426) was none other than the Roman aristocrat Flavius Anicius Auchenius Bassus, who as *comes rerum privatarum* received the laws about the ecclesiastical restorations—not an area with which he would usually officially be much concerned.[31] It therefore seems at least possible that he might have temporarily been administering the central functions of the praetorian prefect until the regime of the child Valentinian III was firmly in the saddle, and that the basic law on the ecclesiastical restoration was thus never issued to a praetorian prefect of Italy and so could not be found by the compilers of the Code.

However that may be, the procedure is clear enough. A central decision was communicated to the directly dependent officers responsible for applying it in different but similar forms of words, texts that might even include identical passages, but did not need to. If this was the case within the jurisdiction of a single emperor, it goes without saying that such communication between the *partes* was even more complicated and could be at all effective only under specific circumstances where cooperation had been formally agreed to (as happened, it seems, for certain common issues in the early years of the regimes of Valentinian and Valens). Thus despite the impression given by the formal structure of all imperial pronouncements—that they were issued in the name of all the reigning emperors—in practice all legislation was in the first place in some sense regional legislation. The same applies in principle also to legislation addressed to the other senior palatine officials whose areas of responsibility were not restricted to the regional prefectures, the master of the offices (*magister officiorum*), and the two financial ministers, the *comes rerum privatarum* and the *comes sacrarum largitionum*, who each, however, served only one emperor in one of the *partes* and had an area of responsibility limited to the regions ruled by his emperor. Knowledge of legislation addressed to them therefore also normally became known initially only in the area governed by the legislating emperor.

Knowledge of legislation outside the region for which it was initially issued was thus with rare exceptions either haphazard, purely accidental, or due, for instance, to the private initiative of enterprising lawyers and teachers of law or other interested parties, who saw advantage in trying to cite laws that—as the prescript always suggested and according to the juristic theory of academic lawyers—were theoretically valid everywhere in the empire. This separation of responsibility in principle did not prevent occasional individual but concerted action in specific areas of common interest, but since there was no regular exchange of information, neither was there any central official collection of all official legal pronouncements. At the time of Diocletian two lawyers, Gregorius and Hermogenianus, had independently made efforts to collect and publish civil-law rulings,[32] but thereafter decisions in the whole field of public law received no form of codification until the reign of Theodosius II.

In March 429 the emperor (naming his fellow emperor Valentinian III, as convention demanded, as co-responsible) sent a message to the Senate in Constantinople announcing his first plan for a codification of the law, which resulted in the Theodosian Code, completed and published in 438.[33]

The basic aim of the Code was practical: to provide judges with a single valid collection of past law, on which they were to base their judgments. Once the Code was completed, no law not included in it was to be citable in court, except such rulings as had been made after its publication.[34] For the future a distillation of the legal content of the new collection and of the earlier collections of Gregorius and Hermogenianus, meant to cut out mistakes and contradictions and to provide a "rule for life" (*magisterium vitae*), was planned but never completed, and the volume that was finished in 438 and put into circulation was no more than the first step of the original program, a collection of raw material abbreviated and ordered according to subject matter and date of issue, but inevitably full of matters of mere historical or local interest, since it contained outdated, superseded, and contradictory rulings from Constantine to Theodosius II. For the modern historian the Code is, therefore, a mine of information, but it can have been of only limited practical value for the judges and lawyers for whom it was intended. We are not here concerned with the making of the Code as such, to which John Matthews has recently devoted a whole book, but one clause expressed in the emperor's statement of his aims helps one to understand the lawgiving process and supports my interpretation of laws as being essentially of regional purpose and validity: for the future, new laws made in one part of the empire were to be valid in the other only if they were officially transmitted and then received and published by the administration of the other part; the right to make changes to the transmitted text or even not to accept and publish it at all was explicitly reserved.[35]

This statement marks the introduction of a new method of systematic exchange of information, and provides clear proof for the view that before this there had been no regular and systematic attempt to inform the other *pars* of legislation issued—the fact that even the new system did not function adequately merely illustrates the practical difficulty of the process. Since these difficulties remained virulent under Theodosius II and Valentinian III (the current Western emperor, successor of Honorius), who had fixed permanent residences in, respectively, Constantinople and Ravenna, which they left only rarely and where the bureaucratic administration had its permanent residence and central archives, any exchange of information under their more distant predecessors, for whom these favorable conditions did not yet apply, must have been even more haphazard, since before Theodosius I the emperors, as active military commanders, normally had no regular long-term place of residence, and the relationship between the two *partes imperii* was additionally often strained. There was, therefore, once the geographical division of responsibilities of the three praetorian prefects had been established and especially after the division of the empire under Valens and Valentinian, no regular comprehensive communication of information about legislation between the prefectures. This demands the historically important conclusion that the often invoked "general law valid for the whole empire" in practice could hardly exist, at least for the period with which we are concerned, but was only a theory of universalist academic lawyers with little base in historical reality. All laws from this period, and probably from others as well, therefore need to be interpreted in their immediate local or regional historical context. That is perhaps the most important general lesson from recent studies of the Code.

Government and Legislation

The division of powers and personnel that Valentinian and Valens agreed on at Naissus and Sirmium in the summer of 364 had an immediate effect on administrative practice at the highest level of the government of the empire. Ammianus Marcellinus, whose hostility to Valens is manifest, loses no chance to make clear that Valens was only in power thanks to his brother's will and decision, and at first, though bearing the title of Augustus (signifying equality), fulfilled no more than the function of subordinate helper.[36] However true this may have been in a purely political sense in 364, Valentinian's refusal to send help to his brother during the revolt of Procopius made it brutally clear that the senior Augustus expected his brother to stand on his own feet and to look after his own area of responsibility independently with the aid of those forces and administrators he had given him.

This meant neither that the two *partes imperii* had no contact nor that in certain areas they did not aim at cooperation. The end of Procopius's usurpation was duly marked by the usurper's severed head being sent by Valens to his brother in Gaul and the transfer to Valentinian for a judicial decision of two Westerners who had supported the usurpation.[37] Formally nothing much changed with the partition. For many generations after it all official imperial pronouncements, publications, and documents of whatever kind continued to be issued in the joint names of all the nominally ruling emperors, wherever they happened to be, even when it is obvious from the contents that merely local or regional problems were involved. For instance, a letter from Valentinian to the prefect of the city in Rome, Praetextatus, in 367 concerning riots that had accompanied the episcopal election of Damasus is formally written in the names of the emperors Valentinian, Valens, and Gratian, although Valens was at Marcianopolis in Thrace, Gratian was only eight years old, and the subject matter concerned only the city of Rome.[38] Just as all legislation formally bore the names of all ruling emperors, although each law was nearly always directed to one particular official who exercised limited responsibility—at its widest extent, as with the palatine financial officials, the *comes rerum privatarum* and the *comes sacrarum largitionum*, or the *magister officiorum*, it was restricted to specific functions within one of the divisions of the empire—so were the formal addressees of any official report to any one emperor all the ruling emperors, although it is usually clear from the circumstances that in practice only one of them can have been intended. This publicistic practice can cause confusion unless adequate attention is paid to ascertaining who was in fact responsible for any specific ruling.

The official communications (*relationes*) that Symmachus as prefect of the city of Rome sent to the court at Milan in 384/85 and which were later edited and published from his own copies give us an inkling of the formal problems posed by this type of protocol. Symmachus's reports were originally all formally directed to the three ruling emperors— Valentinian II, Theodosius, and Arcadius—as occasional unedited addresses in the text as transmitted show; but he had made a private note in his own copies indicating which emperor each communication had actually been sent to, and it is the edited and abbreviated address that is usually found in the manuscripts (though it was sometimes incorrectly recorded or changed in the course of transmission). On one occasion, however, the full unabbreviated address has been preserved.[39] These *relationes* are also valuable for giving us evidence that at least as far as Rome was concerned the prefect of the city, although appointed by the Western emperor, felt at liberty, indeed obliged, to direct occasional formalized polite missives also to the emperor in Constantinople (though all matters of substance went only to Milan). In this way he upheld for his traditional Roman office over and above the mere formal address the pretense that the empire was one.

The emperors for their part also propagated the ideal unity of the empire by agreeing on who was to be consul each year, whereby attention was paid to the adequate representation of both *partes*, without slavishly representing each *pars* each year. And even when tensions were high, as at the time of the usurpations of Magnus Maximus and of Eugenius under Theodosius, Theodosius's refusal to recognize in his own area the consulships of the usurpers, far from meaning that the two *partes* were drifting apart, was a sign of active interest in upholding formal legitimacy in the Western *pars*, and was therefore a form of assertion that the two *partes* really belonged together. As a Westerner on the Eastern throne Theodosius represented in his person both parts of the empire, and his reluctance to abandon the idea of unity is comprehensible enough. Despite all the strains and tensions of the period Orosius, writing in Africa some twenty years after the death of Theodosius, could describe the empire at that time as "joint rule, but with separate seats of government".[40]

Theodosius's heroic attempts to hold the empire together by establishing the rule of his own dynasty were only partially successful, and the effective separation of responsibilities that Valentinian and Valens had reintroduced in 364 developed apace. Particularly important was the gradual development of a separate and largely independent administrative structure in the East. A late but well-informed source, Johannes Lydus, who had served in the office of the praetorian prefect of the East in Constantinople, preserves the invaluable information that the archive of the court of the praetorian prefect of the East began with Valens, not before, and was located in the substructure of the hippodrome, with direct access from the palace.[41] One of Valens's praetorian prefects must therefore have set up this archival system, and this measure seems to imply the intention of making Constantinople a permanent base for the Eastern prefectoral administration, even though the emperor himself was only infrequently in the city and then only for brief periods. The most likely initiator of this important administrative action is Domitius Modestus, who served as praetorian prefect of the East from 369 until 377, after being prefect of the city in Constantinople. As soon as a major central archive existed—this was doubtless not the only one—and the bureaucracy had been built up to administer and use it, the sheer dead weight of a functioning system must have become a major contributing factor in making it permanent.

We do not possess much information about the stages of the development of the Eastern bureaucracy under Valens and Theodosius, though it is clear from the detailed listings of the *Notitia Dignitatum* that by the time of Theodosius's death the bureaucracy was highly developed as an administrative structure that could without difficulty be described, as by the *Notitia*, as an organization in its own right. The area in which we can most easily perceive the separation of functions in operation is that of law making. Since at the time of the compilation of the Theodosian Code in the 430s no central archive for the whole empire existed, and the exchange of information between the *partes* was at best haphazard,[42] it is no surprise to find that under Valentinian and Valens each praetorian prefect (and others, including subordinate officials too, as necessary) received legislation for his own area of responsibility and that there seems to have been little or no general attempt to coordinate legislative policy. This does not, however, mean that coordinated actions could not and did not take place. The need for coordination was more likely felt to be urgent in the areas of private civil law—for instance, in testamentary law[43]—or in economic policy. For example, Valentinian and Valens seem to have carried out a major coinage reform, which must have been agreed-upon policy.[44] Such matters had an automatic relevance stretching beyond a single prefecture. In administrative, organizational, or disciplinary areas (even including details of taxation), where local practice could vary significantly without affecting other areas, the need for coordination was far less pressing. Despite some successful efforts to coordinate policies in some fields of common interest and a general similarity of approach by the administrations of the two brothers to governmental problems, which cropped up in similar fashion in both parts of the empire,[45] the general tendency of the period seems to indicate an ever-increasing legislative and administrative independence of the two *partes*.

This general separation of regional administration and administrative decision making according to prefectures continued under Theodosius and Gratian (and Valentinian II): when Theodosius was in Italy in the years 388–91, he regularly directed separate instructions to Eastern officials in Constantinople, which in most cases can only have been responses to written reports or suggestions that he received from them. Even when the basic idea and purpose of laws were similar for the different parts of the empire, no single legislative text is known to have been issued with the intention of its being applied as issued to the whole empire.[46] Confirmation of the merely local or regional application of imperial rulings may be seen in two closely related Theodosian laws, both issued in Italy in 391, banning bloody sacrifice—in both cases a mere repetition, now, however, with explicit local application, of substantial aspects of earlier legislation—and banning the worship of statues or even the visiting of temples by imperial officials.

The first was issued from Milan and addressed to Albinus, the prefect of the city in Rome, and dates from 24 February. The second, addressed on 16 June to the chief civil and military officials in Egypt, Evagrius, the civilian diocesan officer (*praefectus Augustalis*), and Romanus, the *comes Aegypti*, clearly imitates the earlier text, but differs in its wording, being adapted to the different conditions prevailing in Egypt.[47] Had Albinus's law as preserved been intended for the whole empire, the Egyptian law would have been superfluous; but since it was indeed issued, it was clearly regarded as being necessary. Had it been directed to the *praefectus Augustalis* along with other diocesan officials in the East who were subordinate to the praetorian prefect of *Oriens*, it should have merely borne the name of the prefect as recipient and the notice that it had been posted in Alexandria. The inclusion of the *comes*, who was not a subordinate of the praetorian prefect, as joint recipient shows that the document must have been issued to the named recipients directly from the court chancery. The decision to issue these two similar laws must therefore have been taken separately in each case, the second more than three months after the first, and each separate formulation was intended merely for local application by its recipients. Whether other local versions of this ruling existed, which the compilers of the Code did not find, is not known, but given the localized nature of so much imperial legislation it would be quite misleading merely to assume that these rulings issued for the two major cities Rome and Alexandria and addressed explicitly to the officials responsible for them must have had pendants everywhere in the empire. The fact that the Alexandrian law was dispatched directly to the local officials and not to the praetorian prefect suggests strongly that this was not so. Both laws were most probably found by the compilers of the Code in the central archives.

Occasionally we catch a glimpse of what seems to be common knowledge or in some way a coordinated policy; at other times different rulings on identical, or very similar, problems show the regional administrations' adapting independently to local conditions or traditions. Sometimes a later law includes a back reference to an earlier one, which it emends or restates, but in almost every case the back reference is to a law issued in the later lawgiver's own *pars imperii*. It will be convenient to give some examples of this, particularly since confusion over the status of the dioceses of Illyricum at this period has led to much misunderstanding and to the development of the notion that administrative and legislative separation may not have been as complete as the main body of the evidence suggests. It is not, however, always possible to identify the earlier law to which reference is made. This may be because it was simply not found by the researching compilers of the Theodosian Code or because the editors abbreviated so drastically that the point of reference is no longer recognizable.[48] For the principle this is not in itself important.

The basic facts are, however, not really in doubt. When in 384 Valentinian II's government in Italy felt obliged to address the praetorian prefect Praetextatus on the problem of some men using titles to which they had not been appointed and therefore were not entitled, though they were claiming the privileges that went along with them, he referred to a general ruling issued by his father, Valentinian I. This ruling may possibly be identified as the law addressed to Ampelius, prefect of the city at Rome, on 5 July 372.[49] The back reference to Valentinian incidentally shows, as do all the following examples, that when necessary even in a formal pronouncement an emperor had no hesitation or difficulty in ignoring the normal documentary protocol, which required naming all ruling emperors in official imperial pronouncements, and singling out the one emperor really responsible for a cited precedent. A few years later, in 386, a law directed to Pinianus, the prefect of the city at Rome, addressed the relative status of retired palatine functionaries. The problem was perhaps particularly virulent at Rome, where in the Senate traditional aristocrats met and associated with highly placed ex-officers of the palace. This time Valentinian II was able to refer back to a ruling by Gratian, "our lord brother", issued in 381 to Valerianus, the current prefect of the city at Rome, where the details had already been laid down. Parts of the original law were also included in the Code.[50]

Again, shortly after the death of Theodosius in 395, Honorius's administration addressed a law to one Vincentius—whose post is not recorded, but he may well have been a diocesan officer (*vicarius*)—concerning the financing of public works in the provinces. It seems probable that Vincentius had induced the imperial pronouncement by asking for directions on how to act in certain specific cases, and he was duly supplied with a reference to an earlier ruling by Valentinian I, perhaps the law addressed to the praetorian prefect of the central prefecture, Petronius Probus, in 374.[51] The principle is clear enough. A year later Honorius's officials faced the problem of how to stop unwarranted demands on the local population by troops serving in the provinces, and again referred to a general ruling by the soldier-emperor Valentinian I that regulated such matters (the original law is now lost).[52] The same route was followed up in rulings on the use of lands owned by the financial department of the *res privata*, where Honorius's officials found that their emperor could refer back to regulations issued not only by Valentinian I but also by Gratian, who had himself already followed the precedent of his father's regulation, and in rulings on some more technical financial matters concerning guarantees, where a lost law of Gratian served as point of reference.[53] It seems clear from all these citations of precedents that there must have been a good central archive in Italy, the staff of which was able, when necessary, to find appropriate points of reference for immediate legislation. There is, however, no back reference in any Western law to an Eastern precedent.

In the East back references to precedents from the time of Valens and Theodosius are much rarer. This difference might represent merely a different rhetorical-legal tradition or, perhaps more likely, a less well established and less efficient archive in Constantinople. Since the organization of the archive of the court of the praetorian prefect of the East did not begin until sometime during the reign of Valens, other Eastern administrative archives might well have been begun even later.[54] This fact could perhaps also help to explain why relatively few laws of Valens have found their way into the Code. Thus while a series of later Eastern laws, all issued by Theodosius II, refer back to precedents created by Arcadius,[55] only one citation of precedent in a Theodosian law, a text dated to 383 and issued to the *comes Orientis* Proculus concerning local councillors who illegally achieved senatorial status, goes back to Valens.[56] There is also one imprecise reference to a ruling of "the time of the deified Julian" in a law on a related subject of the same year.[57] Two laws of Arcadius refer back to precedents created by Valens. One concerns the organization of the bureau of the financial minister, the *comes sacrarum largitionum*, which had been given its current form by Valens.[58] The second, issued in 408, concerning the appointment of praetors to pay for the praetorian games in Constantinople, refers back to a law of Valens for the appropriate punishment in case of failure to perform.[59] This is a particularly conclusive case for the essential separateness of legislative activity, since the Code also contains a more recent law issued by Valentinian on 9 June 373 concerning the same problem in Rome, which was clearly unknown to Arcadius's staff, who only found Valens's law from Constantinople in their archive. This may or may not have provided a precedent for Valentinian's Roman law—we just do not know.[60] But the latter was clearly not known in Constantinople until Theodosius II's researchers began work on the Code, long after Arcadius's death.

Two other post-Theodosian back references seem to invoke Theodosian precedents. In 398 Arcadius was called upon by the *comes Orientis* to make a ruling about a detail of property law concerning widows who remarried. He refers to an earlier law (*lex anterior*) in which the point had already been settled, whereby a ruling of Theodosius issued in December 382 to Florus, his praetorian prefect of the East, seems most likely to be meant.[61] In 425 Theodosius II issued a long law on the relative status of persons granted an honorary title—he was specifically concerned about the title of the high court officers, the *comites consistoriani*—and those who had actually held a post and fulfilled the function. For the general point that actual officeholders were to take precedence over honorary bearers of a title, he refers to a law of his grandfather Theodosius—*lex avita* or *avi nostri sanctio*—which is, fortunately, also preserved in the Code. It dates from 383, was issued to the praetorian prefect Postumianus, and contains a general ruling, though it does not mention the *comites consistoriani* explicitly—and no doubt this was the reason why Theodosius II had to legislate forty years later on basically the same subject.[62]

This selection of examples makes it abundantly clear that the two *partes* in general operated independently in administrative matters and seem not to have known even relevant precedents from the other division. It will therefore cause no surprise to find that some issues that *prima facie* seem to affect equally both divisions received rather different treatments in East and West. Two examples from the time of the joint rule of Valentinian and Valens will suffice to indicate the trend. What seems to have been initially an agreed-upon attempt at the very outset of their joint rule to change the way in which some taxes were collected led almost immediately to local variation. We possess only fragments of the legislation, but it is clear that the change was not carried out in a uniform manner, not even within each *pars*. The essence of it seems to have been that the tax collectors responsible for taxes in kind (*susceptores*) and the administrators of the depots (*praepositi horreorum*), who were personally liable for delivery of the tax collected, had traditionally—apparently throughout the empire—been appointed from and by the local council members (*decuriones*). The brothers wished to centralize and have *susceptores* and *praepositi horreorum* appointed from the nonpalatine civil service for one year only—presumably to share the burden and prevent corruption—and to have the appointments made by the office of the provincial governor.[63] The original law (or perhaps it was a series of laws) of Valentinian and Valens is lost; only fragments of consequential subsidiary rulings concerning local details or emendations survive, and they relate to Africa (West) and *Oriens*, especially Cilicia (East), and the rest of the central prefecture, Italy and Illyricum (West). Since all these extant laws date from the summer of 365 and represent official responses to a series of localized objections to the original law (in one case even in the abbreviated text included in the Code this is explicitly said), it seems likely that the original decision to change the system was intended to come into effect at the beginning of the financial year (*indictio*) on 1 September of that year.

The reactions to the local objections varied widely. In proconsular Africa the *susceptor vestium*, who collected the levy of military uniforms, was after all, in contradiction of the new general rule, to be taken from the higher ranks of the councillors (the *principales*) or the "*honorati*" (those men living in the city but holding honorary codicils of rank giving them exemption from service in the council, who without their honorary rank would have been counted as *principales*). Explicitly exempted here are, however, ex-palatine officials or those who had achieved rank by actually holding office. The limit of one year was nevertheless retained, as was the appointment by the proconsul.[64] For the rest of Africa Valentinian capitulated completely and allowed appointments from and by the councils, just as before.[65] He was also pressured to issue an explicit statement to the praetorian prefect that the military bureaucracy was to be spared this job, but that one group of financial officials, who technically belonged to the palatine bureaucracy, though they did not serve in the palace but in the cities (the *largitionales civitatum*), were to be included in the group regarded as eligible.[66]

In parts of the East the situation was no different. The governor of

Cilicia protested that he had no suitable people for the job—presumably, like the proconsul of Africa, he did not want to incur the odium of having to appoint somebody against his will—and in order that someone be made responsible at all, the previous system was temporarily reinstated; but here the praetorian prefect was instructed to investigate and punish anyone sabotaging the new system.[67] How long Valentinian and Valens continued to try to practice their new agreed-upon system is unknown. Only for the central prefecture (without Africa) are detailed rules for making lists of eligible persons known,[68] but sporadic survivals of later decisions suggest that it may not have lasted long even there. In the East by 386, in a general ruling issued to Theodosius's praetorian prefect Cynegius, elections in the local *curia* have in the meanwhile become the norm, and Cynegius is concerned merely that they take place at a well-attended meeting and that the names of those elected are conveyed to the provincial governors—the clear aim is to prevent corruption and mismanagement by the *curiales* chosen.[69] In the West we have two later rulings for proconsular Africa, where the new rules had already been changed by summer 365. One dated to 412 concerns the *susceptio vestium*, as in 365, and Honorius is still trying to change the system: now the office of the proconsul should take on the whole job itself and not leave it to the *curiales*;[70] in 430 the administration of the pork store is removed from the care of the *principales* to the *curia* in general, since, says Valentinian III, this is already the case in the neighboring province Byzacena.[71]

It does therefore seem likely that the centralized system change initially aimed at by Valentinian and Valens collapsed at different speeds in different ways in different areas. In the East by 386 there was no longer any trace of the reform, whereas in the West the idea that normal *curiales* should not be responsible for the administration of at least certain taxes in kind lived on into the fifth century, and there may very well have been areas—Italy, Illyricum, or Gaul, perhaps—where the new system functioned satisfactorily, for the fact is that our information is all concerned merely with those areas which for whatever reason claimed they needed a reform of the reform. Where it functioned satisfactorily, we have by definition no further laws, therefore no information.[72]

A second area in which much variation is manifest is that of curial legislation—laws intended to regulate the obligations and above all the recruitment of the city councils (the *curiae*) throughout the empire. We know from the legislation collected in the Theodosian Code that the emperors were particularly concerned about the maintenance of the city councils in general at this period. Of the 190 general regulations collected by the compilers of the Theodosian Code and ordered under the rubric "On the Decurions" (*de decurionibus*) stretching from 313 to 436, a period of 123 years, no fewer than eighty-three were issued in the thirty-year period from Julian's death to that of Theodosius I.[73] But within this period there are significant differences in regional intensity: whereas until Valens's death the rulings issued in the West dominate the picture, by seventeen (West) to six (East), under Theodosius the East clearly dominates, by forty-eight (East) to thirteen (West); Theodosius also issued laws for Illyricum while it was under his rule during the Gothic war.[74] The figures for Valens may be distorted by the unsatisfactory archival situation for his period of rule, but the domination of the East under Theodosius seems clear enough.

Moreover, a clear trend toward making a general regulation for a whole prefecture, rather than simply reacting to specific local or regional problems, can be perceived, and this tendency is particularly Eastern and most evident under Theodosius. Whereas under Valentinian I almost two-thirds of his extant laws were locally situated (only six were addressed to a praetorian prefect and eleven to other authorities), under Theodosius it was quite the opposite: more than two-thirds of his extant laws on curial affairs were directed to a praetorian prefect (thirty-six) and only sixteen to other authorities. The vast majority were therefore major legislative initiatives intended from the beginning to be valid everywhere within the named prefecture (whatever the precise reason for each law might have been); and the main mass of these general rulings originated with the well-known active Theodosian prefects Cynegius, Tatianus, and Rufinus. A general tendency to centralize initiatives in this area under Theodosius cannot therefore be denied.

The main tenor of this large quantity of legislation was to ensure adequate recruitment to the city councils, since still in the fourth century the curial class remained responsible for the provision of basic civic services, if need be at their own cost, as public "burdens" (*munera*), and as a group the councillors also served as guarantors for the local contributions of imperial taxes, for which their registered property served as collateral. Both functions were, each in its own way, of the greatest importance for the effective running of the empire, and the intensity of the legislation shows that the emperors, particularly Valentinian I and above all Theodosius, were well aware of this. Libanius's evidence for Antioch allows us to see aspects of the problem also from the municipal side in one major Eastern city and obtain an insight into the tense relationship between imperial government and municipal responsibility.[75] But for the present purpose it is sufficient to notice that legislative activity concerning the city councils, to judge by the extant legislation in the Theodosian Code, was much more intense in the East than in the West. It is, of course, only natural that rules for senatorial recruitment, which also affected the city councils, required more attention in the East than in the West under Valens and Theodosius, since the Senate in Constantinople, like the city itself, was new and required consolidation. The recruitment of senators for Constantinople will be treated below in chapter 6.

Let us close this chapter by examining some laws that might seem at first sight to suggest that the Eastern emperor occasionally legislated also for the West. Irrelevant in this respect are, of course, laws from the immediate post–civil war period, 388–391, when Theodosius was in any case resident in Italy, had taken direct responsibility for the central prefecture, and naturally issued laws to the responsible officials there. Other apparent anomalies can, however, be explained easily enough if we remember that Illyricum was the area where the line of partition between the *partes* ran, therefore where immediate joint interests were clearest, and if we also pay attention to the variations in imperial responsibility for the administration of Illyricum during these years.

Common interest in the security of the area resulting in practical military cooperation in Illyricum, particularly against Sarmatians and Goths, is in general well attested. Some cooperation of a different sort, however, is also attested. A law of Valentinian was issued in Trier in 373 to Petronius Probus, praetorian prefect of the central prefecture, concerning recalcitrant miners or quarry workers (*metallarii*) from Thrace

—that is, from Valens's diocese. Having illegally left their workplaces and come over the border to Illyricum, they were to be found especially in the neighboring Western diocese of Macedonia. These men were to be compelled to return to Thrace, and penalties were threatened for anyone employing them in Illyricum.[76] *Metallarii* in the fourth century belonged to those groups of men who were legally tied to their work and workplace, though they remained technically free persons and so could not be bought and sold. The work was extremely hard; the conditions were no doubt appallingly dangerous; and illegal abandonment of their economically important work was frequent. Thracian *metallarii* were among those recruited by Procopius in 365, and some even joined the Goths in the weeks before Adrianople in 378.[77] The maintenance of production in the metal mines, particularly in the Thracian gold mines, was, however, of existential importance to the empire, and Valentinian's law addressed to Petronius Probus shows the cooperation of the *partes* in this important administrative field in the border area of the two *partes*.

However, at the same time the law also demonstrates how slow and ponderous cooperation was in practice, for Valentinian refers back to a law of Valens (which therefore must have been the stimulus for his own legislative action) ordering the search for *metallarii* who had abandoned their workplace and sought agricultural work on private estates. This law is actually preserved in the Code and dates from 30 April 370, almost three years before Valentinian's pendant was issued.[78] In the meanwhile there had presumably been no legal way in which Valens's officers could search for runaway Thracian *metallarii* in the neighboring diocese of Macedonia because it belonged to Valentinian's administration and they had no jurisdiction there. It required, it seems, the cumbersome procedure of having an official travel some two thousand miles from Antioch to Trier with information about the problem, presumably with the text of the Eastern law in his baggage and armed with a request that Valentinian help solve the problem by providing a legal basis for prescriptive action in his Macedonian diocese. This all took some three years, during which runaway *metallarii* could doubtless seek security over the border in the neighboring diocese without serious danger of being sent back. Paradoxically the pair of laws, which indeed show the two *partes* cooperating in tackling a problem that could only be solved by joint action, demonstrate at the same time how effective the real separation of administrative competence had become. Valens clearly felt that without the support of his brother's administration in Macedonia he could not hope to recover his lost Thracian *metallarii*. Moreover this support was anything but automatic; it was achievable, it seems, only through the cumbersome means of diplomatic traffic and the legislative process in the Western division.

One preserved law seems to point in the other direction. In 380 Theodosius issued to his *comes rerum privatarum* Pancratius from Thessalonica a law that explicitly confirmed an earlier ruling of Valentinian (the substance of the law concerned the rights of leaseholders of public land).[79] At first sight this seems to imply that Valens must have formally accepted for his division a minor technical ruling from his brother (the law of Valentinian is itself not preserved), which—given the problems associated with cooperation even in a fairly urgent case, where major economic interests were at stake, like that of the Thracian *metallarii*—seems inherently improbable. However, if this were so, we would have expected Theodosius's reference to have been to Valens's own reissue of the ruling, being both more recent and locally valid, and not to Valentinian's original version. But the reference to Valentinian need not imply this at all, for in 380, when Pancratius received the law, the administration of Illyricum lay in Theodosius's hands, and the official archives of the Illyrican dioceses presumably came with him from Sirmium when he made Thessalonica his headquarters for the war. If therefore his ruling to Pancratius was particularly concerned with Illyricum, there is no problem at all in explaining his finding Valentinian's law in the diocesan archive at Thessalonica and citing it as precedent, since until 379 the West had been administratively responsible for the area.

A similar explanation seems called for in a parallel case that, however, uses Illyricum as a bridge to Italy and the rest of the central prefecture. In May 383 Gratian, in one of his last legislative acts before setting off for his fatal confrontation with the usurper Magnus Maximus, issued a law to Hypatius, his praetorian prefect of the central prefecture, concerning Christians who abandoned their religion and returned to pagan practices. The penalty was to be loss of the right to make a will under civil law.[80] The precise penalty seems to have been new in the West, but it had been proposed two years before for the same "crime" by Theodosius in a law issued to his praetorian prefect for Illyricum, Eutropius, and repeated a week later in a law directed against Manichaeans, also issued to Eutropius and so also intended for Illyricum.[81] The penalty was therefore well known in Theodosius's Illyricum. It is indeed difficult to believe that Gratian's law was not influenced by Theodosius's, and there is perhaps a hidden reference to it to be discovered, for Gratian's law is also directed at Manichaeans, for whom, he says, the punishment had been laid down by his father Valentinian *and by his own decrees.*[82] Now a law of Valentinian concerning Manichaeans addressed to the prefect of the city at Rome, Ampelius, in 372 is included in the Code, although the precise penalty mentioned is not explicit and has to be extrapolated from the general condemnation of Manichaeans as *infames.*[83] From Gratian himself, however, nothing of the sort has been preserved, except for his formal responsibility expressed in the protocol of all laws, also for laws issued in practice by Theodosius. It therefore seems conceivable that he is claiming for himself, as he had a formal right to do, responsibility for Theodosius's Eastern laws issued for Illyricum. But he would have first needed to know about them in order to claim them.

Again there is no pressing need to assume a formal exchange of laws between the *partes* on this relatively abstruse problem, a procedure that, as we have seen, was only envisaged as late as 429 and even then never systematically practiced, though it is, of course, not impossible. The most plausible explanation, however, is to be found in administrative procedures. Eutropius, who received Theodosius's laws in 381, was praetorian prefect of Illyricum at the time, when it temporarily belonged to Theodosius for the duration of the Gothic war. Illyricum returned to Western administration in September 382, and doubtless along with it went the official legislative archive of what had temporarily been a separate Eastern prefecture. Hypatius, a Western official who received Gratian's law in 383, was now Eutropius's direct successor in Illyricum, though in the reunited central prefecture he naturally had responsibility for Italy and Africa as well. What we see here, therefore, seems to be merely the extension of an existing law that Theodosius had issued for Illyricum to the other parts of Hypatius's reunited central prefecture. Of course, there may well have been local pressure on Gratian from ecclesiastical circles to do this; Ambrose in Milan could reasonably be expected to have received information about Theodosius's Illyrican law from, for example, the Illyrican bishops Anemius in Sirmium and Acholius in Thessalonica, with whom he was in regular contact. But that the formal transmission of knowledge of this ruling to the West went via Illyricum and was related to the renewed transfer of responsibility for the area and the associated archival materials back to the West seems most probable.

One last instance which might seem problematic can also be explained in the same way. In 418 Honorius repeated to the proconsul of Africa a ruling about informers (*delatores*) that we find first formulated in the Code in an edict of Theodosius issued "to the provincials" from Thessalonica in 380.[84] Honorius's law contains no explicit reference to a precedent, but it seems clear enough. It is, however, unnecessary to assume a break in the system, for just as knowledge of Theodosius's Manichaean law must have reached Gratian via the transfer of the archive of Illyricum and its associated staff, so Theodosius's ruling about informers must also have reached the West by first having been applied in Illyricum and then becoming part of the Western legislative tradition, being adopted for Italy and Africa when Illyricum and the archive of the Eastern praetorian prefect of Illyricum returned to Western administration in 382.

. . .

As we have shown, apart from the occasional issuing of agreed-upon measures, particularly during the earliest years of the joint rule of Valentinian and Valens, the tendency for the two divisions of the empire each to govern itself and to regulate its own affairs without consulting the other became ever stronger in the latter part of the fourth century, and it can only have been stimulated by the formal division of the empire in 364. The fact that there was no regular systematic exchange of information on legislative activity, which was in any case circumscribed by the prefectoral system, doubtless also favored the general tendency to generate independent legislation. This tendency to engage in effective independent action—necessary, indeed, given the huge distances separating the emperors—could not be seriously counteracted by purely formal public protocol, which maintained the patriotic fiction that all administrative acts emerging from the highest level of the empire were issued in the name of all the ruling emperors. By no means did each know what was being issued elsewhere in his name.

CHAPTER V

ROME

Within the regional government of the empire the city of Rome played a quite anomalous role in the late fourth century. It remained the largest city in the empire—as far as such things can be estimated—with a population of over half a million people; its population retained privileges, including subsidized food, dating back in part to the Republic, when by "Rome" nobody understood anything other than the city and its inhabitants. It was a cause of massive costs for the imperial finances, but for traditional reasons it enjoyed a local administration that was at least theoretically and formally independent of the praetorian prefect of Italy, Africa, and Illyricum—indeed the *praefectus urbi* formally belonged to the same high status group of officials as the praetorian prefect, ranking immediately below him, although his practical competences were less extensive even than those of the vicar of the praetorian prefect.

Rome was the seat of the Senate, the main urban residence of many of the richest families of the empire, and a refuge for imperial traditionalists. The leaders of its Christian population, encouraged by Constantine's building and investment program and relying on their association with the apostles Peter and Paul, were making strides—particularly after 366 under Bishop Damasus—to establish that level of charismatic dominance within the church that in the fifth century produced the phenomenon of the "Papacy." But despite all these aspects, in themselves redolent of the great past and indicative of an influential future, Rome remained politically unimportant, visited in our period only once by an emperor, and then only under the very particular circumstances of post–civil war reconstruction: by Theodosius in 389. Rome was the parasitic name-giving center, feeding on the efforts and products of the heavily taxed periphery, but it was still maintained without serious questioning because of its imperial name, its history, and its tradition, like some great living museum, incorporating long-vanished values and morbid lifestyles, a gigantic costly irrelevance, but splendid in its identity-giving isolation. Reflecting this mixed image is the fact that it is the only city in the empire to which Ammianus Marcellinus in his historical work, which otherwise concentrates on the activity of emperors, pays regular attention; the author himself lived there. For another contemporary, Gratian's teacher, the Aquitanian literary man Ausonius, it is simply "First among cities, home of the gods, golden Rome."[1]

The role of Rome in its relationship with the constantly changing political and administrative center of the empire was not consistent and unchanging; it varied in direct relationship to the stability and aims of the current imperial regime. When the regime was reasonably stable, as it was under Valentinian I and Gratian, Rome was made conscious of its peripheral status and its irrelevance to the immediate problems of the empire, of the uncertain value of its ancient traditions in the modern world, of the insecurity of its privileges. Under weaker emperors or in periods of political tension—especially in the years between the death of Gratian and that of Theodosius—not merely individual influential members of the Roman aristocracy basked in the light of imperial attention, but through them the Senate as a body and the Roman upper class as a whole, and with them the imperial tradition that they represented, received, it seemed, renewed appreciation and support. It is, however, often difficult for the modern historian, given the upper-class bias of our sources, to distinguish between the attitude of the emperor toward the city as such and his attitude toward the rich and potentially influential senatorial class—or even individual members of it—that dominated its social structure. Nevertheless, for my aim of illustrating the relationship of the central government of the empire with the city in the years following the death of Julian and to indicate how this relationship changed under the post-Constantinian emperors, the extant sources are adequate.

The most immediately revealing evidence for the changing relationship is that which shows direct attention being paid to affairs of the *urbs aeterna* by the organs of the central government. Particularly important indications for this are offered by the appointments to the office of the *praefectus urbi*, who was ex officio chairman of the Senate, and his official activities as illustrated by laws directly addressed to him, most or many of which had their ultimate origin in information reaching the emperor from the city, and so reflected the basic governmental pattern of imperial response to locally generated problems. As we have noted, the *praefectus urbi* enjoyed an official status within the empire second only to that of the praetorian prefects. In practice, however, from the time of a reform of the city administration under Constantius II, which made the *vicarius urbis Romae* deputy of the praetorian prefect instead of that of the *praefectus urbi*, there could well be a serious clash of interests between the two officers resident in the city. The one was a high-status senator, the chairman of the Senate and traditional head of the urban administration, whereas the other was merely the local representative of the centralized imperial regional government, of much lower formal and social status but exuding the power of a direct line of communication with the all-powerful praetorian prefect. Moreover, the prefect of the food supply (*praefectus annonae*), whose status had traditionally been equestrian and therefore subordinate to the *praefectus urbi*, had been granted senatorial status by Constans and—under certain circumstances—could also challenge the authority of the *praefectus urbi*. All three officers were imperial appointments—though their career structures and hierarchical status differed widely—so that the central imperial administration in any case retained final control of the personnel.[2]

The treatment of Rome in this period reflects perhaps more clearly than ever the needs and attitudes of the central government, depending on whether it saw advantage or not in a close cooperation with the locally influential representatives of the city. Valentinian I merely administered Rome from his distant residence in Gaul, and paid no more than nominal respect to its representatives. He made no attempt to visit the city. As was the case in regard to other matters, Gratian's attitude was in principle gentler and less abrupt, and he showed some respect to Roman traditions by at least planning a visit (though it probably never took place). But his more assertive Christianity, once he had come to Milan and succumbed to the influence of Bishop Ambrose and others of his ilk, caused a serious rift between the court and the large group of still non-Christian members of the Roman aristocracy, which had not closed when he died. Valentinian II sought cooperation wherever he could find it, including in Rome, in his attempt to master the crisis caused by the usurpation of the catholic Magnus Maximus, but it was the conquering Theodosius who seems to have deliberately and most intensively culti-vated the Roman aristocracy: in 389, for the first time since Constan-tius II's visit in 357, a triumph was celebrated in the eternal city. We shall look at these phases in turn.

Valentinian I

Valentinian I's relationship with Rome was once characterized in an in-fluential book as a conflict of ideas between (essentially) careerist Pan-nonian pragmatists associated with Valentinian's court and Roman tra-ditionalists.[3] This interpretation is perhaps too sharply intellectually stylized to be a wholly accurate description of what actually took place, but there can be little doubt that the Pannonian soldier Valentinian, who had been chosen and acclaimed by the troops in a constitutional crisis following a recent military defeat, seems to have had little sympathy for the parasitic traditionalist rentiers of the eternal city, viewed as a body. The post of *praefectus urbi* had traditionally been virtually reserved for the old Italian nobility, since it carried with it the chairmanship of the Senate. However, Valentinian, once firmly established in the imperial saddle, did not hesitate to appoint his own non-Italian associates to this traditional city office.[4] When the court arrived in Italy from the East, Lucius Aurelius Avianius Symmachus, the father of the orator, was al-ready in office, presumably appointed by Jovian.[5] But of the other ten men who occupied the post during Valentinian's reign, no fewer than five were of non-Italian origin.[6] Three *vicarii urbis*, including Ammianus Marcellinus's own bête noir, the Dacian-born Pannonian Maximinus, who had earlier also been *praefectus annonae* in the city, were also non-Italian.[7] Valentinian therefore made no effort to restrict himself to the traditionalist circles of city administrators for his candidates for high office in Rome. For him these posts seem to have been nothing special, merely normal administrative posts to be filled from the normal pool of competent candidates.

The reign of Valentinian I also provides us with good evidence for the extent to which central government interfered in and tried to exert control of Rome. Laws directly addressed to the *praefectus urbi* reach an intensity and a frequency under Valentinian not seen since the first years of Constantine (who had, after all, conquered the city by military force). Some are indeed merely rules of general application relating to the technical functioning of the law courts, to appeals procedure or to status questions, which cannot in themselves have been specific to the area of responsibility of the *praefectus urbi*, though it is likely enough that a concrete problem arising from his activity gave the impulse for each specific ruling addressed to him. Most of Valentinian's laws sent to Rome, however, have to do with the affairs of Rome in an immediate way—or indeed concern explicitly the duties of the *praefectus urbi*.[8] By far the largest group of rules concerns the food supply in Rome, in particular the financial conditions under which bread was baked and supplied (including the management of the grain depots, the *horrea*), but also the delivery of wine and pork and in general the transport of goods.[9] Another group of rules concerns the games and entertainments, their financing as a financial burden on the senatorial class, various aspects of their shows, and the status of performers in them.[10] Rules were issued concerning public building, whereby emphasis was firmly laid on repairing existing structures rather than on erecting new ones, a matter of general concern to both imperial brothers, which was perhaps particularly acute with regard to Rome.[11] A very tiny group of regulations concerns religious affairs—the renewed expulsion of Manichaeans, a ban on Christian criminals' being condemned to the arena, or a ban on Christians' being detailed to look after pagan temples[12]—and some rules concern the status and obligations of senators.[13]

We gain the irresistible impression from all this that under Valentinian I the intention of the central government to control, to leave little to the initiative of the man on the spot, was as firm as at any time in the history of the imperial city since the emperor no longer resided there. It verges on the ludicrous when the emperor finds it necessary to write from Milan to the *praefectus urbi* Volusianus that old grain from the Roman stores is to be used up before new can be distributed, even if this is part of a larger regulation;[14] or when writing from Trier (twice, to two different prefects) he sets up detailed rules for appointing or replacing public doctors, whose appointment required official imperial approval, even though their area of activity was limited to the city of Rome.[15] The same niggling compulsion to formulate detailed centralizing regulations shows up in the rules governing the presence of students in the city, contained in a law that arrived from Trier in 370: students were to be properly registered with the office of the *magister census*, a subordinate of the prefect of the city, with entries for birthplace, status of parent, course to be studied, and address in Rome. If the student did not study seriously or spent too much time at the games or kept bad company, he could be publicly beaten and returned home. Otherwise an upper age limit of twenty applied, beyond which, if the student did not go home voluntarily, he was to be returned forcibly. The *censuales* were to keep monthly reports on newcomers and those leaving for home; an annual report on the individual students was to be sent to the emperor so that potential recruits for the public service could be identified.[16]

Apart from this last stipulation the regulation concerned only the city of Rome, which even in such a relatively trivial matter clearly had no essential rights of initiative, even if the impetus for the regulation came from a Roman wish to control such young men, who were potential troublemakers. The level of central control and regulation could hardly have been greater if the emperors were still resident in the city. The function of the Roman city administration, despite the formally high status of its representatives within the imperial hierarchy, was thus merely to apply rules and regulations that were formulated in the offices of the central imperial administration and sent down as laws to Rome. This general judgment remains valid, even if the local problems and suggestions for their solution, as must usually have happened, were brought to the notice of the central government by the local authorities themselves, doubtless normally represented by the prefect and his officials. The critical point is that it seems that they could not decide even minor disciplinary matters for themselves without permission from the central administration. This state of affairs was, of course, not exactly new in our period, but the extant laws give the firm impression that Valentinian's administration intended to keep exceptionally close control on how the eternal city ordered its temporal affairs.

Apart from the enactment of laws and appointments to the post of *praefectus urbi*, two further types of events show the imperial government in action at Rome under Valentinian. Neither suggests that Valentinian's administration was particularly sympathetic toward the representatives of the city. The first concerns the tumultuous episcopal election of 366, which took place while the Pannonian Viventius, who also happened to be a Christian, was prefect of the city. One of his official duties was to maintain law and order in the city, so he was ex officio the chief officer concerned with the affair when bloody riots between the supporters of the rival candidates, Damasus and Ursinus, blew up suddenly and without much warning. He obviously could not consult the emperor, who was in Gaul, and his own immediate reaction was to do nothing at all, to sit out the crisis and wait and see which of the battling groups would emerge from the riots as the winner. As soon as it became clear that Damasus's party had won, Viventius threw the weight of the authority of the state he represented onto Damasus's side, and for this pragmatic decision he had the support of the current *praefectus annonae* Julianus. The defeated candidate, Ursinus, and three of his most prominent supporters were expelled from the city.[17]

That might have been the end of the affair had not pressure from the central imperial administration been exerted on the city authorities to allow Ursinus to return, which despite forebodings they were unable to resist. This response to Ursinus's appeal to Trier arrived quite quickly, since Ursinus was already back in Rome by October 367, by which time the pagan Praetextatus was *praefectus urbi*. He, like his Christian predecessor, very soon saw no alternative to expelling Ursinus again, and this had happened within a month of his return.[18] But Ursinus's supporters in the city had been encouraged by the interference of the central government and continued to cause trouble, now, however, outside the city walls, until in 368 a report to Valentinian by the current *vicarius urbis Romae*, Aginatius, elicited imperial instructions to the new *praefectus urbi*, Olybrius, and to Aginatius himself to prevent any further meetings of such persons within the twentieth milestone.[19] A year or so later their successors, Ampelius as *praefectus urbi* and Maximinus as *vicarius urbis*, received official notification that Ursinus had now been banished by imperial instruction to somewhere in Gaul, and that neither he nor a group of named associates were to set foot in Rome or the suburbicarian diocese.[20]

This affair illustrates once more the dependence of the Roman urban authorities on the central instances of the empire, even in such a city-internal matter concerning law and order in which the responsible people on the spot were inevitably in a far better position to assess the situation accurately. Viventius had not been able to prevent the initial bloodshed in 366, but his and Praetextatus's subsequent actions in removing Ursinus from the scene were effective and would probably have remained effective, if the faraway central government had not interfered for whatever reason and asserted its overriding responsibility for the case, issuing binding instructions to the local officials from distant Trier. The fact that after five years the final policy adopted by Valentinian's government was no different from that already initiated by Viventius immediately after the riots can hardly have improved relations with the Roman city administration, which must have been conscious of the mistrust in its competence that existed at the imperial headquarters. It is doubtless a sign of this mistrust that it was only when the local representative of the regional government, the *vicarius* Aginatius, working through the praetorian prefect — currently the influential Roman aristocrat Petronius Probus — sent a report on the affair to Trier that the central government finally accepted the correctness of the decisions of the two *praefecti urbi*.

The affair of Ursinus and Damasus overlapped with a much more serious crisis, which affected a significant number of members of the Roman aristocracy. Its origins go back to the prefecture of Olybrius in 369, and its development was aggravated by an illness that prevented Olybrius from completing his judicial business, some of which was then transferred to the current *praefectus annonae*, Maximinus, who acted as his deputy for this purpose.[21] Maximinus was an outsider in Rome, a man of Pannonian origins who owed his career to his native talents and his early association with the Pannonian emperor Valentinian. He therefore enjoyed no sympathy among traditionalist circles in Rome, who now also suffered from his brutal efficiency and whose reaction to his activities colored the account of our one source, Ammianus Marcellinus.[22] The problem originated in the investigation of certain magical practices that, it seems, were fairly widespread among some sections of the old Roman aristocracy.[23] Olybrius's illness offered Maximinus a first occasion for investigative action, and soon afterward he was promoted to be *vicarius urbis Romae*, a post that allowed him to continue in his own right the investigations he had begun as Olybrius's deputy. Ammianus, reflecting some senatorial opinion, depicts Maximinus as a monster merely looking for an opportunity to suck senatorial blood, but the fact is that magical practices exercised by prominent persons in a major city had always been regarded as a serious matter since Rome had been ruled by emperors, and Valentinian reacted to the news from Rome no differently in this respect than many of his predecessors would have done. The suspicion was always present that prominent people's occult activities could in the last resort only be related to some form of disloyalty, if not conspiracy and therefore treason, against the ruling emperor (*maiestas* was the technical term for the offense).

Three laws issued to the *praefectus urbi* seem to relate to the activities of Maximinus, at least in a general kind of way. The first was directed to Praetextatus, who was *praefectus urbi* from the summer of 367 until the autumn of 368, and it was distinctly friendly toward the Senate, since it instructed the *praefectus urbi* to refer all cases where serious punishment (*austerior ultio*) of senators was appropriate to the emperor himself for final decision.[24] This privileged position soon changed, however. In July 369 a law issued to Olybrius addressed one specific aspect of Maximinus's activity that particularly disturbed Ammianus, the use of torture on senators to procure evidence from them. Privileged persons, that is, especially senators and palatine officials, were to be spared torture—in this respect the law merely formalized what social pressure had long practiced—unless the emperor himself agreed to it, and except for cases of *maiestas*, "in which alone all have equal status".[25] The exact chronology of Maximinus's independent investigative activities in Rome is not clear, but this law would certainly have legitimized his use of torture if he claimed he was investigating cases of *maiestas*. Moreover, there seems to have been little point in issuing the law to the *praefectus urbi* at this time, with its explicit exclusion of *maiestas*, unless *maiestas* was already an immediate issue in the city.

A couple of years later, on 6 December 371, Ampelius as *praefectus urbi* received a ruling that instructed him to conduct trials concerned with senatorial criminality in his own court unless unspecified difficulties prevented a conclusion, in which case they were to be sent to the emperor with full documentation. Maximinus was certainly *vicarius* at the time of the instruction to Ampelius.[26]

These laws issued to the *praefectus urbi* make it clear that the investigation of senatorial criminal behavior was an issue that Valentinian and his court officials took extremely seriously, and was by no means merely a whimsy of Maximinus's, as Ammianus's account suggests. Maximinus's promotion from being *praefectus annonae* to *vicarius urbis Romae* and his subsequent rise to *praefectus praetorio Galliarum* (just as the *notarius* Leo, who served him as legal adviser for a while, received rapid promotion to *magister officiorum*)[27] show clearly that Maximinus was at least in principle carrying out imperial instructions and not merely indulging his own private bloodlust.

Relations between the court and the Roman aristocracy were thus distant and tense during Valentinian's rule. This did not, of course, mean that individual Romans and senators lacked influence. Symmachus, son of the *praefectus urbi* of 364, was well tolerated at court. Just about the time when Maximinus began his investigations in Rome, he visited Trier and addressed Valentinian on behalf of the Senate, congratulating him on his *quinquennalia* in 369, and he was still there, or there again, on 1 January 370 when he praised Valentinian on the occasion of his assumption of his third consulate.[28] Sometime during Maximinus's tenure as *vicarius urbis Romae* Praetextatus and two other senior senators also traveled to Trier in order to object to the use of torture in cases involving senators. The reason for their journey was doubtless Maximinus's broad interpretation of the *maiestas* clause of the law issued to Olybrius. According to Ammianus Marcellinus, whose information must have come from senatorial circles, Valentinian claimed never to have allowed torture of senators but had to be corrected by his quaestor Eupraxius, who might even have been the official who had drafted the law sent to Olybrius—he was certainly in office at the time, and quaestors drafted laws. Thereupon Valentinian allegedly cashiered his earlier ruling.[29] In another case, that of the ex-proconsul of Africa, Hymetius, who was also mixed up by association with a soothsayer (a *haruspex*) in some kind of magical activities, an appeal to Valentinian led to the transferal of the case to the Senate, which then made the formal final decision: not the death penalty, but exile.[30]

Gratian

Under Valentinian and his administration Rome and Roman affairs were clearly not treated with any particular sympathy, even if we acknowledge as too partial a verdict on a complex relationship the positive hostility that Ammianus's account of the activities of Maximinus and his colleagues suggests, which has often enough been believed by modern writers. Valentinian's death, however, brought about an immediate perceived improvement for the Roman senators. The purge of his Pannonian faction from the administration and its replacement by the Gallic-Spanish group headed by Gratian's cultivated teacher, Ausonius,[31] had an immediate effect on the attitude of the central administration toward the eternal city, which for Ausonius, as he expressed it in his later poem "The Ranking of Famous Cities," echoing Vergil on Ilium, was "First among cities, home of the gods, golden Rome."[32] It was thus almost predictable that when a meeting of the emperors Valens and Gratian was planned in order to discuss the future of the empire after the death of Valentinian and after the sudden unexpected acclamation of Valentinian II by the Pannonian military caucus, Rome was chosen to be the setting; to prepare the ground, the senior Eastern senator and imperial envoy Themistius paid a visit with much pomp. The emperors' summit never took place because the Gothic crisis in the East prevented Valens from traveling, and there is no good reason to believe that Gratian ever visited the city alone.[33] But his attitude in principle was less distant than that of his father and in general much more favorable.

One of his first legislative actions, which was read out in the Senate already on 11 February 376, was to regulate court cases in which senators were on trial. Provincial governors, after passing judgment in the first instance, were to refer all such cases, if they originated in the suburbicarian provinces, to the emperor or the *praefectus urbi*, or, if they originated in the other provinces, to the praetorian prefect. If the *praefectus urbi* was involved, he had to consult with a group of five senior senators chosen by lot who formed the court (the *iudicium quinquevirale*).[34] This was clearly a concession aimed at winning senatorial opinion after the troubled relationship under Valentinian. The prefects whom Gratian appointed also served for shorter periods. Whereas Valentinian had appointed eleven *praefecti urbi* in twelve years, Gratian appointed twelve men in eight years, which, of course, meant that more persons served in this prestigious position and enjoyed its prerogatives. Moreover, the first three appointees belonged to that group of men which had particularly suffered under Valentinian: Tarracius Bassus had even been accused of magical practices during Maximinus's reign of terror, though in the end he had been acquitted; Aradius Rufus had been out of office during the whole of Valentinian's reign; and Furius Maecius Gracchus was the son of Cethegus, one of Maximinus's most prominent senatorial victims.[35]

It is also characteristic that Gratian's *praefecti urbi* all belonged to the Roman aristocracy, with three exceptions that, however, prove the rule, for none was in any sense a new man or a careerist outsider and all had prominent Western, even Roman, careers or connections. Martinianus (378) was indeed born in Cappadocia and corresponded with Basil and Libanius, but his career had been exclusively in the West; he had risen to be *vicarius Africae* already under Constantius.[36] Flavius Hypatius, though probably originating in Thessalonica, belonged to the highest level of the imperial aristocracy: his sister Eusebia had been married to the emperor Constantius, and he himself had been consul together with his brother in 359. Under Valens he resided in Antioch, and in 371 he had been suspected of treason, convicted, and condemned, but then reprieved. Immediately after Valens's death he was made *praefectus urbi* in Rome.[37] The third man is Arborius, whose claim to distinction was that he was a nephew of Gratian's éminence grise, Ausonius.[38]

One further feature of Gratian's prefects may be noted. With the exception of the first of them, Tarracius Bassus, all were probably Christians, whereas under Valentinian Christians and non-Christians seem to have alternated.[39] This suggests that for Valentinian religious affiliations had effectively played no part in the selection of his appointees—the alternation was probably more accident than principle—and thus the change under Gratian was the more clearly marked.[40] Nevertheless, the legislation that Gratian's administration directed to the *praefectus urbi*, when compared with that of Valentinian, is small in quantity and consists largely of general rulings on questions of status, of court procedures, and of rules of civil law, which can scarcely have been exclusively Roman problems. Important was certainly the early ruling, preserved in a single lapidary sentence in the Theodosian Code, that senators were not to suffer torture: this was doubtless part of the rollback of Valentinian's perceived antisenatorial attitude.[41] Otherwise Gratian's laws for Rome were concerned with supplies,[42] with the games and entertainments,[43] and with the local civil service.[44] The total impression, however, is that there was far less readiness in this administration to get involved in the minutiae of Roman affairs than there had been under Valentinian.

The one area where Gratian's administration showed active interest in Rome was, however, that of encouraging Christianity. Given the mixed religious composition and pagan traditions of the Roman Senate it can certainly be no accident that all but the first of Gratian's prefects were Christians, and that a long-running tension between the Christian court and the pagan section of the Senate, particularly after the court took up residence in Milan in 381 and came under the influence of Ambrose and other Italian church dignitaries, produced a first serious clash under Gratian. We can be fairly sure that Ausonius would have disapproved of this development, but he and his influence had been left behind in Gaul when the court moved to Milan.[45] In the summer of 384 Symmachus as *praefectus urbi* wrote to Valentinian II—in his Third *Relatio*—asking for a reconsideration of measures taken by Gratian confiscating the property income of the traditional cults and priesthoods of the city of Rome, including that of Vesta; in particular he, representing the non-Christian senators, petitioned for the restoration of the altar of Victoria, which Gratian had caused to be removed from its traditional place in the Senate House.[46]

At the time of its removal Symmachus, as senior senator but without other official status, had led a deputation to Milan and had not even been granted an audience. Exactly when this happened is not clear, but it was sometime in the second half of 382, less than two years before Ambrose's written reply to Symmachus's Third *Relatio*, which dates from the second half of 384.[47] The removal of the altar and the confiscation of the property that financed the cults therefore certainly had to have been carried out by a Christian *praefectus urbi*, since all but one of Gratian's prefects were Christians and it no doubt took place under his personal supervision. In particular an extremely prominent member of the potent Christian Anicii clan, Anicius Auchenius Bassus, who entered office sometime after 1 August 382, comes into question for this initiative.[48] Ambrose later explicitly denied that he himself had inaugurated the idea of confiscating the subsidies of the traditional cults,[49] which, if true, means that the initiative came from Rome itself, therefore inevitably from the Christian *praefectus urbi*, relying on the Christian-friendly climate in Milan and doubtless influenced by his bishop Damasus in Rome. Symmachus indeed claimed even then the support of a majority of senators for his protest, but his démarche was counteracted by a letter written by Damasus that Ambrose brought to the attention of the emperor, and Symmachus did not even receive an audience.[50]

Gratian's refusal to receive Symmachus was a major affront to the Senate and the still rich and influential non-Christian members of the old Roman aristocracy whom he represented, and it would doubtless have soured long-term relationships between the court and Rome had not Gratian had the misfortune to lose his throne and his life less than a year, perhaps even only a few months, after Symmachus's abortive embassy. There is, however, no ancient evidence, either Christian or pagan, for the apparently universally believed modern construct that Gratian further insulted the Roman traditionalists at this time by rejecting the traditional imperial title *pontifex maximus* after taking up residence in Milan.[51] The clash with the Senate was serious enough, even without such a gratuitous insult, and it showed how effective the influence of a Christian *praefectus urbi* could be when making a suggestion backed by a political bishop who had the ear of a dogmatically inclined imperial administration. But for the moment, since Damasus survived Gratian by little more than a year, the non-Christian traditionalists in the city enjoyed an unexpected breathing space, and the city itself, in the feeble and reduced empire of Valentinian II, in which Italy now again played a central role, experienced an almost inevitable increase in prestige, which the stable regimes of Valentinian I and Gratian had felt able to deny it.

Valentinian II

It was certainly no accident that the three *praefecti urbi* appointed by Valentinian II were all prominent Romans and that the first two were non-Christians; they included in 384 none other than the orator Symmachus, so recently denied even an audience at the court of Gratian. Because of Symmachus's appointment we are better informed about the relationship between the *praefectus urbi* and the central government at this time than at any other, since Symmachus kept private copies of his frequent official reports to the emperor (his *relationes*), and when his speeches and letters were published toward the end of his life a book of the *relationes* was included.[52] The forty-nine pieces of official correspondence offer an excellent overview of the type of activities undertaken by a *praefectus urbi*. Symmachus was only in office for some eight months, so that on average a communication from him to the court at Milan—on the assumption that the extant collection is complete—was sent off every four or five days. It is impossible to tell whether Symmachus was a typical *praefectus urbi* in the intensity of his communication with the court. Certainly, the fact that Valentinian was resident in Milan must have made communication less burdensome than it had been earlier, when the court was resident in Trier, but it could simply be that Symmachus was a particularly nervous *praefectus urbi* and that his intensity of communication does not properly reflect the general trend. The mixture of subject material that makes up Symmachus's dossier is, however, in principle characteristic for the office.

Under Valentinian II, as was true of the *praefecti urbi* under Valentinian I, Symmachus was in no way an independent operator in all affairs with which he was concerned; a decision of the central administration in Milan always took priority or could overrule a local decision. When

Symmachus writes, "We are accustomed to respect imperial pronouncements rather than to interpret them,"[53] he is not just passing the buck
in a particularly intractable taxation case where an imperial rescript had
already contradicted normal practice, but rather expressing, it seems, his
own genuine view of his function as *praefectus urbi*. On another occasion when he requests Valentinian to make a final decision, he is, however, clearly avoiding taking responsibility. He argues, "I prefer to reserve
judgment on him for the merciful emperors. Magistrates, if they pass
sentences milder than those prescribed by law, give the impression of
having been corrupted, whereas the power of the divine emperors is different: for it is appropriate for them to ameliorate the harshness of the
law."[54] The attitude of subordination is evident, although the actual recipients of Symmachus's communications, which were, of course, nominally addressed to the emperors, were in practice the high officials of the
imperial administration who made the final decisions and whose formal
status within the imperial hierarchy (except for the praetorian prefect
himself) was actually lower than that of the *praefectus urbi*.

These cases, however, concern matters of law, and the *relationes* contain a sizable number of such cases, in which Symmachus is merely an
intermediate link in the normal chain of judgment and appeal that
ended in Milan. Otherwise, apart from a small number of purely formal
texts—thanks to the emperors for his appointment or for New Year's
gifts—which simply represent the elegance of imperial protocol of the
period, the larger part of the *relationes* concern affairs of the city of
Rome, and they offer a fine illustration of what we have already noticed
in regard to Valentinian I, the extreme centralization of all important
decision making, even though the very appointment of Symmachus as
praefectus urbi was a show of fundamental goodwill by Valentinian II's
administration toward the city and its Senate. The goodwill, however,
did not grant the *praefectus urbi* any further breadth of practical independent competence, only perhaps the hope that matters particularly
affecting the city might be decided in its favor.

This is the case with the two *relationes* that Symmachus (or his editor) placed at the head of the published collection, immediately after
the purely formal protocol letters to Valentinian and Theodosius. The

first is the famous Third *Relatio*, in which Symmachus argues with great eloquence for the restoration of the recently removed altar of Victoria to the Senate House. Whether this text reflects an open senatorial initiative undertaken by Symmachus, or whether he had already had behind-the-scenes contacts preparing the ground for the formal approach to the court, remains uncertain. What does emerge, however, from the violent reaction of Ambrose when he got wind of Symmachus's approach to the consistory, is that, had the bishop not intervened, Symmachus might well have succeeded in obtaining his wish from Valentinian's vacillating regime.[55]

In the second case Symmachus did indeed temporarily gain what he wanted. Under Gratian one of the Christian *praefecti urbi* had succeeded in persuading the emperor that the *praefectus urbi* needed a particularly splendid new four-horse carriage for his official journeys.[56] This initiative may well have been taken by the same prefect who had removed the altar of Victory, and it seems to have been understood by Symmachus as part and parcel of the Christian attempt to "modernize" and replace the old traditions of the city. If the same prefect was involved, one can see why the *relatio* about the carriage was juxtaposed in the published collection of the official correspondence with the *relatio* concerning the altar of Victoria; that also provides an explanation for the extraordinary and otherwise inexplicable intensity of Symmachus's objection to using the new vehicle, employing traditionalistic emotional arguments taken from the oldest history of the city, beginning with Tarquin's arrogance and Camillus's objectionably luxurious conveyance. The implication of Symmachus's disproportionate language is that the action of the initiator of the modernizing new vehicle is to be compared with the famous antiheroes of these historical horror stories. Symmachus's predecessor in office, Anicius Auchenius Bassus, was prominent enough in the city to serve the purpose of the comparison, and whether or not the new coach was originally his idea, he had certainly supported its construction and had been much involved in the financing of it during his term of office. He had used Roman funds that he controlled as *praefectus urbi* as well as some private contributions, but for a purely practical reason he had not touched the imperial funding that Gratian had agreed to: because the local depot of the imperial fiscus in Rome simply did not contain sufficient silver at the time to provide for the extravagant silver decoration foreseen for the coach.[57]

Given the emotional intensity of Symmachus's objection to this extravagant "modernizing," we must at least consider the possibility that the expensive silver decoration, agreed to by the enthusiastic Christian Gratian and ordered, organized, and paid for by an aggressively Christian prefect, might also have included nontraditional—perhaps even Christian—motifs, which the traditionalist Symmachus would inevitably object to without, however, being able to justify his stance openly to the Christian Valentinian. However this may be, Symmachus was successful in his first approach to Valentinian on the subject, since his suggestion to scrap the excessively luxurious new vehicle seemed to save money, but he ran into embarrassing practical difficulties when Valentinian not unnaturally demanded that the costs be returned to the fiscus, on the supposition that Gratian had agreed to the use of imperial funds. Symmachus had to point out that despite Gratian's generosity on paper the fiscus had in the end paid nothing out, and therefore was not entitled to receive anything back. We do not know how the financial question was finally resolved, but the carriage itself, despite Symmachus's attack on its lack of tradition, seems to have survived, since the *Notitia Dignitatum* pictures it as the special iconographic symbol of the *praefectus urbi*.[58]

A further hangover from Gratian's antipagan policy caused Symmachus concern. In recent times some private persons had been quietly privatizing temple possessions in the city, including statues, and since temples were public property, Symmachus had combined duty with inclination and launched an investigation. This brought him a wild accusation at court in Milan that he was persecuting Christians (since only Christians would come into question for the spoliation of temples) and prompted a demand from the administration that he stop doing so. The accusation could have had serious consequences and shows clearly that the aggressive Christian network within the imperial administration, which had functioned so satisfactorily under Gratian, was still operative, despite official attempts at the very highest level to cultivate leading non-Christians to gain their support for the regime of Valentinian II. This time, it seems, Symmachus's Christian opponents had gone too far, and Symmachus was able to elicit a written statement from Bishop Damasus that there had been no persecution, which he included in his official reply to the accusations. But once again it is clear that even in an affair concerning the buildings of Rome the ultimate responsibility lay in Milan, not in Rome itself.[59]

No different picture emerges from the rest of the official correspondence. The greater part of Symmachus's activity was concerned with various aspects of taxation and finance, in particular with regard to the games and the food supply. It seems that in the last resort the *praefectus urbi* could only appeal to the central imperial administration and hope for assistance on these questions, since neither he nor his *praefectus annonae* were able to exert effective pressure on those technically responsible for paying taxes in kind or providing supplies. The city was administratively and financially dependent on the effectiveness of the central government. This is perhaps no surprise, since the laws concerning financial and supply matters—particularly under Valentinian I—also demonstrate central governmental responsibility, but the *relationes* show us indeed some areas where we might have expected a greater level of local decision making than seems to have been practiced.

Even the appointment of staff members to the bureau of the *praefectus urbi* was in the hands of the central government. Symmachus complains on one occasion about the quality of men appointed to supervisory positions, only to provoke the reply, which because of its universal applicability was incorporated in the Theodosian Code, that nobody should dare to question the emperor's choice.[60] The virtually inevitable bureaucratic infighting made Symmachus's life miserable in general and provoked specific problems that he could not resolve without renewed reference back to the central administration. It meant that the *praefectus urbi*, despite his nominal high status, had little chance, in view of how often the officeholder changed, of making his mark against the permanent bureaucracy in Milan. When the central administration made mistakes, or simply chose for whatever reason to ignore its own rules, the *praefectus urbi* was left helpless in his search for an adequate solution for a problem not of his own making. This could involve complex investigations going back over several years,[61] or it could be a relatively simple matter, as in the case of a new appointee as supervisor of the pork market (*tribunus suarii fori*) who presented himself to Symmachus armed with official codicils of appointment at a time when the incumbent had a contractual appointment for a specific period that had not yet ended. Symmachus was left in a quandary and saw no alternative to referring the matter back to Milan, whereby he turned the essentially trivial administrative question into a matter of principle: should he uphold the existing legal contract, which fixed the incumbent's length of tenure, or should he out of loyalty to the administration follow its expressed wishes and remove the incumbent (illegally!) from his post?[62]

The appointment of the pork-market supervisor was not the only case of its kind in Symmachus's eight months in office. Valentinian I had laid down sensible rules for appointing doctors; they were to be elected by other doctors, and precedence within the medical college was to be ordered by simple seniority in office. One Johannes suddenly arrived one day in Rome, unelected but bearing codicils of appointment to the post until recently occupied by the second-place man, Epictetus, who had just died in office. Johannes claimed membership of the palatine service and demanded the place of precedence within the medical college vacated by Epictetus, but he was unable to produce written proof of the date of his appointment to the palatine service. The medical college could not itself resolve the conflict between Valentinian I's clearly formulated rules and Johannes's codicil of appointment, and neither could Symmachus. Again, a matter caused by a conflict between two contradictory imperial rulings had to be referred back to Milan. The *praefectus urbi*, it is clear, did not have the authority to make independent decisions, even in matters directly affecting the city civil service.[63]

Overall responsibility for new public building was also centralized, though the day-to-day supervision inevitably lay in the hands of the local authorities. Their total dependence on the central imperial administration, however, became clear as soon as things went wrong. This had happened with two Roman construction projects, a bridge and a basilica, which had been started some two years before Symmachus became *praefectus urbi* and inherited the problem, and which had already claimed the attention of his two predecessors in office.[64] Two architects, Cyriades and Auxentius, both apparently centrally appointed in Milan, had so far been involved. Why Cyriades had been replaced by Auxentius is unknown, but two problems had emerged during Auxentius's time, one technical, the other financial. Auxentius had not only failed to complete in a competent way work left unfinished by Cyriades when he was relieved of his responsibility, but had also begun a new part of the bridge construction too late in the autumn, so that it had been damaged by the winter high water. He had also used up all the earmarked funds without completing the work.

The two architects blamed each other for the mess, and when Symmachus took office, he appointed technical staff to investigate the damage and report back—his predecessors Anicius Auchenius Bassus and Sallustius Aventius seem to have been content merely to interview the parties concerned—whereupon Auxentius simply disappeared. Cyriades then asked Symmachus to make a report on the affair, as it stood so far, to Milan, and to include with it the papers relating to the investigation carried out by Auchenius Bassus, since he feared machinations against him at court by Auxentius. Symmachus was not disinclined to do this, because the question of financial responsibility, in particular his own, was unclear to him, and he duly reported the affair to Milan. In the meanwhile—the news perhaps even crossing in the post with Symmachus's first report—Milan had appointed a new financial officer for the work, a court official named Aphrodisius, and ordered the inclusion of the *vicarius* of the praetorian prefect in the investigation team, thus taking the matter out of the sole hands of the *praefectus urbi*.[65] Symmachus's second report to Milan concerns merely the technical side of the affair.

This business reveals the same cumbersome administrative procedures as we have seen in other cases. The central administration assigned funds, which were called upon by the centrally appointed architects, but were technically administered locally by the *praefectus urbi*. If the bridge and basilica had been built without technical problems and financial overruns, that would doubtless have been the end of the story; but as soon as something went wrong, the central administration made its interests felt, even to the extent of insisting that the *vicarius* as local representative of the praetorian prefect formally participate in the investigation, although the technical expertise that a successful investigation required was local and, it seems, controlled by the *praefectus urbi*. With some goodwill this system might be regarded as a functional symbiosis of central and decentralist responsibilities, but it is clear that in the last resort it was the distant imperial administration in Milan and not the local *praefectus urbi* in Rome that saw to it that the bridge and the basilica were built.

When Symmachus was *praefectus urbi*, it was already established practice that public statues that the Senate wished to erect to honor its own members or other prominent persons needed the agreement of the imperial government, since such monuments were not merely political statements but also, when erected at public expense, a serious financial commitment.[66] Although the inscriptions on the monuments reflect the working together of emperor and Senate in a quite neutral way,[67] a concrete case pursued by Symmachus shows the extent of senatorial dependence on the imperial administration. The consul designate for 385, the prominent non-Christian and recent praetorian prefect Vettius Agorius Praetextatus, died in Rome a few weeks before entering office, and Symmachus in his official report to Milan transmits a decree of the Senate conferring statues (plural) on Praetextatus together with a *laudatio* and a request that the emperor confirm the Senate's wish. He expects the emperor to be able to offer his own independent evaluation of Praetextatus's qualities.[68] Despite Praetextatus's prominence — which had, however, also brought him enemies — the court did not at once agree to the honor, but wrote back requiring that a list of Praetextatus's contributions to senatorial debate be extracted from the minutes (*acta senatus*). This, as Symmachus pointed out in his justifiably petulant reply, which served also as a covering letter for the documentation demanded, was strictly speaking otiose, since copies of the senatorial minutes were already available in Milan — one of the routine functions of the office of the *praefectus urbi* was to send them along with a monthly report.[69] Whether the petty exchange reflects deliberate delay or is merely an expression of inner-bureaucratic rank pulling between the office of the *magister offi-ciorum* in Milan and the *praefectus urbi* in Rome is uncertain; but the case of Praetextatus shows clearly enough that imperial confirmation of senatorial wishes was by no means automatic, even in local affairs, and that the officials of the central government had no hesitation in letting the authorities in Rome experience their effective inferiority, despite the formal superiority of the status of the *praefectus urbi*.

Symmachus did not bear the pressures of his office lightly, giving it up to his successor, Pinianus, before 24 February 385.[70] Pinianus, as a member of a noble Christian family, the Valerii, must have been a Christian himself, though that fact alone may not have been the primary reason for his appointment. Pinianus was in office for significantly longer than the average term of a *praefectus urbi*, at least until September 387, which meant more than two and a half years; he was replaced, it seems, only when Valentinian fled to Thessalonica after Magnus Maximus invaded Italy in autumn 387. Reliable and Christian, Pinianus proved to be politically unexceptional. He received three extant laws, all of which were concerned merely with technical administrative problems, two of them simply restating the validity of older laws, which must in some way have been challenged.[71]

Magnus Maximus

When Magnus Maximus came to Milan, an invader from the provinces, he replaced Pinianus as urban prefect with Sextius Iulianus Rusticius, a man who had been prominent under Valentinian I as *magister memoriae* in Gaul, where Maximus might well have first come across him; he had also served as proconsul of Africa, but his career had not advanced since 373.[72] Iulianus had enjoyed great prestige and a high reputation while in Gaul: when Valentinian I seemed to be dying in 367, a Gallic faction at court even favored Iulianus, at the time *magister memoriae*, as candidate for the succession.[73] There is, however, no evidence that he was Gallic by birth; his was not a senatorial family, and his geographic origin is simply unknown. Iulianus was a correspondent of Symmachus, and his prefecture in Rome is attested by Ammianus Marcellinus to have been liberal and civilized, though here the direct comparison is with his African proconsulate, which had brought him a reputation, whether justified or not, for gratuitous brutality.[74]

His less authoritarian attitude as urban prefect will have served well enough the needs of Maximus, whose uneasy position in Milan made it advisable to seek support wherever he could find it in Italy, and especially in Rome. While still in Gaul Maximus had already had respectful contact with Siricius, Damasus's successor as bishop in Rome,[75] and once in Milan he seems to have enjoyed the favor of at least some of the Roman senators. None other than Symmachus himself traveled to Milan for the consular celebrations on 1 January 388, as he had a year earlier for Valentinian II,[76] and held one of the official *laudationes*.[77] It would have been useful to know what legislation Iulianus received from Maximus, but since Theodosius, after his success in the summer of 388, declared most of Maximus's *acta* to be invalid, no single law of his was included in the Theodosian Code; so we are in no position to assess Ammianus's view of Iulianus's liberality and gentleness. It is, however, clear that Maximus, just like Valentinian II at the start of his own rule after Gratian's sudden death, saw in Rome a body of established and wealthy opinion that required cultivation in order to gain its support and aid for establishing his power in Italy. His *praefectus urbi*, Iulianus, died while still in office, perhaps also a casualty of the defeat of his master in summer 388.

Theodosius

The arrival of Theodosius in Italy in 388 marked the end of Maximus and his closest supporters, but for Rome and the Roman Senate it brought about the closest imperial attention that the city and its ruling class had experienced for decades. Theodosius, like Magnus Maximus, came to Italy as a conqueror, and he also had no intention of leaving Valentinian II in control of the central prefecture of Italy, Africa, and Illyricum. This meant that he needed to build up personal support and loyalty in Italy, where he had never yet operated, and Rome and the Roman senatorial elite were selected to be one of the pillars of his future program. Religious affiliation played at first no part in this. The elderly, learned pagan intellectual and historian Sextus Aurelius Victor became *praefectus urbi* and used his office to erect a statue of his emperor in the forum of Trajan.[78] The inscription, which praises Theodosius for exceeding the clemency, uprightness, and generosity of the emperors of old, doubtless reflected the relief felt by those senators who had cooperated with Magnus Maximus and their genuine gratitude for favorable treatment.[79] This relief was not just political. The war had disrupted the grain supply to the city, and the shortfall was currently exacerbated by a bad harvest in Italy. Theodosius, whose troops had secured the Roman harbors during the war, in the course of which they had occupied one of Symmachus's properties at Ostia, was immediately confronted by a senatorial request to secure deliveries from Africa. This he seems to have done, and in 389 extra deliveries also reached the city from Macedonia.[80]

In June 389, for the first time since 357, a ruling emperor visited Rome accompanied by his whole imperial entourage, currently including his heavily pregnant adopted niece Serena, who gave birth to his first grandchild, Stilicho's son Eucherius, in the eternal city.[81] Theodosius celebrated his triumph over Magnus Maximus during his residence of nearly three months in Rome, from 13 June until 30 August.[82] Constantius in 357 had only stayed for three weeks. Erected as permanent monuments on this occasion were statues of the three ruling emperors—Theodosius, Valentinian II, and Arcadius (only Theodosius being present)—each with the identical description "exterminator of usurpers and founder of public safety"; they were put up by Victor's successor, the pagan senator Ceionius Rufius Albinus.[83] Theodosius's mother, Thermantia, also received a statue from Albinus, drawing further attention to the rehabilitation of his father, Count Theodosius, who had received equestrian statues in Rome as recently as the prefecture of Symmachus.[84]

Symmachus had endured an especially nervous period following Maximus's defeat, since he had been particularly prominent in courting the usurper, even holding a panegyric on his entry into the consulship—a consulship that, doubtless further increasing Symmachus's embarrassment, Theodosius had no intention of recognizing—and so he was relieved to experience Theodosius's clemency. The precise details of how this happened are unclear. While the imperial entourage was in the city, Symmachus at first seems to have kept out of the way on one of his country estates in Campania; but at the same time he used old contacts at court to gradually improve his image and position there.[85] There is a later report that Symmachus also wrote a formal apologia to Theodosius, which, if he did, was certainly not published with his collected works— did it remain embarrassing still under the rule of Theodosius's sons?— and it certainly has not otherwise survived.[86] Whatever the mechanisms involved, by the end of 389 Symmachus was again persona grata and was invited to Milan for consular celebrations, this time those of his experienced senatorial colleague Neoterius, who was foreseen as representative of Theodosius's interests in Gaul by heading the administration of Valentinian II as praetorian prefect of the Gauls.[87] Symmachus's apologies for not attending the ceremony, officially directed to the emperor personally, conveniently also gave him the opportunity of keeping up epistolary contact with a series of his influential acquaintances at court.[88]

The surest evidence for Theodosius's attitude toward Rome and the Senate is, however, provided by the official speech, cast in the form of an imperial panegyric, delivered by the Gallic orator Latinius Pacatus Drepanius (himself until recently a subject of Maximus) before the assembled court and Senate on some formal occasion during the visit in Rome, perhaps the anniversary of Theodosius's final victory over Maximus.[89] The speaker claims to be representing the Gallic provinces, but it is inconceivable that the Gallic provinces waited nearly a year to congratulate Theodosius on his victory and that their representative was then allowed to dominate Theodosius's imperial visitation in Rome with a long speech, as Pacatus's exordium seems to suggest. Pacatus's claim is a mere rhetorical conceit, and to believe it is to attach too much weight to a *captatio benevolentiae*.[90] He clearly had official information about the war; and he would scarcely have dared on his own initiative to completely ignore Valentinian—whose expulsion from Italy was the ostensible cause of the war and who was now emperor in Gaul, where Pacatus came from! The occasion was far too important to be left to the private lucubrations of a provincial orator, and the speech must have been well prepared and officially vetted. Pacatus's subsequent proconsulate of Africa and his post of *comes rei privatae* in the East in 393 were not merely surprise rewards for a clever speaker; they were stages of a career in the imperial service, of which the preserved panegyric is the first stage known to us.[91]

Within the formal limits imposed by the genre the speech is entirely spin, with the aim of formulating an elegant recommendation of Theodosius to the Senate and an offer of reconciliation and cooperation, which had already been given concrete form by the appointment of the senatorial traditionalists Aurelius Victor and Ceionius Albinus to the prefecture of the city. The Gallic orator chosen to deliver the speech incorporated in his person the reconstructionist theme, for Pacatus gives a scarcely veiled hint that he, like Symmachus, also served Magnus Maximus as *laudator* on some occasion: "Let it be gone and past, that depressing compulsion to a servile eloquence . . . : the time when victims thanked their oppressor, when not to praise the usurper brought the charge of fomenting revolution. Now there is equal freedom to speak, or to be silent."[92] The chosen speaker is thus a living manifestation of the Theodosian imperial qualities already praised in perpetuity in stone by Aurelius Victor: clemency, uprightness, and generosity.

Three further passages of the lengthy speech are of particular interest for its political purpose. Sections 15–16 praise Theodosius's choice of officers and helpers—many of whom will have been present, again providing living evidence of the truth of Pacatus's praise, whether they were past officers like Olybrius and perhaps Neoterius, or the more recent senatorial appointments—and laud his evaluation of personal friendship, which expressed itself in official appointments and promotions, even at the cost of his own family. This was clearly a bid for the future cooperation of the listeners.[93] The second passage occurs toward the end of the speech, where, after relating the official version of the events of the war, Pacatus asserts with particular emphasis that following Maximus's death there had been no further persecution of his supporters, and thus implies, a year after the event, that there would be none starting now. The exercise of clemency was total: no confiscations, no fines, no loss of former (that is, pre-Maximus) status. Theodosius went to pains to ensure that nobody could get the impression of feeling personally defeated through his victory.[94] Again Pacatus is clearly formulating a general policy statement and a bid for future support for Theodosius among the Italian upper classes.

The speech ends, as it must, with Rome, with Theodosius's presence there, and with his attitude toward the Senate and the people:

> But these things were achieved in Rome: the impression you made on the day the city first received you; how you conducted yourself in the Senate House and at the rostra; how you advanced in procession behind the scenes of your victory, now in a chariot, now on foot, equally distinguished in whatever way you advanced, triumphant now in war, now over the arrogance of power; how you presented yourself to all as emperor, to individuals as a senator; how in your frequent and courteous journeyings in the city you visited not only public edifices but also hallowed private houses with your divine tread, moving without your military guard, all the safer through the vigilance of a devoted people. Let all these things be praised by the tongues and voices of these men.[95]

There can be little doubt that Theodosius had invested much in time, energy, and prestige in his visit to Rome and in his bid for support there. And his effort did not end with protocol and promotions: no less than nine laws were issued to (and doubtless suggested by) Albinus while Theodosius was staying in the city. They range from the renewed expulsion of Manichaeans (in a law issued a mere four days after the emperor's arrival),[96] to regulations concerning the holidays of the public courts,[97] to rules fixing punishments for practitioners of magic—especially charioteers: had the problem emerged from complaints during his victory games?[98]—and to laws regulating matters concerning the infrastructure and food supply of the city and the status and rights of those involved in it.[99]

Theodosius's encouragement of Roman senators did not end with his return to the north in September 389. Shortly after his visit to Rome one of the leading pagan intellectuals, Virius Nicomachus Flavianus, a historian who dedicated one of his works to Theodosius and had doubtless made his acquaintance during the visit to Rome, was summoned to

Milan to take the post of imperial quaestor.[100] Symmachus's own invitation to the consular ceremonies on 1 January was surely not restricted to him alone, though he remained persona grata to such an extent that he was chosen to be consul for 391. Nevertheless, he continued to be unable to exert sufficient influence on the Christian court at Milan to overrule Ambrose's objections and achieve the restoration of the altar of Victory to the Senate House.[101] The tensions arising in Milan as a result of Ambrose's continuing insistence that Theodosius pay personal penance for the massacre in Thessalonica sent contradictory messages to Rome in 391, a year that had begun so gloriously for the Roman aristocracy with the consulate of Symmachus and the promotion of Virius Nicomachus Flavianus from quaestor to praetorian prefect.[102]

In Rome the reliable Albinus was still in office as *praefectus urbi* when on 24 February a severely worded law was addressed to him from Milan, forbidding sacrifice and the visiting of temples by imperial officials. It must have worked like a bombshell when it arrived in Albinus's office in Rome a few days later.[103] It is for us, as it was perhaps for contemporaries, an indication that the honeymoon was over and that the Christian establishment in Italy was beginning to hit back at Theodosius's initially undogmatic attitude toward pagan practice. Up to now Rome had always managed to preserve an exceptional position in Italy, despite the growth of Christian tradition and practice in the city in the fourth century. A few years before, Libanius had contrasted the liberal attitude practiced by the imperial government toward Rome with the Eastern praetorian prefect Cynegius's privately driven vigor in promoting even the destruction of temples in Syria;[104] and the traditional Roman cults had also continued to be practiced, none other than Ambrose having recently pointed out that, despite the withdrawal of state subsidies, the Roman cults had enough financial substance to maintain themselves.[105]

Soon afterward Albinus was replaced by the Christian Faltonius Probus Alypius, who in turn was succeeded by the Christian Flavius Philippus. These appointments are a sign of compromise within the senatorial class, since both men were longstanding members of the Senate. Alypius was the younger brother of that famous Olybrius who had been consul in the year of Theodosius's appointment as emperor and then served as his praetorian prefect of the East in 379, the critical first year of his rule. Philippus also belonged to an old consular family, his father (or, possibly, his grandfather) having achieved this rank in 348 while serving under Constantius in the East. The appointments in themselves therefore presented no problem to the self-esteem of the Senate, but in the total context of Theodosius's position in Italy at the time and in the immediate aftermath of the law issued to Albinus they do seem to reflect a swing back to that prewar Christian "normality" which was now re-emerging as a result of Theodosius's struggle with Ambrose in Milan; the appointments also reflect the increasing stabilization of his regime in Italy, which no longer required universal conciliation.[106]

Theodosius's return to Constantinople in the summer of 391 left the false impression in Italy that Valentinian II, though resident in Trier, had been in some sense left in control of the West. Only thus can be explained the approach of a senatorial delegation to him concerning the altar of Victory (or the properties belonging to the traditional cults, or both)—our source, a letter of Ambrose, is very imprecise in detail.[107] But where Theodosius himself had remained hard, they could scarcely expect his man Arbogast to soften, and they achieved nothing. Only after Valentinian's death and Eugenius's usurpation did it seem advisable to the new Western authorities to make some sort of concession to yet another senatorial delegation, though precisely what it was remains unclear. Certainly Eugenius did not grant the full restoration of what Gratian had taken away or confiscated; perhaps he merely made a quiet concession on the application of the law issued to Albinus.[108] This at least might be inferred from Eugenius's decision to appoint as *praefectus urbi* the younger Nicomachus Flavianus, the non-Christian son of the prominent pagan praetorian prefect, who as head of the imperial regional administration in Italy had welcomed Eugenius on his arrival in Milan in the spring of 393 and continued to serve him as praetorian prefect.

Usurpation always put highly placed imperial officials on the spot. Whereas Virius Nicomachus Flavianus, as head of the imperial regional administration in Italy, chose to support Eugenius at a time when it must have seemed perfectly possible that Theodosius might recognize him —the emperor-maker Arbogast was, after all, Theodosius's man—Ambrose read the signs otherwise. Learning from his mistake under Magnus Maximus, he left Milan as soon as Eugenius approached, this time avoiding a confrontation with the orthodox Christian usurper on his home ground. The support of Virius Nicomachus Flavianus, paid for, at least in part, by his son's promotion to *praefectus urbi* in Rome, gave Eugenius's opponents the opportunity to characterize Eugenius's whole regime as pagan-friendly and hostile to Christians when Theodosius set out on his crusade to save the empire for his dynasty. Eugenius's defeat and the suicide of Virius Nicomachus Flavianus marked the temporary end of the prominence of the old Roman aristocracy—both pagan and Christian—in the administration of their city. Theodosius did not even appoint a new *praefectus urbi* after his victory, and until his death he governed the city through the *vicarius* of the praetorian prefect, Flavius Pasiphilus.[109] It was some years before external pressures on the new regime in Milan made it seem advisable to try once again to win over the Roman aristocracy to support the current government.[110]

. . .

The sociopolitical importance of Rome within the empire as a whole depended entirely on how important Italy itself was felt to be by the ruling emperor. For Valentinian I, who chose to reside at Trier, Rome was merely another city—albeit a major city, which posed for him major problems—an entity to be administered from afar. But as soon as the imperial crisis in Illyricum brought one of the ruling emperors to Italy— even if only to Milan—the central importance of the Roman senatorial class within Italy as a whole, and with it their old imperial center, again became a factor that an emperor could ignore only at his peril. In particular weaker or potentially insecure emperors—Valentinian II, Magnus Maximus, and above all Theodosius in the immediate post–civil war phase—cultivated the exquisite Romans of Rome. The city might indeed no longer be the center of the Roman world, but without some cooperation from the Romans of Rome no regime could govern Italy satisfactorily. Rome thus retained a unique political and social ambience within the imperial structure, which, to varying degrees, continued to be the case as long as Italy itself remained a central part of the empire.

CHAPTER VI

CONSTANTINOPLE

The city of Constantinople occupied an exceptional position in the empire of the fourth century.[1] Created by Constantine as New Rome on the Bosphorus in order to cement his dynastic hold on the East, the city enabled the emperor to represent himself as a contemporary name-giving Romulus. When he died, Constantinople was far from being completed, and the tensions and civil wars of the subsequent period hindered its sustained construction. Constantius II nevertheless began or continued construction work on the water supply and some public buildings, including churches, of the steadily growing city, as far as he was able. These investments were necessary both for dynastic reasons and because the new city had already acquired a substantial population, attracted by public subsidies and fresh commercial opportunities. But its long-term function within the empire as a whole was far from clear at the time, and there is little indication that Constantius intended it to be more than yet another place where for shorter or longer periods the emperor and his staff could reside in comfort, along with Antioch and Nikomedeia, Thessalonica and Sirmium, Milan and Trier.

Members of the Constantinian dynasty might like to think of lying after their decease in the dynastic mausoleum in the eponymous city of the dynasty's founder, but this was not a public function that would necessarily outlive the dynasty itself. Constantius certainly took a deliberate step to raise the city's sociopolitical status above that of the other competitors in the East when he decided to install a senate in Constantinople that would parallel the one in Rome. But Constantine's city was still far from becoming the permanent "capital city" in the modern sense, or even the preferred place of residence of the imperial court and the associated administrative offices and their bureaucrats. It is difficult to see how such an aim could even have been seriously conceived at the time, when Constantius, following the old tradition of the soldier-emperors—including not least his father, Constantine—continued to make his headquarters wherever the military requirements of the empire took him.

The creation of an imperial senate for the East in Constantinople does not in itself speak against this, for the Senate in Rome had survived and maintained its social status, though not its political influence, long after the emperors had ceased to regard Rome as an imperial administrative center, to be visited—if at all—only on formal ceremonial occasions. We have seen how rare that was in our period. Since there is no good reason to believe that Constantius viewed Constantinople in a much different light, certainly not as a fixed city of imperial residence, it hardly seems that his new Senate as a body was intended to enjoy more political influence than its Roman counterpart. This did not mean that the infrastructure and public buildings of the ever-growing city would not be further developed. That, at least, he owed to the memory of his father and his dynasty's dissatisfaction with the Romans of "Old Rome." They should learn that they were not unique as cultivators of imperial ceremonial.

The City under Valens and Theodosius

It was thus not the original intention of the Constantinians but the conditions emerging in the empire after Julian's death, precisely in the years of Valens and Theodosius, that created for Constantinople its future status and function as long-term imperial residence and permanent administrative center for a no longer peripatetic emperor, a status that it was to maintain in principle until modern times. The factors conditioning this development were partly accidental, partly deliberately created. Had Julian or Jovian, following Constantius's model and ruling the empire alone without a formally equal imperial partner, lived longer, it might never have happened. But a factor of critical importance for the whole empire, and with it for Constantinople, was the administrative division of the empire between Valens and Valentinian in 364, which created the need for two separate (but at first largely parallel) administrative systems.

Valens might well have been persuaded to reside for longer periods in the city on the Bosphorus that had witnessed his appointment as em-

peror—despite his lack of sophisticated Greek—had not Julian's relative Procopius seemed to find support for his usurpation in the dynastic
city. Thereafter Valens visited Constantinople only for very brief periods, otherwise choosing to be based closer to where the military action
was, whether this was at Marcianopolis in Thrace for the Gothic war or
at Antioch in Syria for the tensions on the frontier with Persia. His decision meant, in effect, that Constantinople's political influence, and that
of its leading men, was far more modest than many of its residents might
have hoped for: just as in the case of Rome senators and their representatives wishing to contact the emperor and gain influence at court had
to make the long journey to the provincial centers to meet him, whether
to congratulate and praise, to deliver a petition or just to lobby for some
favorite scheme. Nevertheless, Valens continued the public investment
program in the infrastructure of the new city; the huge aqueduct that
still bears his name was finally completed; and an additional group of
grain warehouses (*horrea*) was built for the city to help feed its growing
population.[2]

Ironically it was the Gothic war in which Valens died in 378 that
brought Constantinople center stage in the empire, for one of the side
effects of the emperor's defeat at Adrianople was that Constantine's city
was suddenly—and for the first time—exposed to real physical danger:
the frontier, it must have seemed, had come to Constantinople, and the
city required an immediate defense.[3] Moreover, temporarily left alone in
the crisis the Constantinopolitan Senate summoned up the courage to
legitimize preventive military action in Asia Minor. The slaughter by the
magister militum Julius of the young Goths stationed in Asia took place
with the backing and authority of the Senate. Nevertheless the new emperor Theodosius took his time before going to Constantinople: the city
was not yet his top priority. His first year saw him based at Thessalonica,
from where he conducted the war, and it was perhaps not without some
anxiety that the senator Themistius approached him there with a plea
for continuing investment in Constantinople.[4] For if Illyricum, which
Gratian had turned over to Theodosius on his accession for the duration
of the war,[5] were to turn out to be a long-term center of his imperial
activity, Thessalonica was at least as suitable a base for it as Constanti-

nople—indeed for many purposes geographically more suitable, as the tetrarch Galerius had established three-quarters of a century before.

The imperial concentration on Illyricum proved, however, to be temporary, and the war against the Goths came to an end in 382. Theodosius had moved his court to Constantinople in November 380, and the western orientation of his attention over the next few years had a positive effect for Constantinople in that he moved no further eastward, indeed showed no enthusiasm at all for getting to know his Eastern provinces personally, and remained resident in Constantinople. Whatever Theodosius's long-term plans and inclination might have been, his decision to stay in Constantinople was a turning point in the history of the city, for in these Theodosian years it did indeed become a "capital" city in a modern sense, a center of politics, culture, and administration, and not just a ceremonial conurbation or comfortable temporary residence. Theodosius remained resident in the city until 388, when he left for Italy and the confrontation with Maximus. But he left behind his son Arcadius, already formally equal as Augustus, and had in place an efficient Eastern administration headed by the experienced praetorian prefect Tatianus. This meant that the city, even without the personal presence of the senior ruling emperor, now retained not just a ceremonial function but continued to be the administrative center of the eastern parts of the empire. For Constantinople this was a new experience. Valens, like Constantius and Julian, usually took his chief administrators with him when he traveled. Under Theodosius they had a home base, even when the emperor himself was on the move.

Theodosius planned the change deliberately, having seen something similar emerge in the West under Valentinian and Gratian in Trier, which he had probably experienced personally while he served with his father under Valentinian I. There would be, of course, clear advantages in efficiency if a centralized bureaucratic administration could be fixed in one place. Since the death of its name-giver, Constantinople had not experienced such constant attention and imperial favor. Moreover, an ambitious program of public building was begun soon after Theodosius's arrival. Another new harbor, not far from that begun by Julian, was constructed, and in the heart of the city a new forum, the Forum Theodosii (also known as the Forum Tauri) was begun, which seems to have resembled in an uncanny, therefore deliberate way, Trajan's forum at Rome. The Spanish emperor, who claimed kinship with the great Trajan, seems to have been replicating at least some of his Roman work in Constantinople. Even the victory column that was erected in due course in the context of this building program seems likely to have been a pastiche of Trajan's column in Rome, there erected to celebrate the victory over the Dacians, here that over their Gothic successors who had invaded Thrace from what had once been Trajan's Dacia—the territory had been given up in the third century in order to fix the frontier on the Danube. The city was thus not just getting an expensive new infrastructure; at the same time an imperial history and tradition was being constructed for it.[6] Given this intention it was hardly surprising that when the old Gothic leader Athanaric turned up in Constantinople a few weeks after Theodosius's entry into the city, in January 381, to negotiate peace, he was the subject of an extravagant public ceremonial welcome; and when the old man died a few days later, his body received an equally extravagant public funeral.[7] New Rome, the new city of the new emperor, was going to get used to providing the backdrop for major imperial ceremonial.

The long-term presence of the emperor and the imperial family in Constantinople offered the urban population a unique opportunity to exert regular influence on imperial decision making, since the people of the city were by no means simply passive participants to be pushed around for ceremonial purposes as the masters of ceremonies dictated. The place where meetings, even confrontations, between people and court most frequently took place was the hippodrome during the fairly frequent days of races. The imperial palace at Constantinople, following a model based on Rome but already imitated to our knowledge at least in Thessalonica and in Antioch, had been constructed in Constantine's time with direct private access to the imperial loge in the hippodrome. But if no emperor or high official representing him were present at the games, there was no way in which the masses assembled for the races could address or directly influence him by their shouts or even by rioting at the games, as had been characteristic of early imperial Rome while the emperors still resided there. At the same time it was regarded as an essential aspect of public relations that the emperor, when present in the city, be seen to participate in the popular entertainment of the games, whatever his personal inclination. His presence, his visibility in public, and the theoretical possibility of seeming to influence him personally provided an important sociopolitical safety valve in the often tense political atmosphere of an imperial city where the lower classes no longer had any constitutional organ to represent them.[8]

Thus when Theodosius decided to set up a long-term imperial residence in Constantinople, he was at the same time creating the necessary preconditions for a permanent symbiotic political relationship between autocratic ruler and the city population of the ruled, which no city of the empire had enjoyed in quite this way since the emperors ceased to reside in Rome. The permanent residence of the court was what made the city immediately and really imperial, and this is expressed iconographically by the sculptured base on the Theodosius obelisk, set up in 390 in the hippodrome at Constantinople—where it still stands—by the *praefectus urbi* Proculus after Theodosius's defeat of Maximus. One of the four sides shows the emperor, his family, and his entourage in the imperial box at the races, with the emperor holding the starting flag (the *mappa*) in his hand.[9] It symbolizes that the emperor belonged to Constantinople just as much as Constantinople belonged to the emperor. Imperial propaganda certainly, but it could not be denied that with Theodosius the imperial city had won a new political dimension, a new importance, and thus had become the premier city of government for the empire.

The existence of an adequate socioeconomic elite was essential for a ruling city in the empire, and the creation of an effective senatorial class in the East, together with its focus on the new city of Constantinople, turned out to be a major factor in binding the Eastern land-owning classes into the imperial governmental structure and creating vested political and economic interests in its continuation. However, because of the way this was done during the second half of the fourth century, while certainly strengthening the internal cohesiveness of the East and the city of Constantinople, it inevitably led to a weakening of the ties between East and West and to an increasingly independent development in each of the *partes imperii*. Given the external pressures under which the West in particular had to suffer in the fifth century, the development of a separate and increasingly self-assertive mentality in the East caused a decrease of internal cohesiveness in the imperial structure as a whole. This development brought about the paradoxical situation that it was in the West, where the empire began and had its oldest roots and traditions, that the pressures became so great that the empire in effect collapsed in the fifth century, whereas the newer Roman structures in the East, thanks to the consolidation work done by the emperors of the later fourth century and regular flexible adjustments to new circumstances, carried on the name and some of the traditions of the Roman Empire until Constantinople capitulated to the Turks in 1453.

The Senate of Constantinople

Later Eastern writers, beginning already in the fifth century, liked to think that the development of Constantinople into the capital city in the East was intended and foreseen by Constantine, to whom they attributed not merely the foundation of Constantinople but also of the Senate there.[10] In actuality the development of both the city and the Senate seems to have been much more haphazard. Attractive financial offers were indeed made to those prepared to take up residence in Constantinople in the early years, but it was perhaps inevitable that the first prominent people known to have built houses and to have taken up official residence there were existing members of the senatorial class of the empire, who as individuals were closely associated with Constantine and his Eastern policies. Only two of these prominent early settlers can be named with certainty: Constantine's praetorian prefect Flavius Ablabius and the rather younger Flavius Philippus, who served Constantius II as praetorian prefect in the 340s.[11] It cannot be excluded that these men, and others unknown to us, at first participated in the activities of the existing city council of Byzantium, which presumably survived at least for a short period until Constantine's new foundation received its new local governmental structure; but conceivably their role was even less formal than this, and they were spoken of as senators simply because they were the sole representatives of the one-and-only Roman Senate of Rome who happened to be present in Constantine's new city.

They were certainly not members of a formally established Eastern senate in Constantinople, since the impulse to found the institution emerged only from the deadly dispute among Constantine's sons about the succession and the resulting division of the empire on geographical lines. This division effectively cut off Constantius II from Italy and left all senators now resident in the East with embarrassingly divided loyalties: on the one hand, to the emperor—Constantine II, and then after his premature death in 340 Constans—who controlled Rome, where they were supposed to attend meetings, at least occasionally; on the other hand, to their immediate ruler, Constantius, who controlled their prospects of promotion in the imperial service and governed the lands in the East where their estates lay. Since the Constantinian brothers were young, certainly younger than most senators, no significant change in the divided political structure of the empire could reasonably be anticipated in the short term, barring accidents, not even in the lifetime of most existing senators. Constantius therefore had to be committed to finding a solution to this structural problem affecting the political representation and social distinction of his imperial elite class, if he was serious about keeping their loyalty, and he saw it in extending Constantine's initial aims for Constantinople.

The concrete development of his father's name city was for Constantius in any case an act of filial piety, doubtless popular in itself among those who had been attached to Constantine; but turning it into a regional imperial, political, and administrative center could be exploited as a political challenge to his brother in the West. Just as Constans had a Senate in Rome, so would Constantius have one in Constantinople. The first law concerning the organization and recruitment for the new senatorial body—presumably beyond the existing members of the senatorial class in the East, who were now registered as residents in Constantinople—dates from this tense phase in 340 and lays down the formal conditions for entry. Membership was to be open to those willing (and financially able) to hold one of three newly created Constantinopolitan praetorships, the *praetura Flavialis*, the *praetura Constantiniana*, and the *praetura triumphalis*. At the same time, Constantius fixed the costs for the praetorian games—thereby, in effect, setting the entry fee to the Senate—associated with each of these new posts. With this law Constantius not only created a senate for New Rome but also instituted magistracies of a traditional Republican type (but with modernized names) to go along with it. Such praetorships even in Rome were, of course, no longer political offices; they were purely decorative institutions, though enormously expensive for their holders, which nevertheless served as one way of entering the Senate. Their creation for New Rome at this time of political tension therefore emphasizes Constantius's deliberate intention of creating a rival to his brother's institution.[12]

A further source of pressure on Constantius resulted from a change in the functions of senators introduced by Constantine. During the military crises of the third century senators had been gradually excluded from all state functions of any importance, although the prestige associated with being one of the perhaps 600 senators in the whole empire was jealously guarded and awarded only rarely to those born outside traditional aristocratic circles. Under Constantine this had begun to change, not least through the creation of a new type of nobility that had nothing to do with ancient tradition (such as the Senate) or with the public administration (such as the *equites*), but solely with personal service to the emperor. The "companions" (*comites*) developed into a new aristocracy of service that cut across traditional structures and loyalties.[13] The gradual breakdown of traditional status barriers meant that Constantine had also been inclined to treat traditional senators pragmatically, so that capable individual senators once again began to be employed as administrators at various high levels, as governors of provinces, as diocesan officers (*vicarii*), or even as praetorian prefects.

This paradoxically opened the way to a wider recruitment of senators, for if a senator could become a *vicarius* or praetorian prefect, there was no good reason why a nonsenatorial *vicarius* or praetorian prefect should not become a senator. Through the admission of persons who had filled higher posts in the provincial or central palatine administration, imperial service thus led to the Roman Senate's gradual opening to new people and a gradual increase in its numbers. Senatorial status remained attractive because a senator, by contrast with a *comes*, whose honor was merely personal and died with him, passed on his high and privileged status to his children. The expansionist process was well under way in Rome by the time of Constantine's death and the hostile division of the empire among his sons, which effectively cut off from Italy Constantius's own highest officials, who were by definition resident in the East. They would now have had no realistic opportunity of reaching that well-established peak of honor, membership in the senatorial order, which would have been their reward if they had served Constans, unless they abandoned their emperor in favor of his rival and then took their seats in the Senate at Rome. There is no explicit evidence, but we must assume that such people also saw at least a partial solution to their problem in the creation of an Eastern senate, a second assembly of those highly placed men who liked to call themselves "most distinguished" (*clarissimi*) and whom a little later the Roman traditionalist senator Symmachus called "the better part of mankind." [14]

The new Senate in Constantinople did not, however, increase its membership at any great speed. By the late 350s, when systematic major expansion began, it consisted of some 300 members recruited from all corners of the Eastern empire,[15] but this modest number for the elite assembly was perhaps initially intended, since it compared not unfavorably with the Roman Senate at the time of Diocletian, whose members—then taken from the whole empire—have been estimated at some 600. The reasons for the major expansion program at Constantinople, initiated after Constantius's visit to Rome in 357, are nowhere explicitly explained, but imperial dissatisfaction with the attitude of the Senate in Rome seems likely to have played some part. A series of laws following rapidly on the defeat in 353 of the usurper Magnentius, who had eliminated Constans, illustrate imperial disapproval of the senators of the West, many of whom had tolerated the usurper. Some particularly prominent senators, including two ex-consuls and an ex-prefect of the city, had even shown obvious disloyalty to the dynasty by actively supporting Magnentius and accepting posts from him.[16] In 354, very soon after Magnentius was eliminated, both the praetorian prefect Hilarianus and the prefect of the city Orfitus received instructions from the emperor to enforce the rules that obliged senators to give (and pay for) public games: those liable to this extremely expensive service were now to be compelled to come to the city and fulfill their obligation.[17]

At the same time, the city administration of Rome itself suffered a reform that reduced the influence of the *praefectus urbi*, a post that had traditionally marked the peak of a senatorial career. Formally the prefect retained his position as second in the imperial administrative hierarchy after the praetorian prefects, but the *vicarius*, who up to now had been his deputy (with the title *vicarius praefecturae urbis*), now became a deputy of the praetorian prefect of the central prefecture—that is, part of the centralized regional administration. Moreover, the city prefect's right to hear appeals—one of his major judicial functions—was restricted to an area within the 100th milestone from the city, thus deliberately coinciding with the area of his normal primary jurisdiction. Previously he had heard appeals from at least some, perhaps from all, of the provinces of the Italian dioceses.[18] It is difficult not to regard these changes as a mark of imperial dissatisfaction at the disloyal role of prominent senators in recent events.

Meanwhile Constantius had not forgotten Constantinople. In 355 he seized the opportunity offered by his sending an official letter to Constantinople appointing Themistius to the Senate there to issue a programmatic statement committing himself to the further expansion of the Senate in the East.[19] In 356 rules were issued allowing Eastern senators themselves, as long as a quorum of fifty members was reached—explicitly without interference by the imperial authorities—to choose the praetors for Constantinople;[20] and by the summer of 357, after the emperor's ceremonial visit to Rome to mark his victory over Magnentius, the rule was in place bringing about the formal geographical division of the membership of the Senate between East and West according to prefectures, and stipulating this for future recruitment; current members from Illyricum, including the Greek-speaking areas of Macedonia and Achaia, since they belonged to the central prefecture, were put under pressure to actually attend meetings of the Senate in Rome.[21] Themistius, who had visited Constantius in Rome in the early summer of 357 as the leader of a delegation from the Senate of Constantinople, received an imperial appointment as proconsul of Constantinople that was combined with the explicit instruction to expand the numbers of men belonging to the Senate there.[22]

These incidents and activities—senatorial support in Rome for Magnentius, the disciplinary laws, Constantius's visit to Rome with the inevitable personal confrontation with traditionalist Roman senators, and the decision to effectively weaken the Senate in Rome by formally restricting its membership to those resident in the Western prefectures—must be seen in relation to each other. The original foundation of the Senate at Constantinople had indeed occurred as a challenge to Constans and as a focus of ambition for the Eastern upper classes and Eastern functionaries at a time when, it seemed, they were effectively excluded from honor in Italy and would long remain so. However, its continued expansion and increasingly stable structure now by the later 350s conveyed a real sense that the emperor intended it to be permanent, despite the sudden and unexpected reunification of the empire in 353 under Constantius. This development was a direct result of the emperor's reaction to senatorial disloyalty to the ruling dynasty, as shown by the neutral, or even positive, attitude of many Western senators toward the unsuccessful usurper. The decision to further extend and systematize the institutions of Constantinople, above all its Senate, was thus at least in part a deliberate consequence of Constantius's dissatisfaction with Rome.

Themistius's main period of activity as recruiter of senators began around 358, immediately after Constantius's visit to Rome, and his office as proconsul seems to belong to 358/59; but by the time Constantius himself returned to Constantinople, in the autumn of 359, he had taken a further decision to raise the status of both the city and its Senate. The status of the head of the city administration was to be changed by appointing a prefect of the city, thus setting up a direct parallel to Rome. In the imperial administrative hierarchy, the new prefect of the city ranked, as in Rome, immediately below the praetorian prefect, who headed the official list. This was an enormous promotion of status for the Constantinople city administration, since proconsuls belonged to the provincial administration and ranked below all palatine officials. In the East according to the *Notitia Dignitatum* they took the twenty-second position;

in the West the *proconsul Africae* had position twenty-one. Moreover, since the prefect of the city was now always (just as in Rome) appointed from among the members of the Senate, whose meetings he chaired, the rise in status of the chief city administrator brought with it automatically a further rise in status for the Constantinopolitan Senate itself and its members. This administrative change was far from being trivial or merely technical. It was not just a change of name; it was regarded as being so important for the history of Constantinople that the rudimentary city chronicle, the so-called *Consularia Constantinopolitana*, marked only two events of 359 as worthy of record: one was the entry into office of the first prefect of the city, Honoratus, on 11 December, and the other was the birth of the future emperor Gratian.[23]

The expansion of the Senate and the creation of the Constantinopolitan prefect of the city raised many new questions, and a comprehensive law issued to the Senate on 3 May 361, parts of which were included in various rubrics of the Theodosian Code, made a systematic attempt to come to grips with the new situation. In Rome the prefect of the city, even after the reform of 357, had retained his traditional rights as judge of appeal for cases heard within the 100th milestone of the city of Rome. The rule about the 100th milestone was already an anachronism in Italy, having nothing to do with contemporary administrative structures, since it dated from a time when Italy was not divided up into provinces and was still governed from Rome. It obviously made no sense at all in Constantinople. That the prefect of the city should exercise judicial rights in the area immediately surrounding the city, where city interests were most extensive—the original purpose of the rule for Rome—made, however, good sense in principle and limited the judicial burden of the praetorian prefect. In Constantinople the city prefect's area of responsibility had to be defined differently, and it was natural to do this by stipulating certain nearby provinces—three in Europe and six in Asia—for which responsibility for appeals would lie in the future with the prefect of the city and not the praetorian prefect of the East.[24] New senators, who were required to be resident in Constantinople, could not be expected to abandon their property in the provinces, so the Senate was empowered to appoint official representatives (*defensores*) to look after their interests there, especially on questions of taxation and legal representation.[25]

After Themistius's boom years, recruitment was systematized and the first known Eastern limitation on city councillors laid down—senatorial membership was in the future to be possible for such people only if they had already fulfilled their financial obligations to their local community (*munera*).[26] Themistius's recruitment drive must have ignored this problem in the eagerness to build up the Senate with worthy persons, but after three years the problems caused in the provincial cities by the loss to the Senate of wealthy men for their local councils required urgent attention. That senatorial recruitment was also a factor to be taken into account while planning the growth of the city of Constantinople was recognized in a change of the rules fixing the costs associated with the praetorships. These honorable and expensive posts were increased from three to five, the *praetura Romana* and the *praetura Constantiana* being newly created,[27] and the holders of two of the existing posts, the *praetura Constantiniana* and the *praetura Flaviana*, were now instructed to spend 1,000 or 500 pounds of silver respectively on buildings in Constantinople; three posts were therefore, as before, to remain responsible for financing public games. Moreover, in order that candidates might be able to plan for heavy personal expenditures, the Senate was to appoint praetors ten years in advance, with substitutes named in case of premature death. To ensure the appropriate gravity of the Senate meeting at which future praetors were appointed, it was prescribed that at least ten senior senators—proconsuls, ex–praetorian prefects, ex-proconsuls (including the chief recruiter, Themistius), and ex-praetors—should be personally present to give the decision its fitting weight and authority.[28] Various other minor fiscal privileges and other financial rules rounded off this major piece of legislation.[29]

Despite the generality of the language of the law, the new rules were clearly not intended for both Senates, since they made no sense at all in Rome. The law only applied to Constantinople. The two Senates therefore continued to operate under slightly different conditions and rules, though we only catch occasional glimpses of how they worked in practice. It seems likely that existing Eastern members of the Roman Senate were transferred to Constantinople, whether they wanted to be or not. Since Illyricum, including the Greek-speaking dioceses, remained under Western administration, there may not have been so many of them, but one case is better known, thanks to the attempts of Libanius to use his influence to ease the transition of his Antiochene friend Olympius. Olympius was a member of a large curial family from Antioch and had been governor of Macedonia around 356, while the empire was united under Constantius; thereafter he was enrolled in the Roman Senate. He had not, however, taken up residence in Rome and had, perhaps for this reason, so far enjoyed immunity from senatorial expenses. Since Constantius expected his Constantinopolitan senators to attend meetings, which in effect meant being resident in Constantinople, and since one of the socioeconomic functions of a Constantinopolitan senator was to expend parts of his private wealth on improving life in the new city, Constantinopolitan senators enjoyed no fiscal immunity, not even as an exception. In a series of letters Libanius tried to use his personal influence with Themistius and then with his successor as chief administrator, the first prefect of the city, Honoratus, to at least postpone Olympius's duty to occupy one of the expensive praetorships until more senior members of the Senate had fulfilled their obligations. Especially annoying to Olympius was the fact, so he alleged, that he had been confused with another man of the same name in apportioning the financial duties (*munera*). In the end, in 361, intensive string-pulling obtained for Olympius an imperial letter in his favor. But even then the emperor's expressed wish could only be effected in practice if Honoratus, as prefect of the city and chairman of the Senate, was prepared to assert himself in Olympius's interest, since it was not the emperor but the Senate that decided such things, as the recent law had explicitly ruled.[30]

The Senate in Constantinople, at least from the time of Themistius's recruitment drive, remained responsible not only for its own financing but also for its own recruitment, which allowed the large-scale exercise of patronage and social influence. The way Themistius operated is clear enough in general, and another of Libanius's Antiochene protégés, one Julian, who after being a provincial governor in Phrygia had been enrolled in the Senate in 358/59 while Themistius was proconsul, provides a good illustration of the issues and interests involved. Soon after his enrollment Julian's property was assessed for the senatorial tax, the so-called *gleba senatoria* (sometimes known as the *follis*), which meant an annual payment of two, four, or eight pounds of gold, depending on the level of his property assessment. This was the point at which Libanius intervened on his behalf with the praetorian prefect Hermogenes, whose financial staff, the *censuales*, made the official property assessments on which the level of tax was based. The proconsul (after 360 the prefect of the city) then had to confirm their assessment. Libanius therefore also wrote to the newly appointed proconsul Themistius—the letter is extant—to try to influence him to confirm a decision made by Hermogenes to cancel or, perhaps more likely, to reduce, the level of Julian's assessment fixed by the *censuales*.[31] The result of the intervention is not known, but the upper-class network of patronage seems to have functioned quite well.

By the time Olympius's case came to Libanius's notice a few months later in 359, Libanius knew that no total freedom from senatorial taxation (*ateleia*) was possible in Constantinople.[32] Either he was ignorant of the rules when he wrote to Hermogenes and Themistius on Julian's behalf or, more likely, the rules had been tightened up in the meanwhile, perhaps when the city prefecture was created, in order to forestall abuses of patronage. But there is no doubt that even here the final responsibility for such questions formally lay not with the emperor but with the Senate's own administration. Some changes were, however, made by later emperors in the rules governing the praetors. Under Valens in 372 the number was reduced to four[33]—the *praetura Flavialis*, perhaps too redolent of the second Flavian (Constantinian) dynasty, disappeared—only to be doubled to eight by Theodosius in 384. The epithets for Theodosius's new posts, like the old, demonstrated the close public associations of the office with the ruling dynasty and the imperial state. These were the *praetura Theodosiana*, the *praetura Arcadiana*, the *praetura Augustalis*, and the *praetura laureata*, and the holders of the eight praetorships were now paired for the sums of money they were to spend during their period of office, ranging from 1,000 pounds of silver for the highest to 250 for the lowest pair.[34] The pairing of the officeholders was clearly a concession to new senators reaching the Senate via the praetorship, for under Constantius similar sums had had to be paid by each individual.[35] Difficulties in this context had begun to emerge under Valens, who proposed the first penalties for not fulfilling praetorial obligations known in the East.[36] In the West such defaults were, however, an old problem, going back at least to Constantine, from whom two exceptions to the obligations are preserved,[37] and a later law preserves a reference to a fine imposed by Constantine.[38] In Rome pressure had begun in earnest under Constantius II after the revolt of Magnentius,[39] and Valentinian reminded the prefect of the city, Volusianus, of Constantine's penalty again in 365.[40]

The legislative efforts by the imperial chancery to enforce the fulfillment of obligations by future senators did not alter the basic fact of the Eastern Senate's primary responsibility for its own recruitment in our period, despite the many detailed alterations in the rules regarding eligibility for appointment. A well-known case from around 390 shows that neither Valens nor Theodosius had changed the ultimate responsibility, which still lay with the Senate itself. Thalassius was a rich friend and admirer of Libanius's who wished to obtain membership of the Senate in Constantinople; he was a rich man and had no objection to paying all necessary expenses and fulfilling his financial obligations. Before his case was discussed in the Senate, he had already obtained an official letter from the imperial chancellery saying the emperor had no objection to his membership—clearly an attempt to put moral and political pressure on the senators. Yet Thalassius was turned down, despite his imperial letter and witnesses to his suitability having made the long journey from Antioch to Constantinople to testify on his behalf. The negative senatorial decision provoked a series of letters from Libanius to leading senators urging them to reconsider; and when that failed, he composed an angry speech nominally addressed to the emperor Theodosius—but certainly never sent!—complaining about the attitudes and moral qualities of some major senatorial players who had been responsible for the fiasco.[41] This could not have happened at Rome, where a senatorial decision on a potential new member who belonged to a non-senatorial family was taken after hearing speeches by supporting *patroni* before any approach was made to the emperor, who then had to give his approval. Imperial approval was important, since in Rome exemptions from the official praetorian obligations could still be granted to newly elected members (*adlecti*)—though since 383 this did not extend to the *follis*—and the final decision on financial questions remained, it seems, with the emperor.[42]

On one occasion the senatorial tax, the *gleba* (*follis*), was canceled in the East, presumably only temporarily, for the diocese of Thrace—doubtless because of the devastation caused by the Gothic wars after 376. We only know of this cancellation because a later law, dating to 384, orders some senators of Macedonian origin who had joined the Senate in Constantinople to be treated like those of Thrace and be freed from the *gleba*.[43] At first sight it is rather surprising that Macedonian senators should turn up in Constantinople, when Constantius had insisted that they not only remain attached to Rome but also had to attend meetings there, but the reason is not far to seek. If the text of the law (which was damaged in transmission) has been correctly restored, these men were not old Roman senators simply transferred by Theodosius to Constantinople, but rather new recruits (*allecti*), so that their membership can have dated at the earliest from 379, when Theodosius became responsible for Illyricum and his period of residence in Thessalonica began. It would therefore hardly be surprising if some actual or potential senators from the area had used the opportunity offered by the imperial residence there to make themselves known and useful at court and in due course to join the Senate in Constantinople, when their contact emperor Theodosius moved to the city in 380.

Theodosius would have had little inclination to turn them down, since as late as 390 Libanius claimed to know that the emperor still wanted to increase the numbers of senators.[44] The law about the treatment of the Macedonians dates from 384, two years after Illyricum, including Macedonia, had been formally returned to Western administration, and it shows that the new Macedonian senators had remained attached to Constantinople. That they, like the Thracians, needed tax relief, is comprehensible enough, given the wide extent of the ravages caused by the Gothic war, which had also seriously affected Macedonia; but their remaining attached to the Senate in Constantinople draws attention to the increasingly anomalous situation of the Greek-speaking dioceses of Illyricum in the divided empire and their potentially split loyalties. We must therefore assume that during this period, until Theodosius's death, when Illyricum was finally divided at the linguistic boundary between East and West and the Greek-speaking dioceses began to regard Constantinople's responsibility for them as a permanent arrangement, senators from Macedonia could in practice be attached to either the Senate in Rome or the one in Constantinople, depending on when they had been recruited. Whether those who remained attached to Rome also enjoyed tax relief remains unknown, since the extant law concerns only Constantinople. That Greek-speaking men from the Illyrican dioceses still were recruited to the Roman Senate under Theodosius is shown, however, by the following example: in the same year as the Theodosian law about the Macedonians in Constantinople, the Athenian philosopher Celsus, then resident in Rome, was recommended for membership in the Roman Senate by the responsible prefect of the city, Symmachus, in an extant report to the emperor that he wrote on the case.[45]

Over the thirty years following Constantius's reforms, the Senate and its chairman, the prefect of the city, developed into focal points for the social advance of the local aristocracies of the Eastern provinces. As the city continued to expand, so did the importance of the prefect of the city, since his responsibilities were extended to cover all areas that were essential for the civilian functionality of the urban area. In particular the provision of grain, the water supply, town planning, and the maintenance of public order belonged to his domain.[46] As early as Procopius's usurpation attempt in 365, the function of the prefect of the city was so important that Procopius appointed one of his own people, Phronimius, to the post, even though Eastern senatorial support for the usurper was not wildly enthusiastic.[47] The Senate as a body meeting in formal session was regularly regaled with semiofficial policy statements by its own more prominent members, such as Themistius, several of whose surviving public speeches were delivered on such occasions, and senatorial delegations traveled to participate in major ceremonial events at the court when it was not resident in Constantinople. When it was there, the Senate House itself became one of the places where imperial representation was regularly celebrated. In crisis situations the Senate — or at least those members of it permanently resident in Constantinople, who were available at short notice — even participated in major political decisions: after the defeat at Adrianople it was the Senate in Constantinople that formally backed the decision of the *magister militum* Julius to massacre all Goths who were recently enrolled into the Eastern armies; and when Theodosius was deliberating on war with Magnus Maximus in 387/88, discussions with the Senate took place.[48]

The Emperor and His City

Even before Constantinople under Theodosius became the permanent residence of the emperor, the new city and its Senate saw far more of the ruling emperor than did "Old Rome," simply for geographical reasons. Whereas it is not known that "Old Rome" so much as saw an emperor within its walls for the thirty-two years between Constantius's visit in 357 and Theodosius's in 389, Constantinople saw Constantius in 359–60, Julian in 361–62, and Valentinian and Valens in 364, when Valens was appointed Augustus at the Hebdomon barracks and therefore called the city "the mother of his imperial rule"; thereafter Valens was in Constantinople in 364–65, 366, 370, 371, and 378, and Theodosius in principle (and in his absence Arcadius) permanently after November 380. This meant in practice that a quite different and much more intimate kind of relationship could develop between the Senate (and its chairman, the prefect of the city) and the court and the imperial administration than was possible in Rome. There the senators were largely left to their own devices and could communicate with the court only with the greatest difficulty, since Valentinian I preferred to reside at Trier and it was not until 370 that Gratian came a little closer, when he set up his court and administration in Milan. This much more immediate contact with the responsible rulers of the empire meant that a cohesive social ambience could develop in Constantinople, where the central organs of the Eastern imperial administration stood in regular formal and informal contact with the highest echelons of the Eastern imperial aristocracy. Eastern aristocrats may not have been as rich and as jealous of tradition as the senators in Rome, but perhaps for this reason it was much easier to integrate them into the new imperial system.

Constantinople's increasing importance is reflected in the development of the office of *praefectus urbi* there, once the emperor began to live regularly in the city. In the first phase after the creation of the post in 359, it seems to have been closely connected with the provincial administration; its holders, insofar as their earlier careers are known, had gained earlier administrative experience as provincial governors, as indeed was the case with the parallel position in Rome.[49] A change seems to have begun in the later part of Valens's reign with the growth of a closer relationship to the palatine service—though, of course, the two were in no way completely separate career paths—and for Theodosius's urban prefects previous experience in the palatine service, apart from the special case of the senior senator and public orator Themistius in 384, seems to have become the chief qualification for the post. Thus the city administration of Constantinople tended to move gradually closer to the court and the central organs of the empire, and further away from the normal provincial administration. That this tendency began with Valens's appointment in 375 of Vindaonius Magnus, who had previously been *comes sacrarum largitionum*,[50] might suggest that Valens was already thinking along the lines that Theodosius put into practice; this could also be indicated by the fact that the central judicial archive of final decisions taken in the court of the praetorian prefect was established at Constantinople at some time during Valens's reign, probably on the initiative of his long-serving prefect Domitius Modestus.[51]

The same tendency can be observed and the same conclusion drawn from the number and content of general laws contained in the law codes addressed to the *praefectus urbi*. Once again Theodosius's reign marks a change, expressed in an enormously increased tendency to legislate for Constantinople, and this can only reflect the increased importance attached to the city once the imperial court had chosen to reside there, and the resulting increased governmental interest in and attention to the way the city functioned. Whereas for the first twenty years of the urban prefecture at Constantinople (359–379) only six laws addressed to its incumbent are to be found in the law codes, Theodosius's prefects received no less than twenty-six laws in fourteen years.[52] These numbers reflect, of course, only "general laws" (*leges generales*), defined according to the selection criteria of the compilers of the codes. The number of trivial, temporary, or ad hoc rulings cannot now be ascertained, and the difference may also be exaggerated by the greater recovery quota by the compilers of the Theodosian Code of laws directed to Constantinople from the time when a stable imperial administration (with archive) had been established in the city under Theodosius. But we have to work with what we have.

The one question that constantly troubled the *praefectus urbi* throughout the period was that of bread rations (*annona*). Constantine had tried to make his new city attractive for private investment by offering the incentive of free bread rations to those coming to Constantinople with the intention of living there permanently, as long as they demonstrated the seriousness of their intention by investing in building a house. Some time later the incentive seems to have been extended beyond the circle of house builders, since various groups of people enjoying bread rations are known, including members of the administration or some of those on active military service; some even seem, as in Rome, to have received personal rights to free bread independently of house building or office holding. After a generation houses that were lived in by their builders began to change hands, and the first law addressed to a *praefectus urbi* that we know of—to Jovinus in 364—concerns the *annona* rights of such properties. Valentinian, passing quickly through the city that spring, had no hesitation in briskly asserting that the *annonae* once granted were to remain attached to a building as long as the person who had erected it still lived in it; if he sold the house, died, or just moved elsewhere his bread rations were to be annulled (technically they became *caducae*) and be reclaimed by the fiscus.[53] Eight years later Valens allowed his *praefectus urbi* Clearchus to use such annulled rations, *annonae caducae*, to reward copyists working for a public library in Constantinople,[54] while at the same time private rights to bread rations (called now *annona popularis*) were reasserted to be just that: as long as the men entitled to them continued to live in the city, they should continue to enjoy their rights, but these were not transferable to other people. It seems that a regular market for the entitlement tokens to free bread had developed.[55]

This problem did not just go away when Theodosius came to the throne. One of his first legislative actions, taken in 380 before he had even come to Constantinople, was to assert that *annonae* issued to members of the guard corps (the *scholae*), who were now retired from the service or even dead, were to belong to the *scholae* and not remain privatized in the families of the ex-*scholarii* concerned.[56] It was clearly a complicated business, the precise details of which seem to have been unknown to the administration, and in 389 another law instructed the *praefectus urbi* Proculus actively to reclaim for the *scholae* such *annonae* as had been privatized.[57] But further investigation by the efficient prefect, accompanied doubtless by much legal argument, established that at least some rations granted to members of the *scholae* had indeed been initially granted *ad personam*, and this discovery produced another imperial ruling addressed to Proculus: that in each case the original terms of the grant were to be investigated before action was taken.[58] This did not, however, apply to prominent military personnel (*viri militares*) who had received grants explicitly associated with house building: those still not possessing a house were to lose their *annonae*.[59] Proculus's insistence on the accurate investigation of the original terms of each grant was then explicitly upheld by his successor as *praefectus urbi*, Aurelianus, even after Proculus, together with his father, the praetorian prefect Tatianus, had fallen from grace, but new grants that Proculus had made were canceled.[60]

Other aspects of city life at Constantinople were also regulated with increasing intensity under Theodosius, reflecting his existential interest in his city. The Senate received particular attention, though this too seems to have begun under Valens with a law addressed to the *praefectus urbi* Magnus in May 376. Constantius II had allowed the Senate to look after the property rights of its members and their taxation problems in the country by appointing in each province an official as special representative (*defensor senatus*), so that the senators could be present in Constantinople and attend meetings there without having to run the risk of being cited to appear in court in a distant province. In practice this system had not always functioned satisfactorily, and Valens found it necessary to assert that no fiscal decision concerning a senator's property should be taken in a provincial court unless the *defensor* was present.[61] The problem was not so easily solved, and we find a law enacted in 393 that was addressed to the *praefectus urbi* Aurelian asserting the rights of *defensores senatorum* in court against the arbitrary action of ordinary provincial judges, who were hindering them.[62] These laws were addressed to the *praefectus urbi* as chairman of the Senate, who in this respect must have had rights to represent the senators' interests against the normal provincial administration of the praetorian prefect and local tax authorities. Another aspect was senatorial recruitment, which remained of interest, whether from the curial class[63] or with regard to special geographical conditions.[64] Status questions both within and without the Senate attracted Theodosius's attention and produced laws addressed to the *praefectus urbi* concerning such sensitive questions as the relative precedence of *magistri militum* and *praefecti*, the status of honorary ex-quaestors, or that of *agentes in rebus* who had become the heads of administrative bureaus (*principes officiorum*).[65] With all this attention being paid to clearing up questions of formal status and protocol it is not surprising to find a law banning pretense to a status to which one was not entitled.[66]

Theodosius's administration was also particularly concerned with appearances, especially with the public image of the governing classes in the ruling city. In June 382, after a year's experience of observing life styles in Constantinople, Theodosius directed a comprehensive law to the *praefectus urbi* Pancratius regulating questions of dress in public places for senators and government employees (*officiales*). Senators were no longer to wear the short military cape (*chlamys*) in the street, but the more elegant, yet less practical, civilian long coat (*paenula*), while for business meetings of the Senate or a public law court the toga was to be worn. The prescribed street garb of the *officiales* was the *paenula*, but for the office they were to don a two-colored *pallium* over a belted shirt. The clothing of the attendant slaves of nonmilitary men was also regulated. Improperly dressed senators were not to be allowed to attend meetings; improperly dressed *officiales* and slaves were to be banned from the city altogether; and if the office of the *praefectus urbi* turned a blind eye, it was threatened with a penalty of twenty pounds of gold.[67] *Honorati*—highly placed provincials with special tax privileges won through service in the imperial administration—were also required to put their status on public show by always using a suitable carriage when moving about within the city.[68]

This emphasis on public deportment, on creating a corporate image of respectful civilian decency for Constantinople's rulers, was clearly policy, and it went hand in hand with the architectural decoration of the city center, in particular the new Forum Tauri with its architectural reminiscences of Rome. However, practical affairs of the city were by no means neglected. During Theodosius's first hot summer in the city, on 30 July 381, the *praefectus urbi* Pancratius received instructions, under threat of a fine of fifty pounds of gold for his office, to ensure that all supraterrestrial burials, in urns or sarcophagi, were to take place only outside the city walls, and holy places associated with the apostles or martyrs were explicitly to be no exception to this rule.[69]

Attention to public hygiene and controlled use of limited resources (including the public space within the city walls) was also in evidence in regulations concerning water use and building. The completion of the great aqueduct known as that of Valens greatly improved the water supply of the city, but at the same time it made new regulations for the use of the water essential. Theodosius's bureaucracy reacted initially with irritation at private initiatives: a law addressed to Pancratius in 382 threatened those tapping off water from the public aqueducts for private estates with the confiscation of their estates to the public purse (the *res privata*),[70] but a short time later Pancratius's successor, Clearchus, received detailed rules on the use of the water in the city for private bathhouses: depending on the size of the property concerned, the diameter of the water pipes that were allowed to be laid varied from two inches (in exceptional cases up to three inches, but not more) to one-half of an inch. These regulations were to be strictly controlled by the office of the *praefectus urbi*, and his officials were threatened with fines of six pounds of gold if they failed in their duty. Thus the relative importance attached to burial regulations and those concerning water use can be measured by the amount of the fine threatened.[71]

Attempts were also made to control building activity in the public interest: in 389 Proculus received a law asking him to control private buildings that negatively affected the appearance of public ones.[72] The moralizing language used here in referring to the appearance of the public areas seems characteristically Theodosian and fits admirably with his earlier laws concerning the public appearance of imperial officials. Pointing in the same direction were rules insisting that a public building, once begun, had to be completed before a new one could be started[73] and that private buildings up to a value of fifty pounds of gold might be sacrificed for the erection of public buildings on the initiative and responsibility of the *praefectus urbi* alone; more expensive ones required the personal permission of the emperor.[74]

The laws addressed to the *praefectus urbi* during this period illuminate in a unique way the imperial attitude toward Constantinople. The city, for the first time since the initial imperial enthusiasm connected with its foundation, received the continuous personal attention of the emperor and his highest administrative officials, since they were all actually living there. The main emphasis seems to have been laid on creating a representative ambience for the imperial residence, in particular for the public areas, and to encourage in general a public appearance that would elicit pride in the inhabitants and respect and admiration in visitors. The imperial presence was intended to dominate and impress, to persuade those who knew "Old Rome" to believe that "New Rome" was also real Rome. What seems to be missing here is the promotion of the image, notorious in much modern literature following the self-serving Ambrosian description of Theodosius as "most Christian emperor" (*christianissimus imperator*), of the orthodox emperor advancing orthodoxy with missionary enthusiasm. In Theodosius's attitude toward Constantinople, as elsewhere, it is a mirage. Only one law addressed to a *praefectus urbi* shows the least interest in regulating the life of the city according to Christian principles. Near the end of his long period as *praefectus urbi*, the pagan Proculus received on 17 April 392 the instruction that public entertainments in the circus were not to be held on Sundays — with one exception, which, however, for us demonstrates imperial priorities: the birthday of the emperor. Imperial ceremony was simply more important than observing the Sunday peace. Constantinople had under Theodosius certainly taken a large step toward removing the religious ambiguities that had dominated the city since its foundation, but the greatest step it took under "the most Christian emperor" was that toward becoming the city of empire, as it remained for centuries thereafter.

PART III

RELIGION & THE · STATE

CHAPTER VII

JULIAN'S · SUCCESSORS

Julian's brief reign caused turmoil in the religious establishment of the empire. His personal renunciation of Christianity and his official policy of aggressively anti-Christian universal religious tolerance in the empire earned him personally the hatred of most Christian communities and the historical sobriquet "the Apostate." More important, it left his successors, it seemed, with a major problem at several levels, which can be briefly characterized as the relationship between the representatives of the state and those of the multifarious religious communities in the empire. How was the future role of the emperor in religious affairs to be defined, since he still bore the traditional title, going back centuries to the Republic, of *pontifex maximus*, designating him head of the state religion? Constantine had begun the revolutionary policy of officially favoring the Christian church and using the secular law-giving process to issue privileges to favored groups, even intervening personally with the full force of his imperial charisma in internal disputes among the Christian communities. His sons, especially Constantius, had continued this practice, making every effort to bring the so-called Arian dispute to an administratively acceptable solution.

Major doctrinal dispute had, for the emperor, two particularly important aspects. One was theological-salvationist: if the Christian religion was to help to protect and save the empire, with the emperor as God's vice-gerent on earth, then it seemed only reasonable that all right-thinking men should agree on the nature of the God in whose name the emperor claimed to be ruling. The other aspect was administrative-financial: the church and its officials had amassed an enormous amount of capital and enjoyed huge tax privileges; as a result, in many areas they exercised an influence that locally could become comparable with the power of the local representative of the emperor, the provincial governor. It was therefore in the interest of the imperial administration to have a practical definition of who precisely "belonged" to the church, in order to be able to decide who was to benefit from the tax privileges and enjoy the local influence that went hand in hand with them. This implied—and here the two aspects coincided—that it was in the secular interest of the empire that a clear decision be taken on what constituted "the church," which the emperors would officially recognize.

The problem had confronted all emperors since Constantine's impetuous decision to favor Christianity without his fully comprehending the complexity of its theological politics or being able to anticipate the intensity of the internal squabbles of church representatives. Constantius II had been particularly eager to attend to these problems, and in 359 he had pressured ecclesiastical councils meeting at Ariminum (Rimini) in the West and Seleukeia on the Kalykadnos (Silifke) in the East to agree on a formula, which was then confirmed for both parts of the empire by a delegate conference at Constantinople in 360. This declared that the son in the Trinity was "like [homoios] the father who begot him according to the scriptures," not as in the Nicene formula "of one substance [homoousios; in Latin consubstantialis] with the father," and was immediately put into administrative practice, with varying regional success, by the imperial authorities. In the West, where the emperor and his court were not personally present to supervise, little was done before his death in the summer of 361; in the East, where Constantius and his administration could immediately influence what was done, bishops who opposed the unifying formula were deposed and removed to places from which they would have difficulty in causing problems for their "unitarian" successors and the imperial administration.[1]

Had Constantius lived as long as his father, he would have ruled more than twenty more years and might well have managed to create a theological-administrative structure for the church—at least in the East—that would have brought about a symbiosis of church and state, which Constantine initially seems to have thought could be created at the stroke of a pen. But his sudden decease in the summer of 361, followed by Julian's general, undisciplined "tolerance," created chaos. Not only did Julian restore pagan observances to something approaching their old status, at least in places where he and his court were present, but he also declared equal opportunity for all Christian communities—that is, even for those regarded by their Christian opponents as heretics—and he explicitly allowed bishops exiled by Constantius to return to their original places of residence and activity.[2] This inevitably caused strife and dissension within the affected Christian communities, as it was intended to do. Wherever religious strife reached a dimension that affected the law and order of the cities involved—as was the case especially in Alexandria, and threatened to be so in Antioch—the secular authorities could intervene with a heavy hand in order to restore public order, and thus show who in the last resort was the ruler.

Jovian

Julian's sudden death in Mesopotamia in 363 and the resultant emergency election of the Christian Jovian by the army shuffled the cards anew. Jovian was an uncomplicated military man and certainly no religious fanatic, but on returning to Roman territory he was immediately confronted by a crowd of clerics that included the restless Alexandrian bishop Athanasius, who caught up with the new emperor at Hierapolis in Syria. Each of them hoped to persuade the emperor to adopt and support his own favored version of eternal truth.[3] According to our most reliable source, the ecclesiastical historian Sokrates, while Jovian was personally inclined toward orthodoxy—that is, the formula agreed at Nikaia, though this assertion perhaps reflects merely the pro-Athanasius tradition followed by Sokrates[4]—he treated all in friendly fashion. Any bishop deposed under Julian was recalled. Only the pagan excesses encouraged by Julian were officially stopped; in particular bloody sacrifice was banned again. And it seems possible that some kind of ordinance, perhaps at first only for the administrative diocese Oriens centered on Antioch, was issued guaranteeing general tolerance of belief for all Christian believers.[5] Jovian's general attitude is characterized by an anecdote related by Sokrates, whether or not it is historically authentic. A group of so-called Macedonianist bishops from Asia Minor, followers of Macedonius, who rejected Constantius's "homoian" compromise formula agreed to at Constantinople, presented a petition (*libellus*) to Jovian arguing against the "homoian" bishops and asserting that they should now be deposed and that the Macedonianists' own candidates be appointed in their place. The emperor sent them away with their petition unanswered and the remark, "I hate contentious rivalry, but have affection and respect for those working toward concord."[6]

It is clear that Jovian was reluctant to take the initiative in an area where past imperial decisions had continually caused strife and disorder. From this initial reluctance to act it was no great step toward formulating a general policy of religious laissez-faire, which was presented by the senior senator of Constantinople, Themistius, in a programmatic speech delivered in Ankara to celebrate the emperor's first consulate on 1 January 364.[7] Jovian had been held up so long in Antioch that he had just reached as far as Ankara by the time of his consular celebrations, but Themistius made up for the lack of a metropolitan audience for this first official spin-talk of the new regime by repeating the speech in Constantinople before a full house of the Senate there.[8] Among other aspects of the new ruler, his religious policy—or lack of one—plays a major part in the speech, occupying the largest single section, which brings the speech as a whole to a climax: "No single road leads to the one and only winning-post; one way is more difficult, another is rougher, a third is level, but all lead to the same end; our struggling and zeal originate from nothing other than that we are not all marching along the same route."[9] It was a major policy reversal and not merely a return to the status quo before Julian, since not only the differing Christian sects but also the non-Christians, as long as they did not revert to unacceptable sacrificial practices, were officially granted the right to exist and practice their religion. The official attitude toward non-Christians was an aspect later Christian historians preferred to forget when they praised Jovian for reversing Julian's policy of positively encouraging paganism and for restoring the ecclesiastical privileges Julian had abolished.[10] In effect, however, what Themistius announced at Ankara was a general act of tolerance, and at the same time a warning to the many intolerant Christians who openly rejoiced at the death of Julian, that the new regime would neither favor nor tolerate the type of hate-filled triumphalism that characterized their most extreme anti-Julianist utterances, such as the two distastefully vitriolic essays of Gregory of Nazianzos, written immediately after Julian's death.[11]

The East under Valens

We cannot tell what effect, if any, Jovian's new attitude toward religious affairs had, or in the longer term would have had, since a few weeks after Themistius's speech he was also dead and replaced by the Illyrican soldier brothers Valentinian and Valens. Official policy did not change. Themistius's speech officially welcoming Valens to Constantinople, in practice delivering the official policy statement for the new ruler of the East, found it unnecessary even to mention religion;[12] and this reluctance to give an initial line on religion from the imperial government continued and is confirmed by the fact that the Theodosian Code contains not a single general law relating to pagans from the period of rule of the two brothers, either in the East or in the West, and only a very few laws, all of local application, that strictly speaking concern a religious topic at all.[13] This does not mean that the years passed by with no action in the field of religion by the emperors; it does mean, however, that neither of them made a determined attempt to initiate a new policy. Activity, such as it was, was rather reaction of a controlling or disciplinary kind to events or situations occurring somewhere within the empire.

Both ancient and, following them, modern writers take a different view, in particular of Valens. Valentinian was fortunate that in the West, where he chose to rule, interest in dogmatic discussion in the church was limited, and those who departed from the Nicene formula remained largely without influence and certainly posed no long-term threat to the supremacy of those who liked to call themselves catholics. Valentinian therefore had no difficulty in tolerating them, while following what is depicted as his own inclination to the Nicene formulation of the creed, though it might more realistically be interpreted as mere undoctrinaire pragmatism.[14] Valens's problem in the East had a quite different dimension, since although the Nicene Creed had been formulated at an Eastern synod, it had never attained there the level of general acceptability and authority that it quickly reached in the West. It had been so far modified by various ecclesiastical thinkers educated in a tradition of philosophical questioning that a whole series of subtly different formulae for the nature of the Trinity was current, each with its own regional center of favor. The tendency was strong for each group to declare "heretical" all deviations from the version that it chose to favor.

Constantius's efforts to impose his "homoian" compromise in the West failed, but a series of disciplinary actions that placed major Eastern sees under the control of bishops belonging to his "imperial Church" followed in the few months of life remaining to him after the synod of Constantinople in 360. Julian's anti-Christian tolerance, which encouraged bishops expelled by Constantius to return to their cities, created the initial confusion in the church that he desired, and Jovian's brief rule, with its pragmatic but overoptimistic general tolerance, left Valens, when he came to the throne in 364, to pick up the pieces and re-create a systematic imperial policy. It was virtually inevitable that Valens—basically a pragmatist, like his brother—would choose to take up the tradition of Constantius, under whom he had begun his career, and therefore favor the version of the faith that was already predominant in his part of the empire. Anything else would have been a recipe for reviving the ecclesiastical disorder that, it seemed, Constantius had only recently succeeded in resolving. It was, however, equally inevitable, given the vibrant nature of Eastern ecclesiastical controversy, that Valens would be the target of hate campaigns from those churchmen who took another view, and it was a great misfortune for his reputation in religious circles that he was succeeded by a Westerner, Theodosius, who followed the advice of doctrinaire Nicenes in his Western entourage and helped the Nicene formula—with significant aid from the secular arm—to a breakthrough in the East. Once the Nicenes had won and claimed the titles "orthodox" and "catholic" exclusively for themselves, they virtually obliterated memory of other traditions, and Valens went down in mainstream ecclesiastical history as an "Arian" persecutor, just as Constantius was also remembered in these circles as an "Arian." As the most moderate of the later Nicene historians, Sokrates, expressed it, "Valens chose to promote the Arians and did terrible things to those who did not believe in that way."[15]

The Macedonianists · Concrete evidence for Sokrates's "terrible things" is slight. After the Constantian Council of Constantinople in 360 and the synodal condemnation of those who refused to accept the new "homoian" formula, Constantius had vigorously attacked the problem of bishops who did not accept it and removed several of them from their sees. The first of Valens's "terrible things" was that he not only did not restore these people, but in some cases, it seems, in supporting the "homoians," re-exiled some of those who had returned under Julian's troublemaking policy of universal toleration. Although he did not really go much further than Jovian, who had refused to restore the "homoiousian" Macedonianists when they appealed to him in Antioch, Jovian's reputation was saved and he could be claimed by the later Nicene historiography to have been actively Nicene orthodox, largely because he had allowed the Nicene Athanasius to return to Alexandria, and it was the influential Athanasius's version of events that dominated the later ecclesiastical tradition.[16]

Valens tried hard to be pragmatic but was inadequately rewarded. On returning to Constantinople from Sirmium in late 364 he faced the identical problem with the Macedonianists that Jovian had. While traveling westward the new emperors had been approached by the Macedonianists with the request that they might hold a synod. Permission was given—itself a clear sign of basic tolerance in doctrinal matters—and the Macedonianists, led by their figurehead bishop, Eleusius of Kyzikos, met together at Lampsakos. After two months of deliberations they agreed to reject the compromise formula pushed through by Constantius at Rimini in 359 and at Constantinople in 360, that the son was "like [*homoios*] the father who begot him according to the scriptures," and reverted to older formulations that avoided both of the embattled words "*homos*" and "*homoios*."[17] They therefore condemned the results of Constantius's synod of Constantinople. We may imagine that this fact alone would scarcely have disturbed Valens's equanimity had they not also made a serious attempt to persuade him to join them in their condemnation of the synod of Constantinople, and consequently to use his imperial authority to depose Eudoxius, the current bishop of Constantinople and the most influential representative of the "homoian" church created by Constantius and now favored by Valens. The emperor's considered reply, according to Sozomenus,[18] was to exile the troublemakers and order the churches to be handed over to "those around Eudoxius," that is, those accepting the "homoian" formula of Rimini and Constantinople. In fact none of the Macedonianists seems to have been exiled or deposed, so that Sozomenus's statement may well be just another unreflected piece of later anti-Valens tendentiousness.

The precise chronology of these events is not certain. It seems clear, however, that the hostile attitude of the Macedonianists to the attempted usurpation of Procopius in 365 and the resulting military actions in the Hellespontine and Marmara regions where the Macedonianists had their local strongholds—Kyzikos was here particularly important[19]—made their refusal to accept the dogmatic formula favored by Valens seem less threatening to the emperor's desire for peace in the church. The historian Sokrates reports that after the defeat of Procopius—therefore in 366—Valens summoned the leading Macedonianist, Eleusius of Kyzikos, to him at Nikomedeia and put him under pressure to accept the formula of Constantinople; Eleusius embraced it in the presence of the emperor, but he immediately rejected it again as soon as he left him. His congregation found him worthy of continuing in office, despite his dogmatic havering, and he duly remained bishop until his death sometime after 381.[20]

This story can hardly be authentic, since it also confuses the issue by misplacing the extremist ("Anhomoian") Eunomius's period as bishop of Kyzikos to this time (and not under Constantius in 360, as seems correct) and connecting it to this episode concerning Eleusius. It therefore seems likely that the Macedonianist homoiousian traditionalists were doing no more than seeking an explanation for the embarrassment of Eleusius's undeniably *not* having been expelled by Valens after the synod of Lampsakos and his provocation of the emperor, as Sozomenus's all-embracing assertion suggests he should have been, and found it in the conveniently invented story of Valens's favoring the extremist Eunomius. This part of the tale is, however, also quite impossible, a malicious fable aimed at denigrating Valens still further, for Eunomius was no friend of Valens's. Indeed he was quite the opposite, since he had associated with the usurper Procopius and even seems to have helped him in some way; after the failure of the usurpation, even as late as the Gothic war of 367–69, he had severe difficulty in obtaining a pardon from Valens for his disloyalty during the usurpation.[21]

The full truth will never be known, but Kyzikos was one of the cities that offered Procopius serious opposition, and once the town had finally fallen to his troops it was not bishop Eleusius but the extremist leader Eunomius who, because of his established friendship with Procopius, succeeded in persuading Procopius to release Kyzikene prisoners.[22] Eleusius, therefore, can be assumed to have remained loyal to Valens in the civil war, perhaps even leading the local Kyzikene resistance to Procopius's troops. We could therefore perhaps conclude that at Nikomedeia there came about a deal that resulted in Eleusius's being confirmed in office by Valens. This favorable treatment of Eleusius, given Valens's later reputation in orthodox circles as an "Arian" and a persecutor, must surely have become an embarrassment for the orthodox community, which the anti-Valens tradition tried to obscure with the tale of Eleusius's being supported by his people, despite his having bowed to Valens's pressure to join his "heretical" faith. But since Eleusius, as a Macedonianist, was still not orthodox in the full Nicene sense, and could not therefore serve, as did Basil of Caesarea, as a hero of the orthodox resistance, the Nicene tradition followed by Sokrates had no difficulty in allowing him the momentary moral weakness of denying his formula of faith before the "heretical" emperor. The loyalty to Valens shown by the Macedonianist bishops in this secular crisis thus provides the best explanation of why they were pragmatically left in office by Valens once it was over. Part of the agreement reached at Nikomedeia may well also have been that they undertook not to take initiatives that might cause trouble for the emperor's "homoian" church. We certainly hear of no further activity on their part until the reign of Theodosius.

Valens and the "Orthodox" · The later victorious Nicene orthodox anti-Valens tradition had similar difficulties in coming to terms with Valens's basically favorable treatment of the Nicene heroes Athanasius of Alexandria and Basil of Caesarea in Cappadocia. Of all the emperors under whom Athanasius lived, Valens was the only one with whom, after some initial misunderstandings, he achieved a lasting and undisturbed modus vivendi. The initial stages are confusing—and perhaps were deliberately confused by the Athanasian tradition. In May 365 a message described in the anonymous *Historia Athanasii* as a general imperial instruction (*preceptum*)[23] reached Alexandria, ordering those bishops rejected by Constantius who had returned under Julian to leave their churches again; the city councils (*curiae*) were threatened with an unprecedentedly high fine of 300 pounds of gold in case of noncompliance. This order was also known to Sokrates, but perhaps only from the *Historia Athanasii*, not independently, and he attributes its instigation to Eudoxius of Constantinople. Sozomenus, who otherwise follows the *Historia Athanasii*, takes this particular detail from Sokrates, and his account has no independent value.[24] The authenticity of the *preceptum*, at least in the form presented in the *Historia Athanasii*, is dubious, since it seems to have had no practical effect outside Egypt,[25] and even there, after some initial uncertainty, it remained ineffective.

It is thus tempting to regard the account in the *Historia Athanasii* as no more than an extensive interpretation of certain facts by the victorious Nicene propagandists, particularly since the threatened fine for the *curiae*, 300 pounds of gold, is absurdly high, indeed three times as high as that threatened in anger by Julian to the prefect of Egypt in 362/63.[26] Moreover—a point critical for the skeptical view of the *preceptum*—nothing much actually happened to Athanasius (or to anyone else) as a result. The *Historia Athanasii* reports a sophistical discussion of whether the order applied to Athanasius at all, since he had not just been restored but had also been expelled by Julian. Riots, in themselves not an unusual occurrence in Alexandria, are recorded; they were accompanied by a four-month retirement of the bishop to a suburban villa, which lasted until an imperial notary, one Brasidas, arrived in Alexandria on 31 January 366 and confirmed Athanasius's legitimacy as bishop.[27] He then remained undisturbed in the city until his death seven years later on 2 or 3 May 373.

The evidence can perhaps be explained. Valens's confirmation of Eudoxius in office at Constantinople and his pragmatic hopes of restoring Constantius's "homoian" church must have become quickly known in ecclesiastical circles; the emperor's general wish to restore order and peace in the ecclesiastical landscape after the deliberate chaos created by Julian must also have been widely acknowledged, but the discussions with the Macedonianists and their version of events, together with Valens's reaction to their synod of Lampsakos, became known as well. It would therefore have been easy enough for Nicene orthodox rabble-rousers to turn an imperial refusal to restore those expelled by Constantius into an order to reject them anew, had they returned under Julian's dispensation.[28] Partisan discussion of this problem would almost inevitably have caused riots in Alexandria, and the intervention of troops was, as always, the only effective way to quell them. It is then hardly surprising that Athanasius chose to retire from the city center (but not very far), rather than be arrested yet again for causing unnecessary disturbances. In the end he received from Valens exactly the same dispensation he had received from Jovian: to rule the Alexandrian (and Egyptian) church as bishop.[29] This he was able to do for seven whole years without any further interference from the "persecuting" Valens. Valens's *preceptum sent to all the provinces* seems then most likely to be yet another myth deliberately created by Nicene orthodox triumphalism to blacken the emperor's name and enhance the reputations of those bishops who belonged to the faction that in the end won the struggle against his views.

The third example of a heroic bishop being depicted as successfully offering opposition to the "heretical" emperor and his minions is Basil. Accounts here approach more obviously the hagiographic, so that it is even more difficult to separate pious fantasy from the truth, since the original source of all our accounts seems to be a memorial oration delivered sometime in the 380s on the anniversary of Basil's death by his friend Gregory of Nazianzos, and later elaborated for publication.[30] At the time of the composition of this piece Valens was conveniently dead, and his successor Theodosius had already taken major steps to support Nicenes in the East. Nobody in Nicene church circles would therefore have dreamed of challenging Gregory's canonical version of what had allegedly occurred in private audience between the "heretical" emperor and the right-thinking bishop a good decade before.

Yet there is sufficient reason to be skeptical. Gregory offers a heroic picture of a confrontation between Valens's praetorian prefect Modestus and Basil, clothed in the form of a dialogue modeled directly on the Acts of the Martyrs.[31] This rhetorical stylizing was recognized by his first imitator, the Latin ecclesiastical historian Rufinus, who therefore had no hesitation, while in general massively abbreviating Gregory's version, of improving on it by adding a bon mot of his own, which in turn his own Greek successors, Sokrates and Sozomenus, took up and introduced into the Greek tradition.[32] The confrontation with Modestus depicted by Gregory is so carefully stylized that all detail must be regarded as unhistorical. The same applies to Gregory's version of Basil's subsequent confrontation with Valens himself. Here the emperor is so impressed by Modestus's account of Basil that he even attends his epiphany service, and a subsequent tête-à-tête with him much softens his attitude.[33] Despite this favorable impression, Valens decides Basil has to go into exile, which is perhaps the weakest part of Gregory's whole tale, since he makes no attempt to motivate Valens's decision to exile Basil: "The evil ones carried off the victory, and exile was decided against our man." But the exile, of course, does not actually happen, since this part of the story at least has to be consistent with the known facts: the hero is saved by his being able to console Valens and his wife when their son Valentinian Galates suddenly dies.[34] In this hagiographic account the threat of exile and its link with the opportune death of Galates (a real event) are merely literary devices to justify the fact of Basil's undeniable survival in office under the heretical Valens. Basil himself, unconcerned with posterity, asserts unembarrassed that Valens left him in charge of ecclesiastical administration in Cappadocia.[35]

The same literary motif is used to explain Basil's later undeniably friendly relationship with Modestus, to which some of his own extant letters also testify.[36] The standard form of the argument is by now familiar: an alleged threat by the emperor which, never put into practice, is turned to profitable use by the writer in order to uphold the late Nicene tradition that Valens was a serious persecutor, while at the same time explaining why three of the most prominent and influential ecclesiastics who opposed and worked actively against his doctrine neverthe-less maintained their tenure of important sees. Rufinus makes the point most clearly, but, of course, without explanation: "So it happened that while Valens expelled all the catholics [!] Basil survived in the church to the end of his life without compromising the sacrament of commu-nion."[37]

It is not easy to penetrate the thicket of this mythmaking and see what, if any, historical truth might be involved. Caesarea was an impor-tant city on the main east-west road through Anatolia, and it is likely enough that Valens in passing through met the new bishop (Basil had been bishop only since 370), and made efforts to find out what kind of man he was; if so, he would doubtless have wished to know his objec-tions to joining the "homoian" imperial church. It is also perfectly pos-sible that the praetorian prefect Modestus tried to put pressure on Basil in the same direction, though the friendly tone of Basil's letters to him rules out the sort of inquisitorial confrontation depicted by Gregory in his posthumous literary creation. It was clearly not Valens's technique to exile bishops who were well liked by their people and who were com-petent administrators and unlikely to make serious secular trouble. In view of the problems on the Danube and the uncertain situation in Ar-menia it would have been irresponsible to adopt a doctrinaire attitude toward dogmatic questions, and Valens did not do so. Indeed, not only did Basil remain in control of the church in Cappadocia, where he was metropolitan bishop and responsible for organizing the appointment of new bishops in subordinate sees—which he was able to do unhindered by the imperial authorities—but he also received an imperial instruc-tion to help organize the church in the western part of Greater Arme-nia, which at the time fell under Roman influence.[38] Around 375, how-ever, three Cappadocian bishops, among them Basil's brother Gregory of Nyssa, were removed from their sees by the imperial vicar Demosthe-nes. Demosthenes doubtless had administrative reasons for his action, though the evidence for it, coming uniquely from interested parties— Basil himself and his close friend Gregory of Nazianzos—almost inevi-tably depicts Demosthenes's measures as being directed against Nicene orthodoxy as such.[39] Basil's own activities remained unaffected, even when bishops of the currently favored "homoian" imperial church tried to challenge his position before the emperor.[40]

In the administrative diocese Oriens, ruled from Antioch, five "orthodox" bishops are known to have been in exile; the comfortable Nicene orthodox historiographical tradition, in which Nicenes can do no wrong, inevitably attributes their fate exclusively to the dogmatic "homoian" policies of the emperor.[41] The facts, however, though not easy to ascertain, seem to point in a different direction, and skepticism is justified. Under the Christian emperors Antioch, as the apostolic see where the disciples were first called by the name "Christians,"[42] was also of great symbolic value for the role of the church in the empire, especially so after Julian's failed efforts to refurbish the non-Christian cult in the city during his longer period of residence there in 362–63. As a center of Greek traditional culture and associated intellectual life, the city had long been a place where theological controversy was at home, and it could not remain unaffected by the doctrinal discussions associated with Constantius's efforts to create a unified imperial church. Shortly after the "homoian" Councils of Rimini and Seleukeia in 359 and Constantinople in 360 the see of Antioch fell vacant, while Constantius was present in the city preparing for further warfare against the Persians. The person elected bishop was Meletius, an intellectual theologian from Sebasteia in Armenia, who had accepted, so it seemed at the time, the compromise trinitarian formula (the "homoian" formula) favored by Constantius and accepted by his Council of Constantinople. For reasons unknown Meletius rapidly provoked a disagreement with Constantius, who deposed him only a few weeks after his election and sent him back to his native Armenia, where he now lived at Melitene. One Euzoius was then elected in his place, and he was the man who baptized Constantius shortly before his death on 3 November 361.[43]

When Julian allowed bishops deposed by Constantius to return to their sees, Meletius went back to Antioch, just as Athanasius returned to Alexandria. It was, however, in Antioch that the enervating ecclesiastical chaos desired by Julian's policy of general tolerance broke out and dominated the ecclesiastical affairs of the city for the next thirty years, for

Euzoius saw no reason to retire from his throne or his church—and forsake its associated possessions and influence—just because Meletius had come back. This was the beginning of what is known as the "Meletian Schism," or the "Schism of Antioch." But it was more complex than merely a dispute between two men, Meletius and Euzoius, since there existed also a small loyal community of fundamentalist Nicenes in Antioch led by one Paulinus, who chose to recognize no bishop elected in the city since the deposition of Eustathius in 330. Paulinus, in the "chaos days" following Julian's tolerance edict, had been recognized by Athanasius as orthodox, and in a kind of ecclesiastical commando operation was consecrated as bishop in Antioch by the recalcitrant western exile Lucifer of Cagliari. In due course, thanks to the unbending support of Athanasius, Paulinus was also recognized in Rome as the legitimate orthodox bishop of Antioch. Had Julian been a gleeful person, he would surely have chuckled at how "the Galilaeans" were employing the freedom he had granted them.

Meletius, a charismatic intellectual, continued to explore theological questions with those prepared to discuss them with him, and in Antioch he succeeded in building up a sizable following. The ascetic Paulinus and his small community disturbed nobody, restricting their activities to saving their own souls rather than engaging in ecclesiastical politics, so that when Valens came to Antioch in 370 intending to take up long-term residence there, the only obvious rival to his favored "homoian" bishop Euzoius was Meletius, whose presence—as under Constantius— rapidly proved incompatible with that of the "homoian" imperial court as it settled in. Once again Meletius had to leave Antioch, where he had stayed continuously until around 371;[44] he cannot therefore have been affected by any general rule issued by Valens in 365, as asserted by the *Historia Athanasii* for Athanasius.[45] Moreover, an imperial objection in principle to Meletius's form of belief is ruled out by the fact that the other Nicene bishop at Antioch, Paulinus, was left undisturbed in office alongside the "homoian" Euzoius: the Nicene orthodox tradition recorded by the ecclesiastical historians says it was because of Paulinus's especial holiness, which Valens admired;[46] but the historians appear not to have quite realized that this implied that their own Nicene orthodox hero Meletius must therefore have seemed to Valens to be somehow less holy. This tradition is unlikely to represent the full truth. Most probable is that some disciplinary action was deemed necessary by Valens's advisers in order to prevent potential public disorder in Antioch, since the city was being prepared for becoming Valens's main residence from 370 onward. Meletius's community, however, survived as a separate entity despite his exile and was attended to in his absence by two younger associates, Diodorus and Flavianus. An increasingly familiar aspect of the practice of the "Christian Empire" toward the church is illustrated by this affair. In cities where the emperor and his court resided, the church and its local bishops were required to conform to imperial wishes, and certainly no serious competition to the local bishop favored by the emperor was tolerated.

Disciplinary reasons also explain the other cases. Meletius's colleague Eusebius of Samosata was deposed because he offended both ecclesiastical and state authorities by traveling around disguised as a soldier and secretly appointing Nicene priests and deacons.[47] It is hardly surprising that this undercover activity was regarded as troublemaking and led to his deposition. In Jerusalem, where Cyrillus had returned under Julian's amnesty, things remained peaceful until he tried to interfere in the neighboring metropolitan see of Palestinian Caesarea and appoint a person of his own color, and so he also ran afoul of the imperial administration.[48] In Edessa, where Barses was deposed around 373, severe riots had greeted Valens's visit to the city;[49] in the case of Pelagius of Laodikeia, nothing is known, but as he was an associate of Meletius and Eusebius, one cannot rule out that he was subject to similar law-and-order reasons.[50]

Valens's pragmatism was also practiced in Alexandria. Athanasius, like Basil in Cappadocian Caesarea, had been recognized by Valens because he could guarantee peace in the Egyptian church. The "homoian" bishop Lucius was even ejected by the secular authorities when he tried to return secretly in 367, thus demonstrating the unwillingness of Valens's administration to provoke civil disorder, especially during the Gothic war, merely for dogmatic reasons.[51] When Athanasius died, however, in 373 Valens saw his opportunity of winning Egypt for his "homoian" church without serious opposition, and this time sent Lucius, now accompanied by Euzoius of Antioch, with a military escort to take control of the church of Alexandria.[52] This intervention was made all the easier for him by the pagans, who took the opportunity offered by the death of Athanasius and the resultant uncertainty of the Christians to engage in serious rioting; they frightened Peter, whom Athanasius had appointed uncanonically as his successor shortly before his death, so much that he fled the city, making his way to Rome.[53] The imperial military action was thus intended to restore both Lucius to the church and general law and order to the city, since Peter's appointment by Athanasius seemed to show that the "orthodox" were unwilling to abide even by their own procedural rules. Peter was followed into exile by a number of bishops and priests appointed by Athanasius and loyal to Peter, while Lucius with imperial support took measures to "purify" the Egyptian church in Valens's sense. Even the monks of the Nitrian desert, or at least some of them, appear to have suffered from a ruling of Valens, doubtless mainly of local Egyptian application, that young men were not to be allowed to avoid military service by becoming monks.[54]

The exile of the Nicene bishops and their ecclesiastical supporters seems not to have been intended to be permanent, but merely to last long enough for the "homoians" to enjoy a year or two of peace in order to establish themselves firmly. As early as the autumn of 375 the change of policy was floated at court in Antioch by none other than the senior Constantinopolitan senator and imperial adviser, the rhetoric teacher Themistius—ironically enough, himself still a pagan. In a lost speech, which the Greek ecclesiastical historians, taking it at face value, describe as pleading with the emperor for a less extreme policy, the court was being prepared for a change;[55] and two years later the first of the exiled bishops had already returned home.[56] Jerome, resident in Antioch at the time and witnessing the return of Meletius, associates the recall of the bishops with the Gothic crisis, and attributes it to Valens's "late repentance."[57] But Themistius's speech as early as late 375 shows that the connection with the Gothic crisis was merely accidental, the recall of the worthy Nicenes long planned—doubtless an experiment, as with the Macedonianists in the Hellespontine region, on condition that they caused no secular trouble in the cities to which they returned. It was a generous, humanitarian act and the final demonstration that Valens's aim was not doctrinal persecution but disciplined tolerance. As long as his "homoian" bishops and their clergy remained undisturbed and the cities peaceful, the others could in effect believe and do much as they liked.

This attitude did nothing to help his reputation with the triumphalist Nicene orthodoxy under the Theodosian dynasty and later. A start was made by Rufinus, who commented briefly that the emperor's death by fire—one of the versions of his death in the battle of Adrianople—was just punishment for his impiety, and Orosius followed his judgment.[58] By the time Sozomenus was writing in the 440s embroidery had begun. A pious anecdote concerning the Constantinopolitan monk Isaac had by then entered the historiographical tradition, never to depart. Isaac, it was said, had approached the emperor as he was leaving Constantinople for Adrianople and promised him victory if he returned the churches to Nicene believers. On Valens's refusal and his threatening to punish Isaac on his return, Isaac replied: "But you will not return if you do not restore the churches."[59] The anecdote was too good to be true, but also too good to forget, and it lent itself to embellishment. A few years after Sozomenus, the publicist Theodoret doubled its length and added his own pious comment that Valens paid for his crimes in this life.[60] When Theodore Lector took it up, it had already become a standard feature of Byzantine ecclesiastical historiography and was copied by Theophanes and Georgios Monachos,[61] but it was clearly *ben trovato*.

The West under Valentinian

Valentinian's attitude toward ecclesiastical affairs was just as pragmatic as his brother's and was summarized by Ammianus Marcellinus as follows: "His period of rule was famous for its religious policy, in that he took a mediating position amongst the different religious groupings; he caused nobody trouble and issued no orders that this or that should be worshiped; he issued no threats to bend the necks of his subjects to what he himself wanted, but left this area untouched, as he had found it."[62] These words could equally well have been used to describe Valens's basic attitude, had the Eastern church been as unified as the Western on his accession; but whereas Valens had to contend with a bewildering plurality of opinion and organization, Valentinian found a basically Nicene structure, with only relatively minor local "homoian" islands— especially in Illyricum—when he took control of the West, and in general far less enthusiasm for dogmatic battling. This meant that he had a much easier task than his brother, and because his pragmatism favored the status quo, which in his case was Nicene, his reputation with the later Nicene orthodox clerics and ecclesiastical historians was quite different from that of Valens. Sokrates compares him favorably with Valens, and he entered the ecclesiastical tradition as a proponent of Nicene orthodoxy.[63] Yet he was also tolerant of non-Christian religious practices, in this respect following the lead taken by Jovian, and issued laws at the start of his reign explicitly guaranteeing freedom of worship, so long as this was not misused to damage the state.[64] The repeal of central parts of Julian's massively unpopular law against Christian teachers of literature was, however, one of his first imperial legislative acts.[65]

The secular interests of the state were the spring of Valentinian's religious policy, and he was reluctant to give way to partisan interests. Even he was, however, not wholly immune to persistent personal petitioners, who might confront him in his residence. Martin, the ascetic bishop of Tours, offers an example. Our hagiographic source Sulpicius Severus does not say exactly what he wanted, merely that Valentinian did not want to admit him to an audience.[66] After several attempts to gain access to the emperor by normal means had failed, Martin returned to the palace dressed in sackcloth and ashes and staged a hunger strike at the gate. After a week of this he was admitted, Sulpicius Severus says, led on by an angel, still against the will of Valentinian, who was even forced into standing up to greet Martin by the sudden presence of a wondrous hot flame on the seat of his throne, "which set fire to that part of the body on which he was accustomed to sit."[67] Martin achieved his objective, whatever it was, and modestly refused further gifts. It seems clear, however, that Martin's publicity-conscious pressure had achieved its end, and this end was contrary to the official policy of the emperor. It was effective only because the emperor resided in Trier and wished to continue to do so. Considerations of public order are likely to have been decisive here: nobody could tell what might happen if the charismatic ascetic bishop should collapse—or even die!—on the steps of the imperial residence, having been refused access to the emperor to present his petition. Martin of Tours was clearly a special case, and others were understandably reluctant to approach Valentinian with petitions concerning religious affairs. A group of Macedonianists from Asia Minor, who had thought to appeal to the western emperor and the bishop of Rome against Valens in 366, traveled in the end no further than Rome;[68] and Basil of Caesarea's campaign for the Nicene version of the faith in the 370s restricted its diplomatic activity in the West to ecclesiastical circles.[69]

After the initial proclamation of tolerance, laws on religious topics were either local or purely disciplinary. One issued to Ampelius, the *praefectus urbi* of Rome, in March 372 concerns the Manichaeans.[70] This sect originated in Persia and had been persecuted by Diocletian in Africa, where it was particularly strong, apparently because it seemed to threaten Persian subversion of Roman values.[71] The sect did not disappear but gained a reputation for indulging in magical practices, and Valentinian's instruction about them is probably to be interpreted in the context of his ongoing investigations into magical practices within the Roman aristocracy.[72] A second instruction, issued in 373 to the proconsul of Africa during the rebellion of Firmus, attacked the Donatists —an African purist schismatic group, which had originated in Diocletian's great persecution—some of whom supported Firmus, by decreeing that priests who rebaptized, a characteristic Donatist activity, were not worthy of the priesthood. Donatist rebaptism had been an ongoing problem in Africa since Constantine, and it was clearly actualized by the dangerous rebellion of Firmus.[73] Other laws protected non-Christian tradition and explicitly allowed the consultation of the traditional *haruspices*[74] or regulated the election of provincial priests who maintained the pagan tradition.[75] When his proconsul of Achaia, the influential Roman senator Praetextatus, objected that a ban on nightly celebration of ritual—which some regarded as immoral, even potentially dangerous— also negatively affected the prestigious Eleusinian Mysteries at Athens, the ban was lifted for the province of Achaia, where they took place.[76]

Additionally a series of rulings concerned the status or conduct of ecclesiastical personnel, but these were not strictly speaking laws regulating religion or religious activity; the perceptible tendency was indeed to control the freedom of ecclesiastical personnel, but in the interests of discipline and secular order.[77] Only two rulings, both addressed to the elder Symmachus as *praefectus urbi* at Rome in 364 and 365, concerned minor privileges for Christians: they were not to be detailed to protect pagan temples, and judges were not to condemn Christian criminals to appear in the arena.[78]

These privileges were doubtless issues that particularly affected the city of Rome with its sizable Christian proletariat and overwhelmingly pagan infrastructure, and the laws were most probably issued after requests or complaints reached the new emperor on his arrival in Milan, perhaps correcting an abusive practice favored by Julian's supporters. Affairs of the Roman church were, however, to occupy Valentinian repeatedly over the next several years because when bishop Liberius died on 24 September 366 two deacons, Ursinus and Damasus, were each elected by two competing groups of clerics. Each was then consecrated as bishop of Rome in separate ceremonies by a partisan bishop, Ursinus by the bishop of Tibur in the Julian Basilica, Damasus by the bishop of Ostia in the Lateran, which he and his supporters had occupied for the purpose. This was not the first time that the rich and influential church of Rome had experienced schism: Liberius himself had suffered it from his opponent Felix under Constantius II and had only managed to maintain his position in the city with help from the secular authorities. It was the remains of the faction of Felix—who had also died in the meanwhile—that supported Damasus.[79]

This time severe violence broke out, culminating in a three-day siege of the Basilica Sicinini, where Ursinus's supporters had barricaded themselves. When it was over on 26 October, the official count tallied 137 bodies; Ursinus's supporters claimed there were 160.[80] The secular authorities, led by the *praefectus urbi* Viventius, stood aside until the riot was over and it was clear that Damasus, who had in any case occupied the Lateran and with it the central administration of the Roman church, had won. Both parties were subsequently active in propaganda, which has

left traces in the historical tradition, arguing in particular about who was
first appointed and who bore responsibility for the riots and the many
dead. Damasus, who won the battle and the argument, was largely able to
control the orthodox catholic tradition with his version, that he was first
to be appointed and that Ursinus's supporters began the riots, though it
seems likely that this was factually incorrect.[81] For the present purpose,
however, this does not much matter. What is clear is that Viventius, representing the emperor, only became party to the action once it was over
and saw the imperial interest in supporting the winner, whoever it might
be, since only he could offer the chance of future stability and majority
rule. Ursinus and his chief supporters were then exiled, as we have seen
above, and although the next years saw attempts to uphold the schism,
the imperial authorities not only restored the disputed Basilica Sicinini
to Damasus but repeatedly took administrative measures to restrict the
activities of Ursinus's faction and above all to prevent their contacting
their remaining supporters in Rome.[82] In the last of a series of documents that survives from the struggle, the emperor, whose patience was
now at an end, addresses the *vicarius* of Rome Maximinus in 370 expressing his attitude in decisive phrases. If Ursinus's "thankless stubbornness"
should again cause him to break the rules laid down for him by the emperor's decision, the full force of the law was to be applied to treat him
"not as a Christian whose mental instability has separated him from the
religious community, but as a troublemaker and disturber of the public
order, as an enemy of the laws and of religion."[83] The phrase summa-
rizes Valentinian's official attitude toward religious affairs and supports
Ammianus's view of it. Valentinian interfered in religious affairs only by
reacting to given situations, and he was much more concerned with stability and law and order than with setting out a dogmatic program.

Gratian

The sudden death of Valentinian in 375 brought his sixteen-year-old son
Gratian, since 367 bearer of the title Augustus, to the throne as the senior
Western emperor. This meant, in effect, that Gratian's chosen advisers,
in the forefront his teacher Ausonius with his family and associates, took

over responsibility for the empire in the West. Since they had reached the first stages of their influence at court under Valentinian, it is hardly surprising that imperial policy toward religious affairs changed little in Gratian's early years, despite the young emperor's attested personal piety and interest in religious matters. The ecclesiastical historian Rufinus indeed affirms that Gratian is superior to almost all his imperial predecessors in personal piety and attendance to religious affairs;[84] his grateful teacher Ausonius praises to his face his daily attention to prayer;[85] while the same Rufinus also attests to the emperor's reluctance to take initiatives in public affairs—by this, an ecclesiastical historian will mean above all religious affairs—an attitude that is explicitly confirmed in a more general context by the contemporary *Epitome de Caesaribus* and more wordily by Ammianus Marcellinus.[86]

Reactive Legislation · It is therefore hardly surprising that no central initiatives in religious policy can be ascertained for Gratian's period of rule. Like his father and uncle, Gratian did not issue general laws in matters of religion. In May 376 a rescript, an answer to a question, issued to a group of unknown, perhaps Gallic, bishops clarified the existing rules about their rights to perform certain judicial acts, and a ruling addressed to the *vicarius* of Italy a year later, probably also replying to a question posed by the recipient, confirmed that ecclesiastical personnel were to be exempt from taxation in the form of personal service to the state (*munera personalia*).[87] In Africa the Donatists remained suspect even after the collapse of Firmus's revolt, and no less than three laws—of 376, 377 and 379—addressed different aspects of the schism,[88] while in 378 a ruling issued to the *vicarius Romae* expelled the Donatist bishop Claudianus from Rome, though its main function was to deal with ongoing aspects of the old dispute between Damasus and his defeated opponent, Ursinus.[89] In Illyricum, after the battle of Adrianople, Gratian took over for his prefecture Valens's "tolerance edict" of 376, under which expelled Eastern Nicene bishops (including Meletius of Antioch and Peter of Alexandria) had returned to their cities.[90] In the turbulence of those months of imperial crisis Donatists, or perhaps others, had managed to persuade some highly placed person at the court at Sirmium to issue to them an official-looking favorable judgment, which, however, once generally known, was immediately revoked.[91]

A similar rescript was issued on appeal around 382 in connection with the followers of the Spanish ascetic Priscillian, whom their opponents classified as Manichaeans. This case also illustrates Gratian's basically reactive attitude in religious affairs. The Priscillianist controversy, which had begun in southern Spain sometime in the 370s, involved a particular group of ascetically inclined clergy led by Priscillian, whose teachings included the belief that baptism implied "the total abandonment of the fouling darkness of secular activities"[92] and paid particular attention to clerical celibacy. The movement gained scattered support as far afield as Aquitania, but it also provoked opposition among more traditionally minded representatives of the Spanish church, particularly Hyginus, the bishop of Cordoba, and Hydatius of Emerita, who seems to have taken the initiative in calling a small synod to discuss the problem, which met in October 380 in Saragossa and critically assessed the Priscillianists in their absence.[93] In 381 Priscillian was chosen bishop of Avila in an election that was formally sufficiently flawed to allow his opponents not to recognize it,[94] and in the further course of the controversy Hydatius, who had come under some pressure from the ascetic movement on account of his private life, appealed via Bishop Ambrose in Milan to Gratian against "pseudo-bishops and Manichaeans"[95]—disingenuously, it seems, since he had named no names—and a rescript was issued and presented to the responsible Spanish *vicarius*, denouncing such people in general terms.

Hydatius then tried to have the rescript applied to Priscillian and his associates, thereby provoking an appeal also from them, first to Bishop Damasus in Rome. When Damasus showed he wanted nothing to do with them, they traveled on to Milan, where Ambrose also gave them the cold shoulder; but they nevertheless managed to obtain a rescript from the master of the offices, Macedonius—no friend of Ambrose's—asserting that the original rescript did not apply to them.[96] As a result, Hydatius's fellow activist Ithacius of Ossonuba was summoned to the law court of the Spanish *vicarius*, the charge probably including calumny.[97]

Ithacius took to his heels and appealed—illegitimately, since he had not even waited for the trial—to the *vicarius*'s superior, the praetorian prefect of the Gauls in Trier, one Proculus Gregorius, who duly reported the case back to his own superior, the emperor Gratian, who was still in Milan. In Milan the affair came full circle and arrived back with the master of the offices, Macedonius, who not unreasonably again insisted that the correct court for the initial proceedings was none other than that of the *vicarius Hispaniarum*, where the case had begun, and Ithacius was ordered to be taken under military escort back to Spain to stand trial. He escaped from his guards, however, and found refuge in Trier with the local bishop Britto.[98]

As far as the imperial authorities in Milan were concerned, the matter could well have rested there, since they had no primary interest in pursuing it further. Another law from around the same time addressed to Hydatius, the praetorian prefect of Italy, seems at first sight to suggest a governmental initiative, since it was aimed at punishing converts to paganism, Judaism, and Manichaeism, in particular those who induced such apostasy, with loss of testamentary rights, but with the explicit cautious provision that nobody should benefit from a false accusation of those already deceased.[99] Here again, however, Gratian's advisers in fact remained within the legal traditions of the imperial government, since they were merely extending to the rest of the central prefecture a measure that Theodosius had already formulated for Illyricum, where the problem had come to his notice during the turbulences associated with the Gothic war.[100] None of this legislative activity shows the emperor taking the initiative.

Bishop Ambrose · The Gothic crisis in the Balkans had other accidental side effects on Western religious policy that could hardly have been foreseen. Gratian's periods of residence in Illyricum and northern Italy that the war made necessary, culminating in the permanent removal of the court from Trier to Milan in 381, brought him and his court into immediate personal contact with ecclesiastical problems that from distant Trier had offered a quite different perspective and urgency. These problems were inevitably personified by particularly prominent individuals and so received their characteristic nuances. Three persons—Theodosius, Ambrose, and Palladius—were especially important. Gratian's fellow emperor in the East, Theodosius, appointed in 379 for his military qualities, showed at first a brusque insensitivity to the complexities of Eastern ecclesiastical structures and set out initially, encouraged and helped by his largely Western team of administrators, to impose his own Western Nicene orthodoxy on his realm, much to the satisfaction of Western church leaders.[101] Gratian inevitably came under pressure to do likewise, particularly since the war brought him regularly to the Balkans and/or Italy and into contact with the aggressively Nicene bishop of Milan, Ambrose. These contacts intensified after the court arrived in Milan in 381.[102] During his months in Sirmium Gratian had been confronted, probably for the first time consciously, with the apparent importance of the dogmatic differences between the "homoians" and the Nicene form of Christianity. The nondogmatic attitude of his father Valentinian and his own essentially classical education at the hands of Ausonius in Trier must have largely spared him involvement with the details of theological arguments and hindered his ability to recognize their potential for political explosiveness. Although for the duration of the war he left the secular administration of Illyricum formally to Theodosius, the ecclesiastical structure remained unaffected by this;[103] the leading Illyrican "homoian" bishop, Palladius of Ratiaria, had access to Gratian, and he or other Illyrican bishops—perhaps especially the Nicene Anemius of Sirmium—seem to have brought him the idea of settling the dispute in rational discourse in a general council to be held at Aquileia in September 381.

When this idea was born and when the first instructions to attend were issued are unclear, just as the geographical range of the initial list of those instructed to attend is obscure.[104] It is difficult to imagine that Gratian's advisers can seriously have expected at best more than token representation from the war-torn Greek-speaking East. In a similar situation in 359 Constantius had summoned two councils, one in Rimini for the West and one in Seleukeia on the Kalykadnos for the East, well knowing that anything else was impracticable, but Gratian seems to have assured Palladius that he had summoned "Easterners" (*orientales*) to come—by

which, however, he may simply have meant Palladius's "homoian" associates (*consortes*) from his home in eastern Illyricum, currently under the
secular responsibility of Theodosius and ruled from Constantinople.[105]
This interpretation could be supported by a reference in a letter that Gratian wrote to the praetorian prefect Syagrius in the spring of 381 changing
the instructions of the "convocation." Originally, says Gratian, he had
ordered the bishops "of your diocese" to come; now he had changed his
mind on the advice of Ambrose and thought that a few bishops from
neighboring cities in Italy would be sufficient, and therefore the others
could spare themselves the hazards of the journey, if they so wished.[106]
This reference to the original plan is not easy to make sense of, as the
language must be nontechnical, "diocese" meaning merely "area of responsibility," since a praetorian prefect was responsible not merely for
one but for several dioceses in the technical administrative sense of the
word. Moreover, besides the official representatives (*legati*) of the Gallic
church, some bishops from Gaul, which was not included in Syagrius's
prefecture at all, took part,[107] so that the original official instruction to
attend must in any case have been wider than Syagrius's prefecture of
Italy and Africa. In view of the fact that Gratian also assured Palladius
in the summer of 381—rather disingenuously, since the second letter
had already been sent out—that "Easterners" had been instructed to attend,[108] we must assume that at least the Latin-speaking bishops from
eastern Illyricum, despite the war and Theodosius's formal responsibility
for the secular administration, had been part of the original plan. Only
so could Palladius have gained the impression that the council would be
a general one (*generale et plenum*).[109]

By the time the council met in September 381 the honorable, if naive,
original purpose outlined in Gratian's letter to Syagrius had been tor-
pedoed by Ambrose, who, by recommending restricting summonses to
attend to those loyal to him and the Nicene faith, now intended to trans-
form the council into an orthodox Nicene hunt for heretics. At the end
of it Palladius and his "homoian" associates would be condemned and,
as he hoped, dismissed from their sees by the imperial authorities. The
changed instructions to Syagrius are the first evidence we have for Ambrose's influence on Gratian, now that bishop and emperor were in regu-

lar contact in Milan. The changed instructions duly had their effect: in the event no bishop with a see east of Sirmium, except for the two prominent "homoians" Palladius of Ratiaria and Secundianus of Singidunum (Belgrade) came to Aquileia, but some few came from Gaul, including two official representatives (*legati*) of the Gallic church, and two official representatives from Africa. Together with Ambrose's Italian associates these men made up the thirty-six participants, and all but two of them, Palladius and Secundianus, were Nicenes loyal to Ambrose. When Palladius complained that Ambrose's influence behind the scenes had changed the agenda and the status of the council, and showed reluctance to enter into serious discussion without the presence and support of his fellow "homoians" from eastern parts, whom Gratian had assured him had been instructed to come, Ambrose's answer was that the original instruction still stood, in the sense that nobody had been prevented from coming: they could still have come had they wished to.[110] The council ended, as it had to, with the condemnation of Palladius and Secundianus as heretics, and thirty-four bishops appended their signatures to the minutes—unanimous except for the two who were condemned.

This was in the end a great success for Ambrose, but he had had to struggle for his influence at court. Perhaps in 379—the first occasion when he might have met the emperor personally—Gratian had demanded a statement of Ambrose's view of orthodoxy.[111] Perhaps the court was already contemplating a transfer to Milan, in which case the attitude of the bishop of the place became an important consideration. Ambrose turned this test into an attack on the "homoians," who still possessed an influential community in Milan. A respectful correspondence followed, with Gratian demanding further written evidence of Ambrose's views.[112] At some point a church, the possession of which was disputed—presumably by local "homoians," who until Ambrose's election seem to have dominated Milanese Christianity—was confiscated by the imperial authorities, until they had tested and been convinced of Ambrose's orthodoxy.[113] However, by Easter 381, when the court finally arrived in Milan, Ambrose's two tracts, *De fide* and *De spiritu sancto*, were complete and his influence at court was rising, to the extent that he was quickly able to persuade Gratian to alter the arrangements for the council at Aquileia.

The way in which Ambrose turned the planned plenary Council of Aquileia into a Nicene inquisition can in the last resort hardly have pleased the court, and Ambrose seems to have been aware of potential irritation, for in the subsequent letter he wrote on behalf of the council reporting the outcome—formally addressed to all the emperors, though only Gratian is named in the text of the letter, which suggests that it was forwarded only to Milan—he dwells at excessive length on the positive results of having restricted its participants. Moreover, though the secular arm is now requested to follow up the council's condemnation of Palladius and Secundianus by expelling them from their sees, there is no evidence that anything of the sort actually happened.[114] A further letter shows Ambrose, writing in the name of the council, trying to influence Theodosius to sort out ecclesiastical affairs in his area of responsibility by calling a council at Alexandria[115]—an equally ineffective action, which demonstrates the limits of Ambrose's influence at this time, even after Gratian's court had arrived in Milan. The imperial authorities at Milan had allowed themselves to be influenced by Ambrose, but they were not prepared to cause trouble in the provinces by following up the ecclesiastical decision by further action of their own.

One further action of Gratian's has often been regarded as an imperial initiative, perhaps again under the influence of Ambrose. Since the time of Augustus the Roman Senate House had contained a statue and an altar of the deified Victoria. Meetings of the Senate began with a short offering to her and, moreover, a group of traditional Roman priests had been supported out of public funds since Republican times, a practice kept up in the imperial period by the emperor as *pontifex maximus*. The altar of Victoria had already irritated Constantius II when he visited Rome in 357, perhaps particularly because its presence in the Senate House served to underline the embarrassing support that many prominent senators of the time had offered the recently defeated usurper—the victory over whom he was in effect celebrating there—and he had ordered it removed. After its replacement under Julian, the tolerant Valentinian, supposing he knew about it at all, had allowed it to remain. It can scarcely be an accident that once Gratian's court took up residence in Italy, the emperor repeated Constantius's action (though he never visited Rome himself) and indeed went even further: in the second half of 382 he had the altar removed again, but, despite his function as *pontifex maximus*, he also abolished the public subsidies for the traditional state cults and refused an audience to a senatorial delegation led by Symmachus, which came to Milan to protest.

This action cannot have just happened out of the blue. It was an administrative act and required an instruction addressed to the *praefectus urbi*. Most such localized instructions originated in the suggestions of the recipients, and since Gratian's government had otherwise not shown any initiative in religious affairs, merely reacting as did most other imperial administrations before his to problems or issues brought to their attention, there is no good reason to believe that this case was any different. Ambrose denied explicitly that Gratian's action was originally his idea[116] (though he doubtless supported it, just as he was prepared to defend it later), so it is reasonable to assume that the initiative was presented to Gratian by none other than the current prefect of the city, who would then have to carry it out. As has already been suggested,[117] the likeliest candidate was the great Christian aristocrat Anicius Auchenius Bassus, who doubtless intimated to Gratian that the Senate—which he formally represented—would now welcome this initiative. Since at this time Symmachus had no formal *locus standi*, beyond his membership in the Senate, while Auchenius Bassus as imperially appointed prefect of the city was head of the city administration and chairman of the Senate, it is not altogether surprising that the protest that Symmachus formulated did not receive any attention at court.

These actions under Gratian have become well known as a result of Symmachus's later attempt, when he himself was *praefectus urbi* in Rome in 384 after Gratian's death, to have the case reconsidered by Valentinian II. His Third *Relatio* to the emperor concerning the matter tells us nothing at all about the circumstances of Gratian's decision; but together with Ambrose's two eloquent replies, it seems quite soon to have become fairly well known in Christian intellectual circles in Italy. Outside Italy, however, the whole affair was little noticed, not even deserving a mention by the Eastern pagan writer Zosimus, which suggests that his contemporary pagan source Eunapius did not take note of the matter either.[118] It does, however, once again show the imperial government merely reacting to a suggestion (which, of course, suited it), rather than grasping an ideological initiative. There is, moreover, no convincing ancient evidence for Gratian's having taken the initiative to lay down the title *pontifex maximus* at this time—or ever—despite the almost universal modern assertion that he did so.[119]

Valentinian II and Magnus Maximus

The usurpation of Magnus Maximus and the resulting death of Gratian in August 383 shook the fabric of the Western Empire. In Milan Valentinian's second son, Valentinian II, a twelve-year-old boy, became automatically senior Augustus, though in practice he was totally controlled by his court advisers. Among them his mother Justina, who like her son had been kept in the background under Gratian's regime, attained a position of some influence as soon as Gratian's death became known. She was the offspring of a prominent Italian family, the Vettii; her father Iustus had governed the Italian province Picenum in the 350s, perhaps on behalf of the usurper Magnentius, to whom he was able to marry his daughter. After surviving the defeat of her husband and then the execution of her father, she was taken in marriage by Valentinian I following his elevation, and she bore the emperor a son and three daughters. Her brother Cerealis had been with the army on the Danube when Valentinian I died and was one of the influential clique that organized his young nephew's appointment by the field army as Augustus. Cerealis is not known to have had any further career, and Gratian's court officials were able to prevent Justina and Valentinian II from playing any public role until the usurpation by Magnus Maximus and Gratian's death catapulted Valentinian II into prominence in 383.[120]

The relevance of these events for religious affairs emerges from the fact that Justina, as did her son, favored the "homoian" version of the faith, which she had doubtless learned in her earlier career, and for which—apart from Ambrose and his Nicene catholic congregations—she found an existing tradition and community in Milan.[121] Maximus, on the other hand, played the Nicene card strongly in the hope of winning support for his usurpation from the influential Gallic clergy and from his aggressively Nicene fellow Spaniard, the Eastern emperor Theodosius. Ambrose's formidable, if not unchallengeable, position in Milan, which he had gradually built up under Gratian, now seemed potentially threatened from two sides, which presented the bishop with a dilemma: either he remained loyal to the child emperor in Milan, Valentinian II, despite the "homoian" faith of the boy and his closest entourage, or else he had to explore the possibility of supporting Maximus, who would be an efficient ruler and whose Nicene faith was unimpeachable, but who was a usurper and responsible for killing Gratian. The latter alternative must have seemed particularly attractive politically as long as the Nicene orthodox Theodosius showed no sign of taking serious action against Maximus; indeed in 384 Theodosius even recognized the usurper as Augustus.[122] The straight road of cooperation in religious affairs between Ambrose and the emperor resident in Milan, which he had traveled under Gratian and which had brought him success in the events leading up to the Council of Aquileia, seemed certain to become less smooth, whatever he did. The symbiosis between orthodox religion and legitimate imperial rule was seriously disturbed when a "heretic" embodied imperial legitimacy and an orthodox Nicene embodied usurpation.

The political importance of the influential bishop was, however, immediately recognized by Justina, who in a dramatic confrontation entrusted the boy emperor to him, at least so Ambrose was to assert a decade later, when both she and her son were already dead and could not contradict him.[123] The immediate context was Maximus's demand that Valentinian and his mother return to Trier and accept him as "father," and the contrary wish of the Italian political establishment—both pagan and Christian, it seems—that the young emperor remain resident in Italy.[124] Ambrose traveled to Trier on behalf of the court to gain time, on the pretext of negotiating. Part of his argument was that Valentinian could not be expected to travel with his widowed mother to Trier from Milan during the winter, and without his mother not at all, thus emphasizing the importance of Justina.[125] It was, as far as we know, the first time a bishop had ever been turned to use for a secular political objective at this level of imperial affairs, and it shows Ambrose throwing in his lot with the "heretical" Milanese court. Perhaps in the short term he had no real alternative. As was intended, the negotiations failed—Ambrose was not unreasonably later accused by Maximus of having deliberately misled him—but time was won and negotiations with Theodosius soon produced a temporarily acceptable status quo.

The death of Gratian and the immediate needs of the regime in Milan for Italian support gave the pagans in Rome new hope. In 384 Symmachus was *praefectus urbi* in Rome, and he obtained a majority in the Senate for making a new approach to the young emperor concerning the altar of Victoria and the public financing of the traditional cults. An elegantly formulated petition (his Third *Relatio*) was presented to the boy emperor. Had it not been for a brusque intervention by Ambrose, the general political crisis of the time might have encouraged the regime in Milan to think of winning the support of the rich and influential pagan senators by capitulating to their wishes, but the bishop demanded his pound of flesh for supporting the unloved regime in a virulent attack on Symmachus's request, the text of which he had not even seen. Amid an argument of varying quality, which included an open threat to sabotage the emperor's public appearance in church, he reminded the consistory of his own recent service to the regime and demanded that Symmachus's request be rejected.[126] As he himself formulated it on a later occasion, when the issue again became pressing, "the emperor listened to my proposal and did nothing except what the interest of our faith demanded." [127] In this way Ambrose exploited his secular service to promote his religious policy, but it was a dangerous game, and he could hardly expect to win so easily in a real conflict of interests.

The modern literature on the dispute is extensive,[128] but the matter achieved academic notoriety merely because Ambrose included the text of Symmachus's *relatio* in the tenth book of his own letters,[129] together with his own two eloquent replies to it. Ancient historiography, neither ecclesiastical nor even the pagan Zosimus following the contemporary Eunapius, knows anything of this allegedly major defeat for pagans, though it would have suited well both polemical pagan and triumphalist Christian purposes. Symptomatic is Ambrose's own biographer, Paulinus, who gets both the date and the circumstances quite wrong and only knows of the dispute, it seems, through Ambrose's "*libellus*," which he calls splendid (*praeclarissimus*). For him this literary product was the main lasting achievement of the dispute.[130] It therefore seems that modern writers, many of whom attach an epochal importance to Symmachus's defeat, may themselves be victims of Ambrose's self-centered publicity machine.

Ambrose did not have it all his own way. His influence was dependent on his access to the court, but at the same time limited by it. The ambiguity of his position in Milan emerged clearly the following year when the court requested, perhaps in anticipation of Easter, that he assign a basilica for the services of their "homoian" community, which had recently been strengthened by new arrivals: after Gratian's Western army went over to Maximus at Paris, Valentinian II's generals had taken to recruiting among the Goths from the Balkans, who insofar as they were Christians at all had been converted by "homoian" priests when they entered the empire under Valens. At about the same time, a new leader for the "homoians," the Balkan preacher Auxentius of Durostorum, who had grown up with the famous Ulfila, the missionary of the Goths, was accepted by the Milanese "homoians" as their bishop, and for the first time since his own episcopal election presented Ambrose with a real challenge on his home ground. Auxentius certainly had the support of Justina and Valentinian, but beyond them also of those imperial advisers who may well have felt that Ambrose was overplaying his hand.[131] In 385 Ambrose was invited to a meeting of the consistory in order to receive an official imperial request to be able to use a church outside the city walls known as the Basilica Portiana. He succeeded in turning the occasion into a massive demonstration of public solidarity by refusing the use of the building. A large crowd, doubtless organized by Ambrose himself, collected in front of the imperial residence where the meeting was taking place and resisted even military threats to remove them. Not surprisingly, only Ambrose was able to calm them by the assurance that "nobody would invade any basilica";[132] equally unsurprising, however, is that his personal responsibility for the dramatic scene was surely noted, and that in the last resort the incident failed to strengthen his position at court.

Nevertheless, Ambrose remained useful as an intermediary between Milan and Trier, and he allowed himself to be so used again. A second mission later in 385, possibly even as late as the winter of 385/86, ostensibly to recover Gratian's body for official burial in Italy, ended in a slanging match in Maximus's consistory. The Nicene orthodox usurper charged Ambrose, doubtless with some justice, with having misled him on his first mission and so prevented his entering Italy. The charge rankled Ambrose, and he repeated his reply, denying the charge in detail, in an official letter written to Valentinian on his return to Italy. Some months later, when the dispute about the basilica blew up into a major crisis and Ambrose was himself charged by the court with the tyrannical behavior of a usurper of power, he protested in a private letter to his sister Marcellina, later published, that not even Maximus had charged him with that.[133]

While Ambrose was in Trier, the Priscillianist dispute was approaching its brutal end. Maximus's usurpation and his resultant need for support in Gaul led to his playing the catholic card against the "heretical" Valentinian II in a bid for support for his usurping regime among bishops and the orthodox elite in Gaul. As a result Ithacius, who had taken refuge with Bishop Britto of Trier, now found himself unexpectedly in a position to resuscitate the Priscillianist controversy at the level of central imperial jurisdiction.[134] It must have seemed that the new emperor had come to him as a *deus ex machina*. Maximus's administration was, however, shrewd enough to respect the widespread conviction, most successfully put into practice by Valentinian I, that ecclesiastical matters should wherever possible be decided by the ecclesiastical authorities, and that the secular arm should hold back, unless activities of secular interest were involved. This was often a gray area with overlapping implications; now the Priscillianists were charged with calumny, Manichaeism, and magical practices, which indeed originated in the religious sphere, but touched on both secular and religious areas. The first suggestion for the solution of the problem was that a synod of bishops should decide the case in Bordeaux—outside the Spanish diocese, presumably so that no purely local interests or pressures would play any part, yet close enough to it to avoid unnecessary travel. But the damage had already been done by Ithacius when he first appealed to Gratian and so involved the secular authorities, and no synod of bishops could turn the clock back and ignore the unhappy precedent. This time it was Priscillian and his supporters, despite having some local adherents in Aquitaine, who objected to the synod and brought the matter back to the attention of the new emperor Maximus and his praetorian prefect Euodius in Trier. It was a bad mistake, as it turned out, but like Ithacius they seem to have had no doubts about the legitimacy of the new imperial regime and therefore its authority to judge cases originating in Spain and Gaul; they made no approach to Valentinian II in Milan.

The fact that the "trial of the Priscillianists" took place at Trier meant that Italian influence was effectively excluded. When Ambrose arrived in Trier again in 385, he found the court full of bishops busying themselves with the Priscillianists and had to admit in a letter to his employer in Milan that he had no influence with them.[135] A little later, when Siricius, the new bishop of Rome, wrote to Magnus Maximus objecting to what had happened, he received the polite but decisive reply that when he knew all the facts he would surely have a different opinion.[136] Some Gallic bishops, along with the immediately involved parties, also came to Trier to participate in the investigation, among them Martin of Tours, who, though he felt the church should itself settle its internal affairs, nevertheless was not prepared to desert the orthodox camp; while condemning Priscillian and his supporters, he thought the procedures were wrong and deemed excessive the capital punishment that was finally agreed upon. He was certainly not the only observer to feel this way.[137] In the last resort the decision to condemn the Priscillianists fell to the secular court of the praetorian prefect Euodius, and the decision to execute the central figures and to exile those on the margins of the movement was taken by the figurehead champion of catholic orthodoxy, the emperor Magnus Maximus. He doubtless hoped his decision would encourage the consolidation of Gallic and Spanish orthodoxy in support of his imperial rule.[138] The critical charges were of a secular nature and concerned the magical practices that the investigation had turned up. In investigating these charges and punishing the guilty Maximus was in fact acting no differently than Valentinian and Valens had when they were confronted with magical practices in influential social circles. Maximus's success in wooing the orthodox by his handling of this affair was, however, mixed. It was certainly a success for him that the charismatic Martin of Tours joined those who condemned Priscillian, and that on the sudden death of the bishop of Trier, Britto, Martin joined with Hydatius and Ithacius in choosing and consecrating Felix as his successor.[139] But Martin's participation did not prevent Felix's consecration being widely regarded as stained with the blood of those who had not deserved to die, and thus it caused a schism in the Gallic church.

While these tense events were going on in Trier, the court in Milan worked out a new tactic to settle its burning question of the availability of a suitable church. Ambrose's patent failure in his second diplomatic mission to Trier had drastically reduced his usefulness, and more substantial provocation could now be risked. When the emperor's personal religious needs were seriously challenged, as was now happening, then religious questions attained a particularly virulent secular dimension, which in the last resort could only be resolved by use of secular methods. Ambrose may have won the first round with his judiciously organized riotous demonstration, but in January 386 the imperial authorities employed the full force of the secular apparatus of government and issued a law to the praetorian prefect Eusignius explicitly asserting the rights of the "homoians" to assemble and threatening with capital punishment those who created disturbances or tried to subvert the intention of the law in other ways.[140] The new law was a direct official reply to Ambrose's populist rejection of the court's attempt to solve the problem in what seemed to it a rational and worthy manner. The use of the legislative machinery to solve a local ecclesiastical problem shows how high feelings were running at court, for, leaving military action aside, the state was here employing its most potent means of enforcing civil obedience: if consensual respect for the law did not work, force remained the only option. The stakes were high, and Maximus, after his condemnation and execution of the Priscillianists, stood in the wings in Trier as an active and proven champion of Nicene orthodoxy; now recognized as an emperor by Theodosius — his praetorian prefect Euodius was accepted as a consul in 386 — Maximus was ready to seize any excuse to move on Italy, as Ambrose had already reported to Valentinian a few months before after his second mission to Trier.[141]

The court must have thought Ambrose would respect Valentinian's wishes, expressed as they were in the sonorous rhetoric of an imperial edict, but it was again frustrated. Shortly before Easter the imperial request for a church, as in the previous year, was repeated, this time naming the "New Church" situated within the city walls, which Ambrose used as his cathedral. Ambrose again refused to negotiate, whereupon the imperial authorities simply sequestrated the Basilica Portiana outside the city walls, and workers immediately began to decorate it with purple cloths in preparation for an imperial visit. The challenge was there, and Ambrose took it up, causing the Basilica Portiana to be occupied "spontaneously" by part of his congregation, and stirring up emotions by using language in his preaching to the faithful in the cathedral reminiscent of the time of the persecutions. He rejected every attempt to negotiate. On the Wednesday of Holy Week soldiers were stationed to observe and preserve the peace, which gave Ambrose the opportunity of claiming to be besieged, though in fact any who wished to enter the church were let through the picket lines. However, by the next day, Maundy Thursday, it was clear that Ambrose's congregation could only be moved by force; and as the authorities were not prepared to risk this in a church, the workmen began to remove the imperial decorations. Ambrose had kept himself out of direct participation in the confrontation at the Basilica Portiana by staying in his cathedral. His part was merely to reject offers to negotiate, and so he sought to depict the confrontation as an unorganized expression of popular resistance to an unreasonable imperial demand; but by the end of the affair his pretense could no longer be kept up, and it became obvious that the claimed spontaneity was false and that the guiding responsibility lay indeed with Ambrose. His opponents chose extremely strong language to express what they thought of him, even going so far as to call him usurper (*tyrannus*). He expected the struggle to continue after the Easter celebrations.[142]

After Easter a new tactic was tried. The court suggested a disputation between Ambrose and Auxentius in the presence of the consistory and of "judges" named by each side. Perhaps remembering how he had treated Palladius and Secundianus at Aquileia and fearing that he would now suffer in a similar way, Ambrose shut himself up with the most ardent members of his congregation in one of the city churches and justified his refusal to participate in the "hearing" at court by alleging that his people would not let him go. When the government again posted pickets to guarantee public order—before Easter Ambrose's people had embarrassingly committed some acts of violence, so this may have seemed justified—Ambrose had another opportunity to provoke a siege mentality in his people by preaching resistance to persecutors.[143] In the end the imperial initiative fizzled out, and Ambrose consolidated his prestige with his loyal congregation by conveniently "finding" and escorting into the city the bones of two "forgotten" local Milanese martyrs, Gervasius and Protasius, which he buried in an imposing ceremony in his new church, the Basilica Ambrosiana.[144]

The bruising dispute with the court had produced ominous noises from Trier. Although it does not mention Ambrose by name, an extant letter by Maximus, formally undated but, to judge from its subject matter, clearly belonging to this time, raises objections to Valentinian's recent attacks on the catholic church and the faith that "the whole of Italy and Africa believe in, that Gaul, Aquitania, the whole of Spain, and venerable Rome itself are proud of."[145] The general tone is not immediately threatening, but, in expressing more sorrow than anger, it is decisive enough. Whether Ambrose felt comfortable with this unsolicited support from the unloved Gallic usurper may be doubted. The disastrous mix of secular and religious affairs, which the dispute about the basilicas had brought into the open, did not bode well for either the church or the state. Both the politician Ambrose and his "homoian" opponents in Milan were effectively playing into the hands of the usurper, so much so that when early in 387 Maximus finally made his move into northern Italy he met no resistance, and Valentinian, his mother Justina, and some of their most prominent supporters saw no alternative to fleeing to Thessalonica and appealing to Theodosius for help.[146]

Virtual silence reigns over the eloquent Ambrose's activities during the year in which Maximus occupied the imperial residence in Milan. Nothing is to be gleaned from either his biographer Paulinus or Ambrose himself, whose later edited letters are our primary source of information about his activities under Gratian, Valentinian, and again under Theodosius. Paulinus indeed asserts that Ambrose cut off Maximus from his communion table, advising him that he should do penance for shedding the blood of his innocent master if he wished for consideration before God, but the context is conventionally moralizing, not historical: Maximus refused, and he therefore lost his kingdom and his life. The precise circumstances and details of Ambrose's relationship with Maximus remain obscure; it may even be that Paulinus, who did not know Ambrose well until he became his secretary in 394, had no good information. A false inference that Ambrose had excommunicated Maximus for killing Gratian might, however, have been suggested by Ambrose's report to Valentinian about his second embassy to Trier in 385, in which he says he dissociated himself from those bishops who were demanding the death penalty for deviants (that is, the Priscillianists) while being in communion with Maximus, and was then dismissed by Maximus on their suggestion.[147] It is most improbable that Ambrose never wrote anything to anybody about his relationship with Maximus, yet nothing from this period of his life was ever published by him or his friends. We can only conclude that after Maximus's defeat by Theodosius in 388 it seemed inopportune to remind later generations of the arrangements that the catholic bishop of imperial Milan must surely have made with the efficient catholic usurper residing in his episcopal city: apart from the possibility of excommunication, they cannot have been anything much to be proud of.

· · ·

The post-Julianic emperors, from Valentinian I to Valentinian II, seem not to have adopted a programmatic attitude toward the religious affairs of the empire. In view of the serious difficulties caused by Constantius's and Julian's direct personal interference in the developing religious structure, this benign neglect must have seemed a practical necessity, and none of the rulers took a major initiative. For them security problems clearly had a much higher priority than any attempt to achieve a unified Christian orthodoxy or to persecute the last pagans. This did not mean that no action was taken anywhere; but where development occurred, the steps taken by the imperial court were a response to emerging problems. Questions concerning law and order in the major cities had a clear priority for Valentinian I and Valens, after the massive disturbances caused by Julian's aggressive program of universal tolerance. In Italy even Gratian's removal of the altar of Victoria from the Senate House in Rome and his suppression of the financial support for traditional pagan cults were probably not programmatic; they almost certainly were merely the result of glad compliance with an initiative begun by Christian senators.

Usurpations also had a religious dimension, but only a minor one. When in the East the Macedonianist bishops of the Marmara region refused support to the usurper Procopius and remained loyal to the "Arian" Valens, they profited by being left unhindered in office once the revolt was over. When the "Arian" Lucius tried to exploit imagined imperial support to supplant Athanasius in Alexandria, he was removed from the city for causing a disturbance and was only allowed to return after Athanasius's death, when there was a chance of his taking over without much dispute. During the usurpation of Magnus Maximus his staunch catholic belief might have seemed a recommendation to the catholic establishment in Italy against the legitimate but "Arian" Valentinian II. Yet even for Bishop Ambrose and the Roman bishop Siricius secular legitimacy had higher standing than religious orthodoxy; despite the sporadic tensions that darkened the relationship between Valentinian II and Ambrose at the local level in Milan, Ambrose made no secret of the fact that he regarded Valentinian as his emperor. Programmatic religious change promoted actively by the imperial court must have seemed a thing of the past until Theodosius came to Constantinople. But even there, as we shall see, the status quo conditioned the imperial response.

CHAPTER VIII

THEODOSIUS

Ambrose, preaching a memorial sermon on Theodosius forty days after his death in 395, asserted that Theodosius, even while dying, was more concerned with the state of the church than with his own predicament.[1] Augustine, a couple of decades later, praised his restless energy in aiding the church against heretics "with most just and compassionate laws"; he rejoiced more to be a member of the church than to be ruling on earth, and he ordered the images of the heathens to be overturned everywhere.[2] By the sixth century the Eastern chronicler Marcellinus Comes summed him up as "a very religious man and a promoter of the catholic church," an "orthodox emperor."[3] The church, therefore, following Ambrose's lead, very soon canonized Theodosius into a paragon of ecclesiastical orthodoxy on the imperial throne, but for Ambrose himself Theodosius's personal qualities stood firmly in the foreground, and they dominate the memorial sermon. The emperor had been intimately involved in provoking the crises in which these particular personal qualities, it could be claimed, were above all to be witnessed. The provocations left lingering bruises.

Ecclesiastical praise for a man who had been chosen for the imperial throne above all because it was hoped he might manage to find a solution for the defense emergency caused by the Gothic invasion, as it presented itself after the battle of Adrianople—and who indeed did so— might well cause some surprise. It will therefore be advisable to examine the basis for the ecclesiastical judgments in some detail, as Theodosius undoubtedly gave the Eastern church a direction for development that conditioned its adaptation to the structure of the empire over the next century and created the symbiosis of church and state that characterized the Eastern part of the empire long after the Western part had disintegrated. This was one of Theodosius's greatest long-term achievements, which, however, could play no part in forming the contemporary judgments about him cited above, which were based rather on doctrinal or personal moral factors.

Policy and attitudes toward religious affairs under Theodosius were, perhaps more than at any time since the death of Constantine, conditioned by external secular factors. The emergency created by the misfortunes of the Gothic war had brought him to power; the need to consolidate the empire, once the immediate crisis was over, influenced the imperial response to all other matters, not excluding religion. Theodosius and large parts of his entourage were Westerners and men of action, who in general seem to have had little sympathy for the undisciplined but much-loved theological speculations of Eastern intellectuals in the church that made the church in the East as an institution currently so unsuitable as supporting partner for the imperial government, the role that Constantine had originally conceived for it.[4] The problems, if one took them seriously, were complex, having both structural and dogmatic aspects. The dogmatic turbulence created by Valens's relaxation of the ban on certain undisciplined Eastern Nicene troublemakers, who did not hesitate to depict the form of death of the "heretic" emperor as reasonable punishment for his "heresy,"[5] was the ecclesiastical pendant to the administrative confusion created by the Gothic victory at Adrianople.

Characteristic of the general uncertainty and the inchoate structure of the Eastern empire was the status of the city of Constantinople. Founded by Constantine and piously developed by Constantius and Valens, it was still regarded by many traditionalists as a foreign body on Eastern soil; but, more important, it had never become a standing imperial residence, since all emperors after its foundation had continued to take personal command in wars that—except for the current Gothic crisis—had taken place as far distant from "New Rome" as from "Old Rome." Ecclesiastically Constantinople had no specific outstanding status, its bishop being—as successor to that of pre-Constantinian Byzantium—merely subordinate to the metropolitan of the province Europa, the bishop of Herakleia (the city originally called Perinthos); and this state of affairs continued, despite Constantinople's huge physical growth, which by Theodosius's time had made it economically dominant in the eastern Mediterranean area. It had already, it seems, outgrown the city walls built by Constantine. In the East, however, the apostolic sees of Antioch and Alexandria, followed by that of Jerusalem, were traditionally at the ecclesiastical forefront, and dogmatic disagreements between these sees dominated the discourse of the political-theological establishment of the East. In Constantinople it was hardly surprising that the "homoians" dominated affairs at the time of Theodosius's accession, since Constantius and Valens had seen to it that the prestigious new city on the Bosphorus, even if they did not reside there, was governed ecclesiastically by a member of their "homoian" imperial church. When Theodosius became emperor in 379, the leader was the generally well-respected Demophilus. The Nicene community in the city was tiny and until Valens's "tolerance edict" had been leaderless. By the time of Theodosius's accession, the Eastern Nicenes led by Basil of Caesarea and Meletius in Antioch had pressured Basil's old friend Gregory of Nazianzos to leave his monastic retreat in the Thekla sanctuary near Seleukeia on the Kalykadnos in Kilikia and go to Constantinople. By Easter 379 he had arrived and begun to organize the small Nicene community, which indeed was so small that it met in a private house. All the church buildings of the city and their paraphernalia were controlled by Demophilus and those who shared his "homoian" persuasion.[6]

Some time elapsed before Theodosius and his advisers decided how to deal with the hot potato that was Constantinople. After his appointment on 17 January 379 Theodosius avoided Constantinople and first took up residence in Thessalonica, the main city of southern Illyricum, which under the imperial division between Valentinian I and Valens had remained Western. The well-fortified city, strategically placed and equipped with excellent harbor facilities, provided a practical base with relatively easy sea communications with East and West, should the land routes be threatened by marauding Goths. For the duration of the war Gratian had agreed to transfer Illyricum to Eastern administration.[7] Theodosius's decision not to use Constantinople as his base for the war was doubtless taken above all for strategic reasons; it brought with it, however, the additional advantage that the court won time to inform itself about persons and possibilities in Constantinople, before Theodosius committed himself to a specific course of action. General information reached Thessalonica from Constantinople via frequent visits of leading officials and representative leaders of opinion, such as Themistius,[8] but in ecclesiastical affairs a trustworthy expert was on the spot in Acholius, the local bishop of Thessalonica. Acholius, however, was by no means a neutral and unbiased adviser. As with the secular administration of the Macedonian diocese, the formal ecclesiastical links of the church of Thessalonica were stronger with the West than with the East, so that while Acholius was in regular correspondence with Damasus in Rome and constituted a rare pillar of Nicene orthodoxy in the Greek-speaking parts of Illyricum, the bridge position of his see in Greek Thessalonica made it easy for him to follow developments in the rest of the Greek-speaking East. Given this background, it is hardly surprising that among his closest friends and informants were the Nicene-oriented Alexandrians, who since the time of Athanasius also maintained close relations with Rome.

The long residence of the court in Thessalonica, together with its general Western composition and ecclesiastical orientation, preconditioned Theodosius to favor the Nicenes in the East, even if they were still merely a noisy and publicity-conscious minority. There is no reason to think that Theodosius was initially more committed or knowledgeable in doctrinal matters than his immediate predecessors had been, or — despite the posthumous praise of catholic writers — that he initially indulged in more than a conventional level of piety; whether he regarded himself consciously as "Nicene," rather than generally "Christian," may even be doubted. But it seems clear that he took the view, when confronted by the doctrinally turbulent state of the Eastern church — and advised in Thessalonica by the committed Nicene Acholius — that it would be better for the empire if the church were unified and able to offer solid moral backing for imperial decisions, and that this would be best achieved if all shared the same doctrinal position as the emperor, the commander in chief. This view was by no means new; indeed in principle it had been the basis of all imperial religious policy since Constantine, but Constantius's intense commitment to promoting doctrinal unity by forcing agreement had in practice led to a serious doctrinal split between East and West, which had been accidentally reinforced by the formal administrative division along the same general lines undertaken by Valentinian and Valens.

New, however, were the urgency and energy with which the emperor tackled the problem, the consistent and increasingly authoritarian way he kept at it, and—for the East—the Nicene (Western) doctrine that he proposed as the unifying doctrine for his imperial church. For the first time a systematic attempt was made to use all possibilities offered by the authority of the secular administration, including legislation, to put into power within the church those who supported the doctrinal position favored by the emperor. The urgency did not, however, result primarily from a deeply felt personal dogmatic conviction of Theodosius, as later ecclesiastical mythmakers maintained, but rather from a cool analysis of how the military crisis of the empire was to be tackled and how its structure could be made adequate to withstand the social, military, and economic challenges presented by the Gothic presence in Illyricum and Thrace. This emerges clearly from an analysis of Theodosius's priorities: he was concerned that his administrators be given clear legal guidelines to ensure that only those people of whom he approved should gain control of the churches—their buildings, personnel, and possessions—in the cities of the empire. In the last resort what mattered was the exercise of patronage and local influence that went along with command of the churches' material circumstances. These were to be monopolized and employed in the interest of consolidating the consensual structure of the empire, essential factors for winning the war. Avoidance of the ruinous ecclesiastical competitiveness that had characterized recent times lay therefore in the interest of a common political objective.

It was to be a stony uphill path, not made easier by those of his own persuasion who wished to make use of the "orthodox emperor" for their own ends, as soon as it became clear that Theodosius did not intend to continue Valens's favoring of the "homoians," or by those revanchist extremists who exploited the favorable climate at the center to pursue local agendas of their own in the provinces. The year 379 passed in warfare with the Goths, but by February 380 Theodosius was ready to take up the challenge presented by the state of the Eastern church. His initial step was to tackle the problems presented by the status of the church in

Constantinople: first, the Nicene "orthodoxy" of the bishop, as well as his personal suitability for the post in an imperial residence, had to be guaranteed; second, the status of the bishopric within the grown structure of the church needed adjusting to match the status of the city as future imperial residence; and, third, the hinterland of the city, both in Europe and in Asia, required priority attention in view of the function that the hoped-for ecclesiastical unity was to serve in the consolidation process of the public administration.

All these aims could not be achieved at once — or by the same means. Most urgent were the questions concerning Constantinople itself because once the war was over Thessalonica, Theodosius's chosen base, would according to the agreement with Gratian return to Western administration, along with the rest of Illyricum. The first move was to address the urban population of Constantinople in an edict, doubtless directed to them via the office of the *praefectus urbi*, who must have published it in the city, given that "the people" of Constantinople as such possessed no official organ capable of receiving an official communication. This edict broke new ground, and certainly had to reflect the advisory activity of Bishop Acholius, since it is the first known secular law that included in its preamble a positive definition of what Theodosius chose to regard as religious orthodoxy:

> We wish the citizens of all cities that the moderation of Our Clemency rules to practice that form of religion which, as the religious tradition introduced by himself and reaching out until the present day maintains, Holy Peter the Apostle brought to the Romans, and which it is evident that Bishop Damasus and Peter, bishop of Alexandria, a man of apostolic holiness, follow: that is, that we should believe, in accordance with apostolic teaching and the doctrine of the evangelists, in the single divine being of the Father, the Son, and the Holy Spirit, within an equal majesty and a Holy Trinity. We command persons accepting this rule to embrace the name of catholic Christians; but the rest, whom we judge to be out of their minds and insane, shall suffer the disgrace attached to heretical dogma, their meeting places shall not bear the name "church,"

they are first to be stricken by punishment from God, but later by the vengeance of our passion, which we shall have assumed in accordance with the judgment of heaven.[9]

This edict, there can be no doubt, represented an imperial initiative, much influenced by Theodosius's Western entourage, to attend to the perceived problems of the church in Constantinople and so prepare the way for an imperial residence in the city. There is no suggestion that the initial impetus came from Constantinople itself. Despite the imperial rhetoric of its preamble, which has led to much misunderstanding in modern times, it had a strictly limited function: it was directed explicitly to the people of Constantinople and aimed at putting control of the church of Constantinople into the hands of a bishop whom Theodosius and his Western advisers could accept as representing the Western majority position on the main trinitarian question. There were sufficient precedents to justify secular executive action to remove unsatisfactory persons from bishoprics and to proscribe unacceptable liturgical practices. This was, however, the first time that the secular legislative process had been used to influence the appointment of a bishop by limiting in advance the circle of candidates through a positive formulation defining what exactly a man needed to believe in order to be acceptable to the emperor. The edict was, of course, also a transparent statement of imperial support for the currently very small Nicene faction in Constantinople. The reference to the Alexandrian Peter and Damasus as the two "norm bishops," along with the lack of mention of the two current Antiochian representatives of Nicene orthodoxy, Paulinus and Meletius, is a sign of the strong Western orientation of the edict, which, formulated in Thessalonica, inevitably had to have relied on the advice of Acholius. The bishop of Thessalonica must therefore be seen as having been responsible for the naming of his own close ecclesiastical associates as "norm bishops." This modus operandi, however comprehensible in an edict formulated in Thessalonica with the help of Acholius, can hardly have been wholly pleasing to the Nicene organizer in Constantinople, Gregory of Nazianzos, who had been brought up in the competing Antiochene-Cappadocian tradition, in which his supporters, including Meletius, were all to be found. Their absence from the number of designated "norm bishops" seems to provide proof that Gregory was not consulted in advance about the imperial initiative made in his favor.[10]

Constantinople

The message contained in the edict from Thessalonica was in due course received and understood in Constantinople, and Nicene candidates prepared themselves for an episcopal election. Gregory then obtained a letter from Peter in Alexandria confirming that they were in communion, thus supplying the evidence of his orthodoxy precisely in the form that the edict demanded.[11] But to his chagrin he was not the only candidate. An Alexandrian, a man called Maximus who was nicknamed "the Cynic" because he behaved and dressed like a pagan philosopher, had like Gregory also been resident in Constantinople for some time and moved in Nicene circles. In the course of 380 a group of three Egyptian bishops who happened to be in Constantinople—Gregory alleged they had been sent for the purpose by the wily Alexandrian bishop Peter, who had certainly also issued a communion letter for Maximus—secretly elected Maximus to be bishop, as canon law formally allowed. Maximus promptly ordained some clergy, but the closely bound Nicene community in Constantinople, which had not even been consulted by the three Egyptians, refused to accept Maximus, who thereupon felt it advisable to leave the imperial city in some haste. He soon turned up in Thessalonica, late in the summer of 380, where his appeal to Theodosius personally was turned down. The reason is not known, but it can be guessed at: if Maximus was not even acceptable to the current small Nicene community in Constantinople—for whatever reason—he was clearly unsuitable as an imperial protégé who would need to work hand in hand both with the orthodox community and the imperial government to create a unified church there.

The insensitive attempt by Peter of Alexandria to gain influence in Constantinople for his see by putting his own candidate on the bishop's throne had thus failed. Maximus may have been doctrinally pure, but he was socially unacceptable in Constantinople. However, Maximus did not despair. He first tried his luck in Alexandria itself, where the secular authorities, always conscious of the dangers of civil unrest developing from religious dispute, quickly expelled him; he then turned up in Rome, where Damasus, perhaps informed in advance by Acholius, also rejected him. After successive rejections he found a more sympathetic hearer in Milan, where he presented Gratian with a booklet on the faith, which he claimed to have composed himself. The tract not only convinced Ambrose that Maximus was orthodox and that his appointment in Constantinople was canonical, but even enticed a letter from Ambrose to Theodosius supporting this view, which caused no small irritation at the Eastern court. Theodosius might well have wondered whether with such friends he needed enemies.[12]

Before Theodosius entered Constantinople on 24 November 380, his personal situation was further complicated by his suffering an illness so serious that he felt near death, and in the emergency he let himself be baptized by Acholius.[13] He recovered, as we know, but his baptism put him potentially at a disadvantage in some ecclesiastical matters, at least in argument, were he to run into disagreement with a bishop who chose to exert his moral authority. This situation made it politically even more urgent to find a suitable person for the bishop's throne in Constantinople. Two actions concerning religious affairs mark Theodosius's first weeks in Constantinople. The edict from Thessalonica issued on 28 February 380 had threatened the Constantinopolitans with divine punishment for noncompliance, until such time as Theodosius himself took action. Since the threat of divine punishment alone had so far had no perceptible effect on the "homoians" of Constantinople and there was no obvious sign of its being realized imminently, Theodosius immediately summoned their bishop Demophilus to him.[14]

Demophilus's opponent Gregory was certain that Theodosius's attempt to convince the widely respected and influential Demophilus to accept the Nicene definition of the faith was seriously meant, and he may well have been right, since success would indeed have solved many of Theodosius's problems at one blow.[15] The edict from Thessalonica had made it a secular offense to hold church property in the city while rejecting the Nicene formula, and Theodosius as highest judge in the state and interpreter of his own edict felt naturally empowered by the secular tradition to decide finally whether or not those who held church property in Constantinople complied with his law. To Gregory's satisfaction but Theodosius's disappointment the emperor felt compelled to decide that they did not. Thereupon the popular Demophilus departed from the walled area of the city of Constantinople, leaving behind him an angry and hostile congregation to witness Gregory's takeover of the bishop's cathedral, which was only accomplished with the support of a military escort, commanded by the emperor in person. The Goths had failed to conquer Constantinople, but it must have seemed to many of the faithful that their city had nevertheless been taken by storm. It was no auspicious beginning for the plan to consolidate church and state in catholic symbiosis.[16]

The Council of Constantinople · Once the churches and their administration had been removed from the authority of Demophilus, plans were made to consolidate these initial steps by formally electing a new bishop for Constantinople and dealing with other local problems. Since the time of Constantine the traditional way to resolve ecclesiastical problems serious enough to trouble the emperor had been for him to summon a church council. Theodosius followed precedent and convoked a council, which was to elect a bishop for Constantinople—under the prevailing circumstances, the man elected would, of course, have to be someone approved by Theodosius—and to make decisions about other outstanding ecclesiastical problems. Serious theological discussion of doctrine was ruled out from the start, since only convinced Nicene bishops were instructed to attend, with Gregory and Acholius presumably deciding who was suitable.[17] The only minor exception to the rule was a group of thirty-six "Macedonianists" from the neighboring Asiatic provinces, whose form of belief on the basic trinitarian question was thought to be so close to the Nicene formula that it was felt—not for the first time[18]— that agreement with the sect ought to be possible. It proved not to be, and the Macedonianists went home before the first formal session of the council began, leaving the out-and-out Nicenes to themselves when the council assembled in plenary session in May 381.

The winter prior to the council saw further initiatives. The instigators of the edict of Thessalonica seem to have been satisfied with its effectiveness in providing a basis in secular law for Theodosius's expulsion of Demophilus and his "homoian" clergy from the churches of Constantinople. They therefore constructed a similarly phrased edict for Illyricum, which was issued to Eutropius, the praetorian prefect for Illyricum, on 10 January 381.[19] The differences between them can be explained by the differing historical development and the different geographical structure of the administrative areas affected by the edicts: the edict from Thessalonica was intended to prepare the people of a single city—Constantinople—for change and to give the emperor himself a firm legal basis for immediate action, whereas the edict to Eutropius was a law issued to the head of a regional imperial administration, its formal function being to provide a legal basis for actions in his law court, which might arise from anywhere within his huge prefecture. For Illyricum it was judged appropriate to lay more emphasis on the eradication of heresy, with regard to which the Photinians, the Arians ("homoians"), and the Eunomians—of which the first two are known to have been particularly strong in Illyricum—are explicitly named. There follows a list of specific selected phrases taken from the Nicene Creed, acceptance of which would serve to guarantee orthodoxy (in lieu of the certificates of communion with Damasus or Peter of Alexandria required by the edict from Thessalonica for Constantinople). The purpose of the list in a secular law seems clear: to give a secular judge, who inevitably was not competent to decide on the finer points of theology—he may well not even have been a Christian—clear instructions about the critical features of the Nicene Creed to which he needed to pay particular attention in judging cases brought before his court. Then come the penalties:

> Those who do not follow these same terms of faith should cease to bear the name of true religion, which because of the deceit they practice they are not entitled to, and they should be marked down because of this flagrant delinquency. They shall be removed absolutely from the threshold of every church, since we forbid all heretics to conduct meetings within the cities, and, should any violence break out, we order them to be expelled from the city walls, thus

ejecting their madness, so that catholic churches in the whole world might be restored to all orthodox bishops who hold the Nicene faith.[20]

It seems clear that this edict to Eutropius was aimed against those currently controlling churches and their property in Illyricum — "bishops" and clerics or other leaders of "heresies." Their expulsion from the cities, the main centers of population and economic activity, would remove them from their sources of wealth and influence, and so ensure that the cities remained loyal to the new imperial administration (or, at least, had fewer points of conflict with it). The fact that the rural population was not an objective of this law shows that its main purpose was ecclesiastical-administrative and was not in itself intended as a major step in the conversion of the whole population of the empire to Nicene Christianity, despite the globalizing rhetoric about "the whole world." In Illyricum, where "homoian" Goths in the meanwhile occupied large tracts of land in rural areas, this would have been not only impractical but certainly also provocative; but at least the cities, the major population centers, were to be secured against ecclesiastical fraternization with the enemy. Religious and military policy coincided here. A few months later edicts issued to Eutropius attacked apostates — those who left Christianity to become pagans — and Manichaeans resident in Illyricum. Both groups were deprived of testamentary rights. However, since the edict against the Manichaeans was merely following up an earlier ruling by Valentinian, its formulation was more complex and the penalties were more severe; the definition of the persons concerned named explicitly a group of ascetic communities that the authorities felt were suspicious and undesirable and they conveniently subsumed under the rubric of "Manichaeans."[21]

In the meanwhile the imperial summons to the Nicene bishops to come to Constantinople in May 381 had been sent out shortly after Theodosius's dramatic entry into Constantinople in November 380. Through Acholius, who was one of those summoned, news of Theodosius's plans soon reached Italy. While Ambrose was happy enough to support the claim of the scurrilous Egyptian Maximus to the bishop's throne of Constantinople, Damasus in Rome, who also knew of Theodosius's rejection of Maximus and thoroughly approved of it, wrote back to Acholius urging that he and his colleagues make sure that the person chosen for Constantinople should be formally beyond suspicion. What he really meant was that he should not already be a bishop elsewhere—a type of candidature that a canon of the Nicene Council had banned, though up to now it had not been taken seriously in the East.[22] This explicit reference to canonical legitimacy was, however, in fact nothing more than a disguised objection to the candidacy of Gregory of Nazianzos, a representative of the Antiochene theological tradition, who in an earlier phase of his career had been elected, mightily against his will, bishop of the tiny Cappadocian town Sasima. He himself had refused to accept the validity of the election at the time, subsequently not even visiting the place, and so regarded himself as free and electable elsewhere. Damasus had no really good reason to object to Gregory's doctrinal orthodoxy (though the traditional tensions existing between Antioch and Alexandria, and Rome's much closer relations with Alexandria, might have clouded his judgment), but the disciplinary canon seems to have been important to him.

Neither piece of Western interference—neither Ambrose's support for Maximus nor Damasus's formal insistence on canonical correctness—was immediately effective. One of the first things the Eastern bishops did when they assembled in Constantinople for the council was to declare the election of Maximus and his appointments of clergy null and void, thereby also implicitly rejecting Ambrose's contrary opinion on the matter.[23] Acholius reached Constantinople only after the proceedings had begun[24]—whether he deliberately arrived late or not is unclear—and had no opportunity to present Damasus's view of canonical legitimacy in time, since Gregory had already been elected and consecrated by the time he arrived. Gregory's friends, it seemed, led by the charismatic Antiochene Meletius, who in any case packed the council, had already won this battle. For the Eastern Nicene bishops it was a good, self-confident start into a new era, which, however, was abruptly interrupted by the venerable Meletius's sudden death.[25]

Without Antioch's bishop the council was robbed of its leader of opinion, and its agenda was also dangerously extended, for the question of the succession to Meletius in the apostolic see of Antioch was inevitably thrust upon it. This in itself was far from easy to solve, since from the time of Valens's "tolerance edict," which had allowed Meletius to return to Antioch, two doctrinally "orthodox" Nicene bishops, Meletius and the ascetically inclined Paulinus, each with his own congregation and personal following, had again resided side by side in the city. Valens's concession had, in effect, resuscitated the Antiochene schism. In the meanwhile Meletius had gained possession of the main church building after the "homoians" had been expelled from it, and he also led a much larger congregation. Christian leaders in the West tried to interfere in Antioch, as they were currently doing in Constantinople, again testing the purity of the doctrine of the contenders and making basically unwelcome suggestions for solving the schism. The main idea, which seemed sensible to all except those immediately affected by it, was that the congregation of whichever of the two old men should first die should join with that of the other, and that a new election to the see should take place only after the death of the second.[26] This suggestion, however, ignored the wishes of both orthodox congregations in Antioch and underestimated their personal attachment not just to their own bishop but also to the clergy of their own community. Moreover, Paulinus had not come to Constantinople, and the Meletians who were there, now led by the equally charismatic younger Antiochene presbyter Flavianus, who had kept the Meletian congregation together during Meletius's exile in the 370s under Valens, had their own local agenda. It did not envisage their serving under Paulinus.

After the death of Meletius the newly elected Gregory took over as chairman of the council. He showed an extraordinary lack of sensitivity for the internal politics of the situation at Antioch, and proposed, in effect, the acceptance of the Western solution. His suggestion horrified the Eastern bishops whom Meletius had brought with him and who had just elected Gregory, since they favored Flavianus's election for the see of Antioch and expected Gregory's support for it as a quid pro quo. Discussions on this matter were still continuing when the delayed Acholius and his fellow Macedonians arrived together with Timotheus of Alexandria. Timotheus was brother and successor of Peter, who had died suddenly in the interval between his receiving Theodosius's summons to the council and the departure date. These "Westerners," as Gregory called them,[27] began by articulating Damasus's objection to the formal *translatio sedis* involved in Gregory's election; and although they must have supported in principle his suggestion for solving the Antiochene schism, since it was originally a Western idea, their criticism of the legitimacy of Gregory's election hurt the sensitive bishop so much that he appealed to Theodosius, offering his immediate resignation. His appeal was, of course, a tactical bid for imperial support, an attempt to swing the secular arm behind him, as it had helped him a few months before to take effective possession of the cathedral in the city, and to uphold his own position in the church of Constantinople as well as his solution for the Antiochene schism. He might well have expected the Westerner Theodosius to welcome the plan regarding Antioch, not least because it was a Western proposal. But to his surprise and horror Theodosius simply accepted his resignation.[28]

The emperor and his advisers had to have noted Gregory's tactless treatment of those from the Eastern Nicene churches who had supported his election. These men, as it happened, were also the men on whom Theodosius himself was relying for support and consolidation in the Eastern church, and he could not afford to offend them, as Gregory was doing. The delayed Western objections to Gregory's election—now formulated by the well-trusted bishop Acholius, who had baptized the emperor, and which were doubtless also articulated in private audiences —were the last straw. Gregory had failed his first political test as bishop of Constantinople, and it was to be his last. He had shown himself both hypersensitive and politically incompetent. If influential and trusted bishops cherished genuine doubt about the legitimacy of his election, he was clearly an unsuitable person to guide and represent the church in the main imperial residence city of the Eastern empire at this critical time. Theodosius must have been grateful to be able to correct his initial misjudgment so quickly and (for him) relatively painlessly.

So much is known about this phase of the council because Gregory later wrote a bitter account of it as it affected him personally. His resignation put the succession to the episcopal see of Constantinople back on the agenda of the council, and the ball was in Theodosius's court. From this point on our information is less good, since Gregory was not involved, but the best source, the historian Sozomenus, makes clear the participation of Theodosius in the appointment of Nectarius as Gregory's successor.[29] Nectarius, who originally came from Tarsos, was first suggested by the current bishop of his birthplace, Diodorus, himself a protégé of Meletius, whose role in the activities of the council after Gregory's withdrawal seems to have become more prominent. Nectarius's social qualification for the post was obvious enough: he was a senator resident in Constantinople, was rich enough to have been *praetor* there, which brought with it both the opportunity and the obligation to expend some of his private wealth on public display,[30] and he was generally popular, perhaps not least for his outlays. Furthermore, he had not been involved in the ecclesiastical battles of the last decades. He was, however, a layman, and as a resident of Constantinople with a Nicene inclination was presumably part of the select Nicene community that had originally invited Gregory to come to Constantinople after Valens's "tolerance edict." When his name began to circulate, such general enthusiasm was expressed for the popular socialite that the participants of the council were prepared to overlook what might have seemed a fairly basic objection to him: the fact that Nectarius was not even baptized at the time of his election. This was a clear infringement of a further canon of the Nicene Council (canon II), though it was a canon that even in the West had not been universally observed: none other than Ambrose himself had infringed it, which, however, did not prevent that political cleric from subsequently challenging Nectarius's suitability from a safe distance.[31]

In this case the Westerners present in Constantinople were happy enough to ignore a canon that did not suit them, and they seem to have raised no objection to a person whose social network made him so obviously suitable to exploit the possibilities offered by the church to help consolidate the Eastern empire under the rule of Theodosius. His electors must have hoped that he would also use his social competence to exploit the Theodosian empire to consolidate the Eastern church. Both ecclesiastical and secular interests were satisfied. Nectarius, therefore, had the support not only of the strong Meletian contingent at the council but also of the emperor and the most influential sections of society in Constantinople and the East. The appointment of a senator as bishop bound in the person of Nectarius the highest echelons of Constantinopolitan secular and ecclesiastical society together in a practical and symbolic way, which could only have a positive effect on both parts and favor Theodosius's general stabilization program and the acceptability of his own rule. Given these overwhelming advantages it would have been foolish to press formalistic objections, and the council represented Nectarius's election as having been unanimous.[32]

The urbane Nectarius, as Gregory's successor, evidently chaired the remaining sessions of the council, which continued until 9 July; this emerges from his heading the preserved list of signatories.[33] He seems to have had no difficulty in pushing through Theodosius's program. The Nicene Creed was reaffirmed in a slightly modified form, which took account both of a doctrinal letter circulated earlier by Damasus,[34] a text that the Meletians meeting at Antioch in 379 had already accepted, and of certain Eastern discussions on the nature of the Holy Spirit. Particularly prominent "heresies" were explicitly named and marked with anathema.[35] The Antiochene problem was solved by accepting the majority view of the council and electing Flavianus as successor to Meletius, a decision that the council also presented as unanimous: "For the senior and truly apostolic church of Antioch in Syria, in which the honored name of 'Christians' was first used, the bishops of the province and of the diocese Oriens came together and elected the most respected and god-beloved Flavianus as bishop, and the whole church agreed as if with one voice in honoring this man."[36]

With canons II and III we return to Theodosius's long-term structural agenda. Canon II laid down local ecclesiastical responsibility within each of the secular administrative dioceses by banning bishops from interfering in elections or other ecclesiastical affairs outside their own dioceses, unless explicitly invited to do so.[37] This was an attempt to adapt their functional status in canon law to parallel that of a secular diocesan administrator (*vicarius*), who also had automatic rights only within the diocese to which he was appointed, though he could, of course, ask a colleague for help or advice. The canon was clearly aimed at preventing the sort of haphazard external interference from Rome, Milan, and Alexandria that had led to the electoral problems associated with Maximus the Cynic and Gregory of Nazianzos in Constantinople and with the schism in Antioch.

Canon III broke quite new ground in arguing from the secular importance of Constantinople for the empire that it must have an equivalent ecclesiastical status. Theodosius, once he had recognized the political importance of ecclesiastical affairs, was not prepared to accept that his city, where he the emperor now intended to reside, should have only a minor ecclesiastical status, just because it had not functioned as an imperial residence in apostolic times. Nectarius, as a man of the world and ex-senator of Constantinople, undoubtedly saw the question in a similar way. The canon was brief and to the point: "The bishop of Constantinople shall have primacy of honor after the bishop of Rome, since Constantinople is New Rome."[38] Traditionalists must have shuddered, but Theodosius and Nectarius had in the meanwhile put virtually all participants in the council one way or another into their debt. Moreover, the two Eastern apostolic sees that theoretically might have been prepared to offer objections to this revolutionary assertion were currently weak. Timotheus of Alexandria was newly elected, still feeling his way in general, and still suffering from Theodosius's displeasure at the attempt of his brother Peter to capture the see of Constantinople with the disreputable Egyptian Maximus the Cynic. Flavianus was indeed already elected to the see of Antioch but not yet consecrated, therefore formally also in too weak a position to raise any serious objection, and in any case was now morally bound to Theodosius and Nectarius, who had made his election possible. Canon III is incidentally also the earliest concrete evidence we have that Theodosius intended to promote Constantinople to attain secular primacy among the cities of the East. If the bishop was declared to be second in prestige to the bishop of Rome, only practical preeminence in the secular field could make up for the lack of apostolic tradition. With this ecclesiastical coup Theodosius therefore also announced a new and enduring secular future for Constantine's city.

Postconciliar Legislation · By 9 July Nectarius could close the council and send a written report of its proceedings to the emperor Theodosius, who had summoned it. The bishops asked him to give a formal statement of his agreement with their decisions, and—since most of the decisions were on matters dear to Theodosius, ones that had fallen out as he had planned—this cannot have been problematic.[39] The decision of the council had given the emperor a moral legitimization for solving his third urgent ecclesiastical problem, the largely non-Nicene incumbency of bishoprics in the cities of western Asia Minor. Of the three provinces belonging to the proconsulate of Asia—Insulae, Hellespontus, and Asia—not one was represented in the council by a bishop. That can only mean that none of the bishops in question could be classified as Nicene and thus qualify for an imperial summons.[40] We know that the Macedonianists were particularly strong in western Asia Minor and that they were one of the "heretical" groups explicitly rejected in canon I. The time had come for action: after the close of the council the imperial government hastened to draft an edict addressed to the current proconsul of Asia, Auxonius, instructing him to arrange the transfer of all churches in his provinces to Nicene incumbents.[41]

Auxonius was instructed on how he should ensure and assess the orthodoxy of potential candidates: they were to share communion with at least one of a list of named persons, all of them participants of the council, the list being headed by Nectarius himself. This was the same legitimizing technique that had been successfully tested at Constantinople the year before. The authors of the law clearly expected that no suitable candidate would be available locally, since "heresies" were so widespread in the proconsulate that no bishop from any city within Auxonius's provinces could be named as guarantor of orthodoxy. It was inevitable then that the minor clergy of the proconsulate, who would normally have provided candidates for promotion, were tainted by the same "heresies" and therefore disqualified as future Nicene bishops. Otherwise every Eastern diocese outside the proconsulate was represented. Candidates from these areas could obtain their certificates of orthodoxy locally, and Auxonius's secular staff in the proconsulate was doubtless given guidance on how to recognize them when presented. The secular administrative machinery for the ecclesiastical turnaround was in place.

The next year saw the issue of a series of imperial edicts that named once again, made more precise, or increased penalties for "heresies" explicitly condemned at Constantinople in 381, and added to them some other minor or subordinate groups that had not been named in canon I. The historian Sozomenus, himself a lawyer, summed up this material in these words: "By issuing legislation the emperor forbade the heterodox to meet in churches and to teach about the faith and to appoint bishops or other clergy; some he ordered to be driven out of the cities and the country estates; others were to be dishonored and deprived of equal civil rights with the rest of the people. He prescribed severe penalties in the laws, but did not impose them, for he was anxious not to punish but to frighten his subjects, so that they would come to agree with him in religious matters. For this reason he also praised those who converted voluntarily."[42] That Theodosius preferred to try to persuade had already been remarked on by Gregory of Nazianzos; and an event of 383, which provided the context for Sozomenus's statement, shows that even in the environs of Constantinople, however successful Theodosius might have been in transferring church property and rights to Nicene bishops, there still existed a great range of sects that found the Nicene Creed for one reason or another inadequate.

In June 383 Theodosius summoned the leaders of the main regional sects to Constantinople. Apart from Nectarius, who represented the Nicene catholics, named in the summons are the Novatian Agelius (who, however, accepted the Nicene Creed, while differing on some historical disciplinary questions), the "homoian" Demophilus, the "Anhomoian" Eunomius, and the Macedonianist Eleusius of Kyzikos.[43] After some procedural wrangling each was asked to provide a written statement of his basic beliefs concerning the critical trinitarian question of the relationship of the Son to the Father, and after receiving the statements Theodosius tore up all but the Nicene texts. This was a severe blow to the supporters of the sectarian leaders, who now began to accept imperial authority and turn to the Nicene faith. Yet, says Sokrates, "one must know this, that the emperor Theodosius persecuted none of them, except that he ordered Eunomius to be exiled, since he was holding meetings in private houses in Constantinople and declaiming his written speeches, whereby he damaged many people with his teachings. Theodosius molested none of the others, and forced nobody into communion with himself. He agreed that each might assemble in his own place and extol the Christian religion, just as each was able to comprehend its doctrine."[44] That Eunomius was exiled from his residence in Chalkedon opposite Constantinople to Halmyros in Moesia and then later to Cappadocia is confirmed by one of his followers, the historian Philostorgius, who had met him in Cappadocia.[45] He was clearly regarded as a troublemaker and a threat to law and order in the city, but the others were not. The three laws that followed in the six months after this confrontation with the leaders of the main sects, which were aimed principally against the Eunomians, the "homoians," and the Macedonianists, were unknown to Sokrates; though they were known to Sozomenus—from the Theodosian Code, not from historical tradition—the laws were in his estimation intended only to frighten.[46]

More than general disappointment at Theodosius's treatment, it may well have been the legislation that led to the depression felt by the leaders of the sects and the dwindling of their following, if Sokrates's assertion about the decline of the sects is based on fact and not merely on wishful thinking. On 25 July the praetorian prefect Postumianus received a law forbidding a long list of named sects—headed by the Eunomians, the "homoians," and the Macedonianists—from meeting together in large or small groups, from declaring any building to be a church, or from carrying out any activities that even looked like a catholic service. Right-thinking men were encouraged to expel them.[47] On 3 December the main three groups of "heretics," with the addition of the Apollonianists (explicitly condemned at Constantinople by the council), were the subject of another law directed to Postumianus; it added to the list of banned activities—which were in general more extensively formulated—the right to appoint priests. The penalty for transgression was now not just expulsion for the cult leaders, after they had been hunted out; nonresident associates of the heresiarchs would be ordered to return to their registered places of residence and remain there. Meeting places were to be confiscated, and local officials of the government and members of the city councils were made responsible for ensuring that the rules were obeyed.[48] On 21 January 384 the new praetorian prefect Cynegius received a ruling that the priests and teachers of the Eunomians, the Macedonianists, the "homoians," and the Apollonianists were to be expelled from Constantinople; while they might live elsewhere, they were to be prevented from meeting with "good men."[49]

It is important not to take the rhetorical verbiage of these laws too seriously, since competent contemporary judges thought that Theodosius did not take it seriously either. Sozomenus, who knew the Code, asserted that Theodosius did not actually apply the penalties laid down in his laws, and his slightly older contemporary, the Constantinopolitan resident Sokrates—who was unfamiliar with the Theodosian Code— knew nothing of any such general local persecution of "heretics" in his own lifetime, though it would have suited his orthodox agenda and he would have had no reason for concealing it. Indeed, he explicitly denied it, making clear that the exile of the particularly extreme and troublesome Eunomius was an exception. Any centralized action at this time must therefore have been much more restricted in scope than the extant laws suggest.

Pagan Policy

A remarkable feature of imperial religious policy during the first five years of Theodosius's reign is that it was almost exclusively concerned with trying to sort out differences among the Christians themselves and paid little attention to the classic fight with the non-Christians. Theodosius indeed shows no initial awareness of paganism having been a problem at all, for he followed the child emperor Valentinian II in simply not adopting the traditional title *pontifex maximus* on his accession. By now the old title, which had long outlived its function, must have seemed a simple irrelevance, and no contemporary writer, either Christian or pagan, appears to have even noticed its absence or thought it worth mentioning.[50] Three rulings from this period show the emperor's general attitude. On 21 December 381 an edict was issued to Florus, the praetorian prefect of the East, banning prognostication through forbidden sacrifice under penalty of confiscation of goods (*proscriptio*), and the ruling was repeated in May 385 to the praetorian prefect Cynegius, using more dramatic language and threatening crucifixion as the penalty. The principle, however, was almost as old as the empire itself: magical investigation of the future, at least by members of the upper classes, had always been at least as much a political as a religious act, and the laws have nothing to do with antipaganism.[51] In 382 an instruction issued to Palladius, the military commander (*dux*) of Osrhoene, concerning a famous temple, doubtless the one at Edessa, allowed it to stay open because of its artistic value, but the decades-old ban on sacrifice was reasserted. A locally applicable instruction of this sort was usually the answer to a question posed by the responsible local official (a *consultatio*). Palladius's question must therefore have been concerned with whether he was under an obligation to close the temple. While closing it would have pleased local Christian pressure groups, that would have risked provoking serious communal disturbances by offended traditionalists in an important frontier city. The emperor's answer was pragmatic, aimed at trying to satisfy both sides.[52]

From various sources it is known that there was strong Christian pressure in major Eastern cities to attack the visible remains of the pre-Christian past, however valuable these might have been as architectural elements or as works of art; it was often difficult to decide whether or not a particular object or practice was "pagan" or merely pre-Christian and therefore traditional. There was an enormous gray area here, and some of Theodosius's senior advisers and officials turned out to be far less sensitive and conciliatory toward traditional Eastern values and susceptibilities than those responsible for the cautiously formulated instruction sent to Palladius concerning Edessa. Their attitude gave influential moral and political, if not always legal, backing to local Christian radicals throughout the East, who in the 380s began a series of vandalizing actions, the most spectacular of them being the destruction of the temple complex of Sarapis in Alexandria in the winter of 391/92. These activities contributed to Theodosius's later reputation as the emperor who dealt the deathblow to pagan religion in the empire,[53] but the history of pagan religion's demise was not so straightforward.

Between 385 and 387 the Antiochene teacher Libanius wrote a speech nominally addressed to Theodosius concerning local Christian activity directed against temples; never sent to the emperor, it was delivered to a small private audience in Antioch.[54] The main perpetrators of the widespread local destruction of pagan cult buildings, according to Libanius, were the ever-increasing numbers of radical monks living in the hill country to the east of Antioch. Fueled by an anti-aesthetic ascetic fundamentalism, they carried out frequent raids on shrines situated on estates and in villages in the hinterland and enjoyed the tacit approval of Bishop Flavianus, who used all his influence to cover their activities.[55] These actions occurred, says Libanius, despite the fact that no official instruction directed against temple buildings had been issued by Theodosius and even though general obedience toward the old official ban on bloody sacrifice was observed. The proof of this obedience was that though allegations that sacrifice had taken place were made, no case was ever brought before a court. Libanius's arguments illustrate the conflict between two lifestyles. Country festivals and celebrations did not stop just because bloody sacrifice was banned: people continued to meet and enjoy themselves, and grilled meat continued to be prepared and eaten on these occasions, though sacrifice at the altar was omitted.[56] On the other hand, humorless hermits, whose lifestyle was directed to eternal salvation through the mortification of the flesh, could hardly be expected to appreciate that popular communal festivities were fundamentally social activities and chose to interpret them, since they disapproved of joy in this world in principle, as illegal pagan celebrations.

Some highly placed persons, however, were ready to latch onto fundamentalist Christian sentiments and provide moral authority for the vandalizing activities instigated by the soldiers of Christ. It is perhaps no surprise that the most prominent of these people under Theodosius were sober Westerners who had no personal attachment to, or even interest in, the social function of Eastern pre-Christian traditions. In the 380s a man who came with Theodosius from Spain, Maternus Cynegius, was the rising star of the antipagan movement; he quickly rose to be praetorian prefect of the East, an office that he held for an exceptionally long period, from 384 until his death in 388.[57] Religious policy was only a minor part of his job as praetorian prefect, as the extensive extant legislation on a multitude of subjects shows, and it hardly played a role in his legislative activity. But it was an aspect that caught the imagination and certainly guaranteed his reputation as an assertive Christianizer outside government circles in the East.

Cynegius liked to travel.[58] Shortly after his appointment in 384 he was in Egypt, to which he brought the official imperial portrait of Magnus Maximus.[59] The main reason for his being in Egypt was purely administrative, having to do with the reorganization of the local city councils, but what was remembered was his misusing his authority to close temples and interfere with local cult practice.[60] Nevertheless, his reputation with the Alexandrian councillors was such that they obtained permission from the emperor to set up a statue of him in civilian dress, the inscription from which survived into the eighteenth century.[61] Whether on this journey or a later one, he visited Antioch, where he greeted Libanius with respect and imposed some administrative measures of which Libanius approved;[62] but he won no long-term admiration, for it was the same Cynegius who failed to discourage the vandalizing Syrian monks and who participated personally, it seems, in the destruction of a major temple in Osrhoene, at Edessa or Carrhae.[63] He also accompanied Bishop Marcellus of Apameia with his military escort on an initial inspection of the great Apameian temple of Zeus with a view to pulling it down. It turned out, however, to be too big a job to be done while he waited.[64] Cynegius's activities were brought to an abrupt end by his sudden death early in 388, the year that had begun with his gaining the highest honor in the empire, the consulate.[65] After his death Libanius dared make more generally known the bitter complaints he had formulated in his speech "On Behalf of the Temples," written a couple of years earlier and formally addressed to the emperor, in which he alleged that some of Theodosius's officers and friends were engaged semiprivately in antipagan activities that went far beyond the range of actions sanctified by the law. Not only were they not controlling local antipagan activity in the East; they were even encouraging it, while the pagans obeyed the law and suffered injustice at their hands. Libanius explicitly points out, incidentally, the double standard that was involved: even sacrifice had not yet been officially banned in the city of Rome.[66]

In 388 Theodosius had more important things on his mind, since he had by now decided to fight a war for the West against Magnus Maximus. The war between the two baptized Spanish catholic emperors had in itself no confusing religious dimension, and Theodosius demonstrated that he was far from automatically identifying religious conformity with dynastic loyalty when he appointed the pagan aristocrat Fl. Eutolmius Tatianus as praetorian prefect, in succession to the rabid Christian Cynegius, and made Tatianus's son Proculus *praefectus urbi* at Constantinople. Both remained in office for the duration of Theodosius's absence in the West and for some time after his return in 391. We shall meet them again.[67]

Italy

After the war against Maximus was won in the summer of 388, Italy presented Theodosius with political problems different in detail but similar in their structure to those he had initially met in the East. He arrived as a conqueror, however hard he tried to sell himself as the liberator. Most of the Italian aristocracy had in the end probably accepted Maximus, whether willingly or not. Whereas the "homoian" Valentinian II had offended both catholics and pagans, Maximus was a catholic, but he had also offered the pagans some hope. Symmachus, the influential pagan senator and ex-prefect of the city, doubtless still smarting from his defeat by Ambrose in 384 on the question of the traditional cults and the altar of Victory, seems not to have hesitated long before traveling to Milan to greet Maximus and deliver a panegyrical speech in his presence.[68] Since Maximus's propaganda emphasized his agreement with Theodosius, and even hinted at a blood relationship with his fellow Spaniard,[69] it must have come as an unpleasant surprise to many Westerners who thought they could arrange themselves comfortably with Maximus to find that Theodosius was after all taking up arms against him, nominally in the interest of the unloved Valentinian II and his "heretical" clique.

Valentinian in the meanwhile, under pressure from Theodosius in his dire emergency, had embraced the Nicene faith, only to be sent off to Trier soon after the victory to rule in Gaul under the eagle eye of Theodosius's man Arbogast.[70] Theodosius stayed almost three years in Italy, clearly intending to find some way of keeping it under his own rule. For that he needed loyal and competent officials, their personal religious affiliation being a secondary consideration, or even quite irrelevant. In particular he needed to cultivate two opposing elements, the catholic church in northern Italy and the rich and influential Roman aristocracy, many members of which were still pagan in sentiment. The combination was not going to be easy to handle.

A good relationship with the grandees of the Italian church, especially with Ambrose in Milan, where the court took up residence, would be critical for Theodosius's success. Freed of his bête noire, Justina, who had died during the war, Ambrose faced the problem of changing his domineering attitude toward Valentinian because of the young emperor's nominal acceptance of Nicene "orthodoxy." But, as it turned out, the pliable Valentinian disappeared to Trier as soon as the winter was over, and even before that Theodosius seems to have kept him in the background. Ambrose needed to establish a modus vivendi with the new conquering emperor and his staff, for the greater glory of the church and Ambrose its servant, while Theodosius had to win over the bishop and turn him and his substantial local influence to use for his post–civil war regime. Ambrose was important not merely as bishop of the imperial residence city but also because he enjoyed a wide range of elite contacts in Italy and beyond, both inside and outside the church, and therefore could be a very useful voice in helping to coordinate the Theodosian grasp on power in the West.

For both parties it was important that the symbiosis should be widely known to function: that Theodosius be seen to visit the bishop's cathedral and that the bishop be seen to have access to the palace. A letter from Symmachus asking Ambrose to intervene at court on behalf of a friend who—like Symmachus—had compromised himself under Magnus Maximus shows the role that some highly placed contemporaries expected Ambrose to be able to play while the emperor was in Milan.[71]

A problem of imperial protocol presented itself immediately and tested the willingness of both sides to adapt to each other. In church in the East the emperor normally took his place among the priests behind the altar, but this was not Western practice. After some initial irritation a mutually acceptable compromise on this formal question was easily reached, and the emperor found a suitable place for worship right at the front of the congregation, before the lay public, where he could be seen by everybody, but without his penetrating the altar screen. The compromise served well enough: imperial respect for the especial holiness of the sanctuary was made visible and could be observed by all present, and this was in the interest of both parties.[72]

The first serious disagreement between bishop and emperor occurred during the autumn or winter, and it showed how the sheer presence of the emperor and his court offered those living in his immediate environment a chance to gain political profile in areas that would otherwise not be accessible to their influence. Ambrose had for many years made efforts to gain sufficient influence to be able to intervene effectively in ecclesiastical affairs in the East, and had consistently failed. Now that the emperor responsible for the East was resident in Italy, information about Eastern affairs arrived officially and speedily in Italy, and decisions about Eastern governmental problems were inevitably also made in Italy. This potentially opened the door to local Italian influence on them. Ambrose was not the man to pass up such an opportunity. His first chance arose out of a particularly serious incident of unofficial persecution by local Christians in the area of responsibility of the *comes Orientis*, based at Antioch. In Kallinikon, a town on the middle Euphrates, the local bishop had led an attack on a synagogue and burned it down. Since the death of Cynegius, Tatianus, as the praetorian prefect of the East, was the minister in Constantinople responsible for imperial administration in the area. Whereas Cynegius might well have shrugged his official shoulders and privately rejoiced that his example was being followed, Tatianus dutifully sent on the report of the *comes* to Theodosius in Italy. Theodosius's reaction was automatic and immediate: the *comes* himself ought to have shown initiative and acted at once; those responsible for the severe disturbance of public order in the sensitive frontier district were to be punished; the victims were to be compensated; and the bishop was to be forced to rebuild the synagogue at his own expense. In a separate incident violently aggressive monks had beaten up a peaceful community of gnostic "Valentinians," and they were also to be disciplined for their unprovoked breach of the peace.[73]

As soon as Ambrose heard of this affair, he recognized his chance of making his influence felt at court. He approached Theodosius directly and pointed out the moral and practical dangers inherent in the emperor's reaction. The bishop of Kallinikon, said Ambrose, would, if he accepted the punishment, be betraying his faith by building a synagogue; and if he refused to do so, Theodosius might well have a martyr on his hands.[74] Theodosius had no appetite for a battle of theoretical principles and of authorities on the distant Euphrates frontier, and he therefore canceled the specific punishment of the bishop, doubtless moved more by local Milanese political considerations than by religious concerns. Ambrose, by winning access to Theodosius, had thus given good advice that showed both bishop and emperor in a favorable light; but when he tried to persuade Theodosius in an eloquent letter to drop the whole business—a letter that he published in edited form after Theodosius's death—his plea fell on deaf ears. Although the emperor certainly did not wish to risk provoking a messy martyrdom, it was equally necessary to protect the large and important Jewish population in the labile frontier district against deliberate perpetrators of communal violence, and Ambrose's academic ecclesiological arguments were not of this world.

So far so good. Ambrose, however, thought he needed a more visible success, one that would show his admirers that he could influence and impose his views on Theodosius's court, as he had on Valentinian II's— particularly after he had manifested an ambiguous attitude toward the catholic usurper Maximus. He therefore provoked another confrontation with Theodosius, this time on his own ground. Its immediate short-term success, however, did not lead to the stable long-term influence at court he had hoped for. Ambrose's congregation was used to anti-Jewish sermons and can hardly have anticipated an immediate political intent when the preacher again took up the familiar theme in the presence of Theodosius. In the peroration of his sermon, however, Ambrose suddenly made clear that he was not just dealing with ancient history but was directly addressing the emperor on the currently sensitive subject of the vandalizing Christians of Kallinikon and demanding an imperial pardon for them. Theodosius was not amused, and even less so when after the sermon the bishop approached the imperial party, placed conveniently for Ambrose at the front before the eyes of the whole congregation, as the earlier agreement had foreseen, and indicated that he expected Theodosius's public submission on the spot.

Our source for this incident is a letter that Ambrose wrote to his sister Marcellina, in which the bishop naturally paints his own view of the affair. He does not, however, deny Theodosius's assertion that his original change of mind on the punishment of the Kallinikon bishop after Ambrose's initial intervention at court had in his view been an entirely adequate response to Ambrose's wishes; moreover, he emphasized that the destructive activities of the Eastern monks—Ambrose had at the same time also claimed pardon for the vandalizing monks who had attacked the Valentinians—were a serious problem of law and order in the East. He was vigorously seconded in this view by his general Timasius, who was with him in the church. But the emperor could not win by quiet argument, for Ambrose's whole dramaturgy had made the large Milanese congregation—even if they could not hear the details of the altercation—expect him to exact some further concessions from the emperor, and Theodosius, who had extended his *clementia* to the supporters of a usurper, could not afford to be seen to be less than generous to those— so Ambrose's populist claim—who had merely been pursuing the legitimate interests of the church in distant lands. Ambrose got his way and won his concessions, but his extortionist methods erected a sizable barrier to his becoming persona grata at the court.[75]

Theodosius might have his problems with Ambrose, but the pagan senators of Rome came running to his call, doubtless relieved that the pragmatic Theodosius did not intend to have them suffer for their ambivalent attitude toward Maximus. Theodosius visited Rome in June 389, as we have seen, and among other things paid his respects to the Senate as a body, letting his official orator announce in a well-prepared panegyrical speech the emperor's future policy, while also drawing the official picture of the events of the recent civil war.[76] There is no sign of any religious dimension to Theodosius's political activities there. His attitude was conciliatory, for he knew well enough that without the support of the Roman aristocrats a new government in Italy would have a hard time achieving that traditional political consensus among the ruling classes without which no Italian government could function satisfactorily. After the usurpation and the civil war a traditional imperial *clementia* had to be the initial guiding principle of Realpolitik, and this showed through in Theodosius's treatment of the Roman senatorial aristocracy. The new appointment as *praefectus urbi* for Rome was a clever compromise: Ceionius Rufius Albinus, a leading intellectual among the senators, was still a pagan, but not so doctrinaire as to keep him from marrying a Christian.[77] The prominent pagan littérateur Virius Nicomachus Flavianus was invited to put his literary talents to public use by serving as quaestor in the imperial service, and after a test period at court he was appointed praetorian prefect of Italy, Africa, and Illyricum shortly before Theodosius's return to the East in 391.[78] The estimable Symmachus, whose polished periods had failed to move Valentinian II over the altar of Victoria, but who had most recently praised Maximus with no little success, was graciously pardoned for his faux pas and in 391 allowed to advance even to the consulate, which he shared with his fellow pagan Tatianus, the Eastern praetorian prefect.[79]

It is ironic that Theodosius found it easier to reach a working relationship with the pagan aristocracy in Rome than with the ecclesiastical baron in Milan, but the seat of government in Italy was by now not Rome but Milan, and by the autumn of 389 Theodosius and his entourage had returned there. Two major episodes from this second phase of Theodosius's residence in Milan involved Ambrose. Roman traditionalists, who might well have thought they had earned the emperor's favor, made some kind of request to Theodosius in connection with the traditional Roman cults; perhaps it had to do merely with being allowed to make appointments to vacancies in the traditional priestly colleges, a function that for centuries had at least as much to do with social status as with religious practice. Ambrose, however, got wind of their approach

and put pressure on Theodosius, brusquely emphasizing the purely religious side of the request. His argument, once formulated in public, inevitably prevailed, but its perpetrator incurred the lasting wrath of the
emperor, who through this harmless bit of patronage had been concerned to strengthen his ties to the Italian aristocracy.[80] One immediate
result of this successful piece of lobbying was that Theodosius imposed
strict rules about the confidentiality of future meetings of the consistory;
their aim—so Ambrose's version—was to cut him off from his "natural
right" to information.[81] The representatives of church and state in the
residence city were again at loggerheads.

But the all-purifying political thunderstorm was at hand, ready to as-
sist in creating the historical symbiosis that rescued Theodosius's reputation among Western Christians. At the same time, however, there developed a myth that cast an obscuring veil over the critical details, making
them impenetrable for future historians. The precise timescale of the
chain of events is unclear. They most probably ended at Easter in 391,[82]
but the first incident began months previously in Thessalonica, where in
the course of a riot connected with the games the imperial military governor, a Goth called Buthericus, had been lynched. Such violent actions
against the public authorities traditionally provoked strong disciplinary
measures, and a decision of the consistory, the exact terms of which are
not known, was interpreted by the officials on the spot as a license to
let the troops loose on the civilian population. The result, whether intended or not, was an indiscriminate massacre in which large numbers
of citizens were killed.[83] In its origins this incident had no religious dimension. When the news reached Milan, it received one. The main question for the moralist Ambrose concerned the moral responsibility of the
emperor personally for this "massacre of the innocents";[84] but the politician Ambrose was concerned to exploit the general horror at what had
happened at the behest of the emperor in order to reestablish himself
and the church he represented as the highest moral instance in the empire, and be recognized as such by the secular authorities.

Details are obscured by later Christian writers, who were concerned
to make heroes out of both Ambrose and Theodosius, the former for
insisting Theodosius do personal penance, the latter for accepting the

need even for an emperor to do so.[85] The reality was probably more pro-saic and political on both sides. Ambrose helped Theodosius overcome public antipathy, at least in Milan, by representing Theodosius's pub-lic role in the events at Thessalonica as a mere personal failing, a sin that could be washed away by public penitence, and Theodosius in the end accepted the way out offered him by Ambrose. For the officiating bishop the publicity attached to the act of imperial penitence, com-pleted on Maundy Thursday in full view of the pre-Easter congregation in the cathedral—for a private person, an act involving shame and em-barrassment[86]—was the political attraction because with it the church publicly took over responsibility for washing away the sin and restor-ing the moral caliber of imperial rule. The emperor's involvement in the massacre of the innocents in Thessalonica could thus be interpreted as a forgivable personal sin, as long as the accompanying music of the spheres was orchestrated by a politically ambitious Ambrose seeking a role to play in the running of the state.

However, if Ambrose had hoped for intimate long-term influence at court as a result of his help in stage-managing Theodosius's public penance, he was to be disappointed. Easter Sunday fell on 6 April; by 27 May the court had left Milan and already reached Vicenza en route for Constantinople.[87] The praetorian prefect whom Theodosius left in charge of Italy was the pagan Virius Nicomachus Flavianus, whose pagan friend Symmachus had already given his name to the year as consul. Am-brose's Easter triumph was thus extremely short lived. As far as could be foreseen, Milan would no longer be an imperial residence, its bishop therefore without effective access to imperial decision making. Theodo-sius's last months in Italy, however, saw a series of laws ruling on religious matters, which might conceivably have been influenced by the Milanese church. An edict sent to Albinus, still urban prefect in Rome, on 24 Feb-ruary—during Theodosius's period of penance—used extremely violent rhetoric to forbid public officials in Rome and suburbicarian Italy access to temples for the purpose of sacrifice, under threat of significant penal-ties for the official himself and for his subordinates, if they did not stop him. As recently as 388 Libanius had been able to inform his Antiochene audience that sacrifice in Rome was still allowed. At least for public officials that had now changed. Whether Ambrose had anything to do with this edict is unclear, but he cannot have been dissatisfied with it.[88]

Shortly before the court left Milan in the spring of 391, a general ruling was posted in Rome, perhaps as one of several cities, which — again using extreme but imprecise language — banned "the polluted contagion of heretics" from the cities and forbade their maintaining meeting places.[89] The basic model for this law was Eastern, but it echoed an instruction directed at the praetorian prefect for Italy, Africa, and Illyricum, Trifolius, from Stoboi in June 388 at the outset of the war with Maximus — perhaps intended at that time above all for Illyricum, where it was issued — and two edicts from 389 that were addressed to Albinus, one explicitly directed against the old enemy, the Manichaeans, the other against magicians.[90] Before the court left Italy to be administered by the new pagan praetorian prefect Virius Nicomachus Flavianus, he also received a warning shot across the bow. On 19 June, when the court was in transit and had already reached Concordia, Theodosius's lawyers ruled on apostates, using the kind of aggressive language that suggests the involvement of the same hands that had drafted the two earlier laws intended for Rome.[91] Despite Theodosius's favorable treatment of individual members of the pagan senatorial aristocracy, as a group they were clearly to be allowed no room for maneuver in extending their clientele at the cost of the Christian community.

Constantinople Again

Theodosius had not been cut off from Constantinople during his period of residence in Italy. A series of laws issued in Italian cities but directed to Eastern officials demonstrate his determination not to neglect Eastern affairs. The area of religion was no exception, and no less than six laws on religious topics reached the pagan praetorian prefect of the East, Tatianus, during these years, none of which, however, was concerned with paganism. Before the war was won, Tatianus received an instruction from Theodosius from Illyricum threatening dire punishment for those who chose to dispute about religious affairs in public, and this may be linked to an event first recorded by Sokrates, who said that "Arians" provoked riots in Constantinople "while Theodosius was involved in the war," during which Bishop Nectarius's house was burned down. An immediate reason for the edict is otherwise not apparent, but it would fit well enough into this context.[92] One might suspect the influence of Milanese catholicism on a law of 4 May 389 withholding from "Euno-mians" the right to make or benefit from a testament; and the same might be conjectured for a very generally formulated ruling dating from November of the same year, which urged the expulsion from city and suburbs of all those claiming clerical office in associations of "perverse belief"—a law that was presumably intended above all for the city of Constantinople, though Tatianus's area of responsibility was, of course, much wider than this.[93]

A law fixing a minimum age for deaconesses issued at Milan on 21 June 390 was repealed a mere two months later, on 23 August,[94] and a ruling issued on 2 September 390 confining monks to "the desert and great empty spaces" was repealed, once Theodosius had returned to Constantinople, on 17 April 392, in a law that again allowed them free access to urban areas.[95] The background in both cases is obscure, though the damage done by marauding monks in the East, about which Libanius protested and which Theodosius explicitly acknowledged in his dispute with Ambrose concerning the bishop of Kallinikon, was well enough known and the ban on their entering cities only too well justified. More-over, it would have been a particularly appropriate initiative for the pagan law-and-order man Tatianus.[96] If it had been his reasonable intention to curb these "black-robed vandals" in the cities, in the primary interest of upholding public order, then the repeal of the law, once the court had taken up residence again in Constantinople and was exposed to Eastern Christian lobbyists, could well have been the first sign of the orthodox Christian backlash that soon swept Tatianus (and with him his son Pro-culus) out of office by late summer and replaced him with the fanatical Western Christian Flavius Rufinus.[97]

Rufinus had accompanied Theodosius to Italy as his master of the offices (*magister officiorum*) and had clearly gained the emperor's trust. In 392 he advanced to the consulship, which he occupied together with the young Augustus Arcadius—an exceptional honor. By the end of August 392 he had replaced Tatianus as praetorian prefect. The literary tradition reveals the tensions at court caused by Rufinus's presence there,[98] and if the relaxation of the rules about the presence of monks in the city issued in April were in some way his initiative, then the much brisker attitude toward punishing "heretics" might well also reflect the changed climate of opinion associated with his rising influence: a law issued to Tatianus in June threatened all those who participated in the ordination of "heretical clerics" with heavy fines, and not just with expulsion from urban areas.[99] This certainly introduced a new dimension into the official persecution of "perverse believers" in the East, previously known only from Italy, and even there only in connection with members of the ruling class and their officials.

Rufinus's rise to power in Constantinople after the return of Theodosius from Italy is presented by Zosimus, following the contemporary pagan historian Eunapius, as a coup d'état against Tatianus, his family, and his supporters. This interpretation is in general confirmed by Rufinus's issuing an extraordinary law depriving all Lykians—Tatianus and his family belonged to the Lykian aristocracy—access to public office and all advantage from civil honors already achieved, a law that, after his death, was quickly repealed.[100] The text of this law is not preserved, but that of another of Rufinus's laws is, dating from 8 November 392, the beginning of the persecution of the Lykians—an action that lasted longer than a year and culminated in the execution of Proculus on 6 December 393 and the formal condemnation of Tatianus (though in his case the penalty was not executed).[101] This second ruling purports to be an antipagan law (which it indeed is) and allows for no exception: "nobody of whatever quality of men, whether in power or having held office," is to be unaffected.[102] The law repeats the old ban on sacrifices for purposes of prognostication under penalty of death, but it goes much further in detailing a whole range of pagan practices that are now officially banned and fixing extremely high penalties (fines of up to thirty pounds of gold for provincial governors thought to tolerate such activities). No immediate motivation emerges from the preserved text of the law itself; but the date of its issue, merely a few months after the fall of Tatianus and Proculus, is highly suggestive, as is the fact that it explicitly includes highly placed persons in or out of office, at a time when Tatianus and

Proculus were certainly the most prominent pagans in the Eastern Empire. Moreover, given that another contemporary law issued by Rufinus attacked Tatianus and Proculus by an unprecedented disfranchising of all Lykians (whereby only Tatianus, Proculus, and their Lykian clan were really meant), it is difficult to believe that Rufinus's equally unprecedented global law nominally attacking all pagans was not simply an additional blunt and brutal weapon in his missionary persecution of the Lykian pagan clique at Constantinople.

Once the Lykians were deposed from power, the law attacking all pagans seems to have been forgotten until it was discovered in the archives of the praetorian prefect by the compilers of the Theodosian Code. Certainly most later historians know nothing at all of this law or any practical effect it might have had. Although Sozomenus knew it from the Code, as we do, he attributed no great significance to it as a measure that advanced the interests of the church. For him, though a lawyer by profession, it was not Theodosius's legislative activity but the destruction of temples, depriving the pagans of their meeting places, that was the emperor's major contribution to the furtherance of the church.[103] It would therefore be wrong to be led by the violence of the rhetoric to exaggerate the importance of this law and deem it a major step in advancing Christianity throughout the East. The type of antipagan activity in the East regarded as effective by Sozomenus was, as we have clearly seen, not the deliberate considered policy of Theodosius's imperial government; it began with a semiprivate initiative of Cynegius. This particularly alarmed Libanius precisely because it was not covered by official ordinances from Constantinople, merely being backed by the personal authority of the current praetorian prefect, acting indeed *ultra vires*, but because of his personal prestige unchecked and uncheckable. Despite Sozomenus's view that the emperor "at the beginning of his reign stopped them entering the temples, and at the end destroyed many of them,"[104] there is no ancient evidence for any general imperial initiative at this time either for closing temples or for destroying them. Sozomenus is clearly influenced here by the later orthodox myth that claimed Theodosius as the superorthodox emperor and made him personally responsible for everything that occurred during his reign that later generations chose to regard as positive.[105]

In fact, Theodosius seems to have done no more in this respect than to create a general climate of opinion within which highly placed Christian extremists, whether bishops or court officials, could act virtually uncontrolled. The climax of temple destruction, the tearing down of the world-famous Sarapeion complex in Alexandria in 391/92, was no exception to this, though not all details of the action are clear. The story begins while Theodosius was still in Italy. From Aquileia on 16 June 391 a law was addressed to the two senior officials resident in Alexandria, the diocesan administrator, the *praefectus Augustalis* Evagrius, and the military commander, the *comes Aegypti* Romanus. It imposed penalties on all provincial officials and their staffs if they dared so much as to enter a pagan temple, still less to offer sacrifice while in office: "If any provincial governor during the time of his office relies on the privilege granted by his power to enter polluted places as a sacrilegious violator, he shall be compelled to pay to our treasury fifteen pounds of gold; his *officium*, unless it has tried to prevent him with united force, shall pay an equal sum."[106] The hyperactive Italian clergy, perhaps via a contact with Bishop Theophilus, may well have played a part in stimulating this imperial initiative, since a parallel law with similar provisions had been issued a few months earlier to the *praefectus urbi* at Rome, Albinus; at the ecclesiastical level contacts between Rome and Alexandria were close and regular.[107] These two laws suggest that Theodosius's experiences in Italy, not least his mutually bruising brushes with Ambrose, had convinced him and his advisers that the time had come to make a serious attempt to sanitize in a Christian sense the public administration of the two major cities with the strongest remaining pagan traditions, Rome and Alexandria.

Evagrius and Romanus, themselves Christians, were hardly reluctant servants in this respect. Evagrius, representing the emperor's civilian administration in Egypt, had recently taken the decision to let Bishop Theophilus use an old basilica that had earlier been occupied by an "Arian" congregation at the time of Constantius, but in the meanwhile had fallen into disrepair. During the work of restoration the discovery was made of cavelike cellar rooms that were still used for some kind of pagan ceremonial rites and contained ritual equipment. Theophilus and his associates exposed the pagans and their ritual paraphernalia to public mockery in the streets, and the result was serious communal rioting, in which several people who were inevitably claimed to be Christian supporters were killed, whereupon the ringleaders of the pagan faction took refuge in the huge rambling ancient temple complex of the Sarapeion.[108] After initial negotiations with them brought no satisfactory result, Evagrius, feeling that the implications of the situation were stretching the limits of his authority, sent a report to Theodosius, who by now had returned to Constantinople from Italy.

This all took some time, and the next—and crucial stage—of the affair seems to have occurred during the winter of 391/92.[109] In due course an imperial reply arrived from Constantinople. The text is not preserved, but it was doubtless decorated with the modishly drastic rhetoric of such official pronouncements at this period.[110] All reports of it in the literary sources are ambiguous, offering variously biased and anachronistic interpretations in the light of what actually followed on the ground; but the earliest and most detailed account, that of the ecclesiastical historian Rufinus, himself a contemporary of the events, suggests that the emperor's main aim was to avoid further provocation. Those responsible for the deaths of the Christian rioters, who are already designated by Rufinus as martyrs, were not to be hunted out, but the causes of the troubles—presumably the pagan ritual impedimenta and the possession of the ritual chambers were meant—were to be eradicated.[111] It is easy enough to imagine the pragmatic hand of the praetorian prefect Tatianus being behind the formulation of this essentially conciliatory response.

It did not satisfy, however, the Christian mob, which was now further provoked by Theophilus to physically attack the pagans, who were still holed up in the Sarapeion complex, by doing violence to the ancient buildings themselves; in one form or another—there had been massive remodeling and rebuilding under the Severi—those structures had dominated the prominent hill of Rhakotis in the southwest of the city for some 700 years. Later, when the famous cult statue had been destroyed and the huge temple reduced to a sordid ruin by the vandalizing mob, the triumphalist Christian orthodoxy boldly claimed that the emperor had intended exactly such to occur when he had ordered the roots of the intercommunal discord be eradicated. The defeated pagans saw no reason to contradict this view, since the two main representatives of imperial authority in Alexandria, Evagrius and Romanus, had made no serious attempt to interfere with, still less to prevent, Theophilus's destructive mobilization of the Christian mob: indeed the bitter pagan writer Eunapius made them, together with Theophilus, directly responsible for the attack on the Sarapeion.[112]

The vandalizing of the Sarapeion in the late winter of 391/92 was a dramatic event, which went extravagantly far beyond the normally cautious Theodosian Christianizing policy and tipped the balance of influence in Alexandria in favor of the orthodox Christian community, though a large pagan minority continued to flourish for generations thereafter.[113] The destruction of the complex did not, however, represent imperial policy; it resulted from the exploitation of an accidental find by a rabble-rousing bishop seeking to extend his own influence in the city, even at the cost of endangering the public safety. Evagrius had been replaced as *praefectus Augustalis* before April 392 by the experienced Hypatius, who had already been prefect ten years before,[114] and to our knowledge had made no further career. Hypatius's seems to have been an emergency appointment intended to relieve Evagrius at the peak of the crisis, and not a normal period of duty, since his successor Potamius was already in office on 5 May.[115] We may perhaps conclude from this that Evagrius ceased to be regarded in Constantinople as an adequate incumbent of the post, after his failure to control Theophilus and his mob, and had been replaced as soon as the news reached Constantinople and a halfway adequate successor could be found.

The first months of 392, which were also the last months of Tatianus's praetorian prefecture, saw more laws addressed directly to the *praefectus Augustalis* (six in all, between April and July) than for any comparable period covered by the Theodosian Code, and at least three of them seem related, more or less closely, to the religious rioting of the preceding months. On 9 April a law addressed to Hypatius imposed a heavy penalty of no less than thirty pounds of gold on the governor's bureau for allowing appeals for revision or pardon concerning criminal offenses; no intervention of bishop, cleric, or people was tolerable: "For it is not just to reduce the appropriate severity of punishment for those who by rioting and undisciplined disobedience have seriously disturbed the public peace."[116] The point of reference seems clear enough. As a result of the riots the secular public courts had allowed themselves to be swayed by outside ecclesiastical or mob pressure—clearly exercised in the expectation that extrajudicial influence might again sway the appeals judge— to allow unjustified appeals against convictions. This was to cease. Since bishops and clerics surely only intervened in cases in which Christians (or those who claimed to be such) had been convicted, we must assume that once the riots were over, the imperial authorities had tried to use the normal procedures of the criminal courts to address charges emerging from the troubles, and in doing so had found themselves exposed to illegitimate Christian pressures. News of this must have reached Constantinople, and Theodosius's government, still headed by the moderate pagan Tatianus, reacted by insisting that the laws of the land be applied unequivocally. As late as 18 July an order was issued to Hypatius's successor, Potamius, allowing him to deport religious troublemakers who refused to obey the laws, thus showing that even months later local intransigence was still preventing a return to normal conditions.[117] In May Potamius received an instruction concerning the so-called *defensores civitatis*, who were originally intended to protect the lower authorities and the taxpayer against the illegitimate use of influence by the rich and powerful, but who had themselves begun imposing fines and conducting investigations under torture. This was to stop, and they were to revert to the job implicit in their name. The direct connection with recent events in Alexandria is less easy to perceive here, but it is difficult to imagine that the imperial instruction to the *praefectus Augustalis* that the *defensores* were "to protect the people and the decurions from the annoyance and foolhardiness of wicked men" in the Alexandrian context of 392 had nothing to do with the recent crisis.[118]

Italy Once More

Theodosius's last campaign, his return to Italy in 394 to annihilate the usurper Eugenius, gave later Christian orthodox writers, now claiming Theodosius as one of their own uncompromising heroes, a final chance to characterize a major military campaign as "Christians against pagans" and to stamp on history their tendentious view that the religious difference was the heart of the matter. Widespread modern acceptance of this view, for whatever reason, has stimulated research into Italian paganism of the period and led to the assertion of a "pagan revival."[119] A critical look at the evidence, however, shows that this notion is a chimera relying excessively on dating an undated aggressive anonymous poem, "Against the Pagans," to this time and then identifying the person attacked in it as the pagan praetorian prefect Virius Nicomachus Flavianus. But a date in the 390s is very unlikely. The poem most probably belongs to the preceding decade, and the person attacked is best identified as Vettius Agoratus Praetextatus.[120] Once this is recognized, there is no significant source left supporting the view of a reactivation of paganism at this time, apart from the hostile Christian tradition, and the whole idea of a pagan "revival" — as opposed to a well-enough documented low-level continuity — should be abandoned.

The main reason why the Christians could choose and stick to their interpretation was that neither the Frank Arbogast, who led Eugenius's army at the battle of the Frigidus, nor Eugenius's praetorian prefect, Virius Nicomachus Flavianus, was a Christian. But this fact was essentially unimportant. Both men had been initially appointed by Theodosius, who knew well enough that they were not Christians, and until Valentinian's death they had clearly enjoyed his trust. A more convincing argument can hardly be needed for the fact that for Theodosius their religious affiliation played no serious part in his assessment of their characters and their suitability for their functions in government. Only when they involved themselves with the usurpation of Eugenius, therefore with treason, did they become enemies of Theodosius, just as the strictly orthodox Maximus had become his enemy in 388. But the fact of their not being Christian, as Eugenius himself was, gave interested contemporary Christian publicists a great chance for making propaganda — once

Eugenius was defeated and dead, who was to challenge it?—and now it is not easy to sort out fact from fiction. There is, however, no reason to believe that either side regarded the war primarily as a religious crusade. This motif occurs in its developed form for the first time half a century later in the highly tendentious *Ecclesiastical History* of Theodoret, which is notorious for its novelistic inventiveness and cannot be regarded as giving an authentic picture. Theodoret's more serious contemporaries, Sokrates and Sozomenus, are much more cautious. Although the preliminary signs of this kind of stylizing can be found in Ambrose and his circle, it was Theodoret who first let his fantasy run and massively influenced the later historiographical tradition up to the present day, which found his interpretation clear cut and, since it reflected well on the catholic winner, sympathetic. To the victors the spoils.[121]

The outstanding and undeniable fact, which all interpreters had to contend with, is that the battle of the Frigidus on 5–6 September 394 was no walkover and that Theodosius's army won only after an extremely hard fight. We might reasonably accept the tradition that the emperor had prayed for victory. This was a perfectly normal act for a general, whether pagan or Christian, before a battle, but on this occasion the result of the fight favored the propagation of the naive interpretation that Theodosius's prayer had been answered, that his God had granted him the victory. Such an interpretation was further encouraged by the fortuitous occurrence of a well-known local weather phenomenon that still occurs, the "bora," a sudden gale-force wind blowing down from the pass where the battle took place into the faces of Eugenius's soldiers, which seriously hindered their comfort and effectiveness. Yet another factor encouraged (or, perhaps, failed to discourage) mythmaking: none of the three most prominent enemy protagonists survived the clash of arms. Eugenius was decapitated by Theodosius's troops, and both Arbogast and Virius Nicomachus Flavianus committed suicide, so leaving nobody of any prominence prepared to expose himself by perpetuating the views of the defeated. That Theodosius survived his success by a mere four months was the final breakthrough for the mythmakers.

The reality was certainly more complex. Eugenius, himself a Christian, tolerated competent and influential pagans in prominent positions

around him, just as Theodosius did. He had been made usurping emperor by the pagan Arbogast and was doubtless pleased to receive the
support of Theodosius's influential praetorian prefect for Italy, Virius
Nicomachus Flavianus, whom he presumably knew from Rome, when
his court arrived at Milan. But he must have been disappointed in equal
measure to find that Ambrose, now learning from his mistake with Maximus, had decided to abandon his churches and congregations in Milan
rather than face having to decide how to treat the urbane usurper. Ambrose chose to depart precipitately on an extended pastoral visit to Tus-
cany, from which he returned only after Eugenius had left Milan for the
battlefield—though in an extant letter written to Eugenius he tried to
offer a moral justification for his absence. This time Ambrose avoided
compromising himself with the loser in the civil war, for whoever now
won the decisive battle would find the bishop in place to receive him
on his entry into Milan, ready to adapt his welcome to the result of the
war.[122] Eugenius as an educated Italian knew he had to win over the still
largely pagan aristocracy if he were to get anywhere, just as Theodosius
had tried to do in and after 388. He seems to have made some concessions regarding the traditional cults in the city of Rome, including the
disposition of the altar of Victoria in the Senate House, which doubtless
helped convince Virius Nicomachus Flavianus to join him, but which
offered Ambrose a halfway satisfactory excuse for not meeting Eugenius
on his first arrival in Milan.[123]

Given that Arbogast's army was recruited in Gaul and Germany, it
would be surprising if all the soldiers were Christians, but this must have
applied to Theodosius's army too, since he relied to a large extent on
pagan Huns and Goths who, if Christian at all, were—for Ambrose—
heretical "Arians." The orthodox tradition carefully avoided dwelling on
the contribution of the pagans and the "heretics" to Theodosius's victory, and much preferred to point out pagan activities among Eugenius's
partisans. It might well be that after the victory this was the "official version" of the war that Theodosius and Ambrose worked out together, but
it was not attested until after the death of Theodosius. In Ambrose's
memorial sermon on Theodosius held forty days after the emperor's
death, Maximus and Eugenius are placed together in hell for one reason

only, because they risked an insurrection against their legitimate emperor;[124] and while for Ambrose it was Theodosius's faith that gave him the victory, nothing is said of lack of faith among his opponents.[125] This aspect was first ventilated in Ambrose's commentary on the thirty-sixth Psalm, perhaps dating from 396, where the enemy is characterized as "without faith and impious."[126] Rufinus's account, written before 410, is the first to feature Virius Nicomachus Flavianus prominently, but nobody until modern times believed his untenable tendentious assertion that the learned Flavianus thought he deserved death more for his religious error than for his supporting the usurper.[127]

Rufinus was also the first to imply a direct causal relationship between Theodosius's prayer and the "bora," which was first given its extravagant canonical form of turning back the throwing spears of Eugenius's soldiers into the faces of the throwers as a rhetorical conceit in Claudian's court panegyric *On the Third Consulship of Honorius*, written for 1 January 396, almost a year after Theodosius's death. In a similar semiofficial poem written for the consuls Probinus and Olybrius, and recited on 1 January 395 in Theodosius's presence in Milan, Claudian had not yet invented the conceit, nor did he deign to repeat it in 398, when he again came to speak of the battle in a poem celebrating Honorius's fourth consulship.[128] He would doubtless have been amused and astounded to find his facetious invention still alive and regarded as a standard fact today, though the idea clearly appealed to armchair strategists, as is evident from its almost universal appearance in later ancient accounts after Claudian.

Another popular feature of the battle, more so in modern than in ancient accounts, is the presence of pagan statues, images, or symbols (the ancient vocabulary is ambiguous) in Eugenius's army. Here it is important to note that the earliest account within the strong Christian tendentious tradition, that of Rufinus, himself a native of northeastern Italy, where the battle was fought, knows nothing at all of this, nor do the sober Greek historians Sokrates and Sozomenus, who followed him a generation later but also had access to other traditions; nor does Augustine's protégé Orosius. Augustine himself has a short anecdote on images (*simulacra*) of Jupiter with golden, or gilded, thunderbolts, which military scouts persuaded Theodosius to give them as booty by joking that "they would like to be struck by such thunderbolts." The ultimate source was perhaps the recipients themselves, or soldiers who knew them, but the anecdotal contextualizing makes it impossible to know what function the images played for Eugenius and his people, or indeed whose they were at all.[129]

One suspects that the images were merely part of the traditional representative legionary equipment, since the senior palatine regiment was called *Ioviani Seniores*.[130] The same explanation could have served to fuel the one other passage where a pagan god plays a part in an account of the battle. It is again the romanticizing ecclesiastical simplifier Theodoret who dances out of line. He has a lengthy passage, unparalleled in other sources, including invented "own words" of Theodosius and visions of apostles, in which the emperor asserts that "his army was led by the image of the cross, Eugenius's by that of Hercules."[131] The passage ends with another reference to Theodosius's mocking the image of Hercules, before Theodoret rejoins the main historical tradition in recording Theodosius's death.[132] The passage as such cannot be historically authentic. Everywhere else in Theodoret's history where he lets his characters speak their "own words," he has abandoned history for preachy sensation. He could, however, have been introduced to the idea of Hercules through association with the second palatine legion, the *Herculiani Seniores*, who like the *Ioviani* must have had some traditional regimental emblem with them.[133] The same has to apply, however, to the Eastern army, which also included *Ioviani* and *Herculiani*, and it is highly improbable that the pragmatic Theodosius, in setting out for the war, deprived them of their regimental emblems and identifying tradition.[134] The whole story reeks of late tendentious invention by Theodoret, who was writing in Syria two generations after the event. Even the dust, which he alone imaginatively envisages being whirled into the enemy's faces, smells more like late summer Syrian fantasy than subalpine reality. It is time that historians stopped taking Theodoret seriously. The civil war between Theodosius and Eugenius dressed up as a battle between Christianity and paganism has nothing to do with history. For the religious history of the period the war is simply an irrelevance.

. . .

Under Theodosius the Western Nicene establishment that came to the East with him was able to seize the chance to carry out a coup in the East. Theodosius had not even set foot in Eastern territory when he issued to the people of Constantinople his Western instruction about what he wanted his future bishop of Constantinople to believe. But despite this apparently aggressive beginning, once the Gothic war was over and his new regime well established, Theodosius let himself be swayed far more by considerations of power and the future of his dynasty than by his religious beliefs. He doubtless continued to think it desirable in principle that all his subjects should share his beliefs, but competent non-Christian administrators like Tatianus and Proculus counted as being personally so loyal to the imperial system that they were in effect left in control of the empire in the East for the duration of the critical civil war against Maximus; and in Italy itself the old non-Christian aristocracy in Rome was cultivated and advanced at least as much as—if not more than—the Christian establishment, as long as the aristocrats did not parade their non-Christianity in public office.

The most significant developments in this period in the field of religion took place at a societal level below that of the emperor and his court, doubtless encouraged by the private extralegal example of important men such as Cynegius. Local officials may well have chosen to look the other way when local Christian activists began to deface or even demolish established non-Christian monuments, as Symmachus attests was happening in Rome in the 380s and Libanius and others in Syria at the same time. The spectacular act of destruction at the Sarapeion in Alexandria is only a particularly prominent example. Official public policy at the highest level of the state in this period continued to disapprove of such rogue activities; in this regard Theodosius's argument with Ambrose about the Kallinikon synagogue is characteristic. But the local authorities, even if they had the will to intervene, were normally powerless to prevent action, and they could only restore law and order after damage had been done, in this respect as in others merely responding to grassroots challenges. Under Theodosius, as under his immediate predecessors, law and order, which maintained existing social structures and above all preserved the taxation base of the empire, was always the primary consideration; aggressive Christianizing was not.

EPILOGUE

The apparent disaster caused by the death of Julian in Mesopotamia in the summer of 363 stimulated a reaction among the elite in the imperial army that in the end created not only a new dynasty but also a new administrative structure for the empire. The formal division of responsibility between Valentinian and Valens in 364 had above all practical reasons. The creation of two equally legitimate and equally equipped administrations was the immediate answer to the challenges facing the empire, and on the purely military level it allowed an effective response to the military threats. Given the nature of ancient communications, however, the division of equal responsibility led almost inevitably to a gradual separation of administrations, for when there were two recognized centers for appeals or requests for action, a particular request would be directed to only one of them; and, given the responsive, reactive nature of much imperial administration, this meant that in each case the imperial response came only from the center to which the request had been directed. Even if a generally similar attitude to common problems existed, as seems to have been the case at least in the early years of the rule of Valentinian I and Valens, responses to problems that were first formulated regionally would inevitably vary in detail, increasingly so as time advanced and regionally based precedents piled up, so that separate legislative traditions gradually developed in East and West. Even the Westerner on the Eastern throne, Theodosius, seems to have made no attempt to halt this fundamental development.

State policy in the thirty years following the end of the Constantinian dynasty was dominated by this restructuring at the top, which aimed in the last resort at military and administrative efficiency. The apparently unquestioned retention of the three geographical praetorian prefectures, which had emerged in their precise form purely for dynastic reasons under the Constantinian dynasty, favored, on the one hand, a regionally based centralism and, on the other, the gradual separation of the regions. This can be seen in the regional character of most of the legislation collected for the Theodosian Code, which, it has been argued, illustrates both the strengths and the weaknesses of the regional prefectures. A major development of the period was the growth and reorganization of the city of Constantinople, which under Theodosius finally attained the status of the permanent seat of government for the imperial administration of the East.

Imperial policies seem to have been basically reactive, within a general agreed-upon framework set by each center. This is perhaps clearest in military affairs, where no attempt was made to change the status quo on the frontiers. Strategic aims were broadly conservative and defensive, as they had been for generations: to protect the agricultural tax base by maintaining military control of frontier zones (not just frontier *lines*), a policy that merely continued the fundamentally reactive policy of the High Empire. Julian's disaster in Mesopotamia showed how dangerous a change of strategic aims might prove to be. As far as the nonmilitary imperial administration was concerned, we see no important changes in the provincial structure in this period except in Egypt, which as main provider of food supplies in the Eastern empire under Valens received special administrative attention during the Gothic wars, and then under Theodosius — doubtless for the same reason — was given the status of an administrative diocese, the vicar of which received the high-sounding title *praefectus Augustalis*.

As under the High Empire all major policy and administrative decisions of the executive were made centrally, but the information on which they were based was usually regionally generated in one or another province or city. Despite the existence of an administrative hierarchy for the provinces based on the praetorian prefectures, many local officials — provincial governors or vicars — seem to have been able to approach the central administration directly with questions of detail or interpretation and to have received direct replies to their specific problems. The rulings were preserved in central or local archives and thus were available for collection by the compilers of the Theodosian Code and for inclusion in it as general laws, if their substance seemed appropriate. This system meant in practice that much of the administration was not only broadly reactive but also extremely pragmatic, though inevitably operating within the established mental and legal framework of a centuries-old tradition. The government of the city of Rome is a good example of this, since it seems that the city prefects—this is illustrated particularly well by Symmachus's *relationes* directed to Valentinian II—were as dependent on decisions of the central imperial administration, even for many details concerning daily life in the city, as they had been in the past when the emperor and his officials were themselves regularly resident there.

One area in which since the time of Constantine emperors had regularly taken initiatives was that of religious change, including attempts to create some form of centralized imperial Christian church. All emperors except Julian had been concerned to energize Christian communities and their leaders in support of the Roman state; only Julian allowed personal convictions to change this fundamental attitude. After the failure of Julian's attempt at a rollback, further central initiatives meant to favor Christians or to promote ecclesiastical unity might well have been expected, but in practice state policy on religious affairs in the years after the death of Julian was in general conditioned more by pragmatic reaction than by dogmatic initiative. As in all other fields of endeavor, the emperors tended merely to react to religious requests or problems brought to their attention by subordinate officials or private petitioners rather than to follow an active detailed agenda of their own, whereby regular reaction could, of course, be interpreted as policy, if sufficiently often repeated in a similar way. The overriding aim of all ruling emperors was always the stabilization of the political and economic status quo, the means chosen based not solely on personal conviction but also on the consolidated advice of the imperial *consistorium*.

Such political constants explain varying dogmatic positions—as for example between Valentinian I and Valens—and put the religious question into perspective among imperial priorities. The basic interests of all emperors were identical. Two developments of the period from the death of Julian to that of Theodosius had major long-term effects on the empire. The maintenance in principle of the three Constantinian praetorian prefectures gave the empire a rather unwieldy administrative structure, which, however, remained fundamentally unchanged for centuries. The unwieldiness was reinforced by the establishment of the two permanent administrative centers, in Italy for the West and in Constantinople for the East, where each central imperial bureaucracy had its home and each emperor tended to reside. The more the bureaucracy came to dominate the day-to-day running of imperial affairs, the less the emperor could rule without constant contact with it, and therefore he tended to travel away from home and be seen by the people in the regions of the empire much less frequently. This made him into a much more remote figure and increased the difficulty of representing the emperor as a ruler who attended to the needs of his subjects in person. From the time when Gratian left Trier for Milan to cope more easily with the ongoing Gothic war, an Italian city remained the residence of the emperor in the West, as long as the position existed. When Honorius left Milan, he did not leave Italy, but merely transferred to Ravenna, which seemed safer because it was even less accessible, in view of the insecurity caused by the various barbarian threats that affected Italy after Theodosius's death. In the East the parallel decision—with even longer-lasting consequences—to build up Constantinople as the permanent administrative center seems to have been taken in principle by Valens (though he never stayed there for more than a few weeks), but was finally achieved by Theodosius, whose dynasty made the city their permanent home in the East and set an irreversible precedent for all their successors.

Without the Gothic war neither of these innovative developments (and others consequent on them, such as the religious ferment of the time) need have occurred. There can be little doubt that, seen in the long term, the most important single series of events of the period was the entry of the Gothic masses into the empire in 376 and the resulting tensions and wars. Theodosius failed to drive the Goths back over the Danube after Valens's death at Adrianople. In 382 he and his advisers in the end decided to accept the fact that the Goths were there to stay and to seek a lasting modus vivendi with them. From this time on, the various Gothic groups and clans provided a multifaceted and ever-changing challenge to the imperial administration, for they retained their ethnic consciousness and associated social cohesiveness within the empire for centuries, as Theodosius's agreement with them allowed them to do. This conscious separateness of the Goths was further bolstered by the fact that, insofar as they were Christians at all, they belonged to the "homoian" faith of the missionaries who had converted them in the time of Constantius and Valens. Once Theodosius and his Western staff—for reasons associated with their own religious socialization in the West— began to favor and promote the Nicene confession in their new residence in the East, any social integration of the Goths needed to overcome not only the natural ethnic barrier but also an emotional religious one.

The Goths on Roman soil in the lower Danube region thus provided a quite new dimension to Roman strategic thinking, since they presented a problem that, given their numbers, their ethnic and religious identity, and the specific conditions of their settlement, was in the last resort insoluble. Theodosius had agreed with them, as the price for "peace in our time," that they did not need to be integrated into the Roman imperial system, if they chose not to be. In this one decision—prompted by what were doubtless the best of motives and presented to his public as a solution to current security and manpower problems—he had in effect made a major contribution to the future disintegration of the empire, in which the only partially integrated Gothic elements were to play a decisive part.

NOTES

Abbreviations

For ancient texts and reference works, standard abbreviations are used (see, e.g., *PLRE*). The following should be noted.

CAH   *Cambridge Ancient History.* Vol. 13: *The Late Empire.* Edited by A. Cameron and P. Garnsey. Cambridge, 1998.

Chron. Min.
        Chronica Minora. Edited by Th. Mommsen. *MGH Auctores Antiquissimi.* Vols. 9, 11, 13. Berlin, 1892–98.

CIL   *Corpus Inscriptionum Latinarum.* Berlin, 1863–.

CTh   *Codex Theodosianus.* Edited by Th. Mommsen, P. Meyer, and P. Krüger. Berlin, 1905.

CJ   *Codex Justinianus.* Edited by P. Krüger. Vol. 2: *Corpus Iuris Civilis.* Berlin, 1877.

COD   *Conciliorum Oecumenicorum Decreta.* Edited by J. Alberigo, P. Joannou, C. Leonardi, and P. Prodi; advised by H. Jedin. Centro di documentazione. Istituto per le scienze religiose. Bologna, 1962.

CSEL   *Corpus Scriptorum Ecclesiasticorum Latinorum.* Vienna, 1886–.

FIRA   *Fontes Iuris Romani Antejustiniani.* 2d ed. Edited by S. Riccobono, V. Arangio-Ruiz, and J. Baviera. Florence, 1968–72.

ILS   *Inscriptiones Latinae Selectae.* Edited by H. Dessau. Berlin, 1892–1916.

Mansi   J. D. Mansi (cont. I. B. Martin, L. Petit). *Sacrorum conciliorum nova et amplissima collectio.* 53 vols. Florence-Venice-Paris-Leipzig, 1759–1927.

MGH   *Monumenta Germaniae Historica*

Notitia Dignitatum
        Notitia Dignitatum accedunt Notitia Urbis Constantinopolitanae et Latercula Provinciarum. Edited by O. Seeck. Berlin, 1876.

PL   *Patrologiae cursus completus, series Latina.* Edited by J.-P. Migne. Paris, 1844–64.

PLRE   *The Prosopography of the Later Roman Empire.* Vol. 1, edited by A. H. M. Jones, J. R. Martindale, and J. Morris; vol. 2, edited by J. R. Martindale. Cambridge, 1971, 1980.

RAC   *Reallexikon für Antike und Christentum.* Münster, 1950–.

RE   *Realencyclopädie der classischen Altertumswissenschaft.* Edited by A. Pauly, G. Wissowa, and K. Ziegler. Stuttgart, 1893–1978.

SC   *Sources Chrétiennes* Paris, 1942–.

Chapter II

1 For details on this and what follows, see, e.g., Jones, *Later Roman Empire*, and *CAH*, with extensive bibliography.

2 On the traditional consensual basis of Roman imperial rule, which still retained its validity in the fourth century, see, e.g., Ando, *Imperial Ideology* 73ff.

3 Themistius, *Or.* 4.62b, is a semiofficial statement to this effect.

4 Of the massive modern literature on Julian, see esp. the biographies of Bidez, Bowersock, and Browning for further details.

5 Amm. Marc. 23.3.2; 26.6.2; cf. Zosimus 4.4.2. See below, text at nn. 22–26.

6 Amm. Marc. 25.5.1–4. On this, see Lenski, "The Election of Jovian."

7 See chapter 3, text at n. 61.

8 Amm. Marc. 25.8.8–12, 9.8.

9 Amm. Marc. 25.8.9.

10 Amm. Marc. 25.10.16; Themistius, *Or.* 5.65a.

11 Themistius, *Or.* 5.65a; the baby Varronianus was "as old as his father's purple" (τῆς πατρῴας ἀλουργίδος ἡλικιώτου).

12 Amm. Marc. 25.10.6–7.

13 Amm. Marc. 25.10.16–17; 25.10.11.

14 The court propagandist Themistius delivered his *Or.* 5 on this occasion: see Errington, "Themistius" 874–78; Heather and Moncur, *Politics, Philosophy* 149f.

15 Amm. Marc. 25.10.12–13.

16 Sources on Valentinian before his elevation in *PLRE* 1 s.v. Fl. Valentinianus 7; after it in *RE* s.v. Valentinianus I.

17 Amm. Marc. 26.2.3–4; Zosimus 4.1. Cf. Lenski, *Failure* 24–25.

18 Amm. Marc. 26.4.3.

19 So Amm. Marc. 26.4.5–6. See below, chapter 3.

20 Amm. Marc. 26.5.1–5. Ammianus speaks of "parts" (*partes*), whereas a few years later, once the system had proved itself, Symmachus (*Or.* 1, 14) talks more elegantly and traditionally of "areas of special responsibility" (*curae*). On the practical effects of the division, see chapter 4.

21 Themistius, *Or.* 6. See Errington, "Themistius," 879–81; Heather and Moncur, *Politics, Philosophy* 173f.; Vanderspoel, *Themistius* 157–61.

22 Cf. Amm. Marc. 26.9.10.

23 The main sources are Amm. Marc. 26.6–10; Zosimus 4.4.2–4.4.8.

24 Symmachus, *Or.* 1, 19; Amm. Marc. 26.5.13.

25 Eunapius of Sardis is the ultimate source of Zosimus 4.7.4.

26 Amm. Marc. 26.10.6–8.

27 *Or.* 7. For the interpretation, see Errington, "Themistius" 881–83; see also Vanderspoel, *Themistius* 162–67.

28 Amm. Marc. 27.4.1: *ut consulto placuerat fratri*. See below, chapter 3, text at n. 42.

29 *AE* 1965, 156: *Romani status ac libertatis propugnatori*.

30 *Or.* 3.

31 *Versus paschales* 24ff. Misunderstood by Green, *The Works of Ausonius* 273, who thinks the three Augusti are Valentinian, Gratian, and Valentinian II, and dates the piece (269) between 371 and 375. But Valentinian II, born in 371, was never Augustus in his father's lifetime.

32 *Or.* 9.121c: σοὶ γὰρ δὴ μόνῳ τὸ πέρας τῆς ἐν ἀνθρώποις τιμῆς ἁπάσης ἀρχὴ γίνεται καὶ ὑπόστασις; ibid. 127b: ἑκάτερος γὰρ τῆς ἀσφαλείας τῆς ἑαυτοῦ φύλακα τὸν ἕτερον κέκτηται, καὶ δυοῖν ἑνὸς μέλει, μᾶλλον δὲ ἤδη τρισί, μελήσει δὲ ὅσον οὐδέπω καὶ τέτταρσιν ἑνός; cf. Errington, "Themistius" 885–87.

33 *Or.* 11.153d.

34 Amm. Marc. 30.6, 10. See Errington, "Accession" 440–47. The consul lists and laws, which in the form we have them were compiled after the date of Valentinian II's general recognition as Augustus later in the year 376, naturally give him the title Augustus when mentioning his consulship, which was strictly speaking incorrect at the beginning of the year. The parallel cases are those of Gratian, Valentinian Galates, and Varronianus under Iovian, who were all child consuls without being Augustus. This was intended also for Valentinian II by his father when he designated him for the consulship. On these events in detail, see also Girardet, "Die Erhebung."

35 Themistius, *Or.* 13; see Errington, "Themistius" 889–93.

36 Amm. Marc. 31.1–9. See below, chapter 3, text at n. 53.

37 Amm. Marc. 30.10.6; see Errington, "Accession" 441–42.

38 Amm. Marc. 31.10–16.

39 Zosimus 4.24.3.

40 On the problem, see Errington, "Accession" 450–51; on the background, see Matthews, *Western Aristocracies* 88–89. On Theodosius, see the modern brief critical biography by Leppin, *Theodosius*; Williams and Friell, *Theodosius*, is merely conventional.

41 On this, see Errington, "Accession" 448–49. Cf. *PLRE* i s.vv. Eucherius 2, Antonius 5.

42 Cf. Errington, "Accession" 448–52.

43 See Errington, "Theodosius and the Goths," 19–22. See also, below, chapter 3, text at n. 57.

44 Sources in *PLRE* i s.vv. Ausonius 7, Olybrius 3, Syagrius 2 and 3, Eucherius 2, Antonius 5, Merobaudes 2, Saturninus 10; cf. Bagnall et al., *Consuls ad ann.*

45 References in *RE* s.v. Gratianus 3; *RAC* s.v. Gratianus. On the altar of Victoria, see below, chapter 7, text following n. 115.

46 Zosimus 4.35.2–3.

47 Sources on Maximus in *PLRE* i s.v. Maximus 39; the main narrative is Zosimus 4.35.2–36, with Paschoud's notes in Budé *Zosime* vol. 112; see also Birley, "Mag-

nus Maximus"; Matthews, *Western Aristocracies* 173–82. On Merobaudes's role, see Prosper Tiro, *Chron. ad ann.* 384 (*Chron. Min.* I, 461).

48 Zosimus 4.37.1. Themistius, *Or.* 18, probably delivered on 19 January 384 (see Errington, "Themistius" 895–96), at 220d–221a says the expedition had already been called off (ἔργον μὲν αὐτῇ οὐκ ἠκολούθησεν ἐμφανὲς τοῖς πολλοῖς, ἡ διάνοια δὲ ὑπερήφανος καὶ βασιλική, τιμωρῆσαι τῷ ἀρχηγέτῃ πρὸ ὥρας ἀνηρπασμένῳ καὶ τὸ λείψανον ἐκείνης περισῶσαι τῆς γενεᾶς. καὶ ὅτῳ τοῦτο μικρὸν δοκεῖ, ἐνθυμηθήτω ὅτι αὕτη ἡ γνώμη μόνη καὶ ἡ ὁρμὴ καὶ ἡ ἐπιβολὴ τὴν τόλμαν ἔστησε τῆς ἑσπέρας ἤδη σφριγώσης). There was therefore no sham expedition in 384, as many scholars think, including the influential Vera, "Rapporti" 290f., who unfortunately misinterprets the "Heraklea" where laws were issued from 10 June to 25 July 384 (Seeck, *Regesten, ad ann.*) as Heraklea Lynkestis in western Macedonia on the Via Egnatia. He therefore thinks that Theodosius was on his way to Illyricum at the time. Heraklea is, however, the old Perinthos on the Sea of Marmara, renamed by Diocletian, a favorite summer retreat of emperors from Constantinople.

49 *Collectio Avellana* 40.1, Maximus to Siricius, bishop of Rome: *qui videlicet et ad imperium ab ipso statim salutari fonte conscenderim*; cf. Orosius 7.34.9, who regards Maximus as worthy of being Augustus, if only he had not come to power by breaking his oath: *vir quidem strenuus et probus atque Augusto dignus nisi contra sacramenti fidem per tyrannidem emersisset.*

50 New Augusti were usually consuls in the year after their elevation, and since Maximus held his second consulate in 388, Seeck, *Regesten, ad ann.* rightly argued that his first must have been in 384.

51 *Or.* 18.220d–221a; see n. 48 above.

52 Zosimus 4.37.3. For the date of this visit of Cynegius to Alexandria, I follow Vera, "Rapporti" 279–82, modified by Paschoud, Budé *Zosime* II, 2 n. 176.

53 Mentioned by Ambrose in a letter reporting on a second mission in 385: *Ep.* 30 (24). On this, see McLynn, *Ambrose* 161–64. See below, chapter 7, text at n. 124.

54 Zosimus 4.19.2 wrongly attributes this division to the time of Gratian: see Paschoud, Budé *Zosime* II, 2 n. 140. On the prefectures, see below, chapter 4.

55 References in *PLRE* I s.vv. Fl. Bauto, Fl. Euodius, Eutropius 2; cf. Bagnall et al., *Consuls ad ann.*

56 Ambrose, *Ep.* 30 (24).11. On the date, see below, chapter 7, text at n. 133.

57 See Matthews, *Western Aristocracies* 179, citing Fl. Neoterius and Gildo.

58 Zosimus 4.42.1.

59 Zosimus 4.42.5; Ambrose, *Ep.* 30 (24).4: *qui etiam barbaros mihi inmisit*; cf. ibid. 8.

60 *Collectio Avellana* 39; 40.

61 See Chadwick, *Priscillian* esp. 111–48; Birley, "Magnus Maximus"; below, chapter 7, n. 133 on date and text at n. 134f.

62 Zosimus 4.43.1. It is often alleged on the basis of Sozomenus, *Hist. Eccl.* 7.13.11, that the ex–praetorian prefect Petronius Probus accompanied the court to Thessalonica. Sozomenus indeed says this (also, obviously wrongly, that Probus was praetorian prefect at the time). But Sozomenus has merely garbled his source Sokrates, which we happen to possess: Sokrates, *Hist. Eccl.* 5.11.11–12, in the context of Maximus's revolt in 383, when Probus was indeed praetorian prefect, says he went to Thessalonica (which was formally part of his prefecture); later in the context of 387 (5.12.9) he says Theodosius went to meet Valentinian and Justina at Thessalonica. Sozomenus has ignored the context and jumbled the two statements, thus creating a factoid, which is accepted, however, by *PLRE* I s.v. Probus 5.

63 Sources in *PLRE* I s.v. Symmachus 4, p. 868.

64 Zosimus 4.43.2–44.1.

65 E.g. Orosius 7.35.2: *itaque iustis necessariisque causis ad bellum civile permotus, cum e duobus Augustis fratribus et ultionem unius interfecti sanguis exigeret et restitutionem miseria alterius exulantis oraret.*

66 *Hist. Eccl.* 11.17.

67 Zosimus 4.44.2–4.

68 Theodosius left Thessalonica sometime after 30 April, probably in early June, since he was in Stoboi on 16 June and Scupi (Skopje) on 21 June (Seeck, *Regesten* 275).

69 The sources for the battles are Pacatus, *Pan. Lat.* 12 (2).34–36; Ambrose, *Ep.* 74 = *Extra coll.* 1a (40).22. An alternative date for Maximus's death is 28 July (*Chron. Min.* I, 245; II, 15), which probably leaves Theodosius inadequate time for the transfer of his large army from Skopje via Emona (Ljubljana) to Aquileia, a distance of more than 1,000 kilometers, and for fighting two battles en route (see Seeck, *Untergang* 5, p. 525). The argument of Perler, *Les voyages de saint Augustin* 197–203, for 28 July, supported by his reconstruction of Augustine's travels, is inconclusive.

70 [Aur. Victor], *Epit.* 48.6; Dessau, *ILS* 788.

71 Valentinian issued a law from Trier on 14 June (*CTh* 4.22.3). On Arbogast's appointment, see Zosimus 4.53.3.

72 *Chron. Min.* I, 245.

73 On this relationship, see chapter 8, text at nn. 71–75.

74 Zosimus 4.53. The circumstances of Valentinian's death are obscure, but suicide seems most probable; see Croke, "Arbogast." It was probably inevitable, in view of subsequent events, that charges of murder were made.

75 Sources in *PLRE* I s.vv. Serena, Stilicho; *PLRE* 2 s.v. Eucherius 1. *PLRE* asserts that Eucherius was already in Rome when Theodosius visited the city in 389, but it is not easy to see how this can be right. The source, Claudian, *De cons. Stil.* 3.176–81, depicts the presentation of the child by its mother to Theodo-

sius, which would usually occur soon after the birth. If *PLRE* is right, the heavily pregnant Serena must have gone to Rome without her husband, since Stilicho, as *comes domesticorum*, was tied to the court and could scarcely accompany her. Why did she not stay with him in Milan? Moreover, a pregnant (or any!) wife would not usually accompany her husband to war, so that Serena cannot have reached Rome until after the war, therefore not before, say, October 388; in order to have given birth significantly before Theodosius's arrival in Rome in June (as *PLRE* postulates), she must have been pregnant when she arrived there. Since she cannot have left Constantinople before mid-September, and Theodosius's army, including Stilicho, left Thessalonica at the latest in early June, her pregnancy must date from May at the latest, which means that when she left Constantinople in late September she was five or six months pregnant, and instead of going to her husband and her friends at court in Milan she went off alone to Rome for the birth. Not a likely story. A better scenario, which is easier to reconcile with biological facts and habits of ancient warfare, can be constructed: after the death of Maximus (28 August) Serena (and Honorius) came to the West, arriving in Milan perhaps in late September. Stilicho and Serena, long separated by the war, enjoyed their reunion to the full, and Serena immediately became pregnant with Eucherius. While the court was at Rome from June to August 389, Serena duly gave birth and respectfully presented her newborn son to Theodosius, as in the scene depicted later by Claudian.

76 In general, see *PLRE* 1 s.v. Eugenius; see *RAC* s.v. Eugenius for sources. All modern works on the period discuss these events. See also below, chapter 8, text at nn. 119–34, for discussion of some religious components.

77 See Seeck, *Regesten, ad ann.*

78 Gregory of Tours, *Hist. Franc.* 2.9; Zosimus 4.56.

79 Zosimus 4.57.3.

80 Zosimus 4.55.1: τούτων τῷ βασιλεῖ Θεοδοσίῳ συναγγελθέντων συνετάραξεν ἡ τούτου γαμετὴ Γάλλα τὰ βασίλεια, τὸν ἀδελφὸν ὀλοφυρομένη· πολλῇ δὲ ὁ βασιλεὺς λύπῃ τε ἅμα καὶ φροντίδι κατείχετο, κοινωνοῦ μὲν τῆς ἀρχῆς ἐκπεσὼν καὶ νέου καὶ ἀγχιστείᾳ συναπτομένου.

81 Zosimus 4.58.1, with Paschoud, Budé *Zosime* II, 2 n. 210.

82 Rufinus, *Hist. Eccl.* 11.34; cf. Claudian, *III. cons. Hon.* 73–84. These contemporary Western sources are decisive. On the battle and its political and literary stylizing, see below, chapter 8, text at nn. 121–34.

83 Claudian, *III cons. Hon.* 142–62, with Cameron, *Claudian* 41–45.

84 Eunapius, followed by Zosimus 4.59.4, asserts that the attribution of the whole of the West to Honorius was Theodosius's original plan, but this is mere extrapolation from what actually happened after Theodosius's death. Sokrates, *Hist. Eccl.* 5.26, and Philostorgius, *Hist. Eccl.* 11.2, set the final decision into the context of Theodosius's fatal illness. Their information on this will be correct.

Chapter III

1 Mann, "Power, Force and the Frontiers" 180: "In military matters as in government, within a broad framework of the simplest form, Rome tended less to *act*, than to wait for things to happen and then *react*." This basic attitude had not changed in the fourth century.

2 Out of the massive literature on ancient frontiers and their nature I name only three thoughtful, fairly recent works: Millar, "Emperors, Frontiers, and Foreign Policy"; Isaac, *Limits*; and Whittaker, *Frontiers*. See also Gutmann, *Studien*, and Lee, *Information*.

3 Amm. Marc. 25.8.8–12.

4 Amm. Marc. 26.5.7.

5 Amm. Marc. 26.5.13.

6 Drinkwater, "Germanic Threat" and "Ammianus," argues convincingly against an empire-threatening menace on the Rhine at this time, but he seems to me to underestimate the importance of the emperor's being seen to be doing something about the raiding parties and showing the civilian tax-paying population that the emperor cared about them and was indeed doing something—not just *ad maiorem gloriam Valentiniani*. Perhaps the contemporary military man Ammianus understood the mentality of the times better, after all, than some of his modern critics. Cf. Matthews, *Ammianus* 306ff.

7 Evidence collected by Lenski, *Failure* appendix I.

8 Amm. Marc. 27.1–2; 28.2.1–10. On Alamannia, cf. Symmachus, *Or.* 2.31: *fasces in provincias novas mittite, trans Rhenum iudices praeparate.* Cf. Pabst, *Symmachus*, 338f.

9 Amm. Marc. 28.5.8–14.

10 Amm. Marc. 29.4.2–7.

11 Amm. Marc. 30.3.4–6: *prope Mogontiacum blandius rex ante dictus accitur, proclivis ipse quoque ad excipiendum foedus, ut apparebat. et venit immane quo quantoque flatu distentus ut futurus arbiter superior pacis dieque praedicto colloquii ad ipsam marginem Rheni caput altius erigens stetit hinc inde sonitu scutorum intonante gentilium. contra Augustus escensis amnicis lembis saeptus ipse quoque multitudine castrensium ordinum tutius prope ripas accessit signorum fulgentium nitore conspicuus et immodestis gestibus murmureque barbarico tandem sedato post dicta et audita ultro citroque versus amicitia media sacramenti fide firmatur. hisque perfectis discessit turbarum rex artifex delenitus futurus nobis deinceps socius et dedit postea ad usque vitae tempus extremum constantis in concordiam animi facinorum documentum pulchrorum.*

12 Amm. Marc. 17.8.3–9.1; Julian, *Epist. ad Ath.* 280B.

13 Amm. Marc. 26.4.5.

14 Amm. Marc. 27.8.5; cf. Gutmann, *Studien* 44–45.

15 Amm. Marc. 28.5.1–7.

16 Amm. Marc. 27.8; 28.3.

17 Pacatus, *Pan. Lat.* 2 (12).5: *redactum ad paludes suas Scotum loquar?*; Amm. Marc. 27.8.8: *isdemque restituta omni praeter partem exiguam impensam militibus fessis mersam difficultatibus summis antehac civitatem [sc. Lundinium], sed subito, quam salus sperari potuit, recreatam ovantis specie laetissimus introiit.*

18 Amm. Marc. 28.3; cf. Cleary, *Ending* 45–46.

19 Amm. Marc. 31.10.1–17.

20 Amm. Marc. 30.3–7; cf. *PLRE* 1 s.v. Mallobaudes.

21 Gregory of Tours, *Hist. Franc.* 2.9.

22 On Arbogast, cf. *PLRE* 1 s.v. Arbogastes; Waas, *Germanen* 70–73. Claudian's vituperative description of him as *barbarus exul* (*III cons. Hon.* 66) or *Germanus exul* (*IV cons. Hon.* 74) cannot, however, be taken at face value as evidence that Arbogast had been expelled from his home (as Zöllner, *Geschichte* 23, claims).

23 Gregory of Tours, *Hist. Franc.* 2.9.

24 *ILS* 790.

25 Orosius 7.35.12.

26 The evidence is a series of vague assertions by Stilicho's panegyrist Claudian, which leave many details quite uncertain: *IV cons. Hon.* 439–46; *I cons. Stil.* 189, 220–27; *in Eutr.* I, 377–95; cf. *Epithal.* 278–81.

27 Amm. Marc. 16.10.20–21, 17.12–13.

28 On events in this area in the fourth century, see Stallknecht, *Untersuchungen*; Gutmann, *Studien*; Dittrich, *Beziehungen*; Barcelò, *Auswärtige Beziehungen*; Heather, *Goths and Romans*; Wolfram, *Goten*; Lenski, *Failure* 116f.

29 Amm. Marc. 29.6.2. On the forts, see Lenski, *Failure* appendix I.

30 Amm. Marc. 29.6.1–16; with Gutmann, *Studien* 86f.; Dittrich, *Beziehungen* 86f.

31 Amm. Marc. 30.5–6.

32 Amm. Marc. 30.6.1: *quaedam utilia rei Romanae.*

33 Themistius, *Or.* 14.182c; *Or.* 15.198a; Pacatus, *Pan. Lat.* 2 (12).10.2.

34 Sokrates, *Hist. Eccl.* 5.11.2; Sozomenus, *Hist. Eccl.* 7.13.1; cf. Gutmann, *Studien* 101f.

35 For modern discussions of the treaty, see Heather, *Goths and Romans* 108f.; Barcelò, *Auswärtige Beziehungen* 113–14; Wheeler, "Constantine's Gothic Treaty"; Lenski, *Failure* 122–25.

36 Jordanes, *Getica* 112.

37 Anonymus Valesianus 1.31.

38 Julian, *Caesares* 329a. In connection with the treaty of 370, Themistius, *Or.* 10.135b, avers that this time nobody will see money paid out or ships loaded with clothing going to the barbarians, which was harder to bear than the burdens of war (οὐδεὶς εἶδε χρυσίον ἀπαριθμούμενον τοῖς βαρβάροις, οὐκ ἀργύρου τάλαντα τόσα καὶ τόσα, οὐκ ἐσθῆτος ναῦς γεμιζομένας, οὐχ ἃ πρότερον ὑπομένοντες διετελοῦμεν, βαρυτέραν τῶν καταδρομῶν ἐκκαρπούμενοι τὴν

ἡσυχίαν καὶ φόρον ἐτήσιον φέροντες, οὗ τὸ ἔργον οὐκ αἰσχυνόμενοι τοὔνομα ἐξηρνούμεθα). Apart from a possible intertextual connection with Julian, *Caesares* 329a (τά γε μὴν εἰς τοὺς βαρβάρους ἦν γελοῖα αὐτῷ· φόρους γὰρ ὥσπερ ἐτετελέκει, καὶ πρὸς τὴν τρυφὴν ἀφεώρα), almost surely known to Themistius, Themistius's rhetorical aim in this speech was certainly to enhance the present by blackening the past, which remains only vaguely indicated but implies recent experience. It is unclear whether Themistius is referring to Constantine's treaty.

39 Amm. Marc. 22.7.7–8; cf. Libanius, *Or.* 12.78.

40 Amm. Marc. 26.6.11–12.

41 Amm. Marc. 26.10.3, 27.4.1, 5.1; Zosimus 4.10.1. For an account with discussion of all details of Valens's relations with the Goths and his military operations, see Lenski, *Failure* 116–52, 320–67.

42 *CTh* 15.1.13.

43 Themistius, *Or.* 8, with Heather, *Goths and Romans* 117; Errington, "Themistius" 883–85.

44 See above, text at n. 11.

45 Amm. Marc. 27.5.7–10; Zosimus 4.11.4–7; Themistius, *Or.* 10.135cd; cf. Gutmann, *Studien* 245; Heather, *Goths and Romans* 118f.; on the date (early 370), see Errington, "Themistius" 902–4.

46 Themistius, *Or.* 10.135b; cf. Julian, *Caesares* 329a.

47 *ILS* 771, from Rome.

48 Cf. Wolfram, *Goten* 84f.; Heather and Matthews, *The Goths* 133f.; Thompson, *Visigoths* 94f.

49 The main source is Amm. Marc. 31.2–4. Cf. Wolfram, *Goten* 73f.; Heather, *Goths and Romans* 122f.; Lenski, *Failure* 320f.

50 The evidence was collected by Ste Croix, *Class Struggle* appendix III, 509f. Eight instances (his nos. 3, 5, 11, 12, 13, 14, 15, 16) concern Thrace.

51 Amm. Marc. 31.4.1: *et daturos, si res flagitisset, auxilia.* Cf. Heather, *Goths and Romans* 122f.

52 Amm. Marc. 31.4.12.

53 Amm. Marc. 31.4.9–11, 5.5–9; cf. *PLRE* 1 s.v. Lupicinus 3.

54 See in detail, e.g., Burns, *Barbarians* 23f.; Heather, *Goths and Romans* 142f.; Wolfram, *Goten* 124f.; Lenski, *Failure* esp. 341f.

55 On contemporary reactions to the defeat, see Lenski, "*Initium mali.*"

56 Themistius, *Or.* 15. On this and Theodosius's war, see, in addition to the literature in n. 49, Errington, "Theodosius and the Goths."

57 Themistius, *Or.* 16.211b–d (οὕτω καὶ Σκύθας ὀψόμεθα ὀλίγου χρόνου· νῦν μὲν γὰρ ἔτι τὰ προσκρούσματα αὐτῶν νέα, ληψόμεθα δ᾽ οὖν οὐκ εἰς μακρὰν ὁμοσπόνδους, ὁμοτραπέζους, ὁμοῦ στρατευομένους, ὁμοῦ λειτουργοῦντας); with Errington, "Theodosius and the Goths" 19f.

58 *Notitia Dignitatum Or.* V.61, VI.61.

59 Themistius, *Or.* 34.24; cf. Liebeschuetz, *Barbarians and Bishops* 26f.

60 It is often asserted that Gratian, before Theodosius's agreement in Thrace, had already settled groups of Goths in Pannonia and thus provided a model for Theodosius. Heather, *Goths and Romans* 334f., has shown convincingly that source confusion has given this impression. There is no reliable evidence for it.

61 Orosius 7.31.1–2: *cum et locorum iniquitate captus et hostibus circumsaeptus nullam evadendi facultatem nancisceretur, foedus cum Sapore Persarum rege, etsi parum ut putant dignum, satis tamen necessarium pepigit: quippe, ut tutum et incolumem Romanum exercitum non solum ab incursu hostium verum etiam a locorum periculo liberaret, Nisibi oppidum et partem superioris Mesopotamiae Persis concessit.*

62 Amm. Marc. 25.7.10: *et cum pugnari deciens expediret, ne horum quidquam dederetur.*

63 Amm. Marc. 25.7.9. On these territories, see Lenski, *Failure* 161f.

64 Amm. Marc. 25.7.12 (for Ammianus this clause is also scandalous!); *Buzandaran Patmut'iwnk'* (earlier known as "Faustus of Byzantium"), IV.21, in Garsoïan, *Epic Histories.*

65 The most recent detailed account of these events is in Lenski, *Failure* 167–85.

66 Amm. Marc. 27.12.4, 16–17.

67 Ammianus gives regular reports on Armenian affairs, which seem to have interested him: 26.4.6, 27.12, 29.1.1–4, 30.1–2; cf. Blockley, *Foreign Policy* 30f. On Armenian society in the fourth century, see Garsoïan, *Epic Histories,* 41f., with further literature.

68 *Buzandaran Patmut'iwnk',* VI.1, in Garsoïan, *Epic Histories,* drawing attention to both the internal pressures and the external—Roman and Persian—diplomacy. The precise date of the agreement is uncertain, but there is a good chance that 387 is right.

69 See in general Blockley, *Foreign Policy* 129ff., esp. 151f.; Lee, *Information* 15f., 109f.

70 See, e.g., *CAH,* 444f.

71 Evidence listed in Lenski, *Failure* appendix A.

72 *Notitia Dignitatum Or.* XXXIV (*dux Palaestinae*) 35, 42; *Or.* XXXVII (*dux Arabiae*) 29, 30.

73 Rufinus, *Hist. Eccl.* 11.6; Sokrates, *Hist. Eccl.* 4.36; Sozomenus *Hist. Eccl.* 6.38.

74 Sokrates, *Hist. Eccl.* 4.36.1; Sozomenus, *Hist. Eccl.* 6.38.1. Accepted as reliable by Bowersock, "Mavia" 485–87; see also Lenski, *Failure* 207–9, who dates the incident to the the winter of 377–78 and speculates that the conflict with Mavia was a response to Valens's demanding recruits for the Gothic war.

75 Theophanes, *Chronographia* a.m. 5867 (p. 64 de Boor) for the peace. Theophanes's year ends on 24 March 377 (according to Mango and Scott, *The Chronicle* lxxiv); so he also does not support Lenski's view, *Failure* 207–9, that events con-

cerning Mavia were late 377; moreover, Theophanes only claims to date the peace treaty, the raids having occurred at some unspecified time before this (πολλὰ κακὰ ʿΡωμαίοις ποιήσασα εἰρήνην ᾐτήσατο). Theophanes probably had in any case no real authority for his date, since he was merely excerpting Theodor Lector, who in turn relied on Sokrates and Sozomenus—who offered a later date—and Theodoret, who does not mention the Mavia episode. Why he rejected their date we do not know, but in putting the Gallic appeal to Valens in the same year (i.e., 25 March 376–24 March 377), he at least got that about right. Given the uncertainty of how long the Saracen raiding continued (even if the peace treaty is accidentally dated correctly by Theophanes), it is perhaps better to assume a longer period of instability in this area (for whatever reasons) than to try to link the specific accounts we have to the Gothic war of 378. Sokrates, and following him here Sozomenus, simply misdated the activity to the time of Valens's leaving Antioch. I cannot find convincing Lenski's argument (ibid.) that Sokrates's bumbling three mentions of Valens's leaving Antioch for Constantinople (*Hist. Eccl.* 4.35.6, 36.1, 37.1) means that he really left (or tried to leave) twice. Sozomenus at least did not think so.

76 Amm. Marc. 31.16.5–6; Zosimus 4.22.1–3; Sokrates, *Hist. Eccl.* 5.1.4–5; Sozomenus, *Hist. Eccl.* 7.1.1. Woods, "The Saracen Defenders" 259–79, argues that the Saracens in Constantinople were members of the *scholae*, perhaps even part of Valens's wife Dominica's escort.

77 Pacatus, *Pan Lat.* 12 (2).22.3.

78 *Notitia Dignitatum Occ.* XXV, cf. XXX, XXXI (*duces provinciae Mauretaniae* and *provinciae Tripolitaniae*). The final date of *Notitia Dignitatum Occ.* is significantly later than our period (c. 420), but this will only affect details, not principles.

79 *Notitia Dignitatum Occ.* XXVI.

80 *Notitia Dignitatum Or.* XXVIII (*comes limitis Aegypti*), XXXI (*dux Thebaidos*).

81 On this, see Errington, "A Note."

82 Amm. Marc. 26.4.5. The attacks were *solito acrius*.

83 Amm. Marc. 28.6.1–15. On Romanus, cf. *PLRE* 1 s.v. Romanus 3.

84 Augustinus, *c. Lit. Pet.* 3.25 (29).

85 Amm. Marc. 29.5.20; Zosimus 4.16.3 (usurpation).

86 Amm. Marc. 29.5 narrates the events of the war at great length, praising in particular Theodosius—*cuius virtutes ut impetrabilis ea tempestate prae ceteris enitebant* (29.5.4)—under the rule of whose son Ammianus was writing.

87 Augustinus, *c. Lit. Pet.* 2.83 (184); *c. Ep. Parm.* 1.10 (16)–11 (17); *Ep.* 87.10.

88 See Honorius's laws of 405: *CTh* 16.5.37, 38; 16.6.3, 4, 5; 16.11.2, leading into the last imperial attempt to stamp out the schism.

89 See *PLRE* 1 s.v. Gildo.

Chapter IV

1 Amm. Marc. 26.5.5, who names the first prefects of Valentinian and Valens: in *Oriens* Salutius Secundus, in *Italia, Africa et Illyricum* Mamertinus, and in *Galliae* Germanianus, so emphasizing the importance of the existing administrative structure.

2 This anomaly remained even after Illyricum was split on Theodosius's death and the East appointed its own praetorian prefect for Illyricum. The prefect of Oriens did not then lose Thrace (*Notitia Dignitatum Or.* II.52–58), as might have seemed logical.

3 *PLRE* I s.v. Probus 5.

4 *PLRE* I s.v. Olybrius 3. In late 378 Olybrius was with Gratian at Sirmium, where he was appointed consul for 379, along with Ausonius (Ausonius, *Grat. act.* XII.55).

5 For argument and evidence, see Errington, "Theodosius and the Goths" 22–27.

6 Details in *PLRE* I s.v. Eutropius 2; cf. Errington, "Theodosius and the Goths" 24 n. 134.

7 Details in Errington, "Theodosius and the Goths" esp. 22–27.

8 *CTh* 8.5.35. The evidence for Ausonius's family in office is damaged in transmission and is in itself complex and not easy to interpret. Ausonius was in office as prefect before Olybrius, with whom he shared the consulship in 379 (*Grat. act.* XII.55), and the one extant law directed to him (*CTh* 8.5.35) dates from 20 April 378. He was thus in office as praetorian prefect of the Gauls perhaps already in 377. In his speech thanking Gratian for his consulship, he mentions the association of his son (Hesperius) with him (*Grat. Act.* II.7); in the letter to his grandson (*Protr. ad nepotem* [VIII Green; *Ep.* 22 Peiper] 91), he boasts of his *praefectura duplex*; and in the poem commemorating his father (*Epiced.* 41–42), he claims to have been praetorian prefect in Gaul, Africa, and Italy. Cl. Antonius (*PLRE* I s.v. Antonius 5) was still praetorian prefect in Italy until sometime in the summer of 378 (a law addressed to him was posted in Ravenna on 18 August: *CJ* 2.7.2, where the manuscripts have *data* = "issued," but we know that Gratian was at Sirmium, so this must be wrong), and the first law received by Hesperius seems to have been issued in December 378 or February 379 (*CTh* 6.30.4).

There is, however, a textual problem connected with this law. The manuscripts give *Dec.* 379, but Gratian was not then in Sirmium, where the law was issued; thus a change is necessary. Seeck (*Regesten, ad ann.*) changed the year, and Mommsen (*CTh* ad loc.) suggested changing *Dec.* to *Feb.*, thus saving the consular dating. One or the other must be right, Mommsen's doing less damage to the manuscript reading. Another law issued to Hesperius as praetorian prefect (*CTh* 1.15.8) is also wrongly dated to 21 January 377, when he was proconsul of Africa. Since the subject concerns the office of the praetorian prefect, the date must be incorrect. It would be best to place it together with Hesperius's other legislation in 379 (so Mommsen's suggestion ad loc.). Seeck, followed by *PLRE* I s.v. Hesperius 2, put it in 378, where it is, however, isolated eleven months before Hesperius's next law and three before the one addressed to his father. The interpretation in the text is a new attempt to make sense of the complex tradition. See also Errington, "Theodosius and the Goths" 4 n. 21.

9 *CTh* 13.1.11 of 5 July 379 explicitly deals with affairs of Illyricum, Italy, and Gaul. See Errington, "Theodosius and the Goths" 24.

10 *CTh* 11.31.7.

11 *CTh* 11.30.38; cf. *PLRE* I s.v. Syagrius 3.

12 *CTh* 16.5.5.

13 *Notitia Dignitatum Or.* III; *Occ.* II.28–34.

14 Jones, *Later Roman Empire* 1417–28, produced convincing arguments for a date around 395, and Constantin Zuckermann, "Comites et duces" 142–7, refined them to arrive at the date 401.

15 See above, chapter 2, text at n. 62.

16 *CTh* 16.5.15.

17 On Trifolius, cf. *PLRE* I s.v. Trifolius. This formal transfer also explains how Theodosius could easily supply Rome with grain from Macedonia in 389 (Symmachus, *Ep.* 3.55.1).

18 See below, chapter 8, text at n. 83.

19 *CTh* 1.1.2 (explicitly Italy and Illyricum).

20 *CTh* 13.5.21.

21 *CTh* 11.30.15.

22 So also, though varying in detail, Grumel, "L'Illyricum" esp. 27f.

23 On all general aspects of the Code, see Matthews, *Laying Down the Law*; Harries, *Law and Empire in Late Antiquity* 59f., with references to earlier literature.

24 Occasionally an imperial initiative addressed several local officials directly, as is shown by the law addressed to the Eastern praetorian prefect Anthemius on 9 April 414 (*CTh* 11.28.9) concerning a major tax concession. The archival note recorded by the compilers of the *Code* is evidence that communications on this same matter (*de eadem re*), which were not textually identical, had been sent to "the people" (*populus*)—perhaps that of Constantinople; to the *comes sacrarum largitionum* and the *praepositus sacri cubiculi* concerning items affecting the income of the imperial house (neither of these men were subordinates of the praetorian prefect, so the separate communication would be normal here); to the provincial governors; on matters relating to quarry-workers (*metallarii*) to "the people in the Illyrican provinces" (*populus per provincias Illyrici*) and to the provincial governors there. Since the provincial governors were in any case subordinate to the praetorian prefect, we must assume that in this case they in due course received via the prefectorial distribution system both the full text of the law addressed to Anthemius and a textually different direct communication from

the emperor on the same matter, or on selected aspects of it. How frequent such a procedure was is impossible to tell, but such a tax concession was a distinctly high-profile imperial act and perhaps therefore an exception to the norm.

25 A good example is the reminder to the provincial governor of Nova Epirus Zosimus posted at Apollonia perhaps in 374, *CTh* 6.31.1 (the MSS actually say it was issued there—*dat.*—but Valentinian was, as far as we know, never at Apollonia in Epirus, and certainly not at this time). The law refers back to an already issued *edictum generale* and confirms to Zosimus that it applies also to his *officium* (most likely it is a reply to an inquiry to this effect), which will be fined if the edict is not properly applied (*officium quoque provinciae tuae. . . . multabitur*). Lenski, *Failure* 266 n. 16, thinks the law refers to itself as *edictum generale*, but this is incorrect: the perfect *misimus* (line 2) and *quoque* (line 7) make it clear that this is a subsequent ruling.

26 Clear cases, which seem to prove the principle, are *CTh* 5.14.34, to Rufinus *PPO* posted at Tyre; 8.1.8, to Mamertinus *PPO* posted at Viminacium; and 8.4.6, to Taurus *PPO*, posted at Milan. Possible other cases are 7.3.1 (Tyre), where the name and function of the recipient have not been preserved, but the text seems to be the copy made by the provincial governor at Tyre and sent on to Beirut, where it was posted, and 16.2.15. On these texts, see Matthews, *Laying Down the Law* 180f. Matthews (163) states, however, that different versions (i.e., varying texts) of laws were passed on by the *PPO* to his subordinates, but cites no adequate evidence for significant textual variation. On whose authority might a *PPO* have made alterations to a general law accepted by the consistory and the emperor and directed to him?

27 See, e.g., the collection of evidence for this in Corcoran, *Empire* 170ff.

28 *CTh* 16.5.7 (381, 8 May, to Eutropius), 16.5.9 (382, 31 March, to Florus). See below, text at n. 81.

29 *Const. Sirm.* 6 (*PPO Gall.*); *CTh* 16.2.47, 64 (*CRP*); 16.5.62 (*PV Romae*); 16.2.46; 16.5.63 (*Proc. Afr.*). On these laws see Matthews, *Laying Down the Law* 155–60.

30 Merely assumed by Matthews, *Laying Down the Law* 158, 160, but he does not appreciate the importance of the formal independence of all the named recipients from the *PPO It.Afr.Ill.* (on this see Jones, *Later Roman Empire* 375).

31 *PLRE* 2 s.v. Bassus 8; on the duties of the *CRP*, see Delmaire, *Largesses Sacrées* esp. 75–80.

32 See Corcoran, *Empire* 25–42.

33 *CTh* 1.1.5; cf. Matthews, *Laying Down the Law* 55f.

34 *CTh* 1.1.6, 3: *ut absolutionem codicis in omnibus negotiis iudiciisque valituri nullumque extra se novellae constitutioni locum relicturi, nisi quae post editionem huius fuerit promulgata, nullum possit inhibere obstaculum.*

35 *CTh* 1.1.5, p. 29, 2–9: *hos a nostra perennitate electos eruditissimum quemque adhi-*

bituros esse confidimus, ut communi studio vitae ratione deprehensa iura excludantur fallacia. in futurum autem si promulgari placuerit, ita in coniunctissimi parte alia valebit imperii, ut non fide dubia nec privata adsertione nitatur, sed ex qua parte fuerit constitutum cum sacris transmittatur adfatibus in alterius quoque recipiendum scriniis et cum edictorum sollemnitate vulgandum. missum enim suscipi et indubitanter optinere conveniet, emendandi vel revocandi potestate nostrae clementiae reservata. declarari autem invicem oportebit nec admittenda aliter.

36 Amm. Marc. 26.4.3: *participem quidem legitimum potestatis, sed in modum apparitoris morigerum*; cf. 25.5.1–2; 27.4.1.

37 Amm. Marc. 26.10.6, 8.

38 *Collectio Avellana* 6.

39 *Rel.* XV. On this problem, see the notes of Seeck in his edition in *MGH Auct. Ant.* 6.1 and the commentary of Vera *ad rel.* 2, p. 9. On Symmachus, see below, chapter 5, text at nn. 52–70.

40 Orosius 7.36.1: *commune imperium divisis tantum sedibus.*

41 *De mag.* 3.19.

42 See above, text following n. 35.

43 Cf. Lenski, *Failure* 267–68, referring to *CTh* 4.6.4 (West) and Libanius, *Or.* 1.145 (East), on the inheritance rights of bastards. Lenski's attention to divorce law, however, is not wholly convincing, since here Valentinian and Valens simply left Julian's law on the subject allowing unilateral divorce untouched and took no new action themselves. Doing nothing hardly amounts to an argument for a coordinated policy.

44 References and useful discussion in Lenski, *Failure* 299f.

45 Despite the detailed evidence that Lenski cites, his assertion, in *Failure* 272, that "a sophisticated system of communication" existed under Valentinian and Valens seems inadequately supported. Most cases can be explained, perhaps more realistically, by postulating an early general agreement on major aspects of policy while the emperors were still together, and some immediate actions resulting from this agreement. Moreover, in general we have to assume a fundamentally similar basic attitude of the administrative staff in each division toward problems that cropped up—their training and administrative socialization must have been very similar, if not identical—and this seems more likely to explain most of the similarities in decisions taken than the difficult assumption of a comprehensive regular exchange of legal texts once the administrations had separated.

46 Gaudemet, "La première mesure" 147, writes of "a certain instability" in ancient legislative texts to encompass this phenomenon of different formulations, each adapted to local conditions, of very similar legislative ideas and purposes.

47 *CTh* 16.10.10, 11. On the content and context of these two laws, see below, chapter 8, text at nn. 106–7.

48 The basic study of this whole question is Gaudemet, "Le partage législatif dans la seconde moitié du IVe siècle," though many details now require a different interpretation.

49 *CTh* 6.5.2 referring back to 6.7.1+9.1+11.1+14.1+22.4. *CTh* 6.5.1, a similar Theodosian law issued in Constantinople to the prefect of the city there, Clearchus, on 29 December 383, does not mention the precedent of Valentinian I.

50 *CTh* 6.35.13 referring back to 6.10.2+22.5+26.2.

51 *CTh* 15.1.33, perhaps referring back to 15.1.18. On Vincentius, cf. *PLRE* 2 s.v. Fl. Vincentius 6.

52 *CTh* 7.4.22, 23.

53 *CTh* 10.5.1, 12.6.25.

54 Joh. Lydus, *De mag.* 3.19.

55 Cf. Gaudemet, "Le partage législatif dans la seconde moitié du IVe siècle" 335f.

56 *CTh* 12.1.90 referring back to 12.1.74.

57 *CTh* 12.1.96.

58 *CTh* 6.30.13 of 28 November 395: *officium . . . eas tantummodo teneat dignitates, quas divae recordationis Valentis constitutio conprehendit.*

59 *CTh* 6.4.34, line 7: *poenam lege divi Valentis statutam imminere praecepimus.* The reference seems to be to *CTh* 6.4.20 of 8 May 372.

60 *CTh* 6.4.22. Lenski, *Failure* 271, thinks they were coordinated, but the explanation may be just imitation.

61 *CTh* 3.9.1, perhaps referring back to 3.8.2.

62 *CTh* 6.22.8 referring back to 6.22.7.

63 Remnants of the original statement of intention are contained in *CTh* 12.6.5 (East): *perpenso prospeximus studio, ut susceptores et praepositi horreorum ex praesidali officio, qui per diversa officia militiae sacramenta gestarunt, congrua ratione crearentur.* See also 12.6.7 (Italy and Illyricum): *ad susceptionem specierum veniant, qui ante omnia sciant se decuriones non esse.* On this coordination attempt, see also Lenski, *Failure* 297–98.

64 *CTh* 12.6.4. The curious phrase expressing the emperor's insistence on appointment by the proconsul, "in such a way that the risk attached to the appointment does not leave the bureau of the proconsul" (*ita tamen, ut creationis periculum a proconsulari officio non recedat*), suggests that the bureau had objected to the inevitable odium that would be attached to this unpopular new function.

65 *CTh* 12.6.9.

66 *CTh* 12.6.6.

67 *CTh* 12.6.5.

68 *CTh* 12.6.7.

69 *CTh* 12.6.20.

70 *CTh* 12.6.31.

71 *CTh* 12.6.33.

72 Jones, *Later Roman Empire* 145–46, assumed that the reform quickly collapsed everywhere, but this is not a necessary conclusion.

73 *CTh* 12.1. I have tried to exclude "double entries"—i.e., laws of which two fragments are listed under different numbers—from this count. These are normally recognizable by being issued to the same person from the same place on the same day.

74 *CTh* 12.1.85, 86 (two fragments issued to *PPO Illyrici* Eutropius on the same day).

75 This is one of the main themes of the standard modern works on Libanius and Antioch: cf. Petit, *Libanius* esp. 63–69, 247–94; Liebeschuetz, *Antioch* esp. 119f.

76 *CTh* 10.19.7.

77 Amm. Marc. 26.8.14, 31.6.6.

78 *CTh* 10.19.5 (the manuscripts date it in 369, but also record it as issued at Antioch, where Valens was first in 370, and as issued to Fortunatianus *comes rerum privatarum*, who was also first in office in 370: so Seeck, *Regesten, ad ann.*)

79 *CTh* 10.3.3.

80 *CTh* 16.7.3.

81 *CTh* 16.7.1, 16.5.7.

82 *CTh* 16.7.3, p. 884 lines 5–7: *eos vero, qui Manichaeorum nefanda secreta et scelerosos aliquando sectari maluere secessus, ea iugiter atque perpetuo poena comitetur, quam vel divalis arbitrii genitor Valentinianus adscripsit vel nostra nihilo minus saepius decreta iusserunt.*

83 *CTh* 16.5.3: *his quoque qui conveniunt ut infamibus atque probrosis a coetu hominum segregatis.* On this and related matters, see Errington, "Church and State" 51–54.

84 *CTh* 10.10.28 referring back to 10.10.13.

Chapter V

1 Ausonius, *Ordo Urbium Nobilium* (XXIV Green) 1. On Rome in the fourth century in general, see Jones, *Later Roman Empire* 687–711; Chastagnol, *Préfecture*; Curran, *Pagan City*; Pietri, *Roma Christiana*.

2 See Chastagnol, *Préfecture* 36–42, 297–300.

3 Alföldi, *Conflict*.

4 On the prefects, see esp. Chastagnol, *Préfecture* 427f.; on the individuals, see Chastagnol, *Fastes* nos. 66–76.

5 Chastagnol, *Fastes* no. 66; *PLRE* 1, s.v. Symmachus 3.

6 Viventius (Siscia: *Fastes* no. 68); Ampelius (Antioch: *Fastes* no. 71); Bappo (?Gaul: *Fastes* no. 72); Eupraxius (Mauretania: *Fastes* no. 74); Isfalangius (Iberia or Illyricum: *Fastes* no. 76).

7 Maximinus was born of a Dacian family in Sopianae in Valeria (*PLRE* 1, s.v. Maximinus 7); Simplicius (Emona: *PLRE* 1, s.v. Simplicius 7); Doryphorianus (Gaul: *PLRE* 1, s.v.).

8 *CTh* 1.6.2, 8.5.19 (364), 10.1.9, 8.5.22, 1.6.5 (365), 1.6.6 (368), 9.16.10 (371), 6.7.1 (372), 11.30.36 (374).

9 *CTh* 9.40.5, 11.1.8, 14.3.3, 14.3.4, 14.3.5, 14.3.6, 14.6.2, 14.15.1, 14.22.1, 15.1.12, 14.21.1 (364), 13.5.11, 13.6.2, 14.3.8, 11.2.1, 14.3.11, 11.2.2, 11.14.1, 14.6.3 (365), 14.3.7, 14.4.4 (367), 3.12.4, 14.3.13, 13.5.13 (369), 13.5.9, 9.40.9, 14.3.9, 14.3.10 (date uncertain, *PV* Olybrius).

10 *CTh* 6.4.18 (365), 15.7.1 (?367), 14.5.1 (?369), 15.10.1 (371), 6.4.21 (372).

11 *CTh* 15.1.11; cf. Amm.Marc. 27.9.10. Lenski, *Failure* 277–78.

12 *CTh* 9.40.8, 16.1.1 (365), 16.5.3 (372).

13 *CJ* 12.1.9; *CTh* 6.4.18 (365), 9.40.10, 6.35.7 (367), 9.35.1 (369), 6.4.17 (?370), 9.16.10, 8.5.32 (371), 6.4.21 (372).

14 *CTh* 11.14.1 to Volusianus; cf. 1.6.5 also issued to Volusianus as *PV* on (it seems) the same day concerning the function of the *PV* in the *annona*. Lenski, *Failure* 279 n. 96, would include in this law 14.17.3 issued to Maximus *Praef. Ann.* posted in Rome on 4 April in a consulate of Valentinian and Valens and arranged wrongly by the compilers after December 365, and 14.7.4 to Mamertinus *PPO* and posted on the same day. But since both the recorded recipients and the subject (*panis gradilis*) are different, this inclusion seems dubious.

15 *CTh* 13.3.8, 9. The rules were made to be bent and could not even be respected by the central administration, as a case referred to the court by Symmachus in 384 shows (*Rel.* 27); see below, text at n. 63.

16 *CTh* 14.9.1.

17 Amm. Marc. 27.3.11–13; *Collectio Avellana* 1.

18 Amm. Marc. 27.9.9; *Collectio Avellana* 5–6.

19 *Collectio Avellana* 8, 9.

20 *Collectio Avellana* 11, 12. On the details of this affair, see esp. Pietri, *Roma Christiana* 1:414–18; Curran, *Pagan Rome* 137–41; below, chapter 7, text at n. 79.

21 On the chronology of these events, see Barnes, *Ammianus Marcellinus* appendix 9, 241–46.

22 Amm. Marc. 28.1. For his career, see *PLRE* 1 s.v. Maximinus 7. For a more sympathetic account of Maximinus, see Szidat, "Staatlichkeit" 481–95.

23 See, e.g., Matthews, *Roman Empire* 204–18.

24 *CTh* 9.40.10: *quotiens in senatorii ordinis viros pro qualitate peccati austerior fuerit ultio proferenda, nostra potissimum explorentur arbitria, quo rerum adque gestorum tenore comperto eam formam statuere possimus, quam modus facti contemplatioque dictaverit.*

25 *CTh* 9.35.1: *nullus omnino ob fidiculas perferendas inconsultis ac nescientibus nobis vel militiae auctoramento vel generis aut dignitatis defensione nudetur, excepta tamen maiestatis causa, in qua sola omnibus aequa condicio est.*

26 *CTh* 9.16.10: *quia nonnulli ex ordine senatorio maleficiorum insimulatione adque invidia stringebantur, idcirco huiusmodi negotia urbanae praefecturae discutienda*

permisimus. quod si quando huiusmodi incideret quaestio, quae iudicio memoratae sedis dirimi vel terminari posse non creditur, eos, quos negotii textus amplectitur, una cum gestis omnibus praesentibus adque praeteritis ad comitatum mansuetudinis nostrae sollemni observationi transmitti praecepimus.

27 Amm. Marc. 28.1.12; cf. *PLRE* I s.v. Leo I.

28 Symmachus, *Orr.* I, 2. See above, chapter 2, text at nn. 24, 30.

29 Amm. Marc. 28.1.24–25; cf. *PLRE* I s.v. Eupraxius.

30 Amm. Marc. 28.1.17–23.

31 See above, chapter 4, text at n. 8.

32 *Ord. urb. nob.* (XXIV Green), I.: *prima urbes inter, divum domus, aurea Roma.*

33 This is often assumed and is argued for in detail by Barnes, "Constans and Gratian," and Girardet, "Die Erhebung" 119, 140–44; but there is no good evidence: see Errington, "Themistius" 889–93.

34 *CTh* 9.1.13. For further details, see most recently Flach, "Das iudicium quinquevirale."

35 Cf. Chastagnol, *Fastes* nos. 77, 78, 79; *PLRE* I s.vv. Bassus 21, Rufinus II, Gracchus 3.

36 Chastagnol, *Fastes* no. 81; *PLRE* I s.v. Martinianus 5.

37 Chastagnol, *Fastes* no. 82; *PLRE* I s.v. Hypatius 4.

38 Chastagnol, *Fastes* no. 83; *PLRE* I s.v. Arborius 3.

39 See the tables in Chastagnol, *Préfecture* 428, 436.

40 The increasing proportion of Christians in the Roman senatorial aristocracy from the time of Gratian onward has been emphasized recently by Salzmann, *Christian Aristocracy.*

41 *CTh* 9.35.3: *severam indagationem per tormenta quaerendi a senatorio nomine submovemus.*

42 *CTh* 11.2.3, 14.3.16, 14.6.4.

43 *CTh* 15.7.4+5, 15.7.6–8, 15.10.2.

44 *CTh* 1.6.8, 8.9.2.

45 See above, chapter 2, text following n. 44; below, chapter 7, text at nn. 84ff.

46 *Rel.* 3; see below, chapter 7, text at n. 116. Here I am only concerned with aspects affecting the relationship between the city (and Senate) and the imperial administration.

47 Ambrose, *Ep.* 72 (17).10: *ante biennium ferme.*

48 Prudentius, *contra Symmach.* I.552, writes: *fertur enim ante alios generosus Anicius urbis | inlustrasse caput (sic se Roma inclyta iactat).*

49 *Ep. extra coll.* 10 (57).2, to Eugenius.

50 Symmachus, *Rel.* 3: *denegata est ab improbis audientia*; Ambrose, *Ep.* 72 (17).10.

51 For the alleged ancient evidence (Zos. 4.36), see below, chapter 7, n. 119. Errington, "Church and State" 33–34 n. 63.

52 Discussion and detailed commentary on these texts (together with text and Ital-

ian translation) in Vera, *Commento storico*; a less satisfactory English edition, with text, translation, and brief notes, is in Barrow, *Prefect and Emperor*.

53 *Rel.* 30.4: *nos venerari potius quam interpretari oracula divina consuevimus.*

54 *Rel.* 49.4: . . . *malui iudicium de eo clementibus reservare. alia est enim condicio magistratuum, quorum corruptae videntur esse sententiae, si sint legibus mitiores, alia est divinorum principum potestas, quòs decet acrimoniam severi iuris inflectere.*

55 On the religious implications of this affair, see below, chapter 7, text following n. 115.

56 *Rel.* 4.1: *haec ratio sola novum statutum benigno tunc persuasit ingenio, ut veterem magistratum dives pompa gestaret.*

57 *Rel.* 20.1.

58 *Rel.* 20 is concerned with this financial question. For the carriage, see *Notitia Dignitatum Occ.* IV and photographs of the three manuscript pictures in Chastagnol, *Préfecture* pl. I–III.

59 *Rel.* 21 with the commentary of Vera, *Commento storico* 153–60.

60 *Rel.* 17; *CTh* 1.6.9: *disputari de principali iudicio non oportet: sacrilegii enim instar est dubitare, an is dignus sit, quem elegerit imperator.*

61 *Rel.* 23.

62 *Rel.* 22: . . . *utrum fas sit novos tribunos servata lege differri an magis veteres oporteat praelata devotione removere.*

63 *Rel.* 27.4: *quare motus ambiguis et neque divi genitoris vestri ausus rumpere sanctionem neque obviam specialibus venire praeceptis, divino arbitrio numinis vestri subditis allegationibus partium summam negotii reservavi, opperiens, quid deliberatio augusta constituat, cui soli fas est de scitis divalibus iudicare.*

64 *Rell.* 25, 26. The architects were also responsible for a basilica (*Rel.* 25.2; *Epp.* 4.70.1, 5.76.1)—not necessarily a church, though it is often identified on inadequate evidence with San Paulo Fuori le Mura—but this was not the main source of the problem that gave cause for the investigation. The identification of the building projects is quite uncertain: see Vera, *Commento storico* 187–88, for detailed discussion.

65 *Rel.* 26.3.

66 Cf. Chastagnol, *Préfecture* 363–68; Niquet, *Monumenta* 77–86.

67 E.g., *ILS* 1221 for Anicius Paulinus, cos. 334 (*PLRE* 1 s.v. Paulinus 14): *petitu populi R., testimonio senatus, iudicio dd. nn. triumphatoris Aug. Caesarumq. florentium.*

68 *Rel.* 12.

69 *Rel.* 24.

70 *Collectio Avellana* 4. On Pinianus, cf. *PLRE* 1 s.v. Pinianus 1; Chastagnol, *Fastes* no. 91.

71 *CTh* 6.35.13, 6.28.4, 13.3.13. The last, dated 22 January 387, confirms the law

of Valentinian I about the modalities of appointment of doctors in Rome, the ignoring of which in Milan had caused Symmachus such headaches (*Rel.* 27).

72 *PLRE* I s.v. Iulianus 37; Chastagnol, *Fastes* no. 92.

73 Amm. Marc. 27.6.1.

74 Amm. Marc. 27.6.2: *lenis . . . et mollior.*

75 *Collectio Avellana* 40.

76 Symmachus, *Ep.* 3.52, 63.

77 Sokrates, *Hist. Eccl.* 5.14.6; cf. Symmachus, *Ep.* 2.28, 30, 31, 32.

78 *PLRE* I s.v. Victor 13; Chastagnol, *Fastes* no. 93. His extant *History of the Caesars* was already published by c. 361.

79 *ILS* 2945: *[ve]terum principum clementiam [sa]nctitudinem munificentiam supergresso, d.n. Fl. Theodosio pio victori semper Augusto Sex.Aur.Victor v.c. urbi praef. iudex sacrarum cognitionum d.n.m.q.e.*

80 Symmachus, *Ep.* 2.52, 3.55.

81 Claudian, *de cons. Stil.* 3.176ff. Cf. above, chapter 2, text at n. 75.

82 *Cons. Const. ad ann.*; *Fasti Vind. Priores* 511 (*Chron. Min.* I, p. 298). For the triumph, see Rufinus, *Hist. Eccl.* 11.17, followed by Sokrates, *Hist. Eccl.* 5.14, and Sozomenus, *Hist. Eccl.* 7.14.7; cf. McCormick, *Eternal Victory* 85.

83 *CIL* 6.31413, 36959, 31313 = *ILS* 789: *extinctori tyrannorum ac publicae securitat[is] auctori.* On Albinus, cf. *PLRE* I s.v. Albinus 15; Chastagnol, *Fastes* no. 94.

84 *CIL* 6.36960 = *ILS* 8950 (Thermantia). On Theodosius senior, cf. Symmachus, *Rell.* 9, 43, with commentary of Vera, *Commento storico* ad loc.

85 For the details, see Pellizzari, *Commento storico* esp. 51–57; Cecconi, *Commento storico* 47–53.

86 Sokrates, *Hist. Eccl.* 5.14, has the story that Symmachus took refuge in a Novatian church and was only pardoned by Theodosius when the Novatian bishop Leontius appealed to Theodosius on his behalf, whereupon Symmachus wrote his apologia to Theodosius (cf. Symmachus, *Ep.* 2.13: *. . . cum civiles et bellicas laudes domini nostri Theodosii stili honore percurrerem*; with Cecconi, *Commento storico* p. 52 and commentary ad loc.). Sokrates in fact had good information about Novatians through his contacts with them in Constantinople, and there may be something in his story. It is certainly remarkable that it is Leontius and not the catholic bishop Siricius who plays the leading role in the affair, which is not at all what we would expect, if the story were a complete invention by ecclesiastical circles: had Siricius perhaps, like Symmachus, also been too ready for his own comfort to welcome the catholic usurper Maximus? Cf. also McLynn, *Ambrose* 311–12.

87 Symmachus, *Ep.* 3.85. On Neoterius, who had belonged to Theodosius's first team in the East, where he had succeeded Olybrius as praetorian prefect of the East in 380, cf. *PLRE* I s.v. Neoterius. He then returned to Italy, where he be-

came Valentinian II's praetorian prefect of Italy, Illyricum, and Africa in 385. His appointment to Gaul fell between 8 November 389, when his predecessor Constantinianus was still in office (*CTh* 6.26.5), and 2 March 390 (*CTh* 10.18.3).

88 E.g., Rufinus (*Ep.* 3.85), the new consul Neoterius himself (*Ep.* 5.38), and one Hephaistius (*Ep.* 5.34). See the commentaries of Pellizzari, *Commento storico*, and Rivolta Tiberga, *Commento storico* ad locc.

89 *Pan. Lat.* 12 (2). The anniversary of Maximus's defeat was still celebrated in Rome under Justinian: Procopius, *Bella* 3.4.16.

90 Often done, however: for a traditional discussion of the circumstances of the speech, see Nixon and Rodgers, *Praise* 443f.

91 Cf. *PLRE* 1 s.v. Drepanius.

92 *Pan. Lat.* 12 (2) 2.2–4: *fuerit abieritque tristis illa facundiae ancillantis necessitas, . . . cum gratis agebant dolentes et tyrannum non praedicasse tyrannidis accusatio vocabatur. nunc par dicendi tacendique libertas . . .* Nixon, in Nixon and Rodgers, *Praise* 449 n. 5, writes acutely, but too cautiously, "One is entitled to wonder whether Pacatus, like Symmachus, had praised Maximus in panegyric." In fact, there is little room for doubt, the wording being as clear as such things can be in a panegyric.

93 Cf. ibid. 15.2: *ut de his sileam quos tibi primus ille nascentis imperii dies obtulit, tantis virtutibus praeditos ut non pro copia sumpti sed ex copia viderentur optati, quos tu postea qualesque legisti, quibus provinciarum custodiam, quibus militaris rei summam, quibus consiliorum tuorum arcana committeres.*

94 Ibid. 45.6–7: *nullius bona publicata, nullius multata libertas, nullius praeterita dignitas imminuta. nemo adfectus nota, nemo convicio aut denique castigatione perstrictus culpam capitis aurium saltem molestia luit. cuncti domibus suis, cuncti coniugibus ac liberis, cuncti denique (quod est dulcius) innocentiae restituti sunt. vide, imperator, quid hac clementia consecutus sis: fecisti ut nemo sibi victus te victore videatur.* The statement is more than slightly disingenuous, especially the mention of *praeterita dignitas*, since honors and status acquired from Maximus were indeed explicitly canceled (*CTh* 15.14.6–8).

95 Ibid. 47.3: *ea vero quae Romae gesta sunt, qualem te Urbi dies primus invexerit; quis in curia fueris, quis in rostris; ut pompam praeeuntium ferculorum curru modo, modo pedibus subsecutus alterno clarus incessu nunc de bellis, nunc de superbia triumpharis; ut te omnibus principem, singulis exhibueris senatorem; ut crebro civilique progressu non publica tantum opera lustraveris sed privatas quoque aedes divinis vestigiis consecraris, remota custodia militari tutior publici amoris excubiis, horum haec linguis, horum, inquam, voce laudentur.* The translation in the text was made by comparing that of Nixon in Nixon and Rodgers, *Praise* 510, to which I am indebted.

96 *CTh* 15.5.18, of 17 June.

97 *CTh* 2.8.19.

98 *CTh* 9.16.11.

99 *CTh* 11.30.49, 6.1.8, 12.16.1, 14.4.5, 14.4.6, 15.2.5.

100 *PLRE* 1 s.v. Flavianus 15, with emendations in Errington, "Praetorian Prefectures."

101 Ambrose, *Ep. extra coll.* 10 (57), 4.

102 The first law addressed to Flavianus dates from 11 May 391 (*CTh* 11.39.11 = 16.7.4). On modern attributions of other laws to him in 390, see Errington, "Praetorian Prefectures" esp. 448f.

103 *CTh* 16.10.10 (text in chapter 8, n. 88).

104 *Pro templis* (30) 35.

105 Ambrose, *Ep.* 73 (18).16.

106 *PLRE* 1 s.v. Alypius 13; Chastagnol, *Fastes* no. 95 (Alypius); *PLRE* 1 s.v. Philippus 8; Chastagnol, *Fastes* no. 96 (Philippus).

107 Ambrose, *Ep. extra coll.* 10 (57).5.

108 Ibid. 6.

109 *PLRE* 1 s.v. Pasiphilus 2; Chastagnol, *Fastes* no. 96. His title is preserved in an inscription from Pozzuoli *ILS* 792: *agens vicem praefectorum praetorio et urbi.*

110 Cf. Chastagnol, *Préfecture* 443f.

Chapter VI

1 See esp. Dagron, *Naissance*; Mango, *Le développement* esp. 13–50.

2 Jerome, *Chron. ad ann.* 373; cf. Themistius, *Or.* 11.151d–152a (aqueduct); *Notit. urb. Const.* Regio V p. 233 Seeck (*Horrea Valentiaca*). See Lenski, *Failure* appendix D, 399–401.

3 Amm. Marc. 31.16.3–7.

4 Themistius, *Or.* 14 with Errington, "Theodosius and the Goths" 8–9; Heather and Moncur, *Politics, Philosophy* 218f.

5 See Errington, "The Accession."

6 On this, see Mango, *Le Développement* 43ff.

7 See above, chapter 3, text at n. 56.

8 See, e.g., Cameron, *Circus Factions* esp. 157f.

9 See, e.g., Cameron, *Porphyrius* plate 19.

10 Philostorgius seems to have been the first, *Hist. Eccl.* 2.9, but he was quickly followed by Sozomenus, *Hist. Eccl.* 2.3.6, 3.34.3. On this whole question, see Dagron, *Naissance* 126f.; also Heather, "New Men," 11–33.

11 Details in *PLRE* 1 s.vv. Fl. Ablabius 4, Fl. Philippus 7.

12 *CTh* 6.4.5–6. The creation of the praetorships is not explicitly stated in the extract of the law as we have it, but it is inconceivable that these posts, the sole function of which was to regulate entry into the Senate, could have existed before their function and conditions were fixed. For another view, see Heather, "New Men" 12; but I still find Jones, *Later Roman Empire* 132–33, convincing.

13 On this and what follows, see Jones, *Later Roman Empire* 522–54.

14 Symmachus, *Ep.* 1.52: *pars melior humani generis senatus.*

15 Themistius, *Or.* 34.13.

16 Among his prefects of the city at Rome were Fabius Titianus (consul 337 [*PLRE* 1 s.v. Titianus 6]), L. Aradius Valerius Proculus (consul 340 [*PLRE* 1 s.v. Proculus 11]), and Aurelius Celsinus (prefect of the city 341 [*PLRE* 1 s.v. Celsinus 4]).

17 *CTh* 6.4.4; 7.

18 On this development, see Chastagnol, *Préfecture* 36–42.

19 This *Oratio Constantii* is preserved in a Greek translation transmitted with the works of Themistius and perhaps translated by Themistius himself. The text is in the Teubner edition of Themistius, vol. 3, 122f. Cf. Errington, "Themistius" 866–68.

20 *CTh* 6.4.8, 9.

21 This is implicit in *CTh* 6.4.11 (12 August 357), which insists that senators from Achaia, Macedonia, and Illyricum in general were not to absent themselves from meetings just because of their distance from the meeting place in Rome. For this interpretation, see Dagron, *Naissance* 127–28, against those, including Jones, *Later Roman Empire* 132 and 1093 n. 49, who interpret the law as an act of transfer of these people to Constantinople.

22 Themistius, *Or.* 34.13. On the proconsulship, see Libanius, *Ep.* 40, with Daly, "Themistius' Refusal."

23 *Cons. Const. ad ann.*

24 *CTh 1.6.1*: the provinces were Bithynia, Paphlagonia, Lydia, Hellespontus, the Islands, Phrygia Salutaris, Europa, Rhodope, and Haemimontus.

25 *CTh* 1.28.1.

26 *CTh* 12.1.48.

27 The names have to be deduced from the fact that these named posts existed already in 384 (*CTh* 6.4.25).

28 *CTh* 6.4.12, 13.

29 *CTh* 7.8.4+11.1.7+11.15.1+11.23.1+13.1.3+15.1.7.

30 On Olympius's career, see *PLRE* 1 s.v. Olympius 3; on his relationship with Libanius, see Seeck, *Briefe*, Olympius II. On this whole affair, see Petit, "Les sénateurs" (= Fatouros-Krischer, *Libanios* 230–32). The most important letters for this affair are nos. 70 (trans. in Loeb *Libanius, Autobiography and Selected Letters*, no. 43), 251, 252, 265.

31 Libanius, *Ep.* 40. Cf. *PLRE* 1, Julianus 14; Petit, "Les sénateurs" (= Fatouros-Krischer, *Libanios* 229–30).

32 *Ep.* 252.

33 *CTh* 6.4.19 (9 May 372).

34 *CTh* 6.4.25 (23 October 384).

35 *CTh* 6.4.13.

36 *CTh* 6.4.20 (8 May 372).

37 *CTh* 6.4.1, 2.

38 *CTh* 6.4.18.

39 *CTh* 6.4.3, 4, 7. These texts have to be redated, as Seeck (*Regesten* 40) showed, from 339 to 354.

40 *CTh* 6.4.18. This is an extremely odd law, as transmitted in the manuscript, since it suggests it was also sent to Constantinople and therefore presumably collected there by the compilers of *CTh*, because a copy preserved in Milan could not have included the transmitted *accepta* notice: . . . *]MED(iolano) [AC]C(epta) III KAL. IVL. CONSTAN(tino)P(oli) VAL(entini)ANO ET VAL(en)TE AA. CONSS.* But the law of Constantine that Valentinian refers to in the text was no longer valid in Constantinople, since already in 340 Constantius II had made a more favorable ruling for Constantinople, that if those responsible for the games should be absent at the time, the fiscus would advance the money required and later recover the sum spent from the absentees. No actual punishment was foreseen (*CTh* 6.4.6). The transmitted reference to Constantinople, if correct, could conceivably be explained by the law's having been received and included in an archive, therefore becoming collectible there, but not posted, since it did not apply to Constantinople; but some kind of error in transmission remains possible, especially because the text is in any case extremely lacunose at this point.

41 *Or.* 42; *Epp.* 922–30, 932, 938–39, 943 (trans. of nos. 922, 923, 925, 926, 938 by Norman in the Loeb *Libanius, Autobiography and Selected Letters*, nos. 161–65). Cf. Petit, "Les sénateurs" (= Fatouros-Krischer, *Libanios* 223–29).

42 See Symmachus, *Rel.* 5, with the commentary of Vera ad loc. The law on the *follis* is *CTh* 6.2.13; final decision of the emperor: Symmachus, *Ep.* 7.96.2.

43 *CTh* 6.2.14.

44 Libanius, *Or.* 42.48: εἶτα σοὶ μὲν ἡ σπουδή, βασιλεῦ, πολυάνθρωπον ἀπεργάσασθαι τὴν βουλήν.

45 Symmachus, *Rel.* 5.

46 Details listed by Dagron, *Naissance* 278–79.

47 Amm. Marc. 26.6.18, 7.4.

48 Zosimus 4.26.6; cf. Eunapius, F45.2 (Blockley); ibid. 43.

49 For details, see Dagron, *Naissance* 275f.

50 *PLRE* I, s.v. Magnus 12.

51 Joh. Lydus, *de Mag.* 3.19: πάντα δὲ τὰ ἀπὸ τῆς βασιλείας Βάλεντος ἐν τοῖς τότε μεγίστοις δικαστηρίοις πεπραγμένα αὐτόθι σώζεται καὶ τοῖς ἐπιζητοῦσιν οὕτως ἐστὶν ἕτοιμα, ὡσεὶ χθές τυχὸν πεπραγμένα.

52 Statistics are taken from the lists in the prolegomena to Mommsen's edition of the *Codex Theodosianus*. Laws that were split up and included in several fragments under different rubrics are only counted once.

53 *CTh* 14.17.1. The restriction of the grant to the period in which the houses were

lived in by their builders seems implied by the phrase *nulli liceat, ut aedes sequantur annonae.*

54 *CTh* 14.9.2.

55 *CTh* 14.17.7.

56 *CTh* 14.17.8.

57 *CTh* 14.17.9.

58 *CTh* 14.17.10.

59 *CTh* 14.17.11.

60 *CTh* 14.17.12.

61 *CTh* 1.28.3.

62 *CTh* 1.28.4.

63 *CTh* 12.1.130, 132.

64 *CTh* 6.2.14.

65 *CTh* 6.7.2, 6.9.2, 6.27.6.

66 *CTh* 6.5.1.

67 *CTh* 14.10.1.

68 *CTh* 14.12.1.

69 *CTh* 9.17.6.

70 *CTh* 15.2.4. The law as transmitted is dated to 389, but was sent to Pancratius, who was *praefectus urbi* in 381–82. I have chosen to retain the name of the recipient because it is less likely to have suffered corruption in transmission.

71 *CTh* 15.2.3.

72 *CTh* 15.1.25: *turpe est publici splendoris ornatum privatarum aedium adiectione conrumpi et ea, quae conspicuae urbis decori vel nostri temporis vel prioris saeculi aetate creverunt, aviditate cogendae pecuniae sociari.*

73 *CTh* 15.1.29. This law, although in the abbreviated form transmitted in the *Code* seemingly more widely applicable to provincial governors (*ne quis iudicum* . . .), must also, perhaps indeed primarily, have affected Constantinople in its full form, since it was addressed to the *praefectus urbi* Aurelian. The *iudices* mentioned will presumably be those of the six suburban provinces, for which the urban prefect served as judge of appeal.

74 *CTh* 15.1.30.

Chapter VII

1 The best modern account of these events is in Brennecke, *Studien.* See also Hanson, *The Search.*

2 Amm. Marc. 22.5.2–3; *Hist. Athan.* 3.2; cf. Brennecke, *Studien* 96f.

3 Sokrates, *Hist. Eccl.* 3.4.1; *Index* to Athanasius, *Festal Letters* (ed. Albert) xxxv p. 265.

4 So Brennecke, *Studien* 178f.

5 Themistius, *Or.* 5.67bc; cf. Seeck, *Die Briefe des Libanius* 301; Errington, "Themistius" 876.

6 Sokrates, *Hist. Eccl.* 3.25.2–4: ἐγὼ" ἔφη „φιλονεικίαν μισῶ, τοὺς δὲ τῇ ὁμονοίᾳ προστρέχοντας ἀγαπῶ καὶ τιμῶ. Sokrates calls the Macedonianists' opponents "those who accept the Anhomoian formula" (τοὺς τὸ ἀνόμοιον δογματίζοντας), but as Brennecke, *Studien* 168 n. 70, points out, this goes back to the prejudices of Sokrates's documentary source Sabinus and cannot be correct, since such people possessed no recognized churches.

7 Themistius, *Or.* 5. See Errington, "Themistius" 874–77, for details.

8 So Sokrates, *Hist. Eccl.* 3.26.3.

9 Themistius, *Or.* 5.69a: ὁδὸν δ' ἐπ' αὐτὸν οὐ μίαν φέρειν, ἀλλὰ τὴν μὲν δυσπορωτέραν, τὴν δὲ εὐθυτέραν, καὶ τὴν μὲν τραχεῖαν, τὴν δὲ ὁμαλήν· συντετάσθαι δὲ ὅμως ἁπάσας πρὸς τὴν μίαν ἐκείνην καταγωγήν, καὶ τὴν ἄμιλλαν ἡμῖν καὶ προθυμίαν οὐκ ἀλλοχόθεν ὑπάρχειν, ἀλλ' ἐκ τοῦ μὴ τὴν αὐτὴν πάντας βαδίζειν.

10 E.g., Rufinus, *Hist. Eccl.* 11.1; Sozomenus, *Hist. Eccl.* 6.3f. The final revision of part of Julian's "law on teachers" is often attributed to Jovian by scholars who retain the date 11 January 364 of *CTh* 13.3.6 (*III. id.ian. divo Ioviano et Varroniano conss.*) following Mommsen ad loc. (*dies nisi fallit, est Ioviani*) and Seeck, *Regesten, ad ann.* But there is reason for doubting the day, as Mommsen hinted. The recipient, Mamertinus, was *PPO Ill.It.Afr.*, to whom Jovian seems to have directed other laws from Antioch, which at the dates given for them (*CTh* 1.22.3, 8.5.16, 8.1.8) was in relatively easy communication with Italy. (Those laws, however, were formally attributed to the deceased Julian.) But on 11 January Jovian was in Ankara, which in midwinter was just about as difficult a place as any to reach Italy from. Since the subject of the law is not specifically Western, indeed might just as well be Eastern, it is not easy to guess why it should have been directed to Mamertinus in Italy. Moreover, the law is explicitly attributed to Valentinian and Valens in the manuscripts, and the consul Jovian is described in the date as *divus*—i.e., he was already dead when the date was written, thus suggesting a date after 17 February. It therefore seems altogether more satisfactory to change the transmitted date of the law from *ian.* to *iun.*, when Valentinian and Valens were at Naissus, or to *iul.*, when they were at Sirmium. From both places other laws were issued to Mamertinus. The change is palaeographically easy.

11 Greg. Naz., *Orr.* 4, 5. On the date of writing, see Bernardi, *Grégoire de Nazianze, Discours* 4–5 (*SC* 309), 11f.

12 Themistius, *Or.* 6; cf. Errington, "Themistius" 879–81.

13 See below, text at nn. 23–27, 64–78.

14 Rufinus, *Hist. Eccl.* 11.2: *pro fide nostra.* Cf. Sokrates, *Hist. Eccl.* 4.1.5, 12.

15 Sokrates, *Hist. Eccl.* 4.1.13: Οὐάλης δὲ Ἀρειανοὺς αὐξῆσαι προαιρούμενος

δεινὰ κατὰ τῶν μὴ τοιαῦτα φρονούντων εἰργάσατο. Lenski, *Failure* 242–63, accepts in principle this orthodox interpretation of the triumphalist winners (p. 213: "without question a religious persecutor"; or even p. 243: "ferocious persecutor"), though in order to accommodate evidence pointing in another, more pragmatic direction he identifies "phases" without, however, being able to offer adequate explanations for them. Yet it should be clear that in a tense situation, in which "correct belief" was intimately associated with control of sources of wealth and influence, ecclesiastical writers (especially people in the fray of the controversy, like Basil of Caesarea or Epiphanius of Salamis and later writers influenced by them) tended to interpret anything done against their view of church interests as being motivated primarily by dogmatic considerations. Understandable as this was at the time, we do not need to believe it today.

16 Sokrates, *Hist. Eccl.* 3.25.2–4; see above, n. 6. See also Brennecke, *Studien* 178f.

17 Sokrates, *Hist. Eccl.* 4.4.1–6, apparently misdated to 365; Sozomenus, *Hist. Eccl.* 6.7.3–6.

18 Sozomenus, *Hist. Eccl.* 6.7.9.

19 Sokrates, *Hist. Eccl.* 4.4.6.

20 Ibid., 4.6.1–8; cf. Brennecke, *Studien* 216f.

21 Philostorgius, *Hist. Eccl.* 9.8.

22 Amm. Marc. 26.8.4–11; Philostorgius, *Hist. Eccl.* 9.6.

23 *Hist. Ath.* 5.1: *preceptum ubique manavit.*

24 Sokrates, *Hist. Eccl.* 4.13.3–6, seems to follow *Hist. Ath.* while heavily abbreviating. He emphasizes that Athanasius retired to avoid being made responsible for rioting; cf. Sozomenus, *Hist. Eccl.* 6.12.5–13.

25 Noted by Brennecke, *Studien* 211, who, however, draws no conclusion.

26 Julian, *Ep.* 112 (376b) to Ecdicius, *Praefectus Aegypti.*

27 *Hist. Ath.* 5.2–6.

28 Cf. Sozomenus, *Hist. Eccl.* 6.7.9, on Valens's reaction to the synod of Lampsakos: those sharing the beliefs of Eudoxius (οἱ ἀμφὶ τὸν Εὐδόξιον, i.e., the "Homoians") should possess the churches.

29 *Hist. Ath.* 5.6: *litteris imperialibus iubentibus eundem episcopum Athanasium reverti ad civitatem et consuete tenere ecclesias.*

30 Greg. Naz., *Or.* 43.48f., with Bernardi's introduction to *Grégoire de Nazianze, Discours* 42–43 (*SC* 384).

31 *Or.* 43.48–50, cf. Brennecke, *Studien* 226f.

32 Rufinus, *Hist. Eccl.* 11.9: the two "quotations" *atque utinam . . .* and *ego crastina . . .* have no parallel in Gregory, but are found in Sokrates, *Hist. Eccl.* 4.26.16f. (who puts the confrontation in Antioch, but otherwise follows Rufinus); Sozomenus, *Hist. Eccl.* 16.4f. follows Sokrates.

33 *Or.* 43.52–53.

34 *Or.* 43.54: ἐνίκων οἱ πονηροὶ καὶ κυροῦται κατὰ τοῦ ἀνδρὸς ἐξορία.

35 *Ep.* 94.

36 Greg. Naz., *Or.* 43.55. Cf. Basil, *Epp.* 104, 110, 279–81; Brennecke, *Studien* 228f.

37 Rufinus, *Hist. Eccl.* 11.9 (p. 1016, 17–19): *sic accidit, ut cum omnes catholicos expulerit Valens, Basilius usque ad vitae exitum intemerato communionis sacramento in ecclesia perduraret.*

38 Basil, *Ep.* 99 (372). See May, "Basilios der Große" 58f.

39 Basil, *Epp.* 225, 231, 232, 237, 239. Cf. Greg. Naz., *Or.* 43.55; May, "Basilios der Große" 62–63. Lenski, *Failure* 259, accepted completely the orthodox view of the sources, saying, "In these instances Demosthenes—and by implication Valens—always used civil laws for religious purposes." But were not civil laws, at least in principle, intended to be applied? Is it really too difficult to believe that the unworldly intellectual theologian Gregory of Nyssa was simply, e.g., a bad financier?

40 Basil, *Epp.* 120, 129 (from 373); 213.2 (from 375). Cf. May, "Basilios der Große" 61f.; Brennecke, *Studien* 229f.

41 Sokrates, *Hist. Eccl.* 4.2.6; Theodoret, *Hist. Eccl.* 4.13.1–3, 24.2–4. In the latter passage from *Hist. Eccl.*, Theodoret accuses Valens of general tolerance—even of pagans—with the single exception of the Nicene orthodox (μόνοις δὲ πολέμιος ἦν τοῖς τὴν ἀποστολικὴν διδασκαλίαν πρεσβεύουσι).

42 *Acts* 11:26.

43 On this in detail, see Brennecke, *Studien* 66f., replacing all earlier accounts.

44 The date of Meletius's renewed exile is uncertain; cf. Brennecke, *Studien* 233 n. 64.

45 *Hist. Ath.* 5.1; see above, text at n. 23. Brennecke, *Studien* 233f., thinks the general *preceptum* mentioned there (a) really existed and (b) started being applied now in the case of Meletius and his colleagues. But he has to admit that in three of the five known cases of exile in Oriens it would have been technically inapplicable (234).

46 Sokrates, *Hist. Eccl.* 4.2.5 (καὶ Παυλῖνον μὲν τὸν ἐπίσκοπον δι᾽ ὑπερβάλλουσαν τοῦ ἀνδρὸς εὐλάβειαν οὐδὲν κακὸν ἐποίησεν), followed by Sozomenus, *Hist. Eccl.* 6.7.10.

47 Theodoret, *Hist. Eccl.* 4.13.4, for whom Eusebius is one of his local orthodox heroes; cf. 4.14–15 for the rest of the story.

48 Cf. Brennecke, *Studien* 42 n. 11, 232–33.

49 *Chron. Edess.* 31 (Guidi 5.32); Theodoret, *Hist. Eccl.* 4.16, who depicts the troubles, according to his own program, as being a *result* of Barses's expulsion (17). Rufinus, *Hist. Eccl.* 11.5, tells the story of the emperor's visit as an episode without context and does not mention Barses; he is followed in this by Sokrates, *Hist. Eccl.* 4.18, and Sozomenus, *Hist. Eccl.* 6.18.

50 Theodoret, *Hist. Eccl.* 4.13.2.

51 *Hist. Ath.* 5.11–13.

52 Sokrates, *Hist. Eccl.* 4.21.

53 Rufinus, *Hist. Eccl.* 11–13; Sokrates, *Hist. Eccl.* 4.22.1–3; Theodoret, *Hist. Eccl.* 4.22.2, 9.

54 According to part of a letter of Peter recorded by Theodoret, *Hist. Eccl.* 4.22.35, eleven Egyptian bishops and other clerics and monks were banned to Diokaisareia in Palestine. On the young monks and the army, cf. Jerome, *Chron. ad ann.* 375: *Valens lege data, ut monachi militarent, nolentes fustibus iussit interfici.* Cf. Brennecke, *Studien* 236f.

55 Sokrates, *Hist. Eccl.* 4.32.2: ἕως ‹οὗ› αὐτοῦ τὴν πόλλην ἀπήνειαν ὁ φιλόσοφος Θεμίστιος μετριωτέραν τῷ Προσφωνητικῷ λόγῳ εἰργάσατο, ἐν ᾧ μὴ δεῖν ξενίζεσθαι ἐπὶ τῇ διαφωνίᾳ τῶν Χριστιανικῶν δογμάτων παραινεῖ τῷ βασιλεῖ. Cf. Errington, "Church and State" 28 n. 38.

56 See Snee, "Valens' Recall" 397f.

57 Jerome, *Chron. ad ann.* 378: *Valens de Antiochia exire conpulsus sera paenitentia nostros de exiliis revocat.*

58 Rufinus, *Hist. Eccl.* 11.13; Orosius 7.33.15.

59 Sozomenus, *Hist. Eccl.* 6.40.1: "ἀλλ' οὐχ ὑποστρέψεις," ἔφη, "μὴ ἀποδιδοὺς τὰς ἐκκλησίας."

60 Theodoret, *Hist. Eccl.* 4.34; 36.2: οὕτω μὲν οὖν ἐκεῖνος κἂν τῷ παρόντι βίῳ ποινὴν ἔτισεν ὑπὲρ ὧν ἐπλημμέλησεν.

61 Theodore Lector, *Epitome* 216; Theophanes 65 (de Boor); Georg. Mon. 557 (de Boor).

62 Amm. Marc. 30.9.5: *postremo hoc moderamine principatus inclaruit, quod inter religionum diversitates medius stetit nec quemquam inquietavit neque, ut hoc coleretur, imperavit aut illud; nec interdictis minacibus subiectorum cervicem ad id, quod ipse voluit, inclinabat, sed intemeratas reliquit has partes, ut repperit.*

63 Sokrates, *Hist. Eccl.* 4.1.12; cf. Sozomenus, *Hist. Eccl.* 6.21.7; Ambrose, *Ep.* 75 (21).2.

64 *CTh* 9.16.9 of 29 May 371, which explicitly allows the traditional consultation of *haruspices* (as long as this was not *nocenter*), refers to *leges a me in exordio imperii mei datae, quibus unicuique, quod animo inbibisset, colendi libera facultas tributa est.* The first person singular used here, when all laws were officially issued in the name of all ruling emperors, emphasizes Valentinian's own attitude, in this respect not necessarily shared by his brother.

65 *CTh* 13.3.6. On the date, see Pergami, *ad* 11 Jan. 364; above, text and note at n. 10.

66 Sulpicius Severus, *Dial.* I (II) 5.5: *hic cum Martinum ea petere cognovisset, quae praestare nolebat.*

67 Ibid. 8: *nequaquam adsurgere est dignatus (sc. Valentinianus) adstanti, donec regiam sellam ignis operiret ipsumque regem ea parte corporis, qua sedebat, adflaret incendium.*

68 Sokrates, *Hist. Eccl.* 4.12.2, 4.

69 See, e.g., Rousseau, *Basil* 294f.

70 *CTh* 16.5.3.

71 *Mos. et rom. legum coll.* 15.3.1 (*FIRA* 2d ed., 2 pp. 580–81); cf. Lieu, *Manichaeism* 91–116.

72 On this, see above, chapter 5, text at nn. 22–26.

73 *CTh* 16.6.1. See Tengström, *Donatisten* 79–83.

74 *CTh* 9.16.7 (May 371).

75 *CTh* 12.1.60, 75.

76 Zosimus 4.3.3. Valentinian's law was not found by the Eastern compilers of the Theodosian Code, but an Eastern law banning nocturnal rituals is preserved, addressed to the Praetorian Prefect Secundus on 9 September 364 (*CTh* 9.16.7). Either this action was part of a policy agreed to by the brothers before they separated at Sirmium in August 364, or Zosimus records a merely local Western dispute, which his pagan source Eunapius interpreted *ad maiorem gloriam* of Praetextatus, who was one of the most prominent Roman pagans.

77 *CTh* 16.2.17, 18, 19, 20, 21, 22.

78 *CTh* 16.1.1 (17 November 364), 9.40.8 (15 January 365).

79 *Collectio Avellana* 1 is an almost contemporary account told from the point of view of Ursinus; cf. Pietri, *Roma Christiana* 1:408f.

80 Amm. Marc. 27.3.12–13, perhaps from the archives of the *praefectus urbi*; *Collectio Avellana* 1.7. On this, see above, chapter 5, text at n. 17.

81 Rufinus, *Hist. Eccl.* 11.10 favored the Eastern orthodox tradition represented by Sokrates, *Hist. Eccl.* 4.29; Sozomenus, *Hist. Eccl.* 6.23.1–2; cf. Jerome, *Chron. ad ann.* 366. The contemporary Ursinian "*Gesta*" in *Collectio Avellana* 1.6 give the other version; cf. the discussion in Pietri, *Roma Christiana* 1:409f.

82 The details are preserved in *Collectio Avellana* 5–12; cf. Pietri, *Roma Christiana* 1:412f.

83 *Collectio Avellana* 12.3: *qui si ingrata pertinacia statutum mansuetudinis nostrae egrediendum putaverit, eundem non iam ut Christianum, quippe quem a communione religionis mentis inquietudo disterminat, sed ut hominem factiosum perturbatoremque publicae tranquillitatis legum et religionis inimicum iuris severitas persequatur.*

84 Rufinus, *Hist. Eccl.* 11.13: *is pietate et religione omnes paene, qui ante fuerant principes, superabat.*

85 Ausonius, *Grat. Actio* 14 (63).

86 Rufinus, *Hist. Eccl.* 11.13: *plus verecundus quam rei publicae intererat*; *Epitome de Caes.*: *cunctisque esset plenus bonis, si ad cognoscendam reipublicae regendae scientiam animum intendisset*; Amm. Marc. 31.10.18.

87 *CTh* 16.2.23, 24.

88 *CTh* 16.5.4, 6.2, 5.5. On these, see Gottlieb, *Ambrosius* 51f., esp. 60f. There has been much discussion of the application of 16.5.5, but even if, as Williams, *Am-*

brose 159f., argues, other "heretical" sects also practiced re-baptism, the prime objective, as Gottlieb has shown convincingly, must have been the Donatists, the only group in 379 that it could be claimed had prompted "frequent" statements from Valentinian and Gratian (lines 11–13: . . . *ea tantum super catholica observatione permaneant, quae perennis recordationis pater noster et nos ipsi victura in aeternum aeque numerosa iussione mandavimus*).

89 *Collectio Avellana* 13.

90 Sokrates, *Hist. Eccl.* 5.2.1; cf. Sozomenus, *Hist. Eccl.* 6.36.6–7, with Errington, "Church and State" 28f.

91 *CTh* 16.5.5, line 11: *denique antiquato rescripto, quod apud Sirmium nuper emersit* . . . ; with Gottlieb's magisterial demonstration, *Ambrosius* 71f., that this *rescriptum* can have nothing to do with Gratian's "tolerance edict," as much of the earlier literature asserted.

92 Priscillian (*CSEL* 18), *Tract.* II.41: *vivi lavacri regeneratione reparati et sordentes saecularium actuum tenebras respuentes.*

93 Chadwick, *Priscillian* 12ff.

94 Sulpicius Severus, *Chron.* 2.47.4.

95 Priscillian, *Tract.* II.50.

96 Sulpicius Severus, *Chron.* 2.47, who is hostile to the Priscillianists, says the original rescript was aimed "not only to exclude all heretics from churches and cities, but to expel them from all lands" (*rescriptum, quo universi heretici excedere non ecclesiis tantum aut urbibus, sed extra omnes terras propelli iubebantur*). The Priscillianists themselves in a petition to Damasus (*Tract.* 2.50) are more precise, asserting the rescript was directed against false bishops and Manichaeans (*rescriptum contra pseudoepiscopos et Manichaeos*), which nobody could have anything against. Sulpicius Severus (ibid. 49) and the Priscillianists (*Tract.* II.51) agree that the Priscillianists were refused audiences with Damasus and with Ambrose, but gained another rescript, Sulpicius Severus says by bribery, from the *magister officiorum* Macedonius and thus retained their churches; but this statement is also tendentious (whether or not corruption played a part). Macedonius's rescript can only have asserted that the Priscillianists were not covered by the earlier rescript against *pseudoepiscopi et Manichaei*. On all this, see Chadwick, *Priscillian* esp. 33f.

97 Sulpicius Severus, *Chron.* 2.48; see Chadwick, *Priscillian* 40.

98 Sulpicius Severus, *Chron.* 2.49.

99 *CTh* 16.7.3.

100 See above, chapter 4, text at n. 81.

101 On this, see in detail below, chapter 8, text at nn. 7–10.

102 The modern literature on Ambrose is enormous. I name here merely three leading recent works through which older literature can be researched: McLynn, *Ambrose*; Williams, *Ambrose*; Gottlieb, *Ambrosius*.

103 In a letter written in late 381, after the Council of Aquileia, Ambrose regarded Dacia Ripensis and Moesia as Western, doubtless because of their largely Latin-speaking population and ecclesiastical affiliation: *Ep. extra coll.* 6 (12).3: *equidem per occidentales partes duobus in angulis tantum hoc est in latere Daciae Ripensis ac Moesiae fidei obstrepi videbatur.*

104 The modern literature regularly speaks of people having been "invited," but Gratian himself (*Acta* 3) says he had instructed them (*iusseramus*), and Palladius (*Acta* 8; 11) uses the same language; so Williams, *Ambrose* 169f., correctly has "convoked."

105 *Acta* 6, 8. See for this suggestion Williams, *Ambrose* 172, who, however, has forgotten that at this time Illyricum was formally not Gratian's but Theodosius's (see Errington, "Theodosius and the Goths" 22–27), which gives additional point to Illyricans' being called *orientales*—though for Ambrose (see n. 103 above) the area, despite its Eastern secular administration, remained "Western."

106 The letter was read out at the council and taken into the minutes, and therefore preserved along with them: *Acta* 3.

107 Theodorus of Martigny, Domninus of Grenoble, Diogenes of Geneva, Proculus of Marseille, and perhaps Amantius of Lodève; the two *legati* were Constantinus of Orange and Iustus of Lyon (list of subscribers to the *acta* with Zelzer's apparatus criticus in *CSEL* 82, p. 325).

108 *Acta* 8, 11. On the date, see Gottlieb, "Das Konzil," 293.

109 *Acta* 6.

110 *Acta* 8. References esp. in the *Gesta Ep.* 2 to saving not only energy but also expense (ibid. 2: *nullus postremo pauperiem in sacerdotibus gloriosam subsidio veniendi destitutus ingemuit*) suggests that once the imperial order to attend was revoked the attendant possibility of using the public post at imperial expense was also withdrawn. It is therefore no wonder that nobody came from the distant, war-torn eastern Illyricum and that Palladius felt cheated.

111 The date is disputed (see Gottlieb, *Ambrosius* 26f.; McLynn, *Ambrose* 100f.; Williams, *Ambrose* 141f.), but the purpose—to test Ambrose's position—was admirably clarified by Nautin, "Les premières relations" 238f. Barnes, "Ambrose and Gratian" 168–71, argues for a first meeting at Sirmium in 378.

112 Gratian's letter *cupio valde* (*CSEL* 79), 3–4; Ambrose, *Ep. extra coll.* 12 (1).

113 Ambrose, *De spiritu sancto* 1.19–21. There has been much modern discussion of the purpose of this action, which Ambrose says was "*ut fidem probares*" ("in order to test my faith"). There is no evidence that it had anything to do with the activities of the "Arian" Justina, whose arrival in Milan was contemporary with the permanent transfer of the court to the city in the spring of 381, and by then the disputed basilica had been returned to Ambrose. McLynn, *Ambrose* 122, considers this possible, putting Justina's arrival without Valentinian II quite unmoti-

vated before the resettlement of the court; but in 383 Ambrose (*Ep.* 30 [24].7) was to argue with the usurper Maximus that Valentinian could not be expected to travel without his mother, which only makes sense if their inseparability were well known. On this problem, see Errington, "Accession" 442 n. 24.

114 *Gesta conc. Aquil. Ep.* 2.

115 *Ep. extra coll.* 6 (12).

116 *Ep. extra coll.* 10 (57).2.

117 See above, chapter 5, text at n. 48.

118 Ambrose, *Epp.* 72 (17) and 73 (18).

119 This opinion is based on a methodologically unsatisfactory explanation of a chaotic passage of Zosimus (4.36). Zosimus says that at the time of his accession Gratian refused the title and "the pontifical robe" (an object not otherwise attested in the whole of ancient literature), but this is simply wrong: in 369 (*ILS* 771) he was already so entitled, and he was addressed as such to his face by his old teacher Ausonius in 379 (Ausonius, *Grat. act.* 42); Zosimus includes in his tale a bon mot punning on the name of the usurper Maximus, which cannot have been in circulation before late 382 at the earliest, when the usurpation might have become known in Rome. Possibly in the context of the cancellation of public funding for the old cults and Gratian's refusal to discuss it (perhaps in 382)—which however Zosimus does not know about—a Roman wit might have joked that "if the emperor does not want to be *pontifex*, then Maximus soon will be," which Zosimus's source took too seriously and interpreted as a refusal of the office. See also Errington, "Church and State" 34 n. 63, for further discussion. For the best statement of the traditional belief, see Cameron, "Gratian's Repudiation."

120 On Justina and her family, see references in *PLRE* I, s.vv. Iustina, Iustus 1, Cerealis 1, and Stemma 4. For the argument that after Valentinian I's death both Justina and Valentinian II came to Trier, see Errington, "The Accession of Theodosius I" 442.

121 On this, see McLynn, *Ambrose*, esp. 22f.; Williams, *Ambrose* 69f.

122 See above, chapter 2, text at n. 49.

123 Ambrose, *De obit. Valent.* 28: *ego te suscepi parvulum, cum legatus ad hostem tuum pergerem, ego maternis traditum manibus amplexus sum.*

124 Ambrose, *Ep.* 30 (24).7; cf. McLynn, *Ambrose* 158f.

125 *Ep.* 30 (24).7: . . . *responderim non esse aequum, ut aspero hiemis puer cum matre vidua penetraret Alpes; sine matre autem tanto itinere dubiis rebus committeretur?*

126 Symmachus, *Rel.* 3; Ambrose, *Ep.* 72 (17). A subsequent reasoned reply by Ambrose to Symmachus's *relatio* (*Ep.* 73 [18]) dominated the later ancient discussion (Paulinus, *Vita Ambrosii* 26, mentions only this later "*libellus*") and modern historiography, but as McLynn points out (*Ambrose* 167 n. 35) there is no reason to believe that the "reasoned reply" played any part in the actual political discussion in the consistory or had any effect on the decision to reject Symmachus's request.

127 Ambrose, *Ep. extra coll.* 10 (57).3: *Valentinianus tunc temporis audivit suggestionem meam nec fecit aliud nisi quod fidei nostrae ratio poscebat.*

128 For further details and older literature, see Mc Lynn, *Ambrose* 166–67; Matthews, *Western Aristocracies* 203–11: texts and commentary with German translation in Klein, *Streit*; Wytzes, *Der letzte Kampf.*

129 *Ep.* 72a.

130 *Vita Ambrosii* 26.

131 On this and for more details of what follows, see the generally excellent account in McLynn, *Ambrose* 170–219.

132 Ambrose, *Sermo contra Auxentium* (*Ep.* 75a [21a].29): . . . *sponderem fidem quod basilicam ecclesiae nullus invaderet.*

133 *Ep.* 76 (20).23: *non hoc maximum dicere quod tyrannus ego sim Valentiniani qui se meae legationis obiectu queritur ad Italiam non potuisse transire. addidi quia numquam sacerdotes tyranni fuerunt sed tyrannos saepe sunt passi.* This reference to Maximus cannot refer to Ambrose's first embassy in 383, where diplomatic politeness was preserved, but can only relate to the bad-tempered second meeting, where Ambrose was openly accused by Maximus of having misled him and having prevented his entering Italy (reported by Ambrose himself: *Ep.* 30 [24].4ff.). Since *Ep.* 76 was composed soon after Maundy Thursday 386 (see most recently Gottlieb, "Der Mailänder Kirchenstreit" 37–49), the embassy to Maximus mentioned in it must be before this, therefore before the Easter crisis of 386. The objection of Chadwick, *Priscillian* 137, that Ambrose was aware before the mission that Maximus distrusted him (so also Birley, "Magnus Maximus" 29–33) is irrelevant, since Ambrose refers explicitly to the open accusation (or, rather, lack of it) during his mission. What was new to Ambrose was not the accusation that he had deceived Maximus, but that this had prevented his entering Italy. This means that McLynn, *Ambrose* 217, and Williams, *Ambrose* 223, who follow Chadwick in placing Ambrose's second mission to Maximus after the crisis of the basilicas in the spring of 386, have severe difficulty in explaining why Ambrose should then still be regarded by the court as a suitable person for the delicate mission. The death of Priscillian and his associates must therefore also be dated to 385, for which the only chronological indication is Ambrose, *Ep.* 30 (24).12. See on this Dörner, "Ambrosius," who argues for early 385. Williams's argument, *Ambrose* 224, is, however, circular. On the trial of Priscillian and its background, see Girardet, "Trier 385"; Chadwick, *Priscillian* 110–69; Birley, "Magnus Maximus."

134 The catholic reporter Sulpicius Severus has no doubts that Magnus Maximus was a legitimate emperor, calling him *imperator.* Maximus's confrontation with Gratian is not mentioned—Sulpicius does not usually refer to secular events—but he makes it clear that the change of government altered Ithacius's prospects (*Chron.* 2.49.5).

135 Ambrose, *Ep.* 30 (24).

136 *Collectio Avellana* 40 is Maximus's reply to Siricius's objection, which itself has not survived.

137 Sulpicius Severus, *Chron.* 2.50.5–6; cf. Ambrose, *Ep.* 30 (24).12.

138 Sulpicius Severus, *Chron.* 2.50.7–51.5.

139 Sulpicius Severus, *Dial.* 3.13.1–2.

140 *CTh* 16.1.4; cf. 16.4.1.

141 *Ep.* 30 (24).13.

142 Evidence for this first, pre-Easter, phase of the struggle is Ambrose, *Ep.* 76 (20), to his sister Marcellina, giving his version of events. See on this McLynn, *Ambrose* 185–96.

143 The main sources are again Ambrose's own writings: *Sermo contra Auxentium* (*Ep.* 75a [21a]) and *Ep.* 75 (21) to Valentinian, explaining his inability to obey the imperial summons.

144 *Ep.* 77 (22). See also McLynn, *Ambrose* 211ff.

145 *Collectio Avellana* 39.4: *Italia omnis atque Africa hoc sacramento credunt; hac fide gloriantur Gallia, Aquitania, omnis Hispania, Roma ipsa venerabilis.* The parallel noted in this passage with Ambrose, *Ep.* 75 (21).14 (*hanc fidem Galliae tenent, hanc Hispaniae et cum pia divini spiritus confessione custodiunt*), by Birley, "Magnus Maximus" 32 n. 130, might seem to suggest that Ambrose had made available to Maximus his arguments sent to Valentinian during the struggle; but no other phrase is reminiscent of Ambrose, and it should not have been beyond the abilities of Maximus's quaestor, or whoever formulated his letter for him, to invent this fairly obvious listing after having heard of events in Milan and the catholic interpretation of them.

146 See above, chapter 2, text at n. 62.

147 Paulinus, *Vita Ambrosii* 19. Cf. Ambrose, *Ep.* 30 (24).12, with Faller's comment, p. 214 on line 141; so also Bastiaensen, commentary ad loc. (p. 301).

Chapter VIII

1 *De obit. Theod.* 35: *"dilexi" virum, qui cum iam corpore solveretur, magis de statu ecclesiarum quam de suis periculis angebatur.*

2 *De civ. Dei* 5.26: *inter haec omnia ex ipso initio imperii sui non quievit iustissimis et misericordissimis legibus adversus impios laboranti ecclesiae subvenire . . . ; cuius ecclesiae se membrum esse magis quam in terris regnare gaudebat. simulacra gentilium ubique evertenda praecepit.*

3 Marcellinus Comes (*Chron. Min.* 2) *ad ann.* 379: *vir admodum religiosus et catholicae ecclesiae propagator*; *ad ann.* 380: *orthodoxus imperator.*

4 See, e.g., the laws *CTh* 16.2.2 (388) and 16.4.3 (392) punishing those who insisted on public disputation. The readiness to engage in intense public discussion in Constantinople had already been remarked on by Gregory of Nazianzos, *Or.* 22 (perhaps 379); cf. Gallay, *La vie* 134; Bernardi, *Saint Grégoire* 185–88.

5 Reflected in Rufinus, *Hist. Eccl.* 11.13: *impietatis suae poenas igni exustus dedit*; cf. Theodoret, *Hist. Eccl.* 5.11; Orosius 7.33.15.

6 For details, see Errington, "Church and State" 33–36; Bernardi, *Saint Grégoire* 175f.

7 See Errington, "Theodosius and the Goths" 1f., 22–27; above, chapter 4, text at n. 5.

8 Themistius's *Or.* 14 was delivered at Thessalonica in 379; see in general Zosimus 4.25.1; 27.

9 *CTh* 16.1.2: *cunctos populos, quos clementiae nostrae regit temperamentum, in tali volumus religione versari, quam divinum Petrum apostolum tradidisse Romanis religio usque ad nunc ab ipso insinuata declarat quamque pontificem Damasum sequi claret et Petrum Alexandriae episcopum virum apostolicae sanctitatis, hoc est, ut secundum apostolicam disciplinam euangelicamque doctrinam patris et filii et spiritus sancti unam deitatem sub parili maiestate et sub pia trinitate credamus. hanc legem sequentes Christianorum catholicorum nomen iubemus amplecti, reliquos vero dementes vesanosque iudicantes haeretici dogmatis infamiam sustinere nec conciliabula eorum ecclesiarum nomen accipere, divina primum vindicta, post etiam motus nostri, quem ex caelesti arbitrio sumpserimus, ultione plectendos.* On this and what follows, see in more detail Errington, "Christian Accounts" 411–16.

10 McLynn, *Ambrose* 107f., however, thinks the impetus for the edict might have come from Constantinople; cf. also Lizzi Testa, "La politica religiosa" 337–48, for further speculation.

11 Greg. Naz., *Carm.* 11 (*De vita sua*) 859–60: Πέτρος αὐτός, ὁ βραβεὺς τῶν ποιμένων | πρῴην μὲν ἡμᾶς ἐγκαθίστη γράμμασιν.

12 Discussion in detail with sources in Errington, "Church and State" 37–38, 67–72.

13 Sokrates, *Hist. Eccl.* 5.6.3–6; Sozomenus, *Hist. Eccl.* 7.5.1; cf. Errington, "Christian Accounts" 416.

14 Sokrates, *Hist. Eccl.* 5.7; see Errington, "Church and State" 39–40.

15 Greg. Naz., *Carm.* 11 (*De vita sua*) 1293–94.

16 Ibid., 1311–95.

17 The Greek ecclesiastical historians agree on the doctrinal purity of those summoned: Sokrates, *Hist. Eccl.* 5.8.1; Sozomenus, *Hist. Eccl.* 7.7.1; Theodoret, *Hist. Eccl.* 5.6.3. On this, see Errington, "Church and State" 41–47.

18 Sokrates, *Hist. Eccl.* 5.8.2f. Communion with Liberius in Rome had once been agreed to by the Macedonianists' leader Eustathius of Sebaste in the 360s: Sokrates, *Hist. Eccl.* 4.12.

19 *CTh* 16.5.6, with Errington, "Church and State" 47–51. Lizzi Testa, "La politica religiosa" 348, does not notice that this law was intended for Illyricum and asserts that it was for "tutte le città dell'impero d'oriente."

20 *CTh* 16.5.6, 3: *qui vero isdem non inserviunt, desinant adfectatis dolis alienum verae*

religionis nomen adsumere et suis apertis criminibus denotentur. ab omnium sub-moti ecclesiarum limine penitus arceantur, cum omnes haereticos inlicitas agere intra oppida congregationes vetemus ac, si quid eruptio factiosa temptaverit, ab ipsis etiam urbium moenibus exterminato furore propelli iubeamus, ut cunctis orthodoxis epis-copis, qui Nicaenam fidem tenent, catholicae ecclesiae toto orbe reddantur.

21 *CTh* 16.7.1 (apostates); 16.5.7 (Manichaeans); cf. Errington, "Church and State" 51–53.

22 Ambrose, *Ep. extra coll.* 9 (13).4, with Errington, "Church and State" 67f.; Damasus, *Ep.* 5 (*PL* 13). The Nicene canon is no. XV; see Errington, "Church and State" 44.

23 Ambrose, *Ep. extra coll.* 9 (13).4; *Conc. Const.* canon IV.

24 Greg. Naz., *Carm.* 11 (*De vita sua*) 1797–1802.

25 Ibid., 1573f.; Theodoret, *Hist. Eccl.* 5.8.2.

26 The standard treatment of the Antiochene schism remains Cavallera, *Le scisme*, who deals with this question on 232ff.

27 Greg. Naz., *Carm.* 11 (*De vita sua*) 1800–02: Αἰγύπτιοί τε καὶ Μακεδόνες, ἐργάται | τῶν τοῦ θεοῦ νόμων τε καὶ μυστηρίων, | φυσῶντες ἡμὶν ἑσπέριόν τε καὶ τραχύ.

28 Ibid., 1819–1904.

29 Sozomenus, *Hist. Eccl.* 7.7.9, 7.8.1–8, 7.10.1–3. On Nectarius's secular career, see *PLRE* 1 s.v. Nectarius 2. Cf. Errington, "Church and State" 58–59.

30 On the praetorships, see above, chapter 6, text at nn. 12, 20, 27.

31 Paulinus, *Vita Ambrosii* 7.2; Ambrose, *Ep. extra coll.* 9 (13) 3.5, written in the summer of 381.

32 Theodoret, *Hist. Eccl.* 5.9.15.

33 Mansi III 568f.; cf. Schwartz, "Bischofslisten" 83f.

34 Damasus, *Ep.* 4 (*PL* 13, 357).

35 For the creed, see Kelly, *Early Christian Creeds* 296; Hanson, *Search* 812; Ritter, *Das Konzil* 132.

36 Theodoret, *Hist. Eccl.* 5.9.16: τῆς δὲ πρεσβυτάτης καὶ ὄντως ἀποστολικῆς ἐκκλησίας τῆς ἐν Ἀντιοχείᾳ τῆς Συρίας, ἐν ᾗ πρώτῃ τὸ τίμιον τῶν Χριστιανῶν ἐχρημάτισεν ὄνομα, τὸν αἰδεσιμώτατον καὶ θεοφιλέστατον ἐπίσκοπον Φλαβιανὸν οἵ τε τῆς ἐπαρχίας καὶ τῆς ἀνατολικῆς διοικήσεως συνδραμόντες κανονικῶς ἐχειροτόνησεν, πάσης συμψήφου τῆς ἐκκλησίας ὥσπερ διὰ μιᾶς φωνῆς τὸν ἄνδρα τιμησάσης.

37 *COD* 27 (Mansi III 560).

38 *COD* 27–28 (Mansi III 560): τὸν μέντοι Κωνσταντινουπόλεως ἐπίσκοπον ἔχειν τὰ πρεσβεῖα τῆς τιμῆς μετὰ τὸν Ῥώμης ἐπίσκοπον διὰ τὸ εἶναι αὐτὴν νέαν Ῥώμην.

39 The address to the emperor (the *prosphonetikos*) is preserved in Mansi III 557C.

Some modern writers (e.g., Ensslin, *Religionspolitik* 34; Lippold, *RE* Suppl. 13 s.v. Theodosius I, 20) think Theodosius turned the canons into secular law, but the ecclesiastical sources merely confirm his formal agreement with the decisions — i.e., he did not reject them: Sokrates, *Hist. Eccl.* 5.8.20; Sozomenus, *Hist. Eccl.* 7.9.5; cf. Errington, "Church and State" 62–64.

40 So Schwartz, "Bischofslisten," 83.

41 *CTh* 16.1.3 (30 July 381). This edict has been much misunderstood in modern times. For the view presented here and discussion of some characteristic misinterpretations, see Errington, "Christian Accounts" 419–21, 440–42; Errington, "Church and State" 64–66.

42 Sozomenus, *Hist. Eccl.* 7.12.11–12: ὁ δὲ βασιλεὺς νομοθετῶν ἐκέλευσε τοὺς ἑτεροδόξους μήτε ἐκκλησιάζειν μήτε περὶ πίστεως διδάσκειν μήτε ἐπισκόπους ἢ ἄλλους χειροτονεῖν, καὶ τοὺς μὲν πόλεων καὶ ἀγρῶν ἐλαύνεσθαι, τοὺς δὲ ἀτίμους εἶναι καὶ πολιτείας ὁμοίας μὴ μετέχειν τοῖς ἄλλοις. καὶ χαλεπὰς τοῖς νόμοις ἐνέγραφε τιμωρίας. ἀλλ᾽ οὐκ ἐπεξῄει· οὐ γὰρ τιμωρεῖσθαι, ἀλλ᾽ εἰς δέος καθιστᾶν τοὺς ὑπηκόους ἐσπούδαζεν, ὅπως ὁμόφρονες αὐτῷ γένοιντο περὶ τὸ θεῖον.

43 Sokrates, *Hist. Eccl.* 5.10.24; Sozomenus, *Hist. Eccl.* 7.12.9.

44 Sokrates, *Hist. Eccl.* 5.20.4–5: τοῦτο δὲ ἰστέον, ὡς ὁ βασιλεὺς Θεοδόσιος οὐδένα τούτων ἐδίωκε, πλὴν ὅτι τὸν Εὐνόμιον ἐν Κωνσταντινουπόλει ἐπὶ οἰκίας συνάγοντα καὶ τοὺς συγγραφέντας αὐτῷ λόγους ἐπιδεικνύμενον ὡς ταῖς διδασκαλίαις πολλοὺς λυμαινόμενον εἰς ἐξορίαν πεμφθῆναι ἐκέλευσεν. τῶν μέντοι ἄλλων οὐδένα οὔτε ἔσκυλλεν οὔτε αὐτῷ κοινωνῆσαι ἠνάγκαζεν, ἀλλ᾽ ἑκάστους συνεχώρει κατὰ τοὺς ἰδίους τόπους συνάγεσθαι καὶ δοξάζειν τὰ τοῦ Χριστιανισμοῦ, ὡς καταλαβεῖν ἕκαστοι τὴν περὶ αὐτοῦ δόξαν ἠδύναντο.

45 Philostorgius, *Hist. Eccl.* 10.11.

46 Sozomenos *Hist. Eccl.* 7.12.11–12 (text in n. 42 above).

47 *CTh* 16.5.11. Since the Roman state possessed neither police nor public prosecutor, it relied on the activity of its citizens to bring cases to the notice of the courts. Only then could a judge begin to apply the law.

48 *CTh* 16.5.12.

49 *CTh* 16.5.13. The text issued to the praetorian prefect seems general, but its restriction in practice to Constantinople emerges from the phrase *omnibus huius urbis latebris . . . pellantur.*

50 It is often alleged that Theodosius was the first emperor not to take the title, but since this "fact" is merely based on the lack of positive evidence for it — an *argumentum ex silentio* — the same applies to Valentinian II, who in the present state of knowledge must be regarded as the first.

51 *CTh* 16.10.7, 9.

52 *CTh* 16.10.8.

53 Cf. Augustine, *De civ. Dei* 5.26; Rufinus, *Hist. Eccl.* 11.19; Theodoret, *Hist. Eccl.* 5.21.1.

54 *Or.* 30 (*Pro Templis*); on the date of writing, see Wiemer, "Die Rangstellung" 123-29.

55 See esp. Liebeschuetz, *Antioch* 234-39.

56 *Or.* 30.17-18.

57 *PLRE* I, s.v. Cynegius 3; cf. Matthews, *Western Aristocracies* 110-11, 140-43; Matthews, "Pious Supporter."

58 The number of his major journeys seems impossible to establish accurately. *PLRE* I s.v. Cynegius 3 might be right in restricting them to two, whereas Matthews, *Western Aristocracies* 140 n. 2, wants to squash all the evidence for travel into one trip. One trip seems unlikely, but the point is not important for the present purpose.

59 Zosimus 4.37.3. That this was shortly after his appointment as praetorian prefect seems to emerge from Libanius, *Or.* 49.3, who says the initial instruction to travel reached him while he was still quaestor: see Vera, "I rapporti," 279-82, and Paschoud, Budé *Zosime* II, 2 n. 176.

60 Libanius, *Or.* 49.3; Zosimus 4.37.3; cf. *Cons. Const. ad ann.* 388: . . . *usque ad Egyptum penetravit et simulacra gentium evertit.*

61 *ILS* 1273.

62 Libanius, *Or.* 1.231; *Or.* 52.40.

63 Libanius, *Or.* 30.44-51. The convincing identification of the anonymous person attacked by Libanius with Cynegius is due to Petit, "Sur la date" 295f., and is generally accepted.

64 Theodoret, *Hist. Eccl.* 5.21.5-7, who, however, leaves the prefect involved anonymous. This was of no importance for his moralizing story, the point of which is that where even a praetorian prefect and all his men failed, a simple mason with the help of God and a hammer succeeded. This means that the identification with Cynegius could be doubted, but it is accepted by *PLRE* s.v. On Cynegius's activities, see also Fowden, "Bishops and Temples," 62f.

65 Zosimus 4.45.1 says he died en route from Egypt, but this is probably merely an attempt to connect up with his only other mention of Cynegius (37.3) when he was active in Egypt. It fits extremely badly with the consulate, which certainly would have required Cynegius's presence in Constantinople on 1 January, since he was colleague of the emperor himself—a quite exceptional distinction—and he was already dead on 19 March. Nobody traveled by sea in winter unless it was unavoidable, and no urgency is apparent for Cynegius to visit Egypt personally at this time. One curiosity deserves mention: The so-called *Consularia Constantinopolitana* (Burgess, *The Chronicle of Hydatius* 215-45) *ad ann.* devote the largest single item in the whole chronicle to Cynegius, whose body, it seems,

was temporarily deposited in the imperial burial church of the Holy Apostles in Constantinople before being conducted by his wife, Achantia, back to Spain in 389 after Theodosius's defeat of Maximus made travel to the West safe again. This laudatory passage in the official chronicle of the city seems to be Achantia's own responsibility (she is even mentioned as having escorted the body to Spain on foot). It is not the sort of thing the very brief chronicle usually mentions, and Achantia is the only woman named in the whole chronicle, except for the dead Constantia, posthumous daughter of Constantius and wife of Gratian, when her body was brought to Constantinople in 383 (*ad ann.* 383). Since our text of the chronicle goes back to a Spanish source, it seems that Achantia herself must have added this personal item to a copy of the chronicle she took with her when she retired to Spain, where it was later used by the Spanish chronicler Hydatius (see Burgess, *The Chronicle of Hydatius* 191–8).

66 Libanius, *Or.* 30.15. On the date of "publication," see Wiemer, "Die Rangstellung" 126–29.

67 *PLRE* 1 s.vv. Tatianus 5, Proculus 6.

68 Sokrates, *Hist. Eccl.* 5.14.6.

69 Pacatus, Theodosius's official panegyrist in Rome in 389, was at special pains to deny this: *Pan. Lat.* 12 (2).24. It must have been widely believed.

70 See above, chapter 2, text at n. 71.

71 Symmachus, *Ep.* 3.33, for one Marcianus, who was *vir optimus sed invidia tyrannici temporis involutus.* On the date (388), see Forlin Patrucco and Roda, "Le lettere" 289–93, but also Pellizzari, *Commento storico* 130–33, who prefers 395.

72 Sozomenus, *Hist. Eccl.* 7.25.9. Later Eastern mythmaking turned this compromise into a confrontation between the two orthodox heroes, in which Ambrose defended his sanctuary and Theodosius demonstrated his humility by retreating: the man of the church won the confrontation, but the emperor won admiration for his humble acceptance of his role in the church. So Theodoret, *Hist. Eccl.* 5.18.20. The story was unknown to the well-informed Sozomenus and is pious fantasy. It is accepted, however, by McLynn, *Ambrose* 298, who has not noticed that the sole source is the mythmaking Christian publicist Theodoret.

73 The events have to be reconstructed from Ambrose's highly tendentious version in *Ep.* 74 (*Ep. extra coll.* 1a) and *Ep. extra coll.* 1. Since *Ep.* 74 (in the original unedited version preserved as *Ep. extra coll.* 1a) was sent to Theodosius, the basic facts related there will be accurate. On the whole affair, see McLynn, *Ambrose* 298–309, whom I follow with minor changes in emphasis.

74 *Ep. extra coll.* 1a (*Ep.* 74). 6.

75 *Ep. extra coll.* 1.27–28 for the confrontation in the cathedral. In fact this confrontation was probably a fairly discreet affair conducted in low tones (so McLynn, *Ambrose* 307). When Ambrose arranged his letters for publication after Theodosius's death, *Ep. extra coll.* 1a, the copy of the original letter to Theodosius that

he enclosed with *Ep. extra coll.* 1 for his sister, received an addition, in which i.a. Ambrose threatened Theodosius with a confrontation in the church (*Ep.* 74.33 is this addition in the edited version of the letter) and inevitably contributed to the prominence of the confrontation in the later literature *ad maiorem gloriam Ambrosii.* It is not authentic.

76 See above, chapter 5, text at n. 81.

77 Sources in *PLRE* I s.v. Albinus 15.

78 *PLRE* I s.v. Flavianus 15. On his career, see Errington, "The Praetorian Prefectures," correcting some modern "corrections." For their retention, see Matthews, "*Codex*," 196–213.

79 *PLRE* I s.v. Symmachus 4; Matthews, *Western Aristocracies* 229f.

80 Ambrose, *Ep. extra coll.* 10.4; cf. McLynn, *Ambrose* 313–15.

81 Ambrose, *Ep. extra coll.* 11.2–3.

82 So McLynn, *Ambrose* 328. On the uncertain chronology, see also Errington, "The Praetorian Prefectures" 450–51.

83 The sources offer many contradictory details. The best detailed modern account is now McLynn, *Ambrose* 315–30, to which I owe much.

84 So Paulinus, *Vita Ambrosii* 24: *plurimi interempti innocentes.*

85 I.e., Augustine, *De civ. Dei* 5.26; Paulinus, *Vita Ambrosii* 24, with the first description of what later developed into the classic myth of Ambrose's rejecting Theodosius at the door of the cathedral; cf. Schieffer, "Von Mailand nach Canossa" 339–42.

86 So Ambrose in retrospect, *De obit. Theod.* 34—but Theodosius was not a private person.

87 *CTh* 1.1.2, 3.1.6, 7.1.13.

88 *CTh* 16.10.10: *nemo se hostiis polluat, nemo insontem victimam caedat, nemo delubra adeat, templa perlustret et mortali opere formata simulacra suspiciat, ne divinis adque humanis sanctionibus reus fiat. iudices quoque haec forma contineat, ut, si quis profano ritui deditus templum uspiam vel in itinere vel in urbe adoraturus intraverit, quindecim pondo auri ipse protinus inferre cogatur nec non officium eius parem summam simili maturitate dissolvat, si non et obstiterit iudici et confestim publica adtestatione rettulerit. consulares senas, officia eorum simili modo, correctores et praesides quaternas, apparitiones illorum similem normam aequali sorte dissolvant.* See also Libanius, *Or.* 30.33; cf. McLynn, *Ambrose* 331–32; Errington, "Christian Accounts" 425.

89 *CTh* 16.5.20. The text is registered in the Code as an *exemplum sacrarum litterarum,* which leaves its exact status uncertain.

90 *CTh* 16.5.15 (Trifolius), 9.16.11, 16.5.18 (Albinus).

91 *CTh* 16.7.4+5. Given the same (wrong!) date in the manuscripts (cf. Seeck, *Regesten* 104, 15) and the same subject, the two fragments must have originally be-

longed to the same law. It is difficult to see why the compilers of *CTh* should have split it up.

92 *CTh* 16.4.2; Sokrates, *Hist. Eccl.* 5.13.

93 *CTh* 16.5.17, 19.

94 *CTh* 16.2.27, 28. Cf. Errington, "Christian Accounts" 428–29.

95 *CTh* 16.3.1, 2. Cf. Caner, *Wandering, Begging Monks* 199–200.

96 Libanius, *Or.* 30 (*Pro Templis*). 8; Ambrose, *Ep. extra coll.* 1.27; cf. Eunapius, F56 (Blockley).

97 *PLRE* 1 s.v. Rufinus 18.

98 Zosimus 4.51–52.

99 *CTh* 16.5.21.

100 *CTh* 9.38.9, with the explicit rehabilitation of Tatianus.

101 Zosimus 4.52; *Chron. Pasch. s.a.*; Eunapius, F57 (Blockley).

102 *CTh* 16.10.12: *nullus omnino ex quolibet genere ordine hominum dignitatum vel in potestate positus vel honore perfunctus, sive potens sorte nascendi seu humilis genere condicione fortuna in nullo penitus loco, in nulla urbe sensu carentibus simulacris vel insontem victimam caedat vel secretiore piaculo larem igne, mero genium, penates odore veneratus accendat lumina, inponat tura, serta suspendat etc.*

103 *CTh* 16.10.12; Sozomenus, *Hist. Eccl.* 7.20.1–2, with Errington, "Christian Accounts" 429–32, for this interpretation.

104 Sozomenus, *Hist. Eccl.* 7.20.1: ἀρξάμενος βασιλεύειν ἐκώλευσε τούτων ἐπιβαίνειν· τελευτῶν δὲ καὶ πολλοὺς καθεῖλεν.

105 I.e., Theodoret, *Hist. Eccl.* 5.21.1; 5.

106 *CTh* 16.10.11: *iudex quoque siquis tempore administrationis suae fretus privilegio potestatis polluta loca sacrilegus temerator intraverit, quindecim auri pondo, officium vero eius, nisi conlatis viribus obviarit, parem summam aerario nostro inferre cogatur.* Discussion in Errington, "Christian Accounts" 426f. Haas, *Alexandria* 166, puts this law after the destruction of the Sarapeion and fails to notice that it is not directed at the general public; despite its rhetorical generalizations, in its specific instruction it aims purely at controlling the activities of imperial officials.

107 *CTh* 16.10.10; cf. above, text at n. 88; chapter 4, text at n. 47.

108 The main ancient sources for these events are Rufinus, *Hist. Eccl.* 11.22–23; Sokrates, *Hist. Eccl.* 5.16–17; Sozomenus, *Hist. Eccl.* 7.15.2–10; Eunapius, *Vit. Soph.* 6.11.1–7 (= F56 Blockley). On the relationship of these accounts to each other, see Errington, "Christian Accounts" 423f. On the Sarapeion complex, see most recently McKenzie, Gibson, and Reyes, "Reconstructing the Serapeum" 72–114. Cf. Fowden, "Bishops and Temples" 69f.; Haas, *Alexandria* 146–48, 159f.; Trombley, *Hellenic Religion* 129f.

109 The usual date given for these events is 391, but the reasoning for it is merely subjective, taken from the general impression given by Rufinus's narrative. The

only date given directly by a text is 392 (Bauer and Strzygowski, *Alexandrinische Weltchronik* 74, lines 23–25), and the events recorded by the other sources provide no reason in themselves for rejecting this. Evagrius's successor is not known to have been in office until April 392, and post-riot legislation (see below) all belongs to the spring and summer of 392: so also Hahn, *Gewalt* 82.

110 This seems to be reflected in Rufinus's description of the introductory passage: *in cuius exordio vana gentilium superstitio culpabatur* (*Hist. Eccl.* 11.23 [p. 1026, 22 Mommsen]).

111 Rufinus, *Hist. Eccl.* 11.23 (1026 13–19 Mommsen): *ille (sc. Theodosius), qui ingenita mentis clementia errantes mallet emendare quam perdere, rescribit illorum quidem vindictam, quos ante aras sanguis fusus martyres fecit, non esse poscendam, in quibus dolorem interitus superaverit gloria meritorum; de cetero vero malorum causam radicesque discordiae, quae pro simulacrorum defensione veniebant, penitus debere succidi, quibus exterminatis etiam bellorum causa pariter conquiesceret.* See also Sozomenus, *Hist. Eccl.* 7.15.7, using Rufinus. See Hahn, *Gewalt* 85f.

112 So Sokrates, *Hist. Eccl.* 5.16.1: "an instruction of the emperor issued under Theophilus's influence ordered the dissolution of the temples"; Sozomenus, *Hist. Eccl.* 7.15.7: "the temples in Alexandria were to be destroyed, since they were the cause of the riots among the population"; see also Eunapius F56 (Blockley). Sokrates may also reflect the pagan view, since he cites as informants the pagan schoolteachers Helladius and Ammonius, who had taught him in Constantinople after their flight from Alexandria. Helladius was said to be proud of having personally killed eleven men in the riot (Sokrates, *Hist. Eccl.* 5.16.14).

113 See, e.g., Haas, *Alexandria* 169f.; Hahn, *Gewalt* 97f.

114 *PLRE* I s.v. Hypatius 3.

115 *CTh* 1.29.5, with Seeck's amendment of the date from March to May.

116 *CTh* 11.36.31: *nec enim eos fas est adimi debitae severitati, qui pacem publicam actuum perturbatione confusam rebelli contumacia miscuerunt.*

117 *CTh* 16.4.3.

118 *CTh* 1.29.7: *plebem tantum vel decuriones ab omni improborum insolentia et temeritate tueantur, ut id tantum, quod esse dicuntur, esse non desinant.* On the *defensores* in general, see Frakes, *Contra Potentium Iniurias.*

119 Most influential was Bloch, "Pagan Revival"; cf. Matthews, *Western Aristocracies* 240f.; Williams and Friell, *Theodosius* 121f.

120 At excessive length, but convincing: Cracco Ruggini, "Il paganesimo" esp. 75–141. So also McLynn, *Ambrose* 165–66. The poem is in the Teubner *Anthologia Latina* 1.1.17–23.

121 All sources for the battle of the Frigidus are conveniently collected by Paschoud in his Budé *Zosime* II, 2 appendix C.

122 Paulinus, *Vita Ambrosii* 27–31; Ambrose, *Ep. extra coll.* 10; cf. McLynn, *Ambrose* 344f.

123 Paulinus, *Vita Ambrosii* 26.3, with Ambrose, *Ep. extra coll.* 10.6, and McLynn, *Ambrose* 345.

124 Ambrose, *De obitu Theod.* 39: *contra autem Maximus et Eugenius in inferno . . . docentes exemplo miserabili, quam durum sit arma suis principibus inrogare.*

125 Ambrose, *De obitu Theod.* 7.

126 Ambrose, *Explanatio psalmi* 36.25: *infideles et sacrilegi.* The *explanatio* is dated by the mention of the battle merely as post-September 394. But because of the inclusion of the dramatic motif of the "bora" turning the spears back against their throwers, which was first popularized in January 396 by Claudian, *Carm.* 7 (*III cons. Hon*) (who, however, did not use it where it would have been appropriate in *Carm.* 1 [*Prob.*] of January 395, thus suggesting that he had not yet invented it), it is probably necessary to date the *explanatio* after January 396, for it is much more likely that Ambrose took the "bora" motif from the court poet than that the pagan Claudian had borrowed it after studying Ambrose's lucubrations on Psalm 36.

127 Rufinus, *Hist. Eccl.* 11.33 (1038, 1–2 Mommsen): *eruditus admodum vir, mereri se mortem pro errore iustius quam pro crimine iudicavit.* Cf. most recently Williams and Friell, *Theodosius* 135: "faced with the devastating failure of all his gods and his cause." There is, however, no good evidence that Flavianus was even present at the battle; as praetorian prefect he had no need to be. On Flavianus and Eugenius, see also O'Donnell, "Career" esp. 136–40, for some reductionist arguments.

128 Rufinus, *Hist. Eccl.* 11.33 (1039, 5–6 Mommsen): *etenim compertum est, quod post illam imperatoris precem, quam deo fuderat, ventus ita vehemens exortus est, ut tela hostium in eos qui iecerant retorqueret*; Claudian, *Carm.* 7 (*III cons. Hon.*) 93–95; absent in *Carm.* 1 (*Prob.*), 103–12, and *Carm.* 8 (*IV cons. Hon.*), 80–93. See also the passages collected by Paschoud, Budé *Zosime* II, 2, appendix C.

129 Augustinus, *De civ. Dei* 5.26 (p. 239, 25–30DK). He says (239, 16) he had information from soldiers who had been present, but he cites Claudian for the "bora."

130 *Notitia Dignitatum Occ.* V.145.

131 Theodoret, *Hist. Eccl.* 5.24.4.

132 Ibid., 5.24.17.

133 *Notitia Dignitatum Occ.* V.146.

134 *Notitia Dignitatum Or.* V.43 and 44, for the *Ioviani Iuniores* and the *Herculiani Iuniores*, dating from the split in the armies under Valentinian and Valens.

BIBLIOGRAPHY

This bibliography contains works that are mentioned in the notes in an abbreviated form. I have not listed editions of ancient texts, for which I have used standard editions. The letters of Ambrose are cited according to the new Vienna edition of Michaela Zelzer; the *Panegyrici Latini* according to the chronological order of Galletier. In both cases the traditional or alternative numbering has been added in brackets to facilitate comparison with older literature. Abbreviations for periodicals are according to *L'Année philologique*.

Alföldi, A. *A Conflict of Ideas in the Late Roman Empire: The Clash between the Senate and Valentinian I.* Oxford, 1952.

Ando, C. *Imperial Ideology and Provincial Loyalty in the Roman Empire.* Berkeley, 2000.

Asche, V. *Roms Weltherrschaftsidee und Außenpolitik in der Spätantike im Spiegel der Panegyrici Latini.* Bonn, 1983.

Ausbüttel, F. M. "Die Dedition der Westgoten von 382 und ihre historische Bedeutung." *Athenaeum* 66 (1988): 604–13.

Austin, N. J. E. "A usurper's claim to legitimacy: Procopius in A.D. 365/6." *Riv. Stor. di Ant.* 2 (1972): 187–94.

Bagnall, R. S., Alan Cameron, S. R. Schwartz, and K. A. Worp. *Consuls of the Later Roman Empire.* Atlanta, 1987.

Baldini, A. "Problemi della traditione sulla 'distruzione' del Sarapeo di Alessandria." *RSA* 15 (1985): 97–152.

Baldus, H. R. "Theodosius der Große und die Revolte des Magnus Maximus—das Zeugnis der Münzen." *Chiron* 14 (1984): 175–91.

Barceló, P. A. *Roms auswärtige Beziehungen unter der constantinischen Dynastie (306–363).* Regensburg, 1981.

Barceló, P. A., and G. Gottlieb. "Das Glaubensedikt des Kaisers Theodosius vom 27. Februar 380: Adressaten und Zielsetzung." In *Klassisches Altertum, Spätantike und frühes Christentum: Adolf Lippold zum 65. Geburtstag gewidmet*, edited by K. Dietz, D. Hennig, and H. Kaletsch, 409–23. Würzburg, 1993.

Barnes, T. D. "Constans and Gratian in Rome." *HSPh* 79 (1975): 328f.

———. *Athanasius and Constantius.* Cambridge, Mass., 1993.

———. *From Eusebius to Augustine.* Aldershot, 1994.

———. *Ammianus Marcellinus and the Representation of Historical Reality.* Ithaca, 1998.

———. "Ambrose and Gratian." *Ant. Tard.* 7 (1999): 165–74.

Barrow, R. H. *Prefect and Emperor: The "Relationes" of Symmachus A.D. 384.* Oxford, 1973.

Bauer, A., and J. Strzygowski. *Eine Alexandrinische Weltchronik.* Denkschriften der kaiserlichen Akademie der Wissenschaften. Vienna, 1906.

Bernardi, J. *Saint Grégoire de Nazianze: Le théologien et son temps.* Paris, 1995.

Bidez, J. *La vie de l'empereur Julien.* Paris, 1930.

Biermann, M. *Die Leichenreden des Ambrosius von Mailand.* Hermes-Einzelschriften 70. Stuttgart, 1995.

Birley, A. R. "Magnus Maximus and the Persecution of Heresy." *Bull. John Rylands Library of Manchester* 66 (1983): 13–43.

Bloch, H. "The Pagan Revival in the West at the End of the Fourth Century." In *The Conflict between Paganism and Christianity in the Fourth Century,* edited by A. Momigliano, 193–217. Oxford, 1963.

Blockley, R. C. *The Fragmentary Classicising Historians of the Later Roman Empire: Eunapius, Olympiodorus, Priscus and Malchus.* 2 vols. ARCA 6 and 10. Liverpool, 1981, 1983.

———. *East Roman Foreign Policy: Formation and Conduct from Diocletian to Anastasius.* ARCA 30. Leeds, 1992.

Bowersock, G. W. *Julian the Apostate.* London, 1978.

———. "Mavia, Queen of the Saracens." In *Studien zur antiken Sozialgeschichte: Festschrift F. Vittinghoff.* Kölner historische Abhandlungen 28, 477–95. Cologne, 1980 (= *Studies on the Eastern Roman Empire: Social, Economic and Administrative History, Religion, Historiography,* 127–40. Goldbach, 1994).

Brennecke, H. C. *Studien zur Geschichte der Homöer. Beiträge zur historischen Theologie* Beiträge zur historischen Theologie 73. Tübingen, 1988.

Browning, R. W. "The Riot of A.D. 387 in Antioch." *JRS* 42 (1952): 13ff.

———. *The Emperor Julian.* Berkeley, 1976.

Burgess, R. W., ed. *The Chronicle of Hydatius and the Consularia Constantinopolitana.* Oxford, 1993.

Burns, T. S. *Barbarians within the Gates of Rome: A Study of Roman Military Policy and the Barbarians, ca. 375–425 A.D.* Bloomington, 1994.

Cambridge Ancient History. Vol. 13, *The Late Empire,* edited by Averil Cameron and P. Garnsey. Cambridge, 1998.

Cameron, Alan. "Gratian's Repudiation of the Pontifical Robe." *JRS* 58 (1968): 96–102.

———. *Claudian: Poetry and Propaganda at the Court of Honorius.* Oxford, 1970.

———. *Porphyrius the Charioteer.* Oxford, 1973.

———. *Circus Factions: Blues and Greens at Rome and Byzantium.* Oxford, 1976.

Campenhausen, H. von. *Ambrosius von Mailand als Kirchenpolitiker.* Berlin, 1929.

Caner, D. *Wandering, Begging Monks: Spiritual Authority and the Promotion of Monasticism in Late Antiquity.* Berkeley, 2002.

Cavallera, F. *Le scisme d'Antioche (IVe–Ve siècles).* Paris, 1905.

Cecconi, G. A. *Commento storico al libro II dell'epistolario di Q. Aurelio Simmaco.* Pisa, 2002.

Chadwick, H. *Priscillian of Avila.* Oxford, 1976.

Chastagnol, A. *La Préfecture urbaine à Rome sous le Bas Empire.* Paris, 1960.

———. *Les Fastes de la Préfecture de Rome au Bas-Empire.* Paris, 1962.

Chauvot, A. *Opinions romaines face aux barbares au IVe siècle après J.C.* Paris, 1998.

Chesnut, G. F. *The First Christian Historians.* Paris, 1977.

Cleary, H. S. E. *The Ending of Roman Britain.* London, 1989.

Corcoran, S. *The Empire of the Tetrarchs: Imperial Pronouncements and Government, AD 284–324.* Oxford, 1996.

Cracco Ruggini, L. *Economia e società nell' Italia annonaria.* Milano, 1961.

———. *Il paganesimo romano tra religione e politica (324–394): Per una reinterpretazione del Carmen contra paganos.* Atti della acc. naz. dei Lincei, classe di scienze morali, storiche e filologiche, ser. 8, vol. 23, fasc. 1. Rome, 1979.

Croke, B. "Arbogast and the Death of Valentinian II." *Historia* 25 (1976): 235–44.

Curran, J. *Pagan City and Christian Capital.* Oxford, 2000.

Dagron, G. *Naissance d'une capitale.* Paris, 1974.

Daly, L. J. "Themistius' Refusal of a Magistracy." *Byzantion* 53 (1983): 164–212.

Delmaire, R. *Largesses sacrées et res privata: L'aerarium impérial et son administration du IVe au VIe siècle.* Collection de l'école française de Rome 121. Paris-Rome 1989.

Demandt, A. *Die Spätantike: Römische Geschichte von Diocletian bis Justinian, 284–565 n. Chr.* Munich, 1989.

Dittrich, U.-B. *Die Beziehungen Roms zu den Sarmaten und Quaden im vierten Jahrhundert n. Chr. (nach der Darstellung des Ammianus Marcellinus).* Bonn, 1984.

Dörner, N. "Ambrosius in Trier." *Historia* 50 (2001): 217–44.

Domenicis, A. M. de. *Il problema dei rapporti burocratico-legislativi tra 'occidente' ed 'oriente' nel basso impero alla luce delle inscriptiones e subscriptiones delle costituzioni imperiali.* Rendiconti di Ist. Lombardo di scienze e lettere, classe di lettere e scienze morali e storiche 87, iv. Milan, 1954.

Downey, G. *A History of Antioch in Syria.* Princeton, 1961.

Drinkwater, J. F. "The 'Germanic Threat on the Rhine Frontier': A Romano-Gallic Artefact?" In *Shifting Frontiers in Late Antiquity,* edited by R. W. Mathisen and H. S. Sivan, 20–30. Aldershot, 1996.

———. "Ammianus, Valentinian and the Rhine Germans." In *The Late Roman World and its Historian: Interpreting Ammianus Marcellinus,* edited by J. W. Drijvers and D. Hunt, 127–38. London, 1999.

Ehrhardt, A. "The First Two Years of the Emperor Theodosius I." *JEH* 15 (1964): 1–17.

Elton, H. *Warfare in Roman Europe, AD 350–425.* Oxford, 1996.

Ensslin, W. *Die Religionspolitik des Kaisers Theodosius d. Gr.* SBAW phil-hist Klasse 1953, 2. Munich, 1953.

————. "War Kaiser Theodosius I zweimal in Rom?" *Hermes* 81 (1953): 500f.

Errington, R. M. "The Praetorian Prefectures of Virius Nicomachus Flavianus." *Historia* 41 (1992): 439–61.

————. "The Accession of Theodosius I." *Klio* 78 (1996): 438–53.

————. "Theodosius and the Goths." *Chiron* 26 (1996): 1–27.

————. "Christian Accounts of the Religious Legislation of Theodosius I." *Klio* 79 (1997): 398–443.

————. "Church and State in the First Years of Theodosius I." *Chiron* 27 (1997): 21–72.

————. "Themistius and His Emperors." *Chiron* 30 (2000): 861–904.

————. "A Note on the Augustal Prefect of Egypt." *Tyche* 17 (2003): 69–77.

Fatouros, G., and T. Krischer, eds. *Libanios* Wege der Forschung, vol. 621. Darmstadt, 1983.

Flach, A. "Das iudicium quinquevirale im Werdegang senatorischer Strafgerichtsbarkeit." *ZSS* 110 (1996): 358–76.

Forlin Patrucco, M., and S. Roda. "Le lettere di Simmaco ad Ambrogio: Vent'anni di rapporti amichevole." In *Ambrosius Episcopus: Atti del Congresso Internazionale di Studi Ambrosiani (Milano 2–7 dicembre, 1974),* 2:284–97. Milan, 1976.

Fowden, G. "Bishops and Temples in the Eastern Roman Empire, A.D. 320–435." *JThS,* n.s., 29 (1978): 53–78.

Frakes, R. M. *Contra Potentium Inuirias: The Defensor Civitatis and Late Roman Justice.* Münchener Beiträge zur Papyrusforschung und antiken Rechtsgeschichte 90. Munich, 2001.

Gallay, P. *La vie de Saint Grégoire de Nazianze.* Paris, 1943.

Garsoïan, N. G. *The Epic Histories attributed to P'awstos Buzand (Buzandaran Patmut'iwnk').* Cambridge, Mass. 1989.

Gaudemet, J. "Le partage législatif au bas-empire d'après un ouvrage récent." *SDHI* 21 (1955): 319–31.

————. "Le partage législatif dans la seconde moitié du IVe siècle." *Studi in onore di Pietro di Francisci* 2:319–54. Milan, 1956.

————. *L'église dans l'empire romain (IVe–Ve siècles).* Paris, 1958.

————. "La première mesure législative de Valentinien III." *Iura* 20 (1969): 129–47.

————. "La condemnation des pratiques paiennes en 391." In *Epektasis: Mélanges J. Daniélou,* 597–602. Paris, 1972.

Girardet, K. M. "Trier 385: Der Prozess gegen die Priszillianer." *Chiron* 4 (1974): 577–608.

———. "Die Erhebung Kaiser Valentinians II.: Politische Umstände und Folgen (375/76)." *Chiron* 34 (2004): 109–44.

Gottlieb, G. *Ambrosius von Mailand und Kaiser Gratian.* Hypomnemata 40. Göttingen, 1973.

———. "Das Konzil von Aquileia (381)." *AAC* 11 (1979): 287–306.

———. "Der mailänder Kirchenstreit von 385/386: Datierung, Verlauf, Deutung." *MH* 42 (1985): 37–55.

Grattarola, B. "L'usurpazione di Procopio e la fine dei Costantinidi." *Aevum* 60 (1986): 82–105.

Gross-Albenhausen, K. *Imperator christianissimus: Der christliche Kaiser bei Ambrosius und Johannes Chrysostomos.* Frankfurt am Main, 1999.

Grumel, V. "L'Illyricum de la mort de Valentinien Ier (375) à la mort de Stilicon (408)." *Rev. des Ét. Byz.* 9 (1951): 5–46.

Gutmann, B. *Studien zur römischen Aussenpolitik in der Spätantike (364–395 n. Chr.).* Bonn, 1991.

Haas, Christopher. *Alexandria in Late Antiquity: Topography and Social Conflict.* Baltimore, 1997.

Hahn, Johannes. *Gewalt und religiöser Konflikt: Studien zu den Auseinandersetzungen zwischen Christen, Heiden und Juden im Osten des Römischen Reiches (von Konstantin bis Theodosius II.).* *Klio* Beihefte, n.s., vol. 8. Berlin, 2004.

Hanson, R. P. C. *The Search for the Christian Doctrine of God.* Edinburgh, 1988.

Harries, J. "Prudentius and Theodosius." *Latomus* 43 (1984): 69–84.

———. "Sozomen and Eusebius: The Lawyer as Church Historian in the Fifth Century." In *The Inheritance of Historiography, 350–900,* edited by C. Holdsworth and T. P. Wiseman, 45–52. Exeter, 1986.

———. *Law and Empire in Late Antiquity.* Cambridge, 1999.

Harries, J., and I. Wood, eds. *The Theodosian Code.* London, 1993.

Heather, P. "The Crossing of the Danube and the Gothic Conversion." *GRBS* 27 (1986): 289–318.

———. *Goths and Romans, 332–489.* Oxford, 1991.

———. "New Men for New Constantines? Creating an Imperial Elite in the Eastern Mediterranean." In *New Constantines. The Rhythm of Imperial Renewal in Byzantium, 4th–13th Centuries,* edited by P. Magdalino, 11–34. Aldershot, 1994.

———. "*Foedera* and *foederati* of the Fourth Century." *Kingdoms of the Empire,* edited by W. Pohl, 57–74. Leiden, 1997.

———. "Themistius: a Political Philosopher." In *The Propaganda of Power: The*

Role of Panegyric in Late Antiquity, Mnemosyne Suppl. 183, edited by M. Whitby, 125–50. Leiden, 1998.

Heather, P., and J. Matthews. *The Goths in the Fourth Century*. Liverpool, 1991.

Heather, P., and D. Moncur. *Politics, Philosophy, and Empire in the Fourth Century: Select Orations of Themistius*. Translated Texts for Historians, vol. 36. Liverpool, 2001.

Heinen, H. *Trier und das Trevererland in römischer Zeit*. 3d ed. Trier, 1993.

Hoffmann, D. *Das spätrömische Bewegungsheer und die Notitia Dignitatum*. Epigraphische Studien 7/I, 7/II. Düsseldorf, 1969, 1970.

Homes Dudden, F. *The Life and Times of St. Ambrose*. 2 vols. Oxford, 1935.

Honoré, A. *Law in the Crisis of Empire, 379–455 A.D.: The Theodosian Dynasty and Its Quaestors*. Oxford, 1998.

Humphries, M. *Communities of the Blessed: Social Environment and Religious Change in Northern Italy, A.D. 200–400*. Oxford, 1999.

Isaac, B. *The Limits of Empire: The Roman Army in the East*. 2d ed. Oxford, 1992.

Jones, A. H. M. "Collegiate Prefectures." *JRS* 54 (1964): 78–89 (= *The Roman Economy*, 375–95. Oxford, 1974).

———. *The Later Roman Empire, 284–602*. Oxford, 1964.

———. *The Cities of the Eastern Roman Provinces*. 2d ed. Oxford, 1971.

Kelly, J. N. D. *Early Christian Creeds*. 3d ed. London, 1972.

———. *Early Christian Doctrines*. 5th ed. London, 1977.

———. *Jerome: His Life, Writings and Controversies*. London, 1975.

———. *Golden Mouth: The Story of John Chrysostom—Ascetic, Preacher, Bishop*. London, 1995.

King, N. Q. *The Emperor Theodosius and the Establishment of Christianity*. London, 1961.

Klein, R. *Der Streit um den Victoriaaltar*. Darmstadt, 1972.

Kohns, A. P. *Versorgungskrisen und Hungerrevolten in spätantikem Rom*. Bonn, 1961.

Lallemand, J. *L'administration civile de l'Égypte de l'avènement de Dioclétien à la création du diocèse (284–382)*. Académie royale de Belgique, Classe des lettres et des sciences morales et politiques. Mémoires, Collection in 8°, vol. 57, fasc. 2. Brussels, 1964.

Langenfeld, H. *Christianisierungspolitik und Sklavengesetzgebung der römischen Kaiser von Konstantin bis Theodosius II*. Bonn, 1977.

Laporte, J.-P. "Les armées romaines et la révolte de Firmus en Maurétanie césarienne." In *L'armée romaine de Dioclétien à Valentinien Ier: Actes du Congrès de Lyon (12–14 Septembre 2002)*, edited by Yann Le Bohec and Catherine Wolff, 279–98. Lyon, 2004.

Lee, A. D. *Information and Frontiers*. Cambridge, 1993.

Lenski, N. "*Initium mali romano imperio*: Contemporary Reactions to the Battle of Adrianople." *TAPhA* 127 (1997): 129–68.

————. "The Election of Jovian and the Role of the Late Imperial Guards." *Klio* 82 (2000): 492–515.

————. *Failure of Empire: Valens and the Roman State in the Fourth Century A.D.* Berkeley, 2002.

Leppin, H. *Theodosius der Große*. Darmstadt, 2003.

Liebeschuetz, J. H. W. G. *Antioch: City and Imperial Administration in the Later Roman Empire*. Oxford, 1972.

————. *Barbarians and Bishops*. Oxford, 1990.

Lieu, S. N. C. *Manichaeism in the Later Roman Empire and Medieval China*. Manchester, 1985.

Lindner, Amnon. *The Jews in Roman Imperial Legislation*. Detroit, 1987.

Lippold, A. *Theodosius der Große und seine Zeit*. Stuttgart, 1968.

Lizzi Testa, R. "La politica religiosa di Teodosio I, miti storiografici e realtà storica." *RAL* 9.7 (1996): 323–61.

Luzzato, G. I. "Ricerce sull'applicazione delle costituzioni imperiali nelle provincie." In *Scritti di diritto romano in onore di Contardo Ferrini*, edited by G. G. Archi, 265–93. Milan, 1946.

MacCormack, S. "Latin Prose Panegyrics: Tradition and Discontinuity in the Later Roman Empire." *Rev.Ét.Aug.* 22 (1976): 29–77.

————. *Art and Ceremony in Late Antiquity*. Berkeley, 1981.

Mango, C. *Le développement urbain de Constantinople (IVe–VIIe siècles)*. Travaux et Mémoires, Monographies 2. Paris, 1985.

Mango, C., and R. Scott. *The Chronicle of Theophanes Confessor*. Oxford, 1997.

Mann, J. C. "Power, Force and the Frontiers of the Empire." *JRS* 69 (1979): 175–83.

Martin, A. *Athanase d'Alexandrie et l'église d'Égypte au IVe siècle (328–373)*. Collection de l'école française de Rome. Rome, 1996.

Mathison, R. W., and H. S. Sivan. *Shifting Frontiers in Late Antiquity*. Aldershot, 1996.

Matthews, J. F. "A Pious Supporter of Theodosius I: Maternus Cynegius and His Family." *JThS* 18 (1967): 484–509.

————. *Western Aristocracies and Imperial Court, A.D. 364–425*. Oxford, 1975.

————. *The Roman Empire of Ammianus*. London, 1989.

————. "*Codex Theodosianus* 9.40.13 and Nicomachus Flavianus." *Historia* 46 (1997): 196–213.

————. *Laying Down the Law: A Study of the Theodosian Code*. New Haven, 2000.

May, G. "Gregor von Nyssa in der Kirchenpolitik seiner Zeit." *JÖBG* 15 (1966): 104–32.

————. "Basilios der Große und der römische Staat." In *Bleibendes im Wandel der Kirchengeschichte*, edited by B. Moeller and G. Ruhbach, 47–70. Tübingen, 1973.

————. "Die grossen Kappadokier und die staatliche Kirchenpolitik von Valens bis Theodosius." In *Die Kirche angesichts der konstantinischen Wende*, edited by G. Ruhbach, 322–36. Darmstadt, 1976.

McCormick, M. *Eternal Victory: Triumphal Rulership in Late Antiquity, Byzantium and the Early Medieval West.* Cambridge, 1986.

McKenzie, J. S., S. Gibson, and A. T. Reyes, "Reconstructing the Serapeum in Alexandria from the Archaeological Evidence." *JRS* 94 (2004): 73–121.

McLynn, N. B. *Ambrose of Milan.* Berkeley, 1994.

Meslin, M. *Les ariens d'occident, 335–440.* Patristica Sorbonensia 8. Paris, 1967.

Millar, F. G. *The Emperor in the Roman World.* London, 1977.

————. "Emperors, Frontiers, and Foreign Relations, 31 B.C. to A.D. 378." *Britannia* 13 (1982): 1–23 (= *Rome, the Greek World, and the East*, vol. 2: *Government, Society, and Culture in the Roman Empire*, 160–94. Chapel Hill, 2004).

Mirkovic, M. "ὑπήκοοι und σύμμαχοι: Ansiedlung und Rekrutierung von Barbaren bis zum Jahr 382." In *Klassisches Altertum, Spätantike und frühes Christentum: Adolf Lippold zum 65. Geburtstag gewidmet*, edited by K. Dietz, D. Hennig, and H. Kaletsch, 425–34. Würzburg, 1993.

Momigliano, A., ed. *The Conflict between Paganism and Christianity in the Fourth Century.* Oxford, 1963.

Nautin, P. "Les premières relations d'Ambrose avec l'empereur Gratien: Le *De Fide* (livres I et II)." In *Ambroise de Milan: XVIe Centenaire de son élection épiscopale*, edited by Y. M. Duval, 229–44. Paris, 1974.

Neri, V. "Ammiano Marcellino e l'elezione di Valentiniano." *RSA* 15 (1985): 153–82.

Niquet, H. *Monumenta virtutum titulique: Senatorische Selbstdarstellung im spätantiken Rom im Spiegel der epigraphischen Denkmäler.* Stuttgart, 2000.

Nixon, C. E. V., and B. S. Rodgers. *In Praise of Later Roman Emperors: The Panegyrici Latini.* Berkeley, 1994.

Noethlichs, K.-L. *Die gesetzgeberischen Massnahmen der christlichen Kaiser des vierten Jahrhunderts gegen Häretiker, Heiden und Juden.* Cologne, 1971.

Norman, A. F. *Libanius: Selected Works.* 4. vols. Loeb Classical Library. London-Cambridge, Mass., 1969–92.

O'Donnell, J. J. "The Career of Virius Nicomachus Flavianus." *Phoenix* 32 (1978): 129–143.

Pabst, A., ed. *Quintus Aurelius Symmachus: Reden.* Darmstadt, 1989.

Palanque, J.-R. *Saint Ambroise et l'empire romain.* Paris, 1933.

Paschoud, F. *Cinq études sur Zosime.* Paris, 1975.

Paschoud, F., and J. Szidat. *Usurpationen in der Spätantike.* Historia Einzelschriften 111. Stuttgart, 1997.

Pavan, M. *La politica gotica di Teodosio nella pubblicistica del suo tempo.* Rome, 1964.

Pellizzari, A. *Commento storico al libro III dell'epistolario di Q. Aurelio Simmaco.* Pisa, 1998.

Pergami, F. *La legislazione di Valentiniano e Valente (364–375).* Milan, 1993.

Perler, O. *Les voyages de saint Augustine.* Paris, 1969.

Petit, P. "Sur la date du 'Pro templis' de Libanios." *Byzantion* 21 (1951): 285–309 [German translation in *Libanios,* edited by G. Fatouros and T. Krischer, 43–67. Darmstadt, 1983].

———. *Libanius et la vie municipale à Antioche au IVème siècle après J.-C.* Paris, 1955.

Pietri, C. *Roma Christiana: Recherches sur l'église de Rome, son organisation, sa politique, son idéologie de Miltiade à Sixte III (311–440).* 2 vols. Rome, 1976.

Piganiol, A. *L'empire chrétien (325–395).* 2d ed. Paris, 1972.

Portmann, W. *Geschichte in der spätantiken Panegyrik.* Frankfurt, 1988.

Rauschen, G. *Jahrbücher der christlichen Kirche unter dem Kaiser Theodosius dem Grossen.* Freiburg, 1897.

Ritter, A. M. *Das Konzil von Konstantinopel und sein Symbol.* Forschungen zur Kirchen- und Dogmengeschichte 15. Göttingen, 1965.

Rivolta Tiberga, P. *Commento storico al libro V dell'epistolario di Q. Aurelio Simmaco.* Pisa, 1992.

Rodgers, B. S. "Merobaudes and Maximus in Gaul." *Historia* 30 (1981): 83–105.

Rougé, J. "La législation de Théodose contre les hérétiques: Traduction de CTh xvi.5.6–24." In *Epektasis: Mélanges J. Daniélou,* 635–49. Paris, 1972.

Rousseau, P. *Basil of Caesarea.* Berkeley, 1994.

Sabbah, G. "De la rhétorique à la communication politique: Les Panégyriques Latins." *Bull. de l'assoc. Guill. Budé* 4 (1984): 363–88.

Ste Croix, G. E. M. de. *The Class Struggle in the Ancient Greek World.* London, 1981.

Salzmann, M. R. *The Making of a Christian Aristocracy.* Cambridge, Mass., 2002.

Schieffer, R. "Von Mailand nach Canossa: Ein Beitrag zur Geschichte der christlichen Herrscherbusse von Theodosius d. Gr. bis zu Heinrich IV." *Deutsches Archiv für die Erforschung des Mittelalters* 28 (1972): 333–70.

Schlumberger, J. *Die Epitome de Caesaribus: Untersuchungen zur heidnischen Geschichtsschreibung des 4. Jahrhunderts n. Chr.* Vestigia 18. Munich, 1974.

Schneider, H. *Die 34. Rede des Themistius.* Winterthür, 1966.

Schulz, R. *Die Entwicklung des römischen Völkerrechts im vierten und fünften Jh. n. Chr.* Hermes-Einzelschriften 61. Stuttgart, 1993.

Schwartz, E. "Zur Kirchengeschichte des vierten Jahrhunderts." *ZNW* 34 (1935): 129–213 (= *Gesammelte Schriften,* 4:1–110. Berlin, 1960).

———. *Über die Bischofslisten der Synoden von Chalkedon, Nikaia und Konstantinopel.* ABAW NF 13. Munich, 1937.

Seeck, O. *Die Briefe des Libanios.* Leipzig, 1906.

————. *Regesten der Kaiser und Päpste für die Jahre 311 bis 476 n. Chr.* Stuttgart, 1919.

————. *Geschichte des Untergangs der antiken Welt.* 6 vols. Stuttgart, 1920–22.

Shahid, I. *Byzantium and the Arabs in the Fourth Century.* Washington, D.C., 1984.

Simonetti, M. *La crisi ariana nel iv secolo.* Studia Ephemeridis "Augustinianum" 11. Rome, 1975.

Sirks, B. "From the Theodosian to the Justinian Code." *Atti dell'accademia romanistica costantiniana* 6 (1986): 265–302.

————. *Food for Rome.* Amsterdam, 1991.

Sivan, H. *Ausonius of Bordeaux: Genesis of a Gallic Aristocracy.* London, 1993.

Snee, R. "Valens' Recall of the Nicene Exiles and Anti-Arian Propaganda." *GRBS* 26 (1985): 395–419.

Soraci, R. *L'imperatore Gioviano.* Catania, 1968.

Stallknecht, B. *Untersuchungen zur römischen Aussenpolitik in der Spätantike (306–395 n. Chr.).* Bonn, 1969.

Straub, J. *Vom Herrscherideal in der Spätantike.* Stuttgart, 1939.

————. *Regeneratio Imperii.* Darmstadt, 1972.

Szidat, J. "Staatlichkeit und Einzelschicksal in der Spätantike." *Historia* 44 (1995): 481–95.

Tengström, E. *Donatisten und Katholiken: Soziale, wirtschaftliche und politische Aspekte einer nordafrikanischen Kirchenspaltung.* Göteborg, 1964.

Thélamon, F. *Païens et chrétiens au IVe siècle: L'apport de l'"Histoire ecclésiastique" de Rufinus d'Aquilée.* Paris, 1981.

Thompson, E. A. *The Visigoths in the Time of Ulfila.* Oxford, 1966.

Trombley, F. R. *Hellenic Religion and Christianization c. 370–529.* Religions in the Graeco-Roman World 115, 1 and 2. Leiden, 1993–94.

Urbainczyk, T. *Socrates of Constantinople: Historian of Church and State.* Ann Arbor, 1996.

Vandersleyen, C. *Chronologie des préfets d'Égypte de 284 à 395.* Collection Latomus 55. Brussels, 1962.

Vanderspoel, J. *Themistius and the Imperial Court: Oratory, Civic Duty, and Paideia from Constantius to Theodosius.* Ann Arbor, 1995.

Vera, D. "I rapporti fra Magno Massimo, Teodosio e Valentiniano II nel 383–384." *Athenaeum* 53 (1975): 267–301.

————. "Le statue del senato di Roma in onore di Flavio Teodosio e l'equilibrio dei potere imperiali in età teodosiana." *Athenaeum* 57 (1979): 381–403.

————. *Commento storico alle Relationes di Quinto Aurelio Simmaco.* Pisa, 1981.

————. "La carriera di Virius Nicomachus Flavianus e la prefettura del' Illiria orientale nel iv. sec. D.C." *Athenaeum* 61 (1983): 24–63, 390–426.

Waas, M. *Germanen im römischen Dienst (im 4. Jh. n. Chr.).* 2d ed. Bonn, 1971.

Wallace-Hadrill, A. *Patronage in Ancient Society.* London, 1989.

Wallraff, M. *Der Kirchenhistoriker Sokrates.* Göttingen, 1997.

Wanke, U. *Die Gotenkriege des Valens.* Frankfurt, 1990.

Wheeler, E. L. "Constantine's Gothic Treaty of 332: A Reconsideration of Eusebius VC 4.5–6." In *Studia Danubiana. Pars Romaniae, Series Symposia I. The Roman Frontier at the Lower Danube 4th–6th centuries. The Second International Symposium,* edited by M. Zahariade, 81–94. Bucharest, 1998.

Whittaker, C. R. *Frontiers of the Roman Empire: A Social and Economic Study.* Baltimore, 1994.

Wiebe, F. J. *Kaiser Valens und die heidnische Opposition.* Antiquitas ser. 1, 44. Bonn, 1995.

Wiemer, H.-U. *Libanios und Julian.* Vestigia 46. Munich, 1995.

———. "Die Rangstellung des Sophisten Libanios unter den Kaisern Julian, Valens und Theodosius: Mit einem Anhang über Abfassung und Verbreitung von Libanios' Rede für die Tempel (Or. 30)." *Chiron* 25 (1995): 89–130.

Williams, D. H. *Ambrose of Milan and the End of the Arian-Nicene Conflicts.* Oxford, 1995.

Williams, S., and G. Friell. *Theodosius: The Empire at Bay.* London, 1994.

Wirth, G. "Jovianus: Kaiser und Karikatur." In *Vivarium: Festschrift für Th. Klauser. JAC Ergänzungsband* 11:353–84. Münster, 1984.

Wolfram, H. *Die Goten.* 3d ed. Munich, 1990.

Woods, D. "The Saracen Defenders of Constantinople in 378." *GRBS* 37 (1996): 259–79.

Wytzes, J. *Der letzte Kampf des Heidentums in Rom.* Leiden, 1977.

Zöllner, E. *Geschichte der Franken bis zur Mitte des 6. Jahrhunderts.* Munich, 1970.

Zuckermann, C. "Comtes et ducs en Égypte autour de l'an 400 et la date de la *Notitia Dignitatum Orientis.*" *Ant. Tard.* 6 (1998): 137–47.

INDEX

Ablabius, 148
Abundantius, 40
Achaia: senators from at Rome, 152,
    290 (n. 21)
Achantia, 307 (n. 65)
Acholius, 109, 215; advises Theodosius,
    217, 221; baptizes him, 220;
    summoned to Constantinople, 223;
    arrives after council begins, 224;
    opposes Gregory of Nazianzos, 226
Actium, 31
Adrianople: battle of, 28, 62, 188
Africa: supplies tax grain to Italy, 71
Africa *proconsularis*, 103
Agelius, 231
Aginatius, 117–18
Alamanni, 23, 32, 45–46
Alans, 31
Alavivus, 61
Albinus, 97, 135, 137; laws issued to,
    138–39, 242, 244–45, 249
Alexandria, 33, 98, 173, 180;
    ecclesiastical status, 214; expels
    Maximus the Cynic, 219–20;
    destruction of Sarapeion, 249–51;
    laws to *praefectus Augustalis*, 251–52
Altar of Victoria. *See* Victoria, altar of
Alypius, 139
Amantius of Lodève, 299 (n. 107)
Amatius, 90
Ambrose, 31, 109, 113, 123, 139, 167; first
    visit to Trier, 33, 202–3; attitude
    toward Magnus Maximus, 36, 210;
    negotiates with Eugenius, 40;
    massacre of Thessalonica, 85, 243–

44; defeats Symmachus's petition,
    124, 200–201, 203; avoids Eugenius,
    141, 255; appeal of Hydatius, 194; at
    Aquileia, 197, 198–99; *De fide*, 198;
    and Gratian, 198–99; urges council
    at Alexandria, 199; tensions with
    Valentinian II, 202–3, 208–9; second
    visit to Trier, 205, 210, 301 (n. 133);
    finds martyrs, 209; attitude toward
    Theodosius, 212, 255–56; supports
    Maximus the Cynic, 220, 223;
    challenges Nectarius, 227; influence
    at court, 238–39; Kallinikon
    incident, 240–41; on bora, 311
    (n. 126)
Amiens, 51
Ammianus Marcellinus, 18, 23; on
    Valentinian I, 46, 188; on Count
    Theodosius, 51; on Goths, 61; on
    peace with Persia, 66; on Romanus,
    72–73; on Valens, 93; on Rome, 112;
    on Maximinus, 114, 119–20; on
    Iulianus Rusticius, 133–34; on
    Gratian, 193
Ampelius, 99, 108, 118, 120, 190
Anastasius, 67
Andragathius, 32
Anemius of Sirmium, 109, 196
Anicii, 30, 124
Ankara, 20, 124
Anthemius, 279 (n. 24)
Antioch, 16, 105, 144, 158, 173, 183;
    Jovian at, 177; schism of, 184–86,
    225–26, 228; Valens's residence in,
    186–87; ecclesiastical status of, 214;

succession to Meletius, 225–26; monks in vicinity of, 235

Antonius, Fl. Claudianus, 29, 30–31

Apameia, 236

Aphrodisius, 131

Apodemius, 85–86

Apollonianists, 232–33

Aquae Mattiacae, 48

Aquileia, 36, 90, 249; Magnus Maximus at, 37; council of, 196–99

Aquincum, 25, 55, 57

Aquitania, 194

Arabia, 68

Aradius Rufus, 122

Arbogast, 38, 39, 53, 238, 253, 274 (n. 22); suicide of, 41, 254; invades Italy, 85; rejects senatorial petition, 140

Arborius, 122

Arcadius: accession of, 13, 30, 32–33, 42; at Constantinople, 37, 41, 161; and legislation, 100–101; statue in Rome, 135

Archives, 89, 100

Ariminum, 172, 184. See also Rimini

Armenia, 67–68, 183, 184

Arsak, 67

Arzanene, 66

Asia: proconsulate, 230–31

Athanaric: persecutes Christians, 58–59; peace with Valens, 59; at Constantinople, 63, 146

Athanasius, 173, 179–80, 211; restored to Alexandria, 177; death of, 179–80

Attacotti, 50

Auchenius Bassus, 90, 124, 200; and bridge, 131; and new carriage, 127–28

Augustine: on Theodosius, 212; on Frigidus campaign, 256–57

Augustus, 60

Aurelian (emperor), 58

Aurelianus (*praefectus urbi*), 164, 292 (n. 73)

Aurelius Victor, 134–35, 137

Ausonius, 122, 123, 192; on emperors, 25; consul, 30; family in office, 83, 278 (n. 8); on Rome, 112, 121; on Gratian, 193

Austoriani, 72

Auxentius (architect), 131

Auxentius of Durostorum, 204, 209

Auxonius, 230–31

Avila, 194

Banat, 55

Barses, 186, 295 (n. 49)

Basilica Ambrosiana, 209

Basilica Juliana, 191

Basilica Portiana, 204, 208

Basilica Sicinini, 191–92

Basil of Caesarea, 122, 179–80, 181–82; campaign in West, 190; pressures Gregory of Nazianzos to go to Constantinople, 214

Bassus. See Auchenius Bassus

Bauto, 34, 35

Bordeaux, 206

Brasidas, 180

Brigetio, 25, 55, 57

Britain, 31

Britto, 195, 205, 207

Bucinobantes, 48

Buthericus, 243

Byzacena, 103

Byzantium, 148

Caesarea in Cappadocia, 183

Caesarea in Palestine, 186

Callinicum, 69. See also Kallinikon

Camillus, 127

Cannae, 62

Cappadocia, 232

Carnuntum, 57
Carpathians, 60
Carrhae, 236
Carthage, 71
Castra Maurorum, 66
Cauca, 29
Ceionius Rufius Albinus. *See* Albinus
Celsus, 160
Cerealis, 201
Cethegus, 122
Chalkedon, 232
Chosro, 67
Cibalae, 20
Cilicia, 102
Civilis, 51
Claudian: on Frigidus campaign, 256–57; on bora, 311 (n. 126)
Claudianus (bishop), 193
Clearchus, 33, 163, 166
Comites, 150
Concordia, 245
Constans, 14, 15, 80, 149, 151
Constantia, 23, 307 (n. 65)
Constantine I, 14; treaty with Goths, 55, 58; dynastic program of, 79; founds Constantinople, 142; and church, 171, 172
Constantine II, 80, 149
Constantinople, 18, 142; Theodosius arrives, 63; Senate, 105, 148–61; hippodrome, 146; praetorships, 149, 155, 157; emperors visit, 161; library, 163; bread rations, 163–64; water use, 166; Council of (360), 172, 177, 184; position in church, 213; Council of (381), 221–22, 224–30; canons, 228–30
Constantinus of Orange, 299 (n. 107)
Constantius Gallus, 16, 17
Constantius II, 14, 15–16; death of, 18; employs Alamanni, 45; operates on

Danube, 55–56; government of, 80–81; reforms Roman government, 113; builds out Constantinople, 142; creates Senate at Constantinople, 142–43, 148–61; at Rome, 151, 152; disapproves of Roman senators, 151–53; institutes *praefectus urbi* at Constantinople, 153–54; at Constantinople, 161; and Arian dispute, 171, 172, 176; and Meletius, 184
Corduene, 66
Crete, 81
Cynegius, 103, 139, 233, 234, 239, 258; in Egypt, 33; legislation addressed to, 103, 104; travels in East, 235–36; antipagan activities of, 248; death of, 306 (n. 65)
Cyrene, 71
Cyriades, 131
Cyrillus of Jerusalem, 186

Dacia, 55, 58, 81, 84
Dacia Ripensis, 58
Dadastana, 20
Dagalaifus, 24
Damasus, 94, 111, 117, 191–92, 193, 217–18, 222; letter to Ambrose, 124; death of, 125; supports Symmachus, 129; and Thessalonica, 215, 224; rejects Maximus the Cynic, 220, 224; letter on schism of Antioch, 228
Danube, 44–45, 54, 74
Dardania, 63
Demophilus of Constantinople, 214, 221; talks to Theodosius, 220, 231
Demosthenes, 183–84, 295 (n. 39)
Diocletian, 151; governmental system of, 79; persecution conducted by, 190
Diodorus, 186, 227

Diogenes of Geneva, 299 (n. 107)

Domitius Modestus. *See* Modestus

Domninus of Grenoble, 299 (n. 107)

Donatists, 73; law of Valentinian I, 190; law of Gratian, 297 (n. 88)

Dulcitius, 51

Edessa, 186, 234, 236

Egypt, 71–72

Eleusinian Mysteries, 190

Eleusius of Kyzikos, 177–79, 231

Emona, 41

Epictetus (Roman doctor), 130

Epiphanius, 294

Equitius, 57

Eucherius (consul in 381), 29, 30

Eucherius (son of Serena), 39; born in Rome, 135, 271 (n. 75)

Eudoxius of Constantinople, 177, 180

Eugenius, 39–40, 53; comes to Milan, 40, 85; death of, 41; recruits Alamanni and Franks, 54; concession on old cults, 140, 255; attitude toward officials, 254–55

Eunapius, 23, 36, 41; ignores Roman cult dispute, 201, 203; on Rufinus, 247

Eunomians, 222, 232–33, 246

Eunomius, 178, 231; exiled, 232

Euodius: consul, 232; condemns Priscillianists, 206

Euphrasius, 24

Euphrates, 44–45

Eupraxius, 120–21

Europa (province), 213

Eusebia, 122

Eusebius of Samosata, 186, 295 (n. 47)

Eusignius, 207

Eustathius of Sebaste, 185, 303 (n. 18)

Eutropius, 90; consul, 34; praetorian prefect for Illyricum, 83, 108, 222–23

Euzoius, 184, 185, 187

Evagrius, 97, 249–51

Faltonius Probus Alypius. *See* Alypius

Faustina, 23

Felix (bishop of Trier), 207

Felix (Roman), 191

Firmus, 73, 190

Flavianus, Nicomachus, 85, 138–39; supports Eugenius, 140–41; suicide of, 141, 254; praetorian prefect of Theodosius, 242, 244, 245; not attacked in "Against the Pagans," 253

Flavianus, Nicomachus (the younger), 140

Flavianus (bishop of Antioch), 186, 228, 229; at Constantinople, 225; approves destruction of pagan shrines, 235

Florus, 90, 101, 234

Forum Tauri, 166

Forum Theodosii, 145

Franks, 47, 50, 53

Fraomar, 48

Frigeridus, 27

Frigidus (battle of), 41, 86, 254

Fullofaudes, 51

Gabinius, 56

Galatians, 64

Galla, 37, 41

Gallus, 80

Georgios Monachos: on Valens, 188

Gervasius, 209

Gildo, 73–74

Goths: request asylum, 26–27; Constantine's treaty with, 55; on lower Danube, 57–58; serve in army, 65; joined by *metallarii*, 106; converted under Valens, 204; "homoian," 223; importance of invasion of, 264; in Pannonia, 276 (n. 60)

Gracchus. *See* Maecius Gracchus

Gratian: accession of, 24–25, 51; at Trier, 25; meeting planned with Valens, 26, 121; sends help to Valens, 27; at Sirmium, 28, 82, 196; consul with Theodosius, 30; moves to Milan, 31; meets Magnus Maximus, 32; death of, 32; combats Lentienses, 52; not at Adrianople, 62; regional legislation, 97; law to Hypatius, 107–8; attitude toward Rome, 113–14, 121–25; legislation on Rome, 121–22; appoints many *praefecti urbi*, 122; removes altar of Victoria and subsidies for Roman cults, 123, 200, 211; refuses to see Symmachus, 124; does not reject *pontifex maximus* title, 124–25, 300 (n. 119); allows new carriage for *praefectus urbi*, 128; birth noted in *consularia constantinopolitana*, 154; attitude toward religion, 192–201; rulings on clerical *munera personalia*, 193; on Donatists, 193; adopts Valens's tolerance edict, 193; adopts Theodosius's law on converts, 195; convokes council of Aquileia, 197; and Ambrose, 198

Gregorius, 91–92

Gregory of Nazianzos: on Julian, 175; on Basil, 181–82; at Constantinople, 214, 218–21; opposes Demophilos, 220; installed in cathedral by Theodosius, 221; bishop of Sasima, 224; elected bishop of Constantinople, 224; appeals to Theodosius, 226

Gregory of Nyssa, 183

Greutungi, 60, 61

Haimos, 65

Halmyros, 232

Hebdomon, 21

Helladius, 310 (n. 112)

Herakleia (Perinthos), 213, 270 (n. 48)

Hermogenes, 157

Hermogenianus, 91–92

Hesperius, 83, 278 (n. 8)

Hierapolis, 173

Hilarianus, 151

Historia Athanasii, 180–81

Honoratus, 154, 156

Honorius, 93, 103, 256; accession of, 13, 30, 40, 42; as consul, 34; at Rome, 38; in Italy, 41; legislation of, 99

Huns, 26, 60

Hydatius (bishop of Emerita), 194, 207

Hydatius (praetorian prefect), 195

Hyginus, 194

Hymetius, 121

Hypatius (*praefectus Augustalis*), 251–52

Hypatius (praetorian prefect), 107–8, 122

Iberia, 67–68

Illyricum, 81–82, 87; Gratian gives to Theodosius, 83, 214; divided up, 84, 86; legislation for, 105–6, 108, 195, 222–23; senators from, 160, 290 (n. 21); "homoian" church in, 189

Isaac, 188

Ithacius of Ossonuba, 194–95, 205–7

Iulianus Rusticius, 133–34

Iustus (father of Justina), 201

Iustus of Lyon, 299 (n. 107)

Jerome, 187

Jerusalem, 186, 214

Johannes (doctor), 130

Johannes (usurper), 90

Jovian, 18; death of, 20; treaty with

Persia, 19, 66; priority in West, 46; appoints Symmachus senior as *praefectus urbi* at Rome, 114; and Christians, 173–74; perhaps revises Julian's law on teachers, 293 (n. 10)

Jovinus, 163

Julian (emperor): death of, 13, 14, 18; as Caesar, 17; as Augustus, 17; neglects West, 45–46; attacks Constantine, 58; attitude toward Christianity, 171–73, 176; law on teachers revised, 293 (n. 10)

Julian (of Antioch), 156, 157

Julianus, 117

Julius: kills Goths, 144; consults Senate, 161

Justina, 26, 27, 35, 299 (n. 113); death of, 37, 238; importance at Milan, 201–3; flees to Thessalonica, 209

Juthungi, 57

Kallinikon, 239–41, 258

Kyzikos, 178, 179

Lampsakos (synod), 177, 178, 181

Lateran Basilica, 191

Legislation: nature of laws, 87–93; agreements between *partes imperii*, 101–3; laws addressed to *praefectus urbi*, 115–16, 119–20, 121–22, 133, 138–39

Lentienses, 52

Leo, 120

Leontius, 287 (n. 86)

Leptis Magna, 72

Libanius, 105, 122, 258; on Rome, 139; on antipagan activities, 148; influence in Constantinople, 156–57; on senators, 159; speech "For the Temples," 235, 236; meets Cynegius, 236; on monks, 246

Liberius, 191

Licinius, 79

London, 51

Lucifer, 185

Lucillianus, 19, 20

Lucius of Alexandria, 69–70, 187, 211

Lupicinus, 61

Lydus, 95–96

Lykians, 247–48

Macedonia, 62–63, 80, 81, 84, 106; supplies Rome, 135; senators from, 152, 290 (n. 21); need for tax relief, 159

Macedonianists, 173–74, 177–79, 232–33; appeal to Rome, 190; support Valens, 211; invited to Council of Constantinople (381), 221

Macedonius (bishop), 173–74

Macedonius (*magister officiorum*), 194–95, 298 (n. 96)

Macrianus, 48–49, 52, 59

Maecius Gracchus, 122

Magnentius, 14, 15–16, 45, 151, 201

Magnus (*praefectus urbi* at Constantinople), 164

Maiestas, 119–20

Main, 48

Mallobaudes, 52

Mamertinus, 284 (n. 14)

Manichaeans, 108, 115, 223; law to Ampelius, 190

Marcellianus, 56–57

Marcellina, 205, 241

Marcellinus Comes, 212

Marcellus of Apameia, 236

Marcianopolis, 25, 59, 61, 94, 144

Marcomanni, 55

Maria, 39

Martinianus, 122

Martin of Tours, 189, 206, 207

Mauretania Sitifensis, 73

Mavia, 69–70, 276 (nn. 74, 75)

Maxentius, 87

Maximinus (*vicarius urbis*), 56, 114, 118–19, 192

Maximus (*praefectus annonae*), 284 (n. 14)

Maximus, Magnus (usurper), 31, 53, 201; negotiates with Theodosius, 32; consulates of, 33, 270 (n. 50); division of empire, 33–34; invades Italy, 34, 35, 84; catholic, 35; death of, 37; relations with Rome, 133–34; demands Valentinian II go to Trier, 202; support of orthodox, 202–3; accuses Ambrose of bad faith, 203; and Priscillianist dispute, 205–6; letter to Valentinian II, 209; portrait shown in Alexandria, 236

Maximus the Cynic, 219–24; supported by Ambrose, 220, 223

Meletius: bishop at Antioch, 184–86; not mentioned in *cunctos populos*, 218; death of, 224; leads Council of Constantinople (381), 224–25

Melitene, 184

Merobaudes, 25–26, 28, 31, 32

Metallarii, 105–6

Milan, 17, 22, 123, 125; residence of Gratian, 31; residence of Eugenius and Arbogast, 40; place of death of Theodosius, 41; residence of Valentinian I, 46; residence under Constantius II, 142; religious problems, 195–99, 201–5, 207–9; "homoians" at, 204

Modestus, 96, 162, 182

Moesia, 29

Moesia Prima, 55

Moesia Secunda, 55

Nabataeans, 69

Naissus, 18, 21, 93

Nannienus, 53

Neckar, 48

Nectaridus, 51

Nectarius, 38; elected bishop of Constantinople, 227–28; chairs Council of Constantinople (381), 228; sends report to Theodosius, 230; heads list of named bishops, 230; house burned down, 246

Neoterius, 136, 137, 287 (n. 87)

Nicene Creed, 175, 222; reaffirmed at Constantinople (381), 228; weaknesses of, 231

Nicomachus. *See* Flavianus, Nicomachus

Nikaia, 20, 173

Nikomedeia, 142, 178, 179

Nikopolis, 60

Nisibis, 66

Noricum, 54

Numidia, 73

Olybrius (Anicius Hermogenianus), 256

Olybrius (Q. Clodius Hermogenianus), 30, 82–83, 117–18, 120, 137

Olympius, 156

Orfitus, 151

Oriens: bishops under Valens, 184

Orosius: on peace with Persia, 66; on empire, 95; on Valens, 188; on Frigidus campaign, 256; on Magnus Maximus, 270 (n. 49)

Osrhoene, 234, 236

Ostia, 191

Pacatus: panegyric on Theodosius, 51, 136–38; mentions Saracens, 71

Palaestina, 68

Palladius (bishop of Ratiaria), 196–98, 209

Palladius (*dux* of Osrhoene), 234

Pancratius, 107, 165, 292 (n. 70)

Pannonia, 35, 37, 55, 81, 84

Pannonia Secunda, 56

Paris, 17, 32, 46

Pasiphilus, 141

Paulinus of Antioch, 185–86, 204, 210, 218, 225

Pelagius of Laodikeia, 186

Peter (apostle), 217

Peter (bishop of Alexandria), 187, 217, 222; supports Maximus the Cynic, 219; death of, 225–26; letter of, 296 (n. 54)

Petronii, 30

Petronius Probus, 82, 118; repairs defenses of Sirmium, 56–57; laws addressed to, 99, 105

Philippus (*praefectus urbi*), 139

Philippus (praetorian prefect), 148

Philostorgius, 232

Photinians, 222

Phronimius, 24, 160

Picenum, 201

Picts, 50

Pinianus, 99, 133

Poetovio, 37, 85

Pontifex maximus, 171; title not refused by Gratian, 201

Postumianus, 101, 232

Potamius, 251

Praefectus Augustalis, 72, 251–52

Praefectus urbi
—at Constantinople: status and functions of, 153–54, 160, 162–67
—general status of, 111, 113, 153–54
—at Rome: functions of, 113–17, 119–20, 122, 125–33, 138–40; functions of

refined under Constantius II, 113, 152; appointments as, 113, 114, 122–23, 125, 133, 135, 139–40, 141

Praetextatus, 94, 99, 190, 253, 297 (n. 76); as *praefectus urbi*, 117–18; at Trier, 120; death of, 132

Praetorian prefectures: development of, 80–87

Priscillianists: rescript concerning, 194–95, 205–6, 298 (n. 96)

Priscillian of Avila, 35, 194–95, 205–6; date of death, 301 (n. 133)

Probinus, 256

Procopius: usurpation, 23, 160, 178–79; employs Goths, 46, 58; news of usurpation reaches West, 46; severed head sent to Valentinian I, 94; recruits *metallarii*, 106; support in Constantinople, 144

Proculus (*praefectus urbi* at Constantinople), 100, 146, 164, 167, 237, 246, 247, 258

Proculus Gregorius, 195

Proculus of Marseille, 299 (n. 107)

Protasius, 209

Quadi, 55, 57

Quintinus, 53

Raetia, 54, 57

Ratiaria, 196

Ravenna, 93, 264

Rehimena, 66

Reims, 20

Rhine, 44–45, 74

Richomeres, 33, 64

Rimini, 172, 177, 184

Romanus (*comes Aegypti*), 97, 249–51

Romanus (*comes Africae*) 72–74

Rufinus (historian), 36; on Mavia, 69–

70; on Basil, 182; on Valens, 183; on
  Gratian, 193; on Sarapeion, 250; on
  Frigidus campaign, 256
Rufinus (praetorian prefect), 104,
  246–48

Sallustius Aventius, 131
Samosata, 186
Saracens, 68–70
Saragossa, 194
Sarapeion, 249–52, 258, 309 (n. 109)
Sarapis, 234
Sarmatians, 29, 55
Sasima, 224
Sassanians, 16, 18
Saturninus, 31, 64
Sauromakes, 67
Saxons, 47, 50
Schism of Antioch. *See* Antioch:
  schism of
Scoti, 50
Sebasteia, 184
Secundianus of Singidunum, 198, 209
Seleukeia on the Kalykadnos, 172, 184,
  196, 214
Serena, 39, 135, 271 (n. 75)
Severus, 50–51
Shapur, 19, 66–67, 75
Siburius, 83
Singara, 66
Siricius, 35, 134, 206; and Magnus
  Maximus, 211, 287 (n. 86)
Sirmium, 21, 29, 55, 81, 93, 107, 142;
  Gratian there, 62, 82, 196; rescript
  on Donatists issued, 194
Siscia, 37
Sofia, 21
Sokrates (historian): on Mavia, 70; uses
  Athanasian tradition, 173; on Valens,
  176, 178–79; on Basil, 182; on

Valentinian I, 189; on Theodosius,
  232; does not know Theodosian
  laws, 232; on Frigidus campaign, 254;
  on Symmachus, 287 (n. 86); on
  Sarapeion, 310 (n. 112)
Sozomenus (historian): on Mavia, 70–
  71; on Valens, 178, 180, 188; on Basil,
  182; on Nectarius's election, 227; on
  Theodosian laws, 231–33; on
  Theodosius, 248; on Frigidus
  campaign, 254
Stilicho, 39, 41; claims guardianship of
  emperors, 41–42; on Rhine, 54; in
  Rome, 135
Stoboi, 84, 245
Strata Diocletiana, 69
Students, 116
Sulpicius Severus, 189
Syagrius, 30, 83, 197
Symmachus (father of orator), 114, 191
Symmachus (orator), 258; at Trier, 23–
  24, 120; praises Magnus Maximus,
  36, 134, 237; negotiations with
  Eugenius, 40; *relationes*, 94–95, 125–
  33; Third *Relatio*, 123–24, 127–28,
  200; refused audience at Milan, 124,
  200; general activities as *praefectus
  urbi*, 125–33; on new carriage, 127–
  28; accused of persecuting
  Christians, 128; reports on bridge,
  130–31; seeks permission for
  Praetextatus's statues, 132; relations
  with Theodosius, 135–36, 287
  (n. 86); property occupied in war,
  135; on Senate, 151; approaches
  Valentinian II, 203; approaches
  Ambrose, 238; consul, 242, 244

Tarracius Bassus, 122
Tarsos, 227

Tatianus, 145, 164, 237, 239, 250, 258; legislation addressed to, 104; consul, 242; receives law on riots, 245; and monks, 246; replaced by Rufinus, 246; condemned, 247

Tervingi, 26, 60, 65; treaty with Constantine, 58; cross to Thrace, 61

Thalassius, 158

Thekla, 214

Themistius: speeches in Senate, 22, 160; on Procopius, 24; at Marcianopolis, 25; on Valens's *decennalia*, 25; at Rome and Trier, 26–27, 121; serves Theodosius, 63; on Saturninus and Goths, 64–66; at Thessalonica, 144, 215; at Rome, 152; appointed senator at Constantinople, 152; proconsul of Constantinople, 153; recruits senators at Constantinople, 153–55; chooses praetors, 155; receives letter from Libanius, 156, 157; *praefectus urbi*, 162; at Ankara, 174; at Antioch, 187; on treaty of 370, 274 (n. 38); *oratio Constantii*, 290 (n. 19)

Theodore Lector, 188

Theodoret (historian): on Valens, 188, 295 (n. 41); on Frigidus campaign, 254, 257

Theodorus of Martigny, 299 (n. 107)

Theodosian Code: character of, 87–93; curial laws, 103–5

Theodosius (*comes*), 29, 135; in Gaul, 50–51; in Africa, 73

Theodosius I
—administrative matters: plans for West, 37–38; agreement on Armenia, 68; creates diocese of Egypt, 72; appointment of Nicomachus Flavianus, 85; rules Illyricum, 82, 83, 84, 87; law on Manichaeans, 90;

regional legislation, 97; curial legislation, 104; law to Pancratius, 107; legislation for Illyricum, 108; relations with Rome, 111, 114, 134–35, 241–42; handling of Symmachus, 135–36; receives Themistius, 144; increases number of praetorships, 157; desires to extend Senate in Constantinople, 159; tax relief for senators from Thrace and Macedonia, 159; consults Senate, 161; Illyrican law on converts, 195; laws for Italy, 244–45

—Constantinople: arrival there, 63, 140, 145; builds out city, 145; avoids Constantinople at first, 214; ecclesiastical edict to Constantinople (*cunctos populos*), 217–18, 220; convokes Council of Constantinople (381), 221–22; accepts resignation of Gregory of Nazianzos, 226; arranges election of Nectarius, 227; program of council, 228; accepts canons, 230

—military affairs: treaty with Goths, 30, 64–65; accepts Magnus Maximus, 33, 202, 208; motives for rejection of Magnus Maximus, 36–37; rejects usurpers' consuls, 40, 95; employs Goths, 46; repels Sarmatians, 56; Gothic war, 62–63; annuls Maximus's *acta*, 134; celebrates triumph, 135; obelisk, 147; literary versions of Eugenius campaign, 253–57

—personal aspects: death of, 13, 41; appointed at Sirmium, 29, 62; consul with Gratian, 30; statue in Rome, 135; imitates Trajan, 146; opinions on, 212; character of, 213; baptized by Acholius, 220; not *pontifex maximus*, 233

—religious matters: dogmatic position of, 196, 215–16; rejects Maximus the Cynic, 219; talks to Demophilos, 220, 222; talks to leaders of sects at Constantinople, 231; exiles Eunomius, 232; disputes with Ambrose, Kallinikon, 239–40; attitude toward Roman cults, 242–43; Thessalonica massacre, 243–44; Sarapeion affair, 250–52

Theodosius II: Theodosian Code, 87–93; legislation of, 100–101

Theophanes: on Mavia, 70; on Valens, 188

Theophilus of Alexandria, 249–51

Thermantia, 135

Thessalonica: as imperial residence, 36, 62, 83, 84, 142, 214; massacre at, 85, 139, 243–44; origin of Hypatius, 122; visit of Themistius, 144; ecclesiastical position of, 214–15; visit of Maximus the Cynic, 219

Thrace, 82; as settlement area, 60; metallarii, 105–6; senators receive tax relief, 159

Tibur, 191

Timasius, 241

Timotheus of Alexandria, 225, 229

Toxandria, 50

Trajan, 146

Trier, 23, 105, 116, 142, 195; Gratian leaves, 31, 195; death of Victor, 38; residence of Valentinian I, 47, 189–90; arrival of Valentinian II, 53; visit of Symmachus, 120

Trifolius, 84, 245

Tripolitania, 72

Ulfila, 204

Ursinus, 117, 191–92

Valens: accession of, 21; at Constantinople, 22, 144, 161; and Procopius, 23–24; and Goths, 24, 58–59, 60; plans to meet Gratian, 26, 121; at Antioch, 27, 60, 185; death of, 28, 188; divides Danubian territories with Valentinian I, 55; makes peace with Athanaric, 59; asks Gratian for help, 62; builds forts in Jordan, 69; brings Saracen troops to Constantinople, 70; changes Egyptian administration, 72; employs Eutropius, 83; legislation of, 96–97, 101–2, 164–65; law on metallarii, 106; at Marcianopolis, 144; reduces number of praetorships at Constantinople, 157; laws for Constantinople, 164–65; religious attitude of, 175–88; regarded as persecutor, 176; and Macedonianists, 177–79; and Basil of Caesarea, 181–84; ruling on monks, 187; recalls bishops, 187, 213; ecclesiastical judgments on, 187–88, 213

Valentinian Galates, 25, 182, 269 (n. 34)

Valentinian I: accession of, 20; coopts Valens, 21, 80; attitude toward Procopius, 23, 93; death of, 25; at Milan, 46; at Trier, 47; actions on Rhine, 47–48; confronts Macrianus, 49; appoints Gratian Augustus, 51; divides empire with Valens, 55, 81, 93; actions on Danube, 57; agrees with Valens on some laws, 91; legislation of, 96–97, 101–2; law on metallarii, 105–6; attitude toward Rome, 114–21; attitude toward religion, 188–92; repeals part of Julian's law on teachers, 189, 293 (n. 10); pressured by Martin of Tours, 189; reaction to Roman

bishops' dispute, 191–92; law on
Manichaeans, 223
Valentinian II: accession of, 26, 201;
unpopular, 32; retains central
prefecture, 34; consul, 34, 269
(n. 34); at Aquileia with Justina, 36;
flees to Thessalonica, 36, 209; at
Trier, 38, 53, 140; death of, 38, 271
(n. 74); relationship with Rome, 114,
125; his *praefecti urbi*, 125; agrees to
scrap new carriage of *praefectus urbi*,
128; statue in Rome, 135; "homoian,"
201–2; demands Milanese basilica
from Ambrose, 204–5, 207–8; not
pontifex maximus, 233; becomes
orthodox, 238
Valentinians, 240, 241
Valeria, 56–57
Valerianus, 99
Valerii, 133
Varronianus, 19, 20
Varronianus II, 20, 269 (n. 34)
Vesta, 123

Vettii, 201
Via Traiana Nova, 69
Victor (*magister militum*): consul, 25;
marries Mavia's daughter, 70
Victor (son of Magnus Maximus), 37
Victoria, altar of, 31, 123, 127; removed
by Constantius II, 199; removed by
Gratian, 200, 211
Vincentius, 99
Vindaonius Magnus, 162
Visi, 65
Viventius, 117–18, 191
Volusianus, 115, 284 (n. 14)

Zabdicene, 66
Zosimus (historian): ignores Roman
dispute about cults, 201, 203; on
Rufinus, 247; on division of empire,
270 (n. 54); on title *pontifex
maximus*, 300 (n. 119)
Zosimus (provincial governor), 280
(n. 25)